Scripta Series in Geography

Series Editors:

Other titles in the series:

World Systems of Traditional Resource Management

Edited by Gary A. Klee

San Jose State University

A HALSTED PRESS BOOK

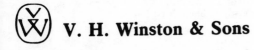 **V. H. Winston & Sons**

John Wiley & Sons
New York

For Helen and Laura

Copyright © V. H. Winston & Sons 1980

First published 1980 by
Edward Arnold (Publishers) Ltd.
41 Bedford Square, London WC1B 3DQ
and published simultaneously in the United States of America by Halsted Press, a division of
John Wiley & Sons Inc.

British Library Cataloguing in Publication Data

World systems of traditional resource management.

(Scripta series in geography).
1. Natural resources   2. Human ecology
I. Klee, Gary A   II. Series
333.7   GN448.3

ISBN 0-7131-6296-1

Library of Congress Cataloging in Publication Data

World systems of traditional resource management.

(Scripta series in geography)
"A Halsted Press book."
Includes index.
1. Natural resources—Addresses, essays, lectures.
2. Environmental policy—Addresses, essays, lectures.
3. Human ecology—Addresses, essays, lectures.
I. Klee, Gary A.
II. Series.
HC55.W68 1980   333.7   80-17711

ISBN 0-470-27008-X

Typeset in America by Marie Maddalena of V. H. Winston & Sons
Printed in Great Britain by
Richard Clay (The Chaucer Press) Ltd,
Bungay, Suffolk

Contents

Contributors

Jacquelyn L. Beyer, Ph.D. (University of Chicago) is Professor of Geography at the University of Colorado. She has done field work on changing land use practices (Lesotho) and river basin development (Orange River) while teaching at the University of Cape Town. Currently her interests include geographic education and environmental impact of resource development in Colorado.

William M. Denevan, Ph.D. (University of California, Berkeley) is Professor of Geography at the University of Wisconsin, Madison. His research interests include traditional tropical agriculture, pre-Columbian agriculture, historical demography, and tropical ecology. He has carried out extensive field work in the upper Amazon in Bolivia and Peru, in central Brazil, in the Orinoco region of Venezuela, and in the highlands of Nicaragua.

Ned H. Greenwood, Ph.D. (Ohio State University) is Professor of Geography at San Diego State University. His principal research interests are soils, human ecology and low-energy agriculture.

W. A. Douglas Jackson, Ph.D. (University of Maryland) is Professor of Geography and member of the School of International Studies at the University of Washington. His research has centered around Soviet agriculture and problems of environmental deterioration. He has travelled extensively in the Soviet Union, although research in agricultural geographical problems in the field is not permitted by Soviet authorities.

Warren A. Johnson, Ph.D. (University of Michigan) is Professor of Geography at San Diego State University. His research has related to the use of land and natural resources. He has done field research on the preservation of the English countryside and on Amish agriculture in Pennsylvania. His current interests focus on industrial society's ability to adapt to resource shortages.

Gary A. Klee, Ph.D. (University of Oregon) is Assistant Professor in Environmental Studies at San Jose State University. His principal research interests are traditional and modern systems of resource management and cultural ecology. He has lived, travelled, and taught widely in Oceania and carried out extensive field research in Micronesia.

Ian R. Manners, D. Phil. (Oxford) is Associate Professor of Geography and Middle Eastern Studies at the University of Texas at Austin. His principal research interests are in the field of environmental impact assessment and decision-making. He has worked extensively in the Middle East, including Egypt, Jordan and Saudi Arabia, on various issues related to water management. Currently he is engaged in a study of the social and environmental impacts of offshore oil development.

Brian J. Murton, Ph.D. (University of Minnesota) is Associate Professor in Geography at the University of Hawaii. His principal research interests center around the historical evolution of agrarian systems. He has carried out field and archival research in southern India and is currently involved in studying the agrarian space economy of Tamil Nadu from 1800 to 1947.

Joseph Whitney, Ph.D. (University of Chicago) is Professor of Geography at the University of Toronto. He teaches environmental sciences and the geography of East Asia. He has lived and travelled widely in East Asia and has recently done field work in both Japan and China. His publications include works on the political and administrative geography of China and environmental and ecological problems of East Asia.

Preface

Two reasons are behind the decision to write and edit this book. First, I became convinced that environmentally concerned students and particularly those bound for resource management positions must have an appreciation and at least an introduction to traditional non-Western means of managing resources. More often than not, the American student graduates from a program (whether it be in natural resources, biology, environmental sciences, environmental studies, or geography) with the misconception that the "U.S. way is the only way." Since many Western trained environmentalists and resource managers end up advising and sometimes even managing resources of other lands and cultures, much damage could be avoided if they understood the cultural ecological foundations behind non-Western systems of resource management.

Secondly, I simply have not been able to find a textbook that could serve as a good foundation for such discussion in my course in human ecology. Although one can gather from the literature various fragmented comments about traditional systems of resource management, no text has attempted to synthesize this information cross-culturally into one volume. Since I could only offer my knowledge of Oceania, other regional specialists were recruited from the ranks of America's cultural geographers to lend their expertise to the subject.

The book is intended primarily for undergraduate students in geography. Classes in *Resource Geography, Conservation Geography*, or *Cultural Geography* will find it particularly useful. Geographers or environmental scientists who teach *Human Ecology*, anthropologists who may teach *Cultural Ecology*, and historical geographers are bound to find this text of interest.

Except for Chapters 1 and 11, the book is organized to cover resource management traditions in each of the major regions of the world. Several regional chapters focus fairly exclusively on agricultural resources, while other, notably that on Europe, chose to illustrate the topic by concentrating on one typical country. Chapter 1 briefly introduces the reader to the need for exploring and evaluating traditional forms of resource management, while the concluding Chapter 11 attempts to draw together some general principles regarding scale, traditional land use planning and decision making, strategies to make systems reliable, perpetual, and productive, as well as implications for the Western development planner.

I particularly wish to thank all reviewers who made major contributions and suggested ideas for the respective regional chapters of this text: Profs. Richard Arvidson, Alvin Urquhart, C. Gregory Knight, and Hartmut Walter (*Africa*); John R. Clark, Gerry A. Hale, and Mutwakil Ahmed Amin (*Middle East*); Alan R. Beals and Chuck Yahr (*South Asia*); Elmer A. Keen and Christopher Salter (*East Asia*); Philip Pryde, Ihor Stebelsky, Robert Picker, and Philip P. Micklin (*Soviet Union*); Clyde Patton, Norman J. W. Thrower, Lester Rowntree, and David E. Kromm (*Europe*); Edward T. Price and Daniel B. Luten (*North America*); Carl Johannessen, James J. Parsons, and Charles F. Bennett (*Latin America*); and Michael McIntyre, Tom L. McKnight, Bryan H. Farrell, and Gordon B. Lewthwaite (*Oceania*).

Gary A. Klee

Chapter 1

Introduction

Gary A. Klee

Western style conservation measures are often not welcome in other countries—simply because they are western. People are understandably unsympathetic to restrictions imposed from outside their culture upon their own resources. Various cultures had (and to a lesser extent still have) their own conservation measures. One can glean from the literature various comments about taboos, hunting and fishing restrictions, marine preserves, wildlife sanctuaries, or sacred forest groves, some of which undoubtedly function in conserving resources. Too often, however, the modern-day resource manager pays little attention to what traditional cultures have to teach. Western resource managers have much to learn from the long standing conservation practices of traditional societies. The purpose of this book is to provide an introduction to these various topics for persons entering the resource management field.

SOME DEFINITIONS

Since the words *traditional, resource, conservation*, and *management* are used throughout the text, it is necessary that we first establish a common ground upon which to build.

By *traditional*, we refer to the "Ecosystem People" described by Raymond Dasmann in his contrasting view of the two major types of people in the world.[1] According to Dasmann, Ecosystem People (traditional people) are members of indigenous cultures who live within a single ecosystem, or at most two or three adjacent and closely related ecosystems. Hunting-and-gathering societies that exploit only their local area, primitive fishing societies that harvest nearby reefs, and subsistence agricultural societies that till local fields would all be considered examples of traditional societies practicing traditional systems of resource management. In contrast, are Dasmann's "Biosphere People" tied in

1

with global technological civilization, drawing support, not from the resources of any one ecosystem, but from the entire biosphere. One look at a representative meal of the average American makes it obvious we are Biosphere People; the beef steak from Argentina, the wheat bread from Canada, and the coffee from Brazil are all elements of a way of life based on global resource exploitation.

Dasmann goes on to say that since traditional cultures are dependent upon local ecosystems for their survival, persistent violation of its ecological rules will inevitably result in the scaling-down or disappearance of the culture. For example, if hunting societies kill more wild game than can be produced by the normal reproduction process, their people will become malnourished and suffer the consequences; if fishing societies overfish their local habitat, their resource base will crumble; and, if subsistence agricultural societies neglect keeping the soil in place and don't restore its fertility, crops will eventually fail. Not being dependent upon any one ecosystem, Biosphere People on the other hand hold to the "myth of superabundance"—a belief that resources are unlimited. As a result, local ecological disasters are considered only a small problem, since these people can simply fulfill the void by drawing more heavily upon the distant ecosystems of the Middle East or Mexico.

Lacking the myth of superabundance, traditional cultures have generally treated their ecosystems gently, trying not to violate their ecological rules.[2] Local constraints in the form of taboos, hunting bans, marine preserves and so on were established so as not to disturb the delicate balances between humanity and nature. Yet Biosphere People, lacking such constraints, often treat their local environment harshly. The mechanical leveling of whole hillsides, the contaminating or actual filling-in of marshlands, the paving-over of prime agricultural lands are all examples of a people engrossed in the myth that there are always other ecosystems on the horizon to exploit.

Furthermore, traditional cultures travel little within the world; they are home based. Unfortunately, their institutions, religions, and long practiced systems of conservation and resource management are being whittled away by the biosphere invaders. A good example is the recent "discovery" of the Tasaday gatherers in the limestone caves of central Mindanao Island in the Philippines. Scenes of government helicopters carrying American newscasters and camera crews to the Tasaday's caves so clearly illustrates how the wealthier Biosphere People travel the globe, invading and breaking-down local traditional ways of life.

Ironically, traditional societies and the conservation lessons they have to teach us are on a decline when people in modern westernized societies struggle to read and use a landscape without harmful consequences. As unbelievable as it may seem, primitive or traditional cultures have insights regarding living with the earth that the technocratic world has lost. Modern resource managers should drop their superior attitude and take a closer look at what these societies did to conserve resources.

We use the word *resources* to refer to all forms of matter or energy considered useful or essential by human societies. *Renewable resources* would be those that can maintain themselves or be continuously replenished if managed wisely, such as soils, food crops and domesticated animals, land or open space, water (abiotic), freshwater (biotic), marine, wildlife, or forest resources.[3] *Nonrenewable resources* are those not regenerated or reformed in nature at rates equivalent to those at which we use them, such as metals, fossil fuels, building materials, fertilizer chemicals, etc.

By *conservation*, we mean the rational use of the environment to provide the highest sustainable quality of living for humanity. Since no two social scientists, theologians, or philosophers can agree on what is meant by "quality of life," we would include in our definition the maintenance of the greatest possible diversity and variety of life on earth. *Management*, when used by this group of authors, refers to both "inadvertent" and "intentional" conservation practices of the society in question. In the case of Oceania, for example, this would include discussing and analyzing magico-religious taboos, bans, seasons, wildlife and marine preserves, land and lagoon tenure systems, social stratification, and such population control measures as overseas voyaging, suicidal voyages, celibacy, prevention of conception, abortion, and infanticide. All such practices, whether inspired by conservation or not, had and still have some effect on the availability and exploitation of local resources.

QUESTIONS TO BE EXPLORED

Each of the following regional chapters is organized to be responsive to five basic sets of questions. In the introductory section entitled *The Resource Base*, we have addressed three basic questions: What are the physical and cultural boundaries of the region? What are the region's principle biomes? What are the implications for traditional resource users? The next section, *Evolution of a Tradition*, attempts to answer four major questions: What are the historical roots of the tradition? What types of traditional conservation practice existed but have now lapsed within the region? Which traditional conservation practices were inadvertent rather than recognized and intentional? To what degree were these conservation measures effective? In the third section, *Existing Traditional Resource-Using Systems*, three major questions are pondered: What types of traditional resource-using systems exist today and where are they located? Which traditional conservation practices are inadvertent rather than recognized and intentional? To what degree are these conservation measures effective and how can they be tested?

In *Region in Transition*, the fourth major section of each chapter, we have endeavored to answer two major questions: What are the elements of cultural change that have the greatest impact on breaking down the traditional ways of conservation mangement? What are the elements of cultural change that might be supportive of these traditional systems of resource management?

The concluding section, entitled *Regional Assessment*, considers a number of important questions: Are there any lapsed attitudes and practices that should be revived? What is the possibility of reviving such lapsed attitudes and practices as they previously existed or in some new slightly modified form? Are there any current attitudes and practices that should be preserved as they now stand? Are there current attitudes and practices that can be made more productive or efficient without being destroyed or without causing disruptive side effects? What methods are available for the conscious preservation of these traditional attitudes, techniques, or technologies from the onslaught of cultural change? What methods are available for regular monitoring of the effects of maintaining or reinstating traditional systems of resource management? What methods are available by which public participation in planning can be increased? What can these older, long standing systems of conservation and resource management teach the modern-day resource manager within the region? And finally, what unifying theories can be applied, if any?

What follows is an introductory survey focused on many questions, answers, and lessons brought about by the long evolutionary experience of traditional societies. Let us begin with Africa, where the genus *Homo* first appeared in the known fossil or cultural record. From there, we will move to Asia, Europe, America, and finally out to the islands of Oceania.

NOTES

[1] R. F. Dasmann, "Ecosystems," Paper delivered at the Symposium on the Future of Traditional Primitive Societies, Cambridge, England, December, 1974. Some societies, however, such as the Soviet Union, do not readily fit Dasmann's assumptions.

[2] It is easy to overstate or romanticize successful traditional societies—those that have been able to adjust to the limitations and potentialities of their bounded ecosystem. Where they could not adjust (and there are too many examples of resource degradation to ignore), they have not survived and we have just as much to learn from these examples as from the successful societies.

[3] However, even renewable resources have constraints in terms of time for recycling or renewing, whether growth rates for trees or energy flows in ecosystems. Also, there is a critical survival threshold for organisms and species. Furthermore, soil resources are renewable in terms of fertility; nonrenewable in terms of erosion, although soils eroded from one site may renew another.

Chapter 2

Africa

Jacquelyn L. Beyer

Physically Africa appears as a compact, discrete region, essentially plateau-like in structure with a coastal plain of limited extent. It is linked to other land masses only by the narrow Sinai Peninsula, a connection interrupted since 1869 by the Suez Canal. Culturally, however, the delineation of Africa as a habitat region is more complex, as there are some significant contrasts between the Arab north and black Africa south of the Sahara. For purposes of this chapter the focus is on Africa south of the Sahara with minimal reference to Madagascar. It is assumed that a better understanding of northern African resource management problems and methods can be gained by the discussion in the chapter on the Middle East.

THE RESOURCE BASE

There are three major natural habitats in Africa (Fig. 1). Contrary to the familiar stereotype, Africa is not a "jungle" continent. The extent of humid, tropical rainforest with consistent high receipts of solar energy and water throughout the year is limited to about 8%. More typical is the savanna or bush-woodland-grass areas where rainfall is concentrated in seasons of varying length. Much of the savanna, however, is "derived" from original woodlands and forests. The third major zone is that of desert or semi-desert where lack of water and/or uncertainty of rainfall are major constraints. There are also small areas of montane forest or grassland, and a limited zone of Mediterranean shrubland in the south. The general picture of temperature as a constant, with low range between average high and average low, is modified by elevation, especially in the high central part of the continent and in southern Africa, where seasonal frost is experienced.

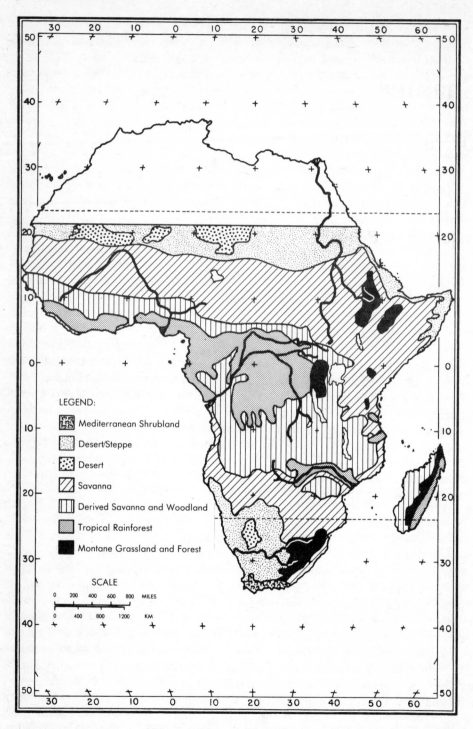

Fig. 1. African vegetation zones.

LEGEND:

- Mediterranean Shrubland
- Desert/Steppe
- Desert
- Savanna
- Derived Savanna and Woodland
- Tropical Rainforest
- Montane Grassland and Forest

SCALE

| 0 | 200 | 400 | 600 | 800 | MILES |

| 0 | 400 | 800 | 1200 | KM |

In traditional Africa topographic barriers were unimportant for migration and diffusion, so that agriculture and pastoralism spread relatively rapidly and easily. The major contrasts in human response between the grain-based agriculture of the savanna and the root culture of the forests represent basic environmental contrasts. Many resource practices reflect the need to cope with the problems of water availability and dependability. These are widespread with 60% of the continent either too dry or with seasonal supplies. Indirectly climate influences human and animal health and productivity so that the distribution of malaria, tsetse fly, bilharzia, trachoma and other diseases and disease vectors accounts in many cases for resource practices as well as population distribution and demographic characteristics. Soils are typically tropical in terms of nutrient and humus deficiencies, in pH, and in tendency toward oxidation when protective cover is removed. Africans over time became highly skilled in assessing varying soil quality, especially by using vegetative indices.

In summary, the physical environment presented a number of complex environmental resistances to traditional resource users. As people in today's African societies work out new patterns of resource use, the environmental challenges remain complex and subject to major research questions. The major problems with respect to the environment are tied in with current population growth rates and political pressures for speed in instituting changes. Changes made under such conditions may irreversibly damage the land or adversely affect human welfare if appropriate techniques are not utilized. But time is required for scientific study, for pilot projects, and for experimentation, and time is not an abundant resource. Part of the necessary analysis and experimentation should certainly involve a careful consideration of traditional resource management techniques to determine those which can continue to contribute to human welfare and progress in a changing Africa.[1]

EVOLUTION OF A TRADITION

It would be trite indeed to say that the human presence in Africa is very old. Recent archaeological evidence points to east central Africa as the home of hominid species. Evidence of tool use by humans, or proto-humans, dates back at least 2½ million years, or 2 million years before such evidence in any other region.[2] Until c. 12,000 B.P. the tools developed to exploit the land animals and plants, and in some cases the aquatic resources, of the natural environments of forests, grasslands and lakes were probably exported from the East African core region, when apparently the Sahara was far less dessicated than it became later, starting about 4500 B.P. Southwest Asia, as a crossroads region, however, became the hearth for development of plant and animal domestication and possibly the kinds of metallurgy later diffused to Africa.[3] This was a major center from which techniques, tools and crops for food producing patterns were brought across the Sahara.

Culture History

Independent development in the forest zone of the upper Niger basin, emphasizing root and tree crops, along with domesticates from the savanna belt and from Southwest

Asia and Egypt, became the basis for West African forms of agriculture. Later crops were probably introduced from Southeast Asia via Madagascar, but Harlan makes a persuasive case for a variety of independently domesticated plants in many parts of West Africa, the eastern Lakes region and Ethiopia.[4]

Population of the continent by agriculturalists and pastoralists with the migrations of the Bantu-speaking peoples, beginning c. the Christian era, must be classified with the great movements of peoples, ideas, and techniques. The migration from the West African hearth is comparable to the spread of Islam, to the African slave trade and to Western European, American Indian and Chinese migrations.[5]

The competitors for the Bantu were the Bushmanoid, Khoisan-speaking peoples, essentially hunters and collectors although a few groups did incorporate some pastoralism very late. The superior technology and tribal organization of the Bantu enabled them to prevail, and the Bushmen were slowly pushed into the remoter and less attractive environments. Today a small remnant group in the Kalahari Desert represents one of the last of such pre-agricultural societies. Eventually the Bantu in their turn were to be slowed and turned back by the confrontation with the more efficient technology and organization of the Europeans who came to the southern tip of the continent.

Metallurgy was brought by the Bantu southward and, as evidenced by numerous sites where mining and smelting took place, was obviously important to the economies of several groups.

During European medieval centuries Africa was becoming a part of the larger world with trade flourishing across the Sahara and the Indian Ocean. The impact of Islam was felt in many ways, and Arabs set up trading posts all along the east coast as far south as present day Mozambique with gold, ivory and slaves from Africa exchanged for the manufactured cloth, utensils and trinkets of Asia. One estimate shows that by 1500 A.D. the sub-Saharan population reached 79 million, compared to about 9 million for a similar sized area in North America.[6] This kind of density helps to account for the more complex societies developed on the continent.

Traditional African production is consistently referred to as "subsistence." This is generally true only insofar as farmers, fishers, and herders did and do indeed produce for their own consumption. But peasants do much more than that. They satisfy their own food needs, and perhaps a majority of other needs such as shelter, clothing, tools and other artifacts, but also produce a surplus with which they enter into trade. By c. 1500 A.D. Africans engaged in exchange almost everywhere. Although such exchange was usually through barter and very localized, there were many examples where a medium of exchange was used and trade was carried out on a regional scale.[7]

One of the frustrating speculations of history is the question of what might have happened to social and economic organization in Africa if the flow of events up to c. 1500 A.D. could have continued without the frightful interruption of the European slave trade. This trade was a major turning point in African history and Davidson has called the 350 years of the peculiar institution the "years of trial." In his analysis he suggests that the slave trade not only cut off normal development of trade and cultural interactions between Europe and Africa, but also failed to be the kind of territorial conquest and occupation which could generate active and innovative resistance.[8] At the least the trade resulted in general stagnation which slowed, if it did not stop, the processes of evolutionary change.

The slave trade led in the 19th century to greater European involvement. Traders and missionaries preceded the troops sent to protect them. Colonial administrators were drawn into the structure in a rather haphazard, almost accidental imperialism. The European presence, except for South Africa, was peripheral and reluctant until the final surge of imperialism in the 1880s. Colonial Africa is the Africa probably most familiar to the Western world, but it is not the most significant era, at least in terms of time.[9] Like a war, colonial occupation undoubtedly provided for intensification of the diffusion of ideas, institutions, and techniques, many of which contribute today to growth and change. There inevitably came a time, however, when racial barriers, insufferable superiority complexes, massive ecological ignorance, official penny-pinching and moral hypocrisy more than negated advantages of roads, civil service, dams and central business districts. The decolonization process itself has been as varied as the continent, ranging from mild referendums to violent guerilla revolution. The process is complete in all but southern Africa, where the looming threat of violent confrontation of new nationalist Africa and the older paternalism and racism promises another traumatic chapter in the evolution of African independence.[10]

There is then a culture history going back for hundreds of thousands of years. The result today, broadly speaking, is a continent essentially made up of three Africas—tribal pre-European Africa, colonial Africa, and post-colonial nationalist Africa. Nowhere is any single pattern to be found exclusively, and the particular mix of types ranges from the isolated, almost purely tribal pockets in some of the more remote or more difficult environments, to sophisticated urban-industrial landscapes comparable to those in the more economically developed regions of the world. The sub-Saharan population is made up of members of more than 277 African societies as well as people of Asian and European descent. In 1978 the estimate of population for all but the 6 northern countries was 333 million with a rate of growth close to 2.6% annually. The rural population makes up 81% of western Africa, 88% of eastern Africa, 73% of middle Africa, and 56% of southern Africa.[11]

The geography of modern Africa must then take into account the distribution of a variety of ethnic groups, languages, religions, economic systems, technologies and settlement patterns. Many of these overlap and affect one another in dynamic ways which tend to make obsolete even the most recent surveys.

Traditional Resource Management and Conservation

Conservation of resources usually involves techniques deliberately designed to preserve, enhance, protect, or reuse those elements of the natural environment perceived as vital for human survival and development. In the traditional African setting the usual inventory of these elements is found in utilization systems, including energy, minerals, water, soil, plants and animals. The determination of whether African resource users were explicitly involved in conservation approaches to solving their resource problems is extraordinarily difficult. More attention to what has been termed "ethnoscience," or shared patterns of thought and belief, can provide better insights into the question of deliberate or inadvertent conservation solutions.[12] The case can be made that long experience, intimate association with the environmental niches used for livelihood, and trial and error experimentation have resulted in a variety of techniques, adaptations and strategies which can only be defined as deliberate efforts to improve and/or protect the value of life-supporting resources and to insure some reasonably secure long term viability.[13] Sometimes, however, actions taken for other reasons have resulted in conservation outcomes. An example of the latter is the use of avoidance as a means of resolving tribal conflict so that the physical buffer zone between two potentially hostile groups became a refuge for wildlife.[14] Certainly to the extent that Africans developed and enlarged their habitat, evolved ever more sophisticated social organizations, and increased in population over thousands of years, we can assume conservation approaches.

Alteration of the environment is an inevitable part of the human presence and even long after the fact can give clues about resource management needs and responses. Major examples of alterations attributable to African resource users before intrustion by Europeans are the vegetative changes resulting from the use of fire, mining sites and terracing.

Fire as a tool. A map of vegetation types for modern Africa is misleading for the plant geographer or ecologist interested in climax ecosystems. It is now generally accepted that most, if not all, of the area designated as "savanna" is derived by the use of fire. Adejuwon has called these "anthropic" savannas and suggests that fire, used for clearing before cultivation, also operates as an equilibrium agent in terms of human use.[15] Whether or not cultivation continues, fire is needed to prevent regeneration of forests. Phillips rejects the criticisms of the present day use of fire as unwarranted as long as alternative methods of controlling woody growth where cultivation or grazing is desirable are neither feasible nor practical. Such alternatives certainly include massive use of herbicides or clean tillage.[16] The fact of efficiency and low relative cost, in labor or capital investment, is reinforced by the continued use of fire for pasture and field clearance even by sedentary farmers.[17] Changes in the drier margins of forests probably date back to pre-agricultural times when hunters and collectors deliberately set fires to develop cleared areas or maintained clearings caused by lightning fires.

Other causes for vegetative changes include trampling by wildlife and grazing livestock, and the use of forests for tree crops or shaded crops in clearings. Fire, however, is the ubiquitous agent and one of the most distinctive aspects of the environment, even today (Fig. 2). Phillips notes that there has been no success in preventing burning, a fact easy to understand when we recognize how important it is even for industrial world farmers (Table 1).

In view of the pervasiveness and antiquity of this management tool, the conventional model for evolution of domestication and agriculture from small beginnings along river courses, possibly succeeding fishing communities, through development of more sophisticated irrigation systems, and then into higher grasslands and finally forests, may not be appropriate. Quite probably for most of Africa south of the Sahara, the progression was the opposite. We would then find lesser population densities plus the use of fire and the development of extensive shifting cultivation and nomadic herding systems not dependent on river basins. Only the growth of population and other pressures or uncertainties, such as trading systems along the East African coast, would turn users to more elaborate systems of water control. In Lesotho, for example, where agricultural-pastoral occupance dates back only to the middle of the 19th century, very little hydrological association is noted. The villages are concentrated on ridge and hill tops, to facilitate communication, rather than along streams to facilitate irrigation or use of alluvial soils.[18]

Fig. 2. Brush fire in Zambia south of Lusaka, 1968.

Mining and smelter sites. Metallurgy supposedly came via Meroe in Egypt to West Africa and then was carried by the Bantu throughout the continent. Recent arguments against this thesis may result in a different time scale and pathway for diffusion, but the evidence is clear that mining and smelting were widespread and very much a part of Bantu and West African economies. In fact a recent study reports good evidence for sophisticated smelting techniques which must have resulted in production of high quality carbon steel in the West Lakes district around Lake Victoria as early as 1500 to 2000 years ago.[19]

Minerals are non-renewable resources and require different management techniques than for renewable resources if conservation goals are to be achieved. As a wasting resource, long term use strategies in theory include beneficiation, wise use, reuse and protection against oxidation as well as development of technology for lesser quality ore extraction. With respect to the first, Schmidt and Avery have offered much in the way of new insights.[20] As far as reuse is concerned Africans are models of recycling abilities. Sites where mining and smelting were carried out are found all through sub-Saharan Africa. Many settlement ruins are associated with mining of iron, copper, tin or gold. Beneficiation, or the improvement in the quality of the ore to reduce impurities and refine out the most workable metal, was carried out through smelting in clay ovens fired with charcoal. Extraction of ores left distinctive alterations in the landscape, sometimes large enough to exclude the sites from present day use.[21] Forests were also affected by demands for fuel wood. It is not strange that modern prospectors and mining companies found these sites valuable indicators of presently worked ores.

Local needs were satisfied by these workings, and in some cases a surplus was produced for trade. The importance of metallurgy for agricultural production is in the

Table 1. Traditional Landscape Altering Practices

Management practice	Examples	Management practice	Examples
Fire as a tool[a]		Beneficiation (smelting)	Widespread
General effects	Widespread and common*	High carbon steel	East Africa
Sub-climax and dryer woodland	East Africa*	Extensive scale[d]	East Africa
Controlled burning	Sierra Leone*	*Rahoniza* furnace[e]	Nigeria
Game control and clearing	Cameroon	Clay furnaces	Rhodesia (Gwembe)*
Brush control after harvest by sedentary farmers	Ethiopia*	Forging, reuse, protection[f]	East Africa
		Spears fashioned from hoes	Uganda
Mining and smelting		Peasants bring scrap metal for blacksmiths	Nigeria*
Extraction	Widespread	Family trained artisans	Zambia (N. Rhodesia)*
Extensive sites	Angola, Katanga, East Africa	European scrap, stolen or bought for forging into axes	Widespread
Evaporation, solar (salt)	Widespread	Recycling waste products[g]	Malagasy
Washing iron ore sands[b]	Kenya	Pride in care of tools[h]	Widespread
Ferrous lumps removed from river mud with sticks	Tete (Mozambique)	Impact on environment	
Shaft and pit mining	Widespread	Deforestation for charcoal	
Gold, tin, copper, iron, salt	Widespread		
Tin[c]	South Africa	*Terracing*	
Gold	Zimbabwe (Rhodesia)	Stone or earth walled	Ethiopia, Cameroon, Togo*
Salt	West Africa	Ruins[i]	East Africa
	East Africa	Contour ridging, grassed	Uganda*
		Contour banks and pits[j]	S. Tanzania*

Notes:

*Pre-European, but often still present.

^aGeneral references on use of fire include Allan (*see note 27*), Bartlett (*see Sources below*) and Phillips (*see note 16*).

^bSand is washed from precipitated ore as a family project, then ore is dried in sun.

^cPre-European workings north of Pretoria covered 40 acres (16 hectares) and produced about 2000 tons of metal, most probably for alloying with copper.

^dA smelting site is described as "a veritable scree slope of broken clay, bellows mouths and lumps of slag." Fosbrooke (*see Sources below*) reported over 800 bellows mouths exposed and suggested as many more could be excavated.

^eClay mixed with grass, built up to 4 or 5 feet (1.5 meters); an eyehole is provided half way up and a charge hole at the bottom; the unit is placed over a pit filled with stones and fired with charcoal (*gawayi*).

^fSimoons (*see note 17*) notes the difference in attitude toward blacksmiths in black Africa, where they were honored craftsmen, and in the Middle East, where they were usually members of lowly, separate groups. Ethiopia straddles these two traditions.

^gRandall (*see Sources below*) notes that "these requests are mixed with a host of other requests such as for rides on a 'lorry' truck, discarded petrol tins, empty tin cans, cigarettes, old clothes, old magazines with pictures, and innumerable scraps and discarded remnants of other symbols of Western civilization."

^hThe narrator reports to Linton (*see Sources below*) that spades are a matter of pride and the farmer polishes the blade and oils and polishes the wood handle. "An old spade that has been tried will bring more money in the market than a new one, for the foreigner's iron is not as good as our own."

ⁱKjekshus (*see note 21*) reports a comment by a late 19th century observer, Freiherr von Schele, that the anti-erosion stone-walled terraces were skillfully constructed and resembled those of German vineyards. The maintenance work was carried out by people dispossessed by cattle-oriented Wahehe.

^jThe remarkable system of the Matengo involves a grid of grass strips which are then covered by topsoil from pits dug from the enclosed squares. The mounded strips are planted and the pits used for compost.

Sources: Adejuwon (*note 15*); Allan (*note 27*); Aubreville, "The Disappearance of the Tropical Forests of Africa," *Unasylva*, Vol. I (1947), pp. 5–11; Bartlett, "Fire in Relation to Primitive Agriculture and Grazing in the Tropics, Annotated Bibliography," Vols. I and II (Ann Arbor: University of Michigan Botanical Gardens, 1955 and 1957); Edel, *The Chiga of Western Uganda* (New York: International African Institute, Oxford University Press, 1957); Fagan and Yellen, "Ivuna: Ancient Salt-Working in Southern Tanzania," *Azania*, Vol. III (1968), pp. 1–45; Fosbrooke, "Further Light on Rock Engravings in Northern Tanganyika," *Man* (1954), pp. 101–102; Hailey, *African Survey*, rev. (London: Oxford University Press, 1956), p. 1053; Jagger, "Kano City Blacksmiths: Precolonial Distribution, Structure, and Organization," *Savanna*, Vol. 2:1 (1973) pp. 11–20; July (*note 24*); Kaberry (*note 36*); Kenyatta, *Facing Mt. Kenya: The Tribal Life of the Gikuyu* (London: Secker & Warbury, 1959), p. 72; Kesby (*note 66*); Kjekshus (*note 21*); Linton, recorder, "Rice, A Malagasy Tradition," in Simon and Phoebe Ottenberg, eds., *Cultures and Societies of Africa* (New York: Random House, 1960); Peltier, *Mineral Resources of South-Central Africa* (Cape Town: Oxford University Press, 1964), p. 17; Randall, *Factors of Economic Development and the Okovango Delta* (Chicago: Department of Geography Research Paper No. 47, 1957), p. 27; Reynolds, *The Material Culture of the Peoples of the Gwembe Valley* (New York: Frederick Praeger, 1968), p. 93; Richards, *Land, Labour and Diet in Northern Rhodesia* (London: Oxford University Press, 1939); Schmidt (*note 19*); Simoons (*note 17*). For correlation of sources with specific management practice forms and examples, *see note 77*.

shaping of new tools as a response to the need for more efficiency and population increases. The shift from digging sticks and wooden hoes to the iron tools necessary for more intensive clearing and weeding practices was a technological response to need and evaluation of resource potentials.

It is doubtful that one can make a claim for the merits of present day implementation of traditional conversion techniques. "Backyard smelters" are unlikely to compete with modern mining complexes, largely run by corporate interests linked to world financial and consumer markets. The traditional skills associated with mining, smelting and blacksmithing, though, are being lost all too rapidly. Schmidt and Avery report on the way blacksmiths in East African villages use scrap iron instead of locally produced iron, but their skills are not being passed on. Schmidt also claims that traditional smelting lasted until at least the 1920s.[22] Traditional methods and values are more likely to be evidenced in the ability of Africans everywhere to reuse and recycle the discards of the industrial economy. Oil drums, cans, bottles, wire, tin sheets are all put to use in creative and ingenious ways.[23] This aspect of current African life is probably the most relevant with respect to non-renewable resources, including, more recently, plastics (Table 1).

Terracing. Although not so widespread as in Southeast and Southwest Asia or in Latin America, there are scattered remnants of ancient systems of terracing as well as areas where present day terraces date back to pre-European days. More intensive research, especially with remote sensing imagery, will undoubtedly fill in many gaps.[24] Present usage and reconstruction through archaeology show erosion control through hill slope terraces or contour ridging in Cameroon, Ethiopia, Kenya, Uganda, Tanzania, and Rwanda (Table 1). Terraces which require major construction and maintenance efforts, such as Simoons reports in Ethiopia, are considered unsuitable for low density shifting agricultural peoples because of labor requirements. Where population increases leads to development of sedentary agriculture, then the labor and capital requirements are deemed feasible. In some cases simpler conservation techniques such as reforestation and contour ridging, or tie-ridges, and planting are better alternatives. Studies in the Uluguru Mountains of Tanzania show that terracing would encourage landslides and expose too much infertile soil.

In modern times the attempts to implement slope control facilities where erosion problems are evident frequently failed in the face of anti-government non-cooperation tactics by nationalists as in Tanganyika and Kenya in the 1950s, or by anti-*apartheid* leaders in South Africa.[25] These are modern examples of how easy it is to "de-develop" where constant maintenance of facilities is required. Eckholm reports on a study made in the Gamu Highlands of Ethiopia where in 1968 a sustainable terraced system was on the verge of breakdown.[26]

On the whole the kinds of structures probably more extensive up to colonial times in many of the more densely settled parts of Africa are not now in operation, and research will be necessary to locate more of these because of dislocation and destabilization caused by internecine warfare and colonial policies.

The European Influence

The impact of the European presence is seen in the spread of cash cropping of such commodities as sugar, cotton, rubber, tea, coffee, pyretheum and cocoa; in large scale mining and smelting; in major multiple-purpose river basin projects, including large irrigation systems; in urban growth; in coal and petroleum based manufacturing; and in the elaboration of transportation and communication systems. The fragmentation of societies with the imposition of arbitrary political boundaries and institutions is also a major factor in destabilization of resource utilization systems. Depopulation because of slave raids and tribal warfare left many areas, especially in West and East Africa, unproductive although they were competently used as late as the 19th century. In South Africa a 325-year experience of Westernization has altered the landscape irreversibly and, along with the impact of racial policies, has left the traditional rural areas of the Bantustans in desperate condition. Efforts to control animal and human diseases have caused serious resource impacts, especially along the desert fringes. Some experiments to modify land use practices in the face of deteriorating environment and population increase, as in the Belgian Congo, showed promise at least as transition modes.[27]

EXISTING TRADITIONAL RESOURCE MANAGEMENT

Europeans contributed to changes in landscape patterns in dramatic ways. African economies were linked to capitalist markets; and European technology, systems of land use and tenure, plus expropriation of resources for metropolitan needs swept the continent. Modern cities, railroads, plantation crops, afforestation, game reserves and irrigation schemes were all imposed on the landscape. All of these were supported by institutions of political order, religious proselytism, and economic structures involving cash exchange, export and mechanization. The medical missionary and the head tax system together probably forced more changes than any other factors. Population growth stressed old systems; taxation forced workers into the cash economy, frequently at the expense of systems stability; and obtuse government agents insisted on trying to implement "more efficient" resource methods, all supported by elaborate justifications about the civilizing mission.

Now that the dust of decolonization has settled, except for the tragic problem of Southern Africa, African nations face problems of environmental deterioration on a massive scale; continuing rapid population growth; and limited decision alternatives in the fact of exogenous forces, including oil prices, market price fluctuations, inflation and international conflict.[28] Yet rural Africa, still the most vital part of Africa's future, remains resilient, open to change, needing more decision-making power, with millions of men and women working to recombine the elements of their beliefs, social values, available resources, new techniques, changing incentives and public guides into new and viable production systems.

What is ancient and/or traditional in the new Africa blends with the modern in some places, contrasts vividly in others, or is difficult or impossible to find without careful research. The following is an attempt to summarize the general nature of these patterns with specific support in the tables for the presence or disappearance of a large number of techniques, methods, tools and values which have made Africa the distinctive region that it is.

Shifting cultivation. This is a common form of land use which is extraordinarily difficult to explain because of the many variations in place and time. Karl Pelzer's definition,

Table 2. Organizational Systems and Tools

Management practice	Examples	Management practice	Examples
Pastoralism[a]		Oil palm for cleaning and beer	Zaire*
Emphasis on quantity as an ecological adjustment	Uganda, Kenya, Tanzania, (Masai), South Africa*	Domestic poultry, hunting, fishing	Cameroon*
		Vegetable salt[g]	Zambia, Sahel*
Shifting cultivation[b]		Storage	Widespread*
Bush fallow	Cameroon, Nigeria (Ibibio), Ghana*	Drying with smoke in house attic	Zaire*
		Mud and raffia bins	Zaire*
Pollarding and burning[c]	Ethiopia, Zambia, Congo-Zambezi watershed*	Baskets or small huts on rocks or stilts	Uganda, Ghana, Ethiopia*
Forest fallow with axe, burning	Zaire, Nigeria (Ibo)*	Grass and clay bins on stones	Nigeria*
Semi-permanent[d]	Kenya, Tanzania, Cameroon*	Wooden racks shaded in barns (*oba*)	Nigeria*
		Dried earth graneries, plant material construction, underground stores; in-hut storage, pot storage, modern silos	Nigeria*
Sedentary cultivation		Groundnuts sun dried and stored in shell	Zambia*
	Ethiopia, Kenya, Nigeria, Zambia, Ghana, Uganda, Tanzania*	Seed stock in gourds, pots, baskets	Ethiopia*
		Cassava, yams stored in ground—harvested when needed	
Combination strategies		Tree crops as storage	Zambia*
Interplanting	Widespread*	Livestock as insurance	Zaire*
Calendars	Widespread*		Tanzania, South Africa, Kenya*
Ants not disturbed; clues to rain	Kenya*	Rat-proof wooden collars on hut posts	Madagascar*
Sequencing of planting, cultivation, harvesting	Widespread*	Other	
Multiple use	Widespread*	Excess land claimed for reserve	Tanzania*
Grass for thatching, composting, fires	Tanzania, Lesotho*	Drought resistant crops	Widespread*
Woodlands for firewood, ash, construction, medicines, source for game and gathering	Zambia*	Seed selection for varying qualities—fast, slow, drought resistant, etc.	Zambia*
Supplements to main food production[e]	Widespread*	Bananas as perennial source	Zaire, East Africa*
Hunting and fishing	Widespread*	Livestock exchanged[h]	Sahel, Kenya, Ghana*
Foraging—plant products, insects[f]	Widespread	*Hoe cultivation*	
Dogs used for hunting	Zambia, South Africa*	General	Widespread*
		Combined with plow and sickle	Ethiopia, Central Africa*
		Primary tool—bent or straight	Widespread*

16

Notes:

*Pre-European, but often still present.

No system of primary production is so subject to stress as nomadic herding. Old ways of accommodating through mobility and quantity of livestock are giving way to pressures to settle permanently and to integrate animal husbandry with other forms of agriculture. Ironically, a way of life which resulted in territorial and political domination in traditional Africa is now associated with some of the poorest societies, e.g., Turkana, Somali, Karimojong, and Maasai.

^bAllan (*see note 27*) and Prothero (*see note 76*) are useful references in explaining not only the nature of traditional systems, but also the numerous forces for and directions of change.

Pollarding is the practice of lopping off branches of trees, collecting them in piles for burning, and leaving the tree trunks, scarred by burning, for soil protection, trellises, etc. A distinctive part of the Central African system known as *citemene*.

^dAccording to Allan, Zambia includes a semi-permanent transhumance associated with the regular flooding of the Zambezi river system in Barotseland where the Lozi transport livestock and village artifacts to higher ground in February–March, returning to the floodplains in June. Agriculture is high risk, so fishing and cattle husbandry are more important activities.

^eAccording to Richards (*see Sources for Table 1*), "The Bemba does not measure land, assess its value in size or productive capacity, or conceive of this value as a figure to be permanently maintained at a given figure by the expenditure of effort and capital. He views the country round him as all one unit, all accessible to him, and all ready to supply his needs—trees to be used for wood, ash for his gardens, building material or medicines, and wild plants, game and fish for food."

^fReynolds (*see Sources for Table 1*) reports how the people he observed would use torches, usually made of *mubalubdu* wood, as a light trap to attract termites from a mound into a pit.

^gEarly observers reported the burning of straw and other vegetable matter, dissolving the ash in water, boiling the lye in small pans to produce salt. This is still a widespread practice, although commercially available salt is replacing this technique.

^hCattle are loaned or leased for grazing and maintenance in areas distant from owners land or village.

Sources: Allan (*note 27*); Benneh, "Small-Scale Farming Systems in Ghana," *Africa*, Vol. 43 (1973), pp. 136–139; Beyer, Jacquelyn, L., personal observation (Lesotho); Cunnison, *The Laupula Peoples of Northern Rhodesia* (Manchester: Manchester University Press, 1959), p. 16; Curwen and Hatt (*note 39*); Douglas, "The Lele of Kasai," in *African Worlds*, Daryll Forde, ed., (London: International African Institute, 1954), p. 2; Dyson-Hudson, "Subsistence Herding in Uganda," *Scientific American*, Vol. 229:2 (1969), pp. 76–89; Eckholm (*note 26*); Edel (*see Sources, Table 1*); Forde and Jones, *The Ibo and Ibibio Speaking Peoples of South-Eastern Nigeria* (London: International African Institute, 1950), p. 70; Gerlach, "Nutrition in its Sociocultural Matrix: Food Getting and Using Along the East African Coast," in Brokensha, ed., *Ecology and Economic Development in Tropical Africa* (Berkeley: Institute of International Studies, Research Series No. 9, 1965), pp. 217–244; Gulliver, "A Land Dispute in Arusha, Tanzania," in Mark Karp, ed., *African Dimensions* (Boston: African Studies Center, Boston University Press, 1975), pp. 1–14; Hays, "The Storage of Cereal Grains in Three Villages of Zaria Province, Northern Nigeria," *Savanna*, Vol. 4 (1975), pp. 117–123; Hill, *The Migrant Cocoa-Farmers of Southern Ghana* (Cambridge: Cambridge University Press, 1963), p. 10; Igbozurike, "Ecological Balance in Tropical Agriculture," *Geographical Review*, Vol. 61:4 (1971), pp. 519–529; Isack (*note 14*); July (*note 24*); Kaberry (*see Sources, Table 1*); Linton (*see Sources, Table 1*); Reining, "Land Resources of the Haya," in David Brokensha, ed., *Ecology and Economic Development in Tropical Africa* (Berkeley: Institute of International Studies, Research Series No. 9, 1965), pp. 217–244; Porter (*note 35*); Reynolds (*see Sources, Table 1*); Richards, *Hunger and Work in a Savage Tribe* (Glencoe, Ill.: Free Press, 1948); Richards, *The Changing Structure of a Ganda Village: Kosozi 1892–1952* (Nairobi: East African Publishing House, 1966), p. 19; Simoons (*note 17*); Talbot, "Ecological Consequences of Rangeland Development in Masailand, East Africa," in M. Taghi Farver and John P. Milton, *The Careless Technology* (Garden City, N.Y.: The Natural History Press, 1972), pp. 694–711; Turnbull (*note 52*); Vermeer (*note 32*). **For correlation of sources with specific management practice forms and examples, see *note 77*.**

"...an economy of which the main characteristics are rotation of fields rather than crops; clearing by means of fire; absence of draft animals and of manuring; use of human labor only; employment of the dibble stick or hoe; short periods of soil occupancy alternating with long fallow periods. . ." gives the essential elements but there are many exceptions or modifications.[29] The important issue is how peasants who utilize some form of shifting cultivation, whether termed bush fallow, forest fallow, rotational bush fallow or semi-permanent cultivation, cope with increased pressure, usually brought about by population increase, or environmental degradation or disaster. There is satisfactory documentation for the fact that accommodation through stable, sedentary farmsteads was a feature well before European interaction in places like Nigeria, Cameroon, and East Africa. Intensification (greater density of permanent fields and/or shorter fallow periods, less crop variety, higher yields, etc.) as Knight points out, is likely to coincide today with the influence of urban demands for food, accessibility to markets along railroads or roads, and resources available, especially water.[30] It is easy to forget that early agriculture everywhere in the world was marked by a form of cultivation suitable for sparse populations and adequate land, and that a form of shifting agriculture was present in North America and Europe well into the 20th century.[31]

The issue of carrying capacity for a stable sedentary system, given present institutions and technology, is crucial. Vermeer, in a study of the Tiv of Nigeria, suggests that a density of $400/mile^2$ or $154.4/km^2$ might well be a critical index of a tipping point toward instability and decline.[32] Much more needs to be done with this kind of analysis. Many experts caution that great care should be taken with evaluation of commercial monocropping as superior to relatively modest modifications of stabilized shifting systems. The assumption which needs to be critically evaluated is that for some unfathomable reasons, persons who utilize shifting cultivation as an appropriate adaptation where land and population ratios are suitable will cling to the system until a final crash and that somehow they must be convinced of their ignorance. Nothing could be farther from the truth as evidenced by many examples of complex evolutionary systems (Table 2).

Combination strategies. One study in the Kamba region of Kenya reported that when one considered the number of crops, patterns of rainfall, available land for each farmer, labor investments, and cultivation needs, there were 243 possible combinations of land, labor, crops and timing.[33] Do African farmers and pastoralists choose? They certainly do. Life is a constant matter of meticulous attention to ways of insuring production in times of drought or crop failure; providing time for supplementing food from cropping and livestock with hunting, fishing and collecting; and utilizing ritual feasting for reward and incentive (Table 2).

Some areas of restricted environmental potential, especially the drier margins of steppelands, were correlated with the dominance of one kind of activity, such as hunting, collecting or grazing. But even here there were institutional adjustments including mobility, raiding, trading or tolerance of lower calorie diets which allowed for some "back up" assurance of continuity.

Few agricultural groups were without domestic animals in some sort of combination, including cattle, sheep and goats in West and East Africa; and sheep, goats and poultry in the forests. Cattle were a major part of the economy for the southern Bantu. Tree crops were combined with gathering and field crops in forested areas, along with supplemental food from insects and fish. Seasonally dry areas were interplanted to assure at least a crop of more drought resistant plants for a given field; timing of planting was adjusted in terms of familiar weather indices to insure maximum moisture availability; and various storage techniques helped bring villagers through severe times. The welfare obligations of tribal leaders combined with storage facilities to contribute a form of insurance, one which is sorely lacking for urban migrants. Forms of storage also contribute to system redundancy (Table 3). Root crops such as yams can be left in the earth until needed, cattle are slaughtered only in times of dire need and only with the support of ritual, and physical facilities are constructed to protect against weather and predatory animals. Sun drying or smoking are used to cut down losses from bacteria, mold and disease (Table 2 and 4).

An important part of the life of peasants and herders is the calendar (Table 2). In a region where temperature allows for year around activities, and only seasonal moisture inputs provide for any rest or dormancy, how do people manage their affairs? There are so many combinations throughout the continent that generalizations or even classification is difficult.[34] A look at any study which describes the work routine will impress one with the variety and omnipresent character of chores and the essential rationality of work performance by groups and individuals. As Porter noted in writing of a semiarid region in Kenya, ". . .the timing of planting, weeding, irrigating and harvesting is carefully worked out so that there is a constant movement between zones and no intolerable peak load of work in any month."[35] For the Cameroon uplands Kaberry utilizes diaries kept by the women of the village to document the work associated with field and garden care, implement maintenance, family care, food preparation and social life. It is a richly textured life which greatly complicates the simplistic notion of peasants living in "harmony with" or "in tune with the rhythms" of nature. Nature matters, but there is a reciprocal relationship with people exerting major kinds of control over environmental factors in an ordered and flexible sequence over a year's time.[36]

To the extent that modernization "rationalizes" or reduces the range of choice for subsistence, it tends also to introduce a larger degree of instability and uncertainty. The extreme example of this is cash cropping for export where disaster can strike no matter how efficient and skilled the local producer may be. Where necessary changes can be incorporated into and become extensions of traditional ways, then there is a better chance for long term productivity.[37]

Hoe cultivation. The absence in most of Africa of both plow and wheel was one of the most persistent irritants for early European observers. This irritation evolved into the perception of Africans as primitive and lacking in technological skills. The usual positive explanation was that techniques dependent upon animal draft power were not adoptable in the face of the tsetse fly barrier. It is true that the presence of a wildlife reservoir, combined with the tsetse fly host, enhances the spread of trypanosomiasis to domestic animals. However, there is increasing evidence that Africans did exert enough control over the wildlife reservoirs in many places to support thriving cattle based economies where now tsetse is a plague.[38] A better explanation may well be that while the diffusion of plow technology was slow in any case, Africans did know about plows and *chose* hoes as preferred tools. This suggests a clear perception of soil management problems where plowing frequently leads to greater oxidation, breakdown of structure, and turns up lower quality soils.[39]

The digging stick tends to dominate in forest cultivation where tillage and weeding

Table 3. Cooperative Management[a]

Management practice	Examples	Management practice	Examples
Soil fertility and texture management; erosion control		*Water management*	
General	Widespread*	Irrigation	
Kitchen gardens	Widespread*	Aqueducts[g]	Kenya*
Mulch from grass household carpet	Tanzania*	Channels	Tanzania
Ash for fertilizer	Widespread*	Drainage ditches and diversion dams	Ethiopia*
Grass dug into mounds and fired[b]	Cameroon, Zambia*	Small dam and diversion system	Zimbabwe (Rhodesia)*
Composting	Widespread*	Seasonal flood paddies	Zambia*
Broadcast sowing—cattle used to tramp in seeds and fertilize	Ethiopia*	Ponding water on hillsides	Madagascar*
Reuse of soil from abandoned villages (*umufundo*)[c]	Zambia*	Flood water, paddy cultivation; *chili* gardens	Zambia*
Grass mounds evolved into contour ridges (*vikuse*)	Zambia*	Wells for permanent field irrigation	Ghana*
Rotation of cattle pens on dry *litongo* soils	Zambia*	Drainage canals in peat soils (*mataba*)	Zambia*
Stumps and stones left in plowed fields as erosion control	Ethiopia*	Irrigation of terraced fields	Togo*
Roots of tree stumps and pollarded trees left against erosion	Rhodesia*	Domestic	
Recognition and classification of soils	Ethiopia, Tanzania*	General	East Africa*
Stall feeding for manure	Ghana, Tanzania*	Cisterns	Ghana*
Grazing animals in fallowed fields	Ethiopia, Lesotho	Convenient water supply as village site factor	Zambia*
Straw from cattle pits	Madagascar*	Swamp pools, swamp-side wells and springs	Zambia*
Ikpezi composting[d]	Nigeria*	Shallow pits and mud puddles	Ghana*
Ant hills used as fertile sites	Zambia*	Water from rivers	Widespread*
Litter to mulch banana groves[e]	Tanzania*	Water troughs to keep leeches from cattle	Uganda*
Field ridges and strip cropping	Nigeria*	*Fishing*	
Mounding with hoe[f]	Widespread*	Nets, baskets, spears, traps	Widespread*
Night soil and composting	Tanzania*	Drumming water, fences or small dams	Widespread*
		Beach seines for sea fishing	Sierra Leone to

Manure	Widespread*
Erosion control by small trenches	Zambia*
Renewal of fertility by alluvial deposits along rivers (cilli gardens)	Zambia*
Manure from goat sheds	Zambia*
Trees as index to soil quality	Zambia*
Torches, spears, hooks on rope across stream, mud and grass dikes, semi-permanent weirs	Angola*
Stick enclosure (nhangu) in river sand; shibaba (reed traps)	Zambia*
Poison, stupefying plants[h]	South Africa*
Fixed fishing villages	Zambia, Ethiopia*
	Zambia*

Notes:

*Pre-European, but often still present.

[a]This term is used to suggest management practices where resources are perceived as those to be protected, maintained and/or enhanced.

[b]New surface hoed into sod piles mixed with soil, burned and ash heaps planted. This is the *vikuse* system of the Ngoni-Chewa.

[c]Richards (see *Sources, Table 1*) observes that while "no Bemba will admit that an adult could ever defecate on a village bed," old village sites are valued for new gardens precisely because it is recognized that refuse from huts and latrines benefits the soil.

[d]A rubbish heap, known as an *ikpezi*, will be started by a family on a path frequently used by villagers. It will be started with fallen leaves, but household garbage, other rubbish, and contributions from passersby will be added. It is turned over with hoes to facilitate decomposition.

[e]As coffee replaces banana trees, only the banana groves near the village continue to receive such care.

[f]This is one of the most common ways to protect and enhance soil quality. These mounds are large—1 to 6 feet (.3 to 2 meters) in diameter and may be as much as 2½ feet, or less than 1 meter, high.

[g]A pair of photographs shows a modern pipe aqueduct, suspended by wire cables, which has replaced an indigenous aqueduct of brush and poles; water carried from Embobut River to floor of Kerio Valley. (See Ministry of Agriculture in *Sources below*).

[h]Simoons (*see note 17*) reports the use of seeds of the *Milletia ferruginea* (*birbiria*) tree, leaves of the shrub *Maesa lanceolata* (*killabo*), the bark of *aura* (*Lantana trifoliata*) and the fruit of *Solanum marginatum*.

Sources: Allan (*note 27*); Benneh (*see Sources, Table 2*); Beyer, Jacquelyn L., personal observations (Zimbabwe, Lesotho); Cunnison (*see Sources, Table 2*); Edel (*see Sources, Table 1*); Forde (*see Sources, Table 2*); Goody, *Technology, Tradition and the State in Africa* (London: International Africal Institute, Oxford University Press, 1971), p. 76; Gulliver (*see Sources, Table 2*); Hill (*see Sources, Table 2*); Hunter (*note 42*); Igbozurike (*see Sources, Table 2*); Kaberry (*note 36*); Linton (*see Sources, Table 1*); Ministry of Agriculture, *African Land Development in Kenya* (Nairobi: English Press Ltd., 1962), pp. 152–153; Ogbu, "Seasonal Hunger in Tropical Africa as a Cultural Phenomenon," *Africa*, Vol. 43 (1973), p. 329; Reining (*see Sources, Table 2*); Reynolds (*see Sources, Table 1*); Richards (*see Sources, Table 1*); Roder, *The Sabi Valley Irrigation Projects* (Chicago: Department of Geography Research Paper No. 99, University of Chicago Press, 1965), pp. 54–55; Schneider, "Turu Ecology: Habitat, Mode of Production and Society," *Africa*, Vol. 36 (1936), p. 254; Simoons (*note 17*); Vermeer (*note 32*); White (*note 49*); Wylie, "Migrant Anlo Fishing Companies and Socio-Political Change: A Comparative Study," *Africa*, Vol. 39 (1969), pp. 396–410. **For correlation of sources with specific management practice forms and examples, see *note 77*.**

are less important, but the hoe in all its variations, along with the axe, bush-knife and spade, is the tool for the bush. The importance of *not* having clean cultivation, except for rare places where it is possible to control erosion and use soils resistant to damage, is suggested by one recommendation for modernization of shifting cultivation. Janzen recommends that judicious use of herbicides be preferred for clearing over plows as modernization and intensification proceeds:[40]

> The 'ultra-low volume' knapsack sprayer is a much cheaper item of advanced technology for the small farmer to use than a tractor and plow, and likely to cause far less damage than the erosion that has so frequently been induced by inadequately managed mechanization schemes. Introduction of machines developed for a different type of farming is not the best way to reduce drudgery in farming. Suppression of weeds by mulching and minimum tillage constitute appropriate technology that achieve the same purpose, and the real need is to develop appropriate tools for the operations involved.

Conservation of human energy and maintenance of productive capacity over a long time with minimal external inputs is the desired goal.[41]

Soil management. A variety of techniques, as elsewhere in the tropics, can be seen as responses to problems of soils and soil erosion (Table 3). Mounding, composting, cover crops, household waste, animal manure and fallowing are widespread and effective techniques. Ash from burning produces potash and is effective enough to offset the adverse effects of heat on structure and humus. The heat can also produce beneficial effects such as increasing soil alkalinity and destroying weed seeds and pests. Kitchen gardens, a widespread feature of farm organization, receive a greater percentage of such inputs as house waste. Latrines may be rotated in garden and field areas so that later reuse will provide benefits. There is usually a discernible gradient of soil quality from house to outer limits of field areas, and this is related to the energy required for composting and manuring away from easy supplies.[42] Frequently old village sites become the preferred new fields with explicit recognition of the value of remnant refuse.[43] It is not clear, however, that the direct and deliberate use of human waste was generally found acceptable, although Hill describes how such cycling is used in northern Nigeria.[44]

Tillage practices protect soil structure and texture, as well as contributing to erosion control, and remain a model for manipulation of fragile lateritic soils. Incorporation of organic materials through various methods is widely recognized as contributing to soil quality. Many micro-scale adjustments are made to control soil erosion.

Water management. Most traditional agriculture is rain dependent although scattered examples of irrigation works can be found, though rarely in operation. Nowhere else in Africa is there an example of pre-European organized irrigation-based economy comparable to that of the Nile Valley. Colonial land use observers seemed to rule our irrigation almost completely as an indigenous technology, but more recent investigations have shown a range of water management techniques associated with use of flood water paddy cultivation, stream diversions, dams and diversion through gravity flow.[45] Whether modern large-scale multipurpose development projects such as Volta and Kariba are everywhere a satisfactory substitute for smaller and more localized projects is questionable[46] Rehabilitation and reconstruction of small scale facilities in many areas could probably contribute much to lessening risks and improving crop production (Table 3).

One explanation for lack of extensive irrigation devices is that it takes work and organization, not always practical for a mobile population. When sufficient production is achieved by concentrating on rain crops and drought resistant crops, clearly it is not worth the effort to extend that production. Also, as Janzen notes:[47]

> ...irrigating between subtropical oases and between wet seasons is tempting, but it elimi- nates the only part of the physical environment that is on the farmer's side in his competi- tion with animals and weeds. The less extreme the dry season (or the more thorough the irrigation), the less extreme are the seasonal dips in insect pest population, with which the farmer can synchronize his crop's growth.

Lesser quantities of water are needed for domestic use or for livestock but good quality supplies on a regular basis are even more crucial (Table 3). Peasants and herders need water for consumption, hygiene, and amenities such as bathing. Locating and developing appropriate sources in streams, ponds, springs, lakes or wells, or cisterns; transferring water to sites of use; and storage of supplies is a major part of the daily workload. Women are usually always responsible for the transport of domestic water. Quality problems, including water borne diseases and mineral content, have been re- current issues and here it is not clear how able rural Africans were in making the connec- tion between health and use of water. In malaria regions the adaptation has been ruth- lessly Darwinian.[48] Modern observers have noted that defecation and urination does take place in water also used for bathing, but whether this is an index of social disequi- librium is not known. Certainly everywhere fishing and bathing bring people constantly into contact with water borne diseases.[49]

The choice of better water over lesser quality where such differences are recognized is complicated by considerations of danger, distance, dependability, conflicting use, ownership and other social factors. The important issue for today's resource users is the extent to which good quality water can be supplied to rural populations in order to reduce the social costs of disease and drudgery as well as meeting new kinds of urban demands. The study by the Whites and Bradley clearly shows the importance of taking into account traditional perceptions and use practices if these ends are to be accom- plished fairly and at reasonable cost.

Fishing. Exploitation of fish was a very early transition mode to a more sedentary pattern of livelihood by hunters and gatherers in most parts of the world. However there are few areas in Africa where pre-European tribes depended predominantly on fishing for subsistence. Murdock maps these and says:[50]

> In no instance, however, does this [fishing] represent a survival from a preagricultural economy but occurs only as a reflection of environmental influences. Coastal Mauritania, inhabited by the Imragen, and the lagoons of the Ivory Coast exemplify one type of favor- able situation—a maritime location with an immediate hinterland unsuited to agriculture. A second conducive situation is presented by the Congo and Niger Rivers and some of their principal tributaries. Here numerous tribes combine fishing with a profitable boat trade and exchange dried or salted fish for the agricultural produce of their neighbors. An occasional insular people, notably the Buduma of the small islets in Lake Chad, has arrived at a comparable economic adjustment.

He also notes that, except for a strongly enforced taboo on eating fish by the Cushites in Northeast Africa, fishing is widely used for supplementary diets. This is still true today.

Table 4. Adversarial Management[a]

Management practice	Examples	Management practice	Examples
Forests		Protection of	
Clearing—fire, axe (pollarding)	Widespread*	Crows and woodpeckers protected for alarm purposes; honey bees and wasps; unclean animals not hunted	Kenya*
Firebreak for huts	Cameroon*	Bees[c]	Widespread
Protection		Utilization	
Special council trees	Kenya*	General	Widespread*
Use rules[b]	Tanzania*	Traps, snares, fall traps, pit traps	Widespread*
Pruning	Tanzania*		
Ownership for fodder, animal bedding, construction		*Weeds, pests, and disease (also toxic food plants)*	
Planting	Tanzania* Cameroon*	Mulching against weeds	Widespread*
Charcoal	Widespread*	Cats for rodent control	Cameroon
		Human scarecrows	Widespread*
Wildlife		Wild meat not brought near cattle	Kenya
Protection against		Weeding with hoe	Widespread*
Living fences and hedges	Widespread*	Medicinal plants protected	Widespread*
Herd boys	Widespread*	Soaking seeds against disease[d]	Zambia*
Shallow holes or pits—*sirikwa*	East Africa*	Hire cattle out to non-tsetse areas	Kenya*
Raised platforms for guards	Ethiopia*	Fermentation and drying	Zaire*
Limits set for herds	Kenya*	Fires to smoke locust flights	Madagascar
Ditch dug around garden against bush pig	Zambia*	Treatment of animals[e]	Ethiopia, Zambia, Zaire*
Ridging instead of mounds against monkeys	Nigeria*		
Flapping leaves—scarecrow against birds or monkeys	Zambia*	Settlement siting to avoid water and animal diseases	Widespread*
Watching platforms (*amopungu*), 10 feet (3 meters) high—muzzle loading guns vs. elephants, buck	Zambia*		

Notes:

*Pre-European, but often still present.

aThis term is used in reference to environmental elements perceived as those to be avoided, eliminated (or cleared), and/or controlled. In many cases the control may include occasional, periodic or regular utilization, e.g., trees.

bScattered trees, left from deforestation for cultivation in the 19th century, may be used for gathering, fuelwood, etc. by owners who do not have other rights to contiguous land.

cAccording to Townsend (*see Sources below*), "It has been estimated that 1/3 of total diet of peoples in developing countries is derived either directly or indirectly from insect pollinated plants;" pictures of log hives in baobab trees, Uganda and Tanzania.

dReynolds (*see Sources, Table 1*) reports that a mixture of pounded kashi fruit, seeds of the wild cucumber (*Cucumis ficifoluis*) and water is used to protect seeds against white ants.

eSimoons (*see note 17*) reports the use of charms from goatskin plus sacrifices to control flies; pack sores are treated with leaves and burdens are rotated to allow time for healing; sores are cauterized with red-hot iron.

Sources: Allan (*note 27*); Beyer, Jacquelyn L., personal observations (Tanzania, South Africa, Kenya, Botswana); Butynski and Richter, "In Botswana Most of the Meat Is Wild," *Unasylva*, Vol. 26 (1974), pp. 24–29); Cunnison (*see Sources, Table 3*); Curwen (*note 39*); de Vos, "Game as Food," *Unasylva*, Vol. 29:116, pp. 2–12; Douglas (*see Sources, Table 2*); Gerlach (*see Sources, Table 3*); Gulliver (*see Sources, Table 2*); Hughes and Hunter, "The Role of Technological Development in Promoting Disease," in M. Taghi Farmer and John P. Milton, *The Careless Technology* (Garden City, N.Y.: The Natural History Press, 1972), pp. 69–101; Isack (*note 14*); Keberry (*note 36*); Linton (*see Sources, Table 1*); Porter (*note 35*); Reining (*see Sources, Table 2*); Reynolds (*see Sources, Table 1*); Richards (*see Sources, Table 1*); Simoons (*note 17*); Townsend, "Beekeeping and Agricultural Development," *World Animal Review*, Vol. 12 (1974), pp. 36–40; Vermeer (*note 32*). **For correlation of sources with specific management practice forms and examples, see *note 77*.**

Other sources and studies report the use of fish as supplements or for trade. In modern times there have been increasing examples of fishing for cash income and, in some instances, very great increases in wealth, not always with completely successful social results. For the most part the techniques now widely used are, with some adaptations, essentially the same as in pre-European times. Nets and baskets, traps, spears, bows and arrows, drumming, fencing of lagoons, dams, grass rolls and poisons, and dugout canoes can still be seen (Table 3). One can note some changes, such as the substitution of gunpowder for drumming, which have meant more rapid depletion of resources, but generally fish resources are underexploited.

Modern planners frequently point to the potential of fresh and saltwater fisheries as reasonable developments to help improve protein-poor diets with little expense (dried fish is over 70% protein). There are destabilizing aspects to this however. Introduction of pond aquaculture on a large scale, as in the Congo in the 1950s, created problems of new water-borne diseases and spread of malaria along with maintenance problems.[51] Rapid infusion of cash into traditional village economies can produce distortions in social relations as well as non-productive investments. As in agriculture, intensification will call for serious attention to the total complex of resource base and human institutions, values and needs.

Forests. Trees are obstacles to farmers and herders. Universally forest clearing has been an historic fact and Africa is no different. The major exception is the Mbuti pygmies of the Ituri rainforest in the Congo basin. Their fear of and distaste for the cultivators who threaten their forests are matched only by their loyalty to their forest habitat.[52] Yet, even for cultivators, paradoxically, trees have been and are valued resources, and become especially so after major deforestation. In equatorial forests, clearings for crops are protected by trees used for cropping and for occasional gathering. Trees are sources for firewood and charcoal, and for building materials. Frequently complicated ownership and use rules, designed to insure continued usage, will be established as guides for exploitation. But nowhere in Africa was afforestation or reforestation applied as a concept on a major scale until Europeans arrived and then there was usually bitter resentment of the expropriation of land for plantation crops or tree reserves.[53]

There were clear examples, however, of ways in which Africans explicitly recognized the value of trees as protectors for water and soils (Table 4).[54] Commercial exploitation of indigenous forests was deterred by the complications of diversity and access, and now many ecologists insist that any timber exploitation should be done with due consideration for other contributions of tropical ecosystems, many of which are realized in traditional systems of tree and plant cropping. These benefits include soil protection, oxygen balance and gene pools for useful food and medicinal products.[55] Firewood scarcity is a growing crisis for many areas, especially in densely settled rural areas and for urban dwellers, so that reforestation as part of other plans to improve land and water and soil use is of primary importance (Fig. 3). Otherwise plantations which remove land from cultivation for export products may not necessarily benefit local inhabitants. Extensive plantations of exotic conifers are common in South Africa and other places where European investors supported development (Table 4).

Wildlife. Like forests, wild animals are typically seen by farmers and herders as antagonists in the struggle for survival. Avoidance and control, if not elimination, are management goals. There are excellent arguments for protection of as diverse a set of natural

Fig. 3. Manure collected and left to dry for fuel, Lesotho. Unfortunately increasing settlement in areas without trees has led to use of manure for this purpose rather than for renewing soil fertility.

systems as possible, especially relating to the advantages of genetic reservoirs to provide resources for many purposes. Africans, however, traditionally want protection from wild animals for themselves, their crops, and livestock. A variety of techniques, including hunting with poison, traps, nets and communal hunts, were and are used. Fencing of ranges to provide corridors for livestock migration has also been built. Avoidance is very much a tactic (Table 4).

Animals are also a resource for food supplements and for non-food products. The modern drive for protection of African wildlife and for setting aside large reserves for their exclusive use is as alien to African tradition as it is for Russian pioneers in Siberia or Nevada sheep ranchers. It is not unusual for claims to be made today that particular societies "owe" the world protection of some valued artifact or environmental resource. England, for example, is said to owe the world its heritage of 18th century landscape planning; Italy owes the world an undamaged and preserved Venice; Brazil is encouraged to think twice or more about plans for clearing the Amazon rainforest; Egypt owes its pyramids and temples; and so forth. Thus African nations are not unique in the demand that they subsidize external values in wildlife preservation. The problem is that the needs of people in East Africa, where the issue is acute, are frequently in conflict with the goal of wildlife maintenance and protection in any kind of ecological security. Game cropping has been proposed and fitfully tried as a compromise solution, but nowhere has this been implemented with continuing success except for some white farms in South Africa. One writer has proposed a program of reserves backed by mandatory environmental impact statements whenever non-African public and corporate agencies operate overseas.

In addition compensatory payments, possibly generated through international bodies, would be made to developing countries where opportunities to exploit nature reserves are foregone. These are beginning steps in what will have to be a hard look at such land use conflicts in terms of who benefits and who pays.[56]

Weeds, pests and disease control. Apparently the biological environment has been the most hazardous and the least amenable to control by traditional Africans. It may be true that as ethnoscientists Africans were less skilled at understanding the intricate linkages for disease pathogens than, say, the workings of the hydrologic cycle. Still there was and is an enormous fund of practical knowledge (Table 4). It is clear now, for example, that pre-colonial East Africans were very aware of the tsetse fly menace and were more familiar with its ecology than whites were to be until well into the 20th century.[57] Folk medicine itself is an important subject and the extent to which the traditional treatment practices should be incorporated into modern medicine is open. This chapter cannot cover such an extensive subject but there is a parallel in the world of medicine for the concern we have here in "listening to the people" to find out what works. Even in western countries there are growing requests for a more comprehensive medical system.[58]

Poisons and mechanical or biological controls have been used against predator insects, birds and animals. Some folk remedies for plant diseases have also been reported. Some insect and weed pests are exotics but most simply are indigenous opportunists. The first patch of grain or row of yams undoubtedly became a chomping paradise and the greater the elaboration of cultivation or herding, the greater the attraction. Monoculture is the extreme case of a happy hunting ground and the problems with chemical control everywhere cast clouds over its extensive usage in the future. Major efforts to develop appropriate biochemical, biological, and genetic controls must be supported.[59] In all cases the total system must be considered. One writer makes a strong case for massive trypanosomiasis control as a major contributor to the Sahel drought in the 1960s and 1970s because there was little consideration for the effects of increased grazing where the fly was controlled.[60] Sometimes, however, the adverse results of a quick technical fix are not because of ignorance but rather because something must be done and comprehensive strategies are difficult and time consuming to implement.

Certainly widespread environmentally caused disease is a major deterrent for human vigor as well as successful and continued food production. Science has much to offer in understanding and control, but there will be a succession of agonizing dilemmas over the issue of a solution producing new and painful problems, as with the medical control of death and subsequent explosions in population growth. These problems for research range from day to day coping with insects, viruses, bacteria, birds, etc. to periodic dramatic invasions by weaver birds, army worms or locusts.

Energy. One can find so many examples in the industrial world, and its extensions into the developing world, of massive environmental insults partly because of the fossil fuel based extention of human and animal powers. African impacts were relatively benign, even taking into account vegetative changes and mining, because relatively fewer people were limited to their own energy, plus a small amount from animals. In addition to the use of fire as a clearing tool, there was the use of wood as a primary fuel for cooking and drying as well as for industrial charcoal (Table 5). Wood is still a primary source of energy.[61] There is little evidence of mechanical power of water having been

Table 5. Energy

Management practice	Examples*
Animal	
Draft and transport animals	Ethiopia, Central Africa, West Africa, South Africa
Wind and solar	
General	Widespread
Threshing	Widespread
Drying	Widespread
Wood	
General	Widespread
Depletion	Widespread

Note:
*Pre-European, but often still present.
Sources: Allan (*note 27*); Arnold and Jongma (*note 61*); Beyer, Jacquelyn L., personal observation (Lesotho, Rhodesia); Eckholm, *The Other Energy Crisis: Firewood* (Washington, D.C., Worldwatch Paper I, 1975); Eckholm, *Losing Ground* (New York: Norton & Co. 1976), pp. 25-45; Makhijani, *Energy and Agriculture in the Third World* (Cambridge: Ballinger Publishing Co., 1975); Simoons (*note 17*). Also see *note 77.*

traditionally harnessed and it is rare to find animals used for work, although they were and are important in the Sahel, Ethiopia and, since the 19th century, in Southern Africa. Gravity was used in some irrigation works and wind for chores such as threshing.

It is hard to deny the thesis that widespread introduction of facilities using fossil or nuclear energy is both unwise and potentially ineffective in satisfying the energy needs of most Africans. These needs will remain for a long time those of rural, small-scale activities. At the same time one cannot deny that these needs include elaboration of traditional energy usage to provide more efficient and labor-saving tools. But again this elaboration is more involved than simply introducing solar cookers, pumps or water heaters. As one energy consultant to the United States Agency for International Development (AID) reminds us:[62]

In fact, renewable energy technologies raise a host of social issues . . . . Renewable energy for Africa is in few important ways a technical issue. Instead, place by place, the signifi-cant questions will be cultural ones. It follows that the people to work on such programs will have to know as much about social realities as they do about technology. The skills required are those of listening, adapting, teaching, collaborating at the village level. These are not skills the development community has in abundance, or knows well where to find. Yet America alone has several groups experienced in building energy technologies with poor communities (and) . . . counterpart organizations exist in Europe, Asia, and Africa itself. If we outsiders wish to assist Africa with renewable energy programs, we will have to rely on groups like these. To help build significant parts of Africa's future on renewable energy systems is a task both inescapable and awesomely complex. The venture is one that many Americans will simultaneously be pursuing, however, since our own energy future must move substantially in the same direction. With good will and a little work, we may all help each other find ways to do the job right.

This statement is an appropriate introduction to a brief consideration of future needs and some of the problems planners, policy-makers and resource users face.[63]

A REGION IN TRANSITION

Characteristics of Traditional Systems

In general the characteristics of African resource management systems include:

(1) Localized scale of operations, including market exchange and the use of local wood, brush, grass, clay and minerals for construction, tool-making and cooking fires.

(2) The redundancy built in through cropping practices, combination strategies, and diversity of skills, giving resiliency and flexibility to socioeconomic patterns of life.

(3) Mobility as expressed in nomadic herding, shifting agriculture, migration to new locations, and seasonal movement in response to floods or drought. Such mobility has decreased significantly in this century so that shifting agriculture, especially, seldom involves locational changes.

(4) Change and adaptability as evidenced in the long history of new crop and livestock introductions, evolution of systems of production, and resiliency and persistence in the face of traumatic dislocations.

(5) Integration of economic activities with political, social and religious institutions and values so that there is a certain holistic integrity to the day to day life of work, ritual, learning and social interactions.

(6) Low Productivity whether measured in yields or returns per person.[64]

(7) Relatively high efficiency as measured by return of food per unit of energy input, in strong contrast to machine based, fossil fuel systems.[65]

(8) Demographic profiles which show low life expectancy and high infant mortality, but consistent growth over time. Such growth has occurred in spite of recurrent drought, epidemics, locust invasions, slaving, war and exogenous economic and political decision-making.

(9) Low capital investments but high labor requirements.

Generalizations are frustrating because so much texture is lost. A reconstruction of the spatial arrangement of different cultural groups in East Africa alone, for example, shows that about 2000 years ago there were seven different associations of economic activity, resource use, environmental niches, ethnicity and social order in what is now Kenya, Uganda and Tanzania. By 500 A.D. there were eight and by 1000 A.D. there were 15.[66] The heritage of such diversity which is still so strong will be hard to homogenize.

There can be no question, however, that pre-European Africa was a success by any conventional standards. There was a rewarding economic and cultural life, population grew and expanded, and a variety of opportunities existed for individual achievement. Africans, as Bohannan notes, were not deprived until European rule opened up new vistas and then denied access to benefits of the colonially controlled structures.[67] In many places complex and relatively dense populations were supported and often at densities far higher than are now present.

Persistence and Change

It is true that much of this success can be attributed to the possibility for migration to virgin, or less intensively used, areas. This was a solution resorted to up until the 20th century, but now growth, change and development must take place by intensification of areas already used. Although there are still opportunities for expansion these increasingly conflict with such resource goals as wildlife preservation or afforestation. Infanticide, coercive practices or lower calorie diets are less and less acceptable responses.[68]

Today traditional patterns of use can still be found with varying degrees of change. It would be accurate to say that integrated systems of traditional resource practices are hard to find than are individual component practices. Because economic activities are so intimately linked with belief systems and forms of social interactions, there are resilient elements in all societies which allow for continuity in the face of all kinds of pressures to change. Also, the kinds of productive systems Africans had developed by the 16th century were reasonably effective except possibly for problems of disease. They allowed for experimentation and innovation, for continued productivity, and for steady population growth and expansion. Now mobility across political boundaries or into virgin lands is very limited and this, combined with rapid population growth and the tighter integration of most economies into a global system, are part of the pressures for increased production.

REGIONAL ASSESSMENT

Africa is so diverse in its institutional forms that a summary of forces supporting or inhibiting the regeneration of and/or support for traditional resource techniques and values must necessarily include many exceptions. Governments vary with respect to their commitments to economic planning, to emphasis on rural needs, to support of education and applied research, and to integration of local folk knowledge with scientific analysis. Fascination with the productive fruits of large scale, high technology frequently obscures the need for patient, human scale developments. Guidelines set by external assistance agencies do not always recognize the value of indigenous methods. Political and educational elitism leads to scorn for peasant labor and a drive to emulate consumer societies, while rural folk are alienated by lack of participation or incentives. There is, however, a growing network of educational institutions, research projects, model developments, and social critics which can tap the traditional willingness of Africans to adopt new techniques, experiment, and take risks while placing high value on social cooperation and on the land itself.

Recombinations and Evolution

Many of the suggestions for ways to insure consideration of traditional methods as components of modernizing resource utilization systems are similar to those for other regions. The interesting issue to consider is the way in which many people in the industrialized world are beginning to question the authority of experts who recommend continuation and expansion of large-scale, technologically complex, energy and materials consuming, and essentially predatory techniques. These questions are framed in the context of persistent examples of impaired environments, insults to health, scarcity, and escalating costs, and are expressed in the appropriate technology movement, in pressures for environmental awareness, and in new social inventions designed to decentralize and organize for strategies which would be less fragile.[69] Western techniques have many things to offer, but for natural resource management in general the same approach should be used as for medicine. The trust, belief, and psychological well being which results from sympathy with folkways in curing are analagous to the cooperation, sense of belonging, and pragmatism which could be gained by more humility and sensitivity to effective traditional approaches.

Examples of ways the technology and characteristics of traditional methods could combine with western modes of analysis and action include:

(1) Controlled burning to allow for reforestation of hill crests, watersheds, and erodable soils while maintaining the clearings necessary for grazing and cultivation.

(2) Planting trees instead of extending a grid of electricity, especially where this must be generated by fossil fuels.

(3) Explore better biological and biochemical controls for insects and disease parasites, with a considerable skepticism about massive eradication programs.

(4) Serious attention to game cropping, especially for marginal areas.

(5) Attention to "humble" plants by plant geneticists and agronomists in order to rationalize the enormous diversity of indigenous foods.[70]

(6) A paramedical approach to training for human and animal health programs, tapping local skills and knowledge.

(7) Pilot projects, research and education programs linking community and formal education and based on a premise that technology is a means, not an end, and that holistic, integrated problem solving is best.[71]

(8) A wide range of "appropriate technology" to expand the present kinds of energy and water use by tapping the ingenuity and skills of Africans to improve their ability to store and prepare food; pump, lift and transport water; care for animals, etc.[72]

(9) Be skeptical of infrastructure facilities and institutional rules which could inhibit development of modern forms of mobility.[73]

Growth and change leading to development is a complex matter, especially for so large an area. It would not be accurate to say that present planners, researchers, or resource users are totally unaware of the fundamental ideas expressed here, although the criticism expressed by Janzen is fair.[74] Where barriers are present they are likely to be psychological (western hubris, elitist viewpoints), practical (there is always a problem of allocation of resources and urban dwellers do have more power), lack of knowledge, lack of will, and failure to distribute decision-making power equitably. Where firewood is harder to find and more costly every day, for example, it is easy to say that planting trees will benefit more peasants than will a major hydroelectric plant. It is harder to achieve because dams are much quicker to build, the results are more immediately apparent, decisions are centralized, and those with the capacity to build dams also have the economic and political power to force the decision.

EPLIOGUE

The ultimate goal for conservation is the enhancement of human welfare. People are involved in resource management techniques as agents of production and creators of tools and institutions. They are also resources of concern with respect to development of those special qualities which support creativity, insure justice and equity, and allow for humane and peaceful social interaction. These are difficult issues for many societies in Africa as the stress of rapid social and economic change increases, but especially so for the Republic of South Africa.

In terms of traditional survivals versus westernization and change, it is easy to refer to data showing how thoroughly changed South African black societies have been by 325 years of interaction with white conquerors and rulers. This interaction has provided few models of sensitivity to traditional modes of resource use or awareness of ways modernization should and could accommodate traditional wisdom. In a large part this is because of the deliberate exclusion of black South Africans from significant decisions about the direction and pace of change. As the bitter confrontation between African and Afrikaner nationalisms in this beautiful and resource abundant country escalates into angry violence it is hard to maintain cool "scientific" objectivity. Reference is made in the Tables to examples of useful techniques in South Africa, but the special case must be made here for the viability and strength of black African institutions and values as shown by the continuing resilience and resistance to oppression in that country. Many of you may wish to explore the special problems of contrasting wealth and poverty or of the allocation of power in the society, but I want to emphasize especially the massive and destructive impact of the *apartheid* ideology on rural women. They live a hard-scrabble, tenuous existence in the neglected and abused reserves or phantom "Bantustan" nations.[75] If Africa is ever to be whole again in its pursuit of increased quality of life, this last trauma of the 20th century must be healed.

NOTES

[1] A fuller explanation of the meaning of "traditional" is given in the Introduction to this book by Dr. Gary Klee.

[2] Patrick J. Munson, "Africa's Prehistoric Past," in *Africa*, Phyllis M. Martin and Patrick O'Meara, eds. (Bloomington: Indiana University Press, 1977), pp. 62–82. More recently the date for the appearance of hominid species has been fixed at between 3–4 million years B.C., but this remains a controversial assertion. See D. C. Johanson and T. D. White, "A Systematic Assessment of Early African Hominids," *Science*, Vol. 203 (1979), pp. 321–330.

[3] The usual explanation for a diffusion route from Turkey to West Africa via Meroe in Egypt has been questioned by B. G. Trigger in a 1969 article, "The Myth of Meroe and the African Iron Age," *African Historical Studies*, II, pp. 23–50. His view is based, in part, on recent radiocarbon dating of human-made iron in Bukoba on the west shore of Lake Victoria. This shows that iron was produced as early as 500 B.C., a greater antiquity than for Meroe.

[4] Jack R. Harlan, "Agricultural Origins: Centers and Noncenters," *Science*, Vol. 174 (1971),

pp. 468–474. His short list of African domesticates shows 7 cereals, 3 pulses, 5 tubers, 5 oil-yielding plants, and 7 others, including watermelon, coffee, and cotton.

[5]Phillips W. Foster, "Migrations and Agriculture," U.S. Department of Agriculture Yearbook, *Farmer's World* (Washington, D.C.: Government Printing Office, 1964), pp. 24–25.

[6]James H. Vaughan, "Environment, Population and Traditional Society," in Martin and O'Meara, op. cit., note 2, p. 22.

[7]Paul Bohannan and George Dalton, *Markets in Africa* (Garden City, N.Y.: The Natural History Library, Anchor Books, Doubleday & Co., 1965).

[8]Basil Davidson, *Black Mother: The Years of Trial* (London: Victor Gollanz, Ltd., 1961).

[9]Roland Oliver and Anthony Atmore, *Africa Since 1800* (London: Cambridge University Press, 2nd ed., 1972).

[10]For a summary see Sheldon Gellar, "The Colonial Era," pp. 132–149 and Edmond J. Keller, "Decolonialization and the Struggle for Independence," pp. 15–165 in Martin and O'Meara, op. cit., note 2. For a more detailed critical view see Walter Rodney, *How Europe Underdeveloped Africa* (Dar-es-Salaam: Tanzania Publishing House, 1972).

[11]Thomas T. Kane and Paul F. Myers, *1978 World Population Data Sheet* (Washington, D.C.: Population Reference Bureau, 1978). Western: Benin, Cape Verde, Gambia, Ghana, Guinea, Guinea-Bissau, Ivory Coast, Liberia, Mali, Mauritania, Niger, Nigeria, Senegal, Sierra Leone, Togo, and Upper Volta; Eastern: Burundi, Comoros, Djibouti, Ethiopia, Kenya, Madagascar, Malawi, Mauritius, Mozambique, Reunion, Rhodesia, Rwanda, Seychelles, Somalia, Republic of Tanzania, Uganda, and Zambia; Middle: Angola, Republic of Cameroon, Central African Empire, Chad, Republic of Congo, Equatorial Guinea, Gabon, Sao Tome and Principe, and Zaire; Southern: Botswana, Lesotho, Namibia, South Africa, and Swaziland.

[12]C. Gregory Knight, "Ethnoscience: A Cognitive Approach to African Agriculture," Paper prepared for the S.S.R.C. Conference on Environmental and Spatial Cognition in Africa (University Park: Pennsylvania State University, May 1974).

[13]D. M. Chavunduka, "African Attitudes to Conservation," *Rhodesian Agriculture Journal*, Vol. 75:3 (1978), pp. 61–63.

[14]Hussein Adan Isack, "An African Ethic of Conservation," *Natural History*, Vol. LXXXV (Nov., 1976), p. 95.

[15]J. Oladipo Adejuwon, "Human Impact on African Environmental Systems," in *Contemporary Africa*, C. Gregory Knight and James L. Newman, eds. (New York: Prentice Hall, 1976), pp. 140–158.

[16]John Phillips, *The Development of Agriculture and Forestry in the Tropics*, rev. (New York: Praeger, 1967), pp. 104–105.

[17]Frederick J. Simoons, *Northwest Ethiopia: Peoples and Economy* (Madison: University of Wisconsin Press, 1960).

[18]Personal observation, 1963.

[19]Peter Schmidt and Donald H. Avery, "Complex Iron Smelting and Prehistoric Culture in Tanzania," *Science*, Vol. 201 (1978), pp. 1085–1089.

[20]Ibid.

[21]Helge Kjekshus, *Ecology Control and Economic Development in East African History: The Case of Tanganyika, 1850–1950* (Berkeley and Los Angeles: University of California Press, 1977), p. 83. Kjekshus reports that Schmidt, in Kianja, was shown a slag heap "120 metres long, 2–3 metres wide and 2 metres high. . . .Scores of pits were found at Kikukwe village in Kiziba some of which were up to 8 metres deep."

[22]Schmidt and Avery, op. cit., note 19.

[23]Betsy Jones, "Recycling at the Grass Roots," *Africa Report*, Vol. 23:3 (1978), pp. 15–17.

[24]Robert W. July, *Precolonial Africa: An Economic and Social History* (New York: Charles Scribner's Sons, 1975). In writing about the migration of Cushitic-speaking peoples (c. 1000 B.C.) from Ethiopia to the lakes region, he notes: "They are also thought to have built a series of agricultural sites noted for the presence of irrigation ditches, terraced fields, graded roads and revetted homesteads, all constructed in fitted stone technique and apparently designed to sustain relatively dense populations in low rainfall areas." (p. 148)

[25]Personal conversation with Chief Albert Luthuli, Stanger, Natal, South Africa, 1961.

[26]Erik P. Eckholm, "The Deterioration of Mountain Environments," *Science*, Vol. 189 (1975),

pp. 764–770. "The villages in this area [Gamu Highlands] are violating their own land management rules and they know it, but they see no alternative."

[27]William Allan, *The African Husbandman* (Westport, Conn.: Greenwood Press, 1965), pp. 441–445.

[28]Douglas L. Johnson, ed., "The Human Face of Desertification," *Economic Geography*, Vol. 53:4 (1977), several articles; Bashir A. Datoo, "Peasant Agricultural Production in East Africa: The Nature and Consequences of Dependence," *Antipode*, Vol. 9:1 (1977), pp. 70–78; Michael Mortimore, ed., "Drought in Africa," *Savanna*, Vol. 2:2 (1973); Ade Akenbode, "Population Explosion in Africa and Its Implications for Economic Development," *Journal of Geography*, Vol. 76:1 (1977), pp. 28–36; James J. Hidore, "Population Explosion in Africa: Further Implications," *Journal of Geography*, Vol. 77:6 (1978), pp. 214–220.

[29]Karl Pelzer, *Pioneer Settlement in the Asiatic Tropics*, Special Publication #29 (New York: American Geographical Society, 1945), p. 17.

[30]C. Gregory Knight, "Prospects for Peasant Agriculture," in Knight and Newman, op. cit., note 15, pp. 195–225.

[31]Ibid.

[32]Donald E. Vermeer, "Population Pressure and Crop Rotational Changes Among the Tiv of Nigeria," *Annals*, Association of American Geographers, Vol. 60 (1970), p. 314.

[33]Judith Heyer, "Preliminary Results of a Linear Programming Analysis of Peasant Farms in Machokos District, Kenya" (Kampala: *Proceedings of East African Institute of Social Research Conference*, Jan., 1965).

[34]A major contribution to typology is Esther Bosrup, *The Conditions of Agricultural Growth* (Chicago: Aldine, 1965).

[35]Phillip W. Porter, "Environmental Potentials and Economic Opportunities: A Background for Cultural Adaptation," *American Anthropologist*, Vol. 67 (1965), pp. 409–20.

[36]Phyllis M. Kaberry, *Women of the Grassfields* (London: Her Majesty's Stationery Office, 1952).

[37]Frank E. Bernard, "Geographers and Peasant Agriculture: Some Random Observations Based on Kenya Experience," pp. 7–12 in *Peasant Agriculture in the 21st Century*, Gene Wilkin and Donald E. Vermeer, eds., papers presented at Special Session of AAG, 1973; K. G. V. Krishna, "Smallholder Agriculture in Africa: Constraints and Potential," *Annals, AAPSS*, Vol. 432 (1977), pp. 12–25.

[38]Kjekshus, op. cit., note 21.

[39]E. Cecil Curwen and Gudmund Hatt, *Plough and Pasture: The Early History of Farming* (New York: Henry Schuman, 1953); July, op. cit., note 24: "...its [the plow] early appearance and continued use in Egypt, Ethiopia and the Mahgrib makes plausible the hypothesis that it failed to appear in sub-Saharan Africa not because the tropical farmer was unaware of its existence but because he felt he possessed more effective alternatives." (p. 285)

[40]Daniel H. Janzen, "Tropical Agroecosystems," *Science*, Vol. 182 (1975), p. 1214.

[41]D. J. Greenland, "Bringing the Green Revolution to the Shifting Cultivator," *Science*, Vol. 190 (1975), pp. 841–844.

[42]John M. Hunter, "The Social Roots of Dispersed Settlement in Northern Ghana," *Annals*, Association of American Geographers, Vol. 57 (1967), p. 341.

[43]Audrey Richards, "A Changing Pattern of Agriculture in East Africa: The Bemba of Northern Rhodesia," *Geographical Journal*, Vol. 124 (1958), pp. 302–14.

[44]Polly Hill, *Population, Prosperity and Poverty: Rural Kano, 1900 and 1970*, (Cambridge: Cambridge University Press, 1977), p. 102: "...it was one of the important duties of farmslaves to fetch household sweepings, as well as latrine manure (*takin masai*) from the city. Although it is usually believed that the use of 'night soil' is abhorrent to the ordinary West African farmers, Dorayl farmers, like those in many Hausa localities...have long been accustomed to apply dry latrine manure to their land, most of which is produced by sealing their own house latrines with earth and ashes for a year or so, when a black, odourless 'earth' may be extracted."

[45]Kjekshus, op. cit., note 21.

[46]W. M. Warren and N. Rubin, eds., *Dams in Africa* (London: Frank Cass, 1968).

[47]Janzen, op. cit., note 40.

[48]Robert S. Desowitz, "How the Wise Men Brought Malaria to Africa," *Natural History*, Vol. LXXXV:8 (1976), pp. 36–44: "Paradoxically and cruelly, in the absence of an effective control

program, a community's welfare and stability often depend on continuous, intense exposure to malaria. Under these conditions, as in the agricultural villages of Africa and Southeast Asia, malaria accounts for high infant mortality; some 40 percent or more of the children under the age of five may die of the infection. Those who survive, however, develop a protective immunity, and adults, the productive segment of the community, remain relatively free of the pernicious clinical manifestations of the infection. Usually, the high infant mortality is compensated by a high birthrate, and so a population equilibrium is achieved in which the workers are sufficiently healthy to provide the community's food requirements." (p. 44)

[49] One of the most comprehensive studies of the ecology of health, technology, culture, and economics associated with domestic water use is Gilbert F. White, David J. Bradley and Anne U. White, *Drawers of Water* (Chicago: University of Chicago Press, 1972).

[50] George Peter Murdock, *Africa: Its Peoples and Cultures* (New York: McGraw-Hill, 1959).

[51] D. F. Owen, *Man in Tropical Africa: The Environmental Predicament* (New York and London: Oxford University Press, 1973), pp. 128-130.

[52] Ibid., pp. 49-52; Colin Turnbull, *The Forest People*, (New York: Simon & Schuster, 1961).

[53] T. R. Batten, *Problems of African Development: Part I, Land and Labour* (London: Oxford University Press, 1960), p. 54: "When a Department of Forestry was established there [Ghana] in 1909 it recommended that the forests should be protected. Chiefs and lawyers of the Aborigines Protection Society at once strongly attacked the proposals, which they said were an attempt by the government to take away the people's land, and they were able to delay the protection of the forests until 1927 by which time very great damage had been done."

[54] For example, R. A. Pullan, "Farmed Parkland in West Africa," *Savanna*, Vol. 3:2 (1974), pp. 119-141: "In West Africa trees are left in cultivated areas for a variety of purposes. Some are kept specifically for fodder and shade for sheep, cattle, and goats. Others provide leaves and fruit for human consumption, while others are used to provide wood and fibre rope for utensils, implements, construction timber and canoes. Many have multiple uses related to the medicinal requirements, the provision of shade, hives for bees, and, in former times, bark cloth. At least one tree has been shown to maintain or increase soil fertility. As a last resort trees supply firewood for the local farm population and near towns a substantial local trade in firewood derived from the pollarding and felling of farmed parkland trees may develop." (p. 119)

[55] Raymond Bouillene, "Man the Destroying Biotype," *Science*, Vol. 135 (1962), pp. 706-712; and A. Gomez-Pompa, C. Vasquez Yanes and S. Guevara, "The Tropical Rainforest: A Nonrenewable Resource," *Science*, Vol. 177 (1972), pp. 762-765.

[56] Norman Myers, "An Expanded Approach to the Problem of Disappearing Species," *Science*, Vol. 193 (1976), pp. 198-202. Also see Erik Eckholm, "Third World Development: A New Goal for Environmentalists?" *Agenda*, Washington, D.C., U.S. AID (Oct., 1978); Norman Myers, "National Parks in Savannah Africa," *Science*, Vol. 178 (1972), pp. 1255-1263.

[57] Kjekshus, op. cit., note 21.

[58] George L. Engel, "The Need for a New Medical Model: A Challenge for Biomedicine," *Science*, Vol. 196 (1977), pp. 129-136.

[59] Owen, op. cit., note 51, pp. 84-108; Jerrold Meinwald et al., "Chemical Ecology: Studies from East Africa," *Science*, Vol. 199 (1978), pp. 1167-73; P. T. Haskell, "Integrated Pest Control and Small Farmer Crop Protection in Developing Countries," *Outlook on Agriculture*, Vol. 9:3 (1977), pp 121-6.

[60] W. E. Ormerod, "Ecological Effects of Control of Trypanosomiasis," *Science*, Vol. 191 (1976), pp. 815-821; Robert S. Desowitz, "The Fly that Would be King," *Natural History*, Vol. LXXXVI:2 (1977), pp. 76-83; "As trypanosomiasis is conquered, overgrazing, soil erosion, social disruption, and faunal extinction may result. Until such time that scientists and their technical-administrative partners appreciate the grand strategy to act sanely and effectively to protect the well-being of all Africa's citizens, both two-legged and four-legged, we might applaud the cosmic wisdom that has made the tsetse, rather than man, Africa's custodian." (p. 83)

[61] J. E. M. Arnold and J. Jongma, "Firewood and Charcoal in Developing Countries," *Unasylva*, Vol. 29:118, pp. 2-9. The authors calculate total fuelwood and charcoal use in all of Africa at 282 million m^2 (93 million tons of coal equivalent) or 66% of total energy, excluding other organic fuels and human/animal labor. (p. 3)

[62] David French, "Energy for Africa's Future," *African Report*, Vol. 23:3 (1978), pp. 9-14.

[63]Norman L. Brown and James W. Howe, "Solar Energy for Village Development," *Science*, Vol. 199 (1978), pp. 651-657.

[64]Jen-hu Chang, "Tropical Agriculture: Crop Diversity and Crop Yields," *Economic Geography*, Vol. 53 (1977), pp. 241-254. His data show an average production of 862 kg. per hectage for tropical African production, compared to 896 in Southwest Asia, 1055 in South America, 1159 in South Asia, 1307 in Central America, and 1782 in Southeast Asia. All of these compare to 2107 for temperate zone agriculture.

[65]Peter J. M. McEwan and Robert B. Sutcliffe, eds., *Modern Africa* (New York: Thomas Y. Crowell Co., 1965), p. 139: "...the African is quite well aware of the difference in yield per unit area and has deliberately chosen the low yielding methods because they give a higher return per unit of labour."

[66]John D. Kesby, *The Cultural Regions of East Africa* (London: Academic Press, 1977), maps 17-19.

[67]Paul Bohannan and Philip Curtin, *Africa and Africans* (Garden City, N.Y.: The Natural History Press, 1971), p. 15.

[68]Len Berry, "Dynamics and Processes of Rural Change," Knight and Newman, op. cit., note 15, pp. 212-225.

[69]V. A. Fernando and M. Pugh Thomas, "The Role of Technology in Agriculture: A Short Ecological Appraisal," *International Journal of Environmental Studies*, Vol. 11 (1977), pp. 35-38.

[70]Noel D. Vietmeyer, "The Plight of the Humble Crop," *Ceres*, Vol. 11:2 (1978), pp. 23-26: "In a recent questionnaire sent out by the National Academy of Sciences for its studies of underexploited tropical plants, neglected tropical legumes, and trees for energy plantations, respondents named over 2000 species that deserve much greater recognition." There are almost 4,000 items listed in: Claude Jardin, *List of Foods Used in Africa* (Rome: FAO, 1970).

[71]See, for example, William S. Saint and E. Walter Coward, Jr., "Agriculture and Behavioral Science: Emerging Orientations," *Science*, Vol. 197 (1977), pp. 733-737; Daniel M. Dvorkin, ed., *Environment and Development* (Indianapolis: SCOPE, Miscellaneous Publication, 1974).

[72]One report, limited in design but with along bibliography is: Richard S. Eckaus, *Appropriate Technology for Developing Countries* (Washington, D.C.: National Academy of Sciences, 1977).

[73]Carl Kraenzel, *The Great Plains in Transition* (Norman: University of Oklahoma Press, 1955). A useful set of recommendations for encouraging flexible and mobile institutions and facilities in semiarid regions.

[74]Alternatives includes, for example, Richard Deutsch, "New Wave in Washington," pp. 39-42 and Richard B. Ford, "Putting the Problems in Context," pp. 4-8 in *Africa Report*, Vol. 23:3 (1978); and Uma Lele, *The Design of Rural Development: Lessons from Africa* (Baltimore: John Hopkins University Press, 1975). Janzen, op. cit., note 40, notes: "Short-term exploitation is particularly easy in contemporary tropical societies. Government attitudes are generally 'frontier exploitative' and the 'tragedy of the commons' is promoted by undefined ownership of resources despite the fact that much of the land has been under stable subsistence agriculture for thousands of years . . . By assuming that technological ignorance is the sole cause of agricultural problems in the tropics, we allow this ignorance to become the scapegoat for all ills of the agroecosystem. In fact, the scientific and folklore communities know quite enough to deal with most of the technological problems in tropical agroecosystems, or if not, how to get that information." (p. 1212)

[75]Hilda Bernstein, *For Their Triumphs and For Their Tears*, (London: International Defense and Air Fund, 1975), and Liz Clarke and Jane Ngobene, *Women Without Men*, (Durban: Institute for Black Research, 1977).

[76]R. Mansel Prothero, ed., *People and Land in Africa South of the Sahara* (New York: Oxford University Press, 1972).

[77]In the manuscript, each specific management practice and each example thereof was correlated with a detailed bibliographic entry. In order to conform with the presentation of similar tables in other chapters of this book, all sources pertaining to Tables 1, 2, 3, and 4 were set in type in an abbreviated form. Researchers interested in any complete bibliographic reference pertaining to any specific form of management practice and example thereof can obtain it by writing to Dr. Gary A. Klee, Department of Environmental Studies, School of Social Sciences, San Jose State University, San Jose, CA 95192.

Chapter 3

The Middle East

Ian R. Manners

To many people the Middle East is identified in terms of continuing political ferment. The crises that have dominated the headlines in recent decades have arisen as the independent states of a strategically and economically important region have sought a more equal relationship with the West. Familiar as the term "Middle East" may be as a result of these crises there continue to exist ambiguities in its usage and application. The failure to distinguish between the very different concepts of the Islamic World, the Arab World, and the Middle East region, for example, frequently leads to confusion over the specific geographical or political boundaries that should be assigned to the region.[1] As defined in this chapter, the Middle East includes the northern tier states of Iran and Turkey, the Arab states of South West Asia, as well as Israel and Egypt. It is a region defined in terms of political boundaries and strategic interests. In this respect it must be recognized that the Middle East is a particularly ethnocentric (or perhaps more accurately Eurocentric) expression that in the political lexicon of the first half of the twentieth century represented a projection of European, particularly British, thinking. Traditionally sensitive to any threat to the routeway to India, British strategic interests in the area extending from the Arabian/Persian Gulf to the Suez Canal were reinforced by the discovery of oil and by commercial involvement in its exploitation. With the passage of time, the expression became both familiar and institutionalized, first in the military commands of the Second World War and later in the specialist agencies of the United Nations.[2]

Designation of any area as a region, however, implies some degree of homogeneity. In the contemporary Middle East any such unity based on political or cultural considerations is difficult to discern. Even among the more culturally homogeneous Arab states of the Middle East there exist differences in ideologies, often reinforced by traditional rivalries as between the Nile Valley and Mesopotamia, that have so far impeded every effort to give substance to the oft-expressed desire for political unity.[3]

Despite these elements of disunity, there do exist certain shared concerns that serve to unite the inhabitants of this area. The dominant feature of the physical environment is aridity. Throughout the summer drought only the lush greenery of the irrigated fields interrupts the overall aridity and barren hillsides and bare steppe dominate the landscape. Rainfall, whether scanty or abundant, is everywhere restricted to the winter months.[4] In such an environment, water is the critical "life-sustaining" resource and human activities reveal a close adjustment to spatial and temporal variations in water supply. "We have made from water every living thing" states the Qur'an and everyone, from nomadic pastoralists to sophisticated urbanites share an interest in the sources and availability of water. In this respect, traditional methods of water management, ranging from the *qanats* of Iran to the *shadufs* of Egypt, from the hand dug wells of the Bedu to the basin irrigation systems of the fellaheen, have had a common purpose—by ameliorating the problem of water scarcity, they have enabled societies to survive and flourish under conditions of uncertainty and adversity.

THE RESOURCE BASE

In an absolute sense, the water resources of any region consist of the moisture which falls as precipitation plus any inflow of water, whether in surface streams or underground aquifers.[5] In the Middle East, the Nile represents such an exogenous supply accounting for nearly 60% of all surface water available for development. This potential supply will be substantially diminished by such physical factors as evaporation. Moreover, within the physical limits of the available supply, the actual pattern of water use will be influenced by a range of human factors, particularly the technology used to conserve and redistribute water.

A glance at the annual rainfall map immediately reveals one critical dimension of the water supply situation in the Middle East; the marked disparities in resource endowment within the region (Figure 4). In particular, the duration and intensity of the summer drought increases southwards until steppe merges imperceptibly into desert. A basic contrast exists therefore between the higher elevations of Asia Minor, Iran and the Levant, where winter rains are prolonged, abundant, and reliable, and the extreme aridity of interior Arabia and Iran, where rainfall, when it does occur, is likely to be in the form of intense and highly localized storms.

Since surface streamflow is essentially a residual item, representing the balance of rainfall remaining after evaporation and transpiration have taken place and after allowance has been made for changes in soil moisture and groundwater storage, it is hardly surprising that spatial and temporal variations in precipitation are reflected in river regimes. Most of those perennial rivers originating within the Middle East have their sources in the more northerly and mountainous areas which experience a water surplus on an annual basis (i.e., the sum of monthly differences between precipitation and potential evapotranspiration).[6] Over most of the Middle East, however, there is an annual moisture deficit. In this respect, the major river systems convey water from the regions of moisture surplus to more arid steppes where a supplementary irrigation supply is necessary to sustain any form of intensive agriculture.

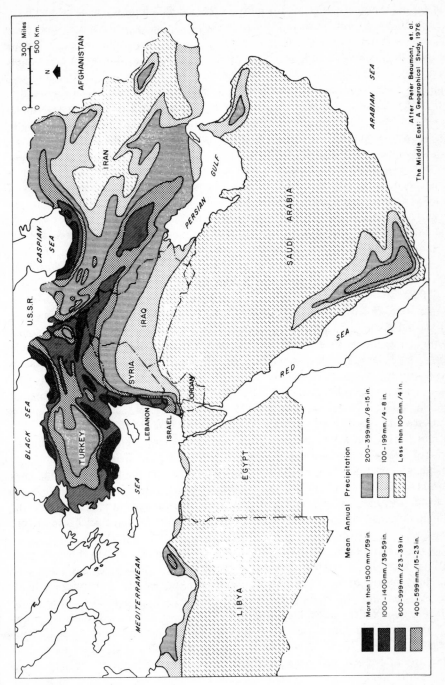

Fig. 4. Mean annual precipitation.

Mean Annual Precipitation

More than 1500 mm./59 in.
1000 - 1400 mm./39 - 59 in.
600 - 999 mm./23 - 39 in.
400 - 599 mm./15 - 23 in.
200 - 399 mm./8 - 15 in.
100 - 199 mm./4 - 8 in.
Less than 100 mm./4 in.

After Peter Beaumont, et. al.
The Middle East: A Geographical Study, 1976

41

The highly seasonal nature of streamflow is exemplified by the regime of the Tigris-Euphrates (Figure 5). Both rivers exhibit a marked early summer maximum when snow-melt accounts for by far the greatest contribution to streamflow. The Tigris in particular is notorious for its sudden and violent spring floods, heavy rainfall over elevated, snow-covered portions of the catchment producing high rates of run-off and rapid rises in discharge in the tributaries draining the Zagros Mountains. The regimes of the Orontes, Litani, Jordan and Yarmuk, which drain more southerly catchments of lower elevation, show a closer relationship to the seasonal distribution of rainfall. Streamflow is greatest during the winter months, the rivers exhibiting pronounced depletion curves from April through September during which time discharge is derived almost entirely from ground-water. As rainfall decreases in amount and reliability, surface streamflow becomes in-creasingly ephemeral. Short periods of moisture surplus still occur immediately after a rainstorm or a wet spell lasting several days, but the brief duration and localized extent of the surplus nourishes only irregular wadi flow in the form of sudden flash floods.

The Nile, its flood season coinciding with the summer months of greatest irrigation need, is something of an anomaly in Middle Eastern terms. In this respect the Nile's regime reflects the influence of heavy summer rainfall over the highlands of Ethiopia. The Nile illustrates a further critical characteristic of streamflow in the Middle East; marked fluctuations from one year to the next. Thus although the flood is an annual phenomenon it is highly variable. The mean annual discharge of the Nile at Aswan (1871–1965) was 84.35 billion cubic meters, yet annual streamflow in 1879 amounted to 137 billion m^3 while the year 1913 saw the smallest flood on record, a mere 45 billion cubic meters.[7] The Nile is therefore something of a mixed blessing. A low Nile flood has traditionally been a source of anxiety to all those engaged in agriculture. In 1877, for example, nearly one million acres remained unirrigated during one of the lowest re-corded Nile floods of the 19th century.[8] Yet the following year saw the second greatest flood on record posing a major threat to Lower Egypt where the river channel frequently stood four to five feet above the level of the surrounding land. "The flood . . . eventually breached the left bank of the river midway between Zifta and Samanud and destroyed the standing crops and every village that lay between it and the sea."[9] All other rivers in the Middle East exhibit similar annual fluctuations in streamflow. Thus, while adjust-ment to aridity provides an overall unifying theme for the region, actual water supply conditions vary markedly and pose very different opportunities and challenges to human occupancy.

Other resources besides water are necessary to sustain life. In any predominantly agricultural society, soil conservation practices are a critical issue since mismanagement can all too quickly destroy the basis of subsistence. Of particular significance in the Middle East are the potentially productive Terra Rossa soils derived from limestone parent material. Widely distributed throughout the Fertile Crescent these soils have a good moisture retention capacity, yet they are highly susceptible to erosion should the vegetation cover be removed. Unfortunately, the Middle East provides a classic example of the way in which clearance of the natural vegetation cover, when combined with exploitive land use practices, will result in accelerated soil erosion.[10] In the foot-hills of Asia Minor and the Levant in particular, the drastic destruction of forests for lumber and fuel, the burning of scrub and woodland to clear land for cultivation, the grazing of excessive numbers of livestock, have over the centuries combined to alter the

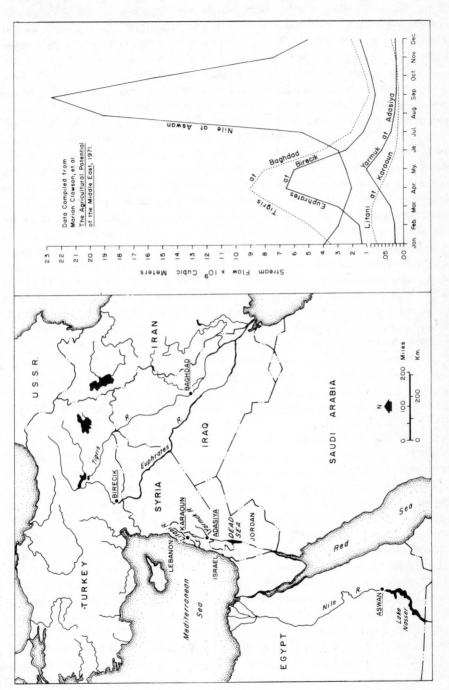

Fig. 5. Streamflow regimes.

ecological balance.[11] The net result is a spectacularly degraded landscape with bare limestone hills which retain only a trace of their former vegetation and soil cover.[12]

The general pattern of land use reflects the continuing efforts of Middle Eastern societies to manage the resource base and to come to terms with the uneven distribution of water. The cultivated zone, for example, is affectively determined by the amount and variability of annual rainfall. In the better watered areas, the coincidence of the rainy season with the winter months of lowest evapotransporation results in a short period of moisture surplus when cultivation is possible without irrigation (dry farming or rainfed agriculture). Wheat and barley, with olives, figs and some vegetables in the more humid areas, represent the major dry-farmed crops producing a typical Mediterranean mixed tree and field crop pattern of land use. In the more mountainous areas, poorer soils, steeper slopes, and the shorter growing season may restrict the opportunities for farming but elsewhere within the cultivated zone villages are clustered closely together. Where topography is a limiting factor, terraces are a conspicuous feature of the rural landscape, reducing soil erosion to an acceptable minimum and ensuring that every conceivable acre of cultivable land, no matter how steep or small, is brought under the plough.

It is frequently suggested that the minimum amount of annual rainfall necessary for successful rainfed cereal cultivation is 180 mm. In the Middle East as in other arid areas, however, the dependability of rainfall is inversely related to amount (Figure 6). As a result of the annual variability in rainfall conditions, dry farming in the Middle East involves some degree of risk even in areas with a mean annual rainfall of 300 mm.[13] Moreover, while the likelihood of drought can be calculated in terms of probabilities and while a farmer, based on his own personal experience, will have a rough idea of the risks involved, in any particular year land use decisions must be made against a background of uncertainty and with no guarantee that that season's rainfall will be adequate.[14]

Thus from the farmer's perspective it is variability that poses the greatest threat. Yields in the dry-farmed lands vary markedly from year to year. Where a farmer must depend on rainfall alone, reduction in yield due to drought brings severe hardship. In this context, the character of stream discharge is ill-suited to agricultural needs. The unpredictability and rapid fluctuation in flood flow considerably diminishes its utility—it is "lost" in the sense that it does not immediately contribute to an increase in agricultural productivity since storage is frequently beyond the economic and technical capabilities of local communities. Without storage facilities, it is the reliable, low-water discharge of perennial rivers that effectively determines the extent of the irrigated area. During the summer drought, when the disparity between supply and demand is greatest, this base flow is likely to be fully appropriated for local domestic and irrigation needs. In this fluctuating and uncertain environment, where the individual has limited access to "buffering technologies," it is hardly surprising that decisions affecting the area to be planted and irrigated, the crops to be grown, even the date of sowing, have traditionally been made to minimize risk.

Taking into account a farmer's ability to withstand limited, though not repeated, crop losses, and the need for a reasonable distribution of rainfall throughout the crop-growing season, a United Nation's study concluded that the critical outer limit for viable rainfed agriculture in the Middle East is a mean annual rainfall of 240 mm with an annual variability of no more than 37.5% (Figure 6).[15] According to these criteria most of the

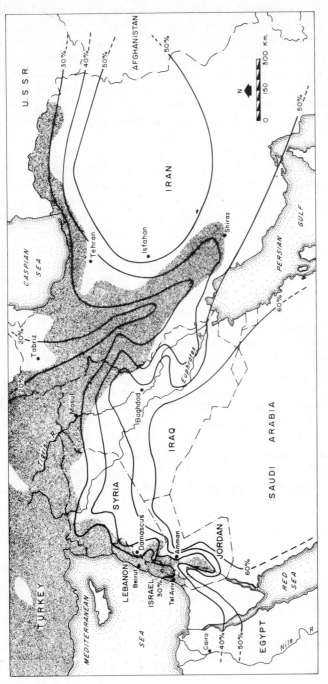

Fig. 6. Variability of annual rainfall and theoretical limits of dryland farming.

20% —— Percentage Relative Interannual Variability of Annual Rainfall

Area of Dryland Farming — Outer limit defined as mean annual rainfall of 240 mm with annual variability of no more than 37.5%.

After C. C. Wallen and G. Perrinde Brichambaut, A Study of Agroclimatology in Semi-Arid and Arid Zones of the Near East, 1962.

45

Middle East is uncultivable by rainfed methods. Only where a reliable irrigation supply is available is it possible to overcome the deficiencies of the rainfall regime and realize the agricultural potential of frequently fertile soils. Outside these irrigated oases, extensive grazing is the only practical form of land use.

It must be emphasized that there is no clear cut boundary between the desert and the sown, the former the preserve of the herder and the latter the domain of the farmer. Instead, there exists a gradual transition as environmental conditions impose increasingly severe restraints on human occupancy. Land use patterns reflect this transition, with herding playing an increasingly important role as conditions become marginal for dryland farming. Indeed, Johnson views pastoral nomadism and settled agriculture as the end points on a continuum of numerous potential economic possibilities.[16] In this respect, the movements of the herder, like the activities of the farmer, are of a seasonal nature, reflecting a close adjustment to the rainfall regime. In interior Arabia, for example, the migratory cycle involves a summer "retreat" to permanent wells, frequently along the margin of the cultivated area, and a winter "advance" into the desert following the onset of the rainy season to take advantage of regenerated pastures. Uncertainty is just as much a factor in the life of the nomad as it is in that of the farmer. Nomadic pastoralism is geared to the seasonal availability of pasture, but at the scale of the individual nomad or herding unit migration routes must be sufficiently flexible to respond to year to year variations in the distribution of pasture.[17] Moreover, as suggested by Johnson "In his grazing activities the nomad is primarily concerned with placing a hedge between himself and potential disaster from natural or human causes."[18] Not unlike the farmer, many nomadic decisions, about herd size and composition, even about the amount of time to be devoted to agricultural pursuits, will reflect a desire to minimize risk in an uncertain and hazardous environment.

Thus as far as management of the resource base is concerned, the practical problems confronting the farmer and the herder alike result not so much from inadequate rainfall as from the *variation* in rainfall and *uncertainty* over its time and place of occurrence. It is the fluctuating nature of the physical environment, with marked seasonal and annual variations in rainfall and streamflow, that make the Middle East region a hazardous one for human occupation. In these circumstances, traditional methods of water management may be regarded as an adjustment to uncertainty at a particular technological level.

EVOLUTION OF A TRADITION

Wherever drought represents a threat to human occupancy, the primary effort of society has been directed towards controlling and making the fullest possible use of surface and groundwater sources. Nowhere has this concern been more evident, nor has the pattern of adaptation to the conditions of the supply been better exemplified, than in the Nile Valley (Figures 7 and 8).

Quite literally, Egypt is the Nile's creation, the river's sediments providing the fertile alluvial soils that have allowed the establishment and survival of a settled agricultural society. The transition from seasonal inundation of the Nile's flood plain to a more controlled form of irrigation undoubtedly occurred before the end of the Predynastic period.[19] It seems probable that the earliest forms of water management represented

Fig. 7. Nile Valley. Low mud walls divide the Nile's flood plain into smaller basins. The embankments serve to retain irrigation water on the land and to mark property lines for landowners. These fields in the Sudan were submerged beneath the water impounded by the Aswan High Dam (From *Nubians in Egypt*, University of Texas Press, 1973, courtesy of Georg Gerster).

little more than refinements on the natural system of irrigation. Deepening natural flood channels, digging ditches through low points of natural levees, constructing earthen dams and barriers, would have served to retain and redistribute the summer flood waters over a larger area, allowing cultivation to take place beyond the immediate confines of the flood plain. Excellent descriptions of the basin system of flood irrigation, as it existed in Egypt at the end of the nineteenth century, are to be found in the reports of British irrigation engineers transferred to Egypt after the occupation of 1882:[20]

> Upper Egypt, with the exception of the Ibrahimia Canal system and the Fayoum, is divided into basins by earthen dykes running transversely to the direction of the river, starting from its bank and reaching the desert. A dyke running parallel with the river...encloses the basins on the river-side, while the desert generally forms the fourth side...Each system of basins depends on one or more canals for its irrigation; some of the canals are insignificant, and feed only a few basins; while some, like the Sohagia, discharging 30 million cubic metres per 24 hours, are veritable rivers, and irrigate a very extended system.

As the flood stage moved northwards, the last basins in Lower Egypt (usually defined as encompassing the delta) would normally be flooded by late September, some four to

Fig. 8. Nile Valley. A traditional method of irrigation in the Nile Valley involved the use of animal-operated water wheels. The wheels raise leather buckets filled with water to the level of the irrigable terraces. Two water wheels are in operation to the right; a third water wheel is under construction in the left foreground of the photograph (From *Nubians in Egypt*, University of Texas Press, 1973, courtesy of Georg Gerster).

six weeks after the basins in southern Egypt. Each basin system possessed an "escape" allowing the surplus water to be drained back into the Nile as the level of the river dropped. Winter crops planted in the saturated alluvial soils included wheat, barley, lentils, beans, berseem (Egyptian clover) and occasionally tobacco and opium. Harvesting took place in March or April, after which time basin land lay fallow until the next flood. Thus in the Nile Valley, as elsewhere in the Middle East, perennial irrigation was limited by the low water discharge of the Nile and the area that could be commanded from lifting devices such as the *shaduf*, the *saqiya* and the Archimedes screw.

Basin irrigation, by ensuring a reliable and controlled flow of water and by maintaining the fertility of the soil, contributed to the development of a highly productive agricultural system. Equally critical from the point of view of the long-term stability of that system, the flushing action of the annual floods prevented the accumulation of salts harmful to crop growth. The obvious merits of this method of irrigation were readily apparent to British engineers:[21]

> One cannot study the principals of basin irrigation without admiring the skill and order of the whole operation. However much fault may be found with the unskillful treatment of the new summer irrigation in lower Egypt, the basin irrigation of Upper Egypt, gradually developed through 500 years, commands sincere admiration. If a fraction of the money spent on Lower Egypt, or on the Ibrahimia Canal in Upper Egypt, had been spent in completing the masonry works needed in the chains of basins extending down the Valley of the Nile in Upper Egypt, the benefits reaped would have been astonishing as compared to what has been done in Lower Egypt. The crop in Lower Egypt is 33% more valuable per acre than what it is in Upper Egypt; but the cost of raising it is so great, that the peasantry of Lower Egypt are not better off than those in Upper Egypt, while the Treasury receives positively less per acre from Lower Egypt than what it does from Upper Egypt.

Willcocks' observations were made at a time when the switch from basin to perennial irrigation was already far advanced in Lower Egypt. And although basin irrigation continued to be practiced on a considerable scale in Upper Egypt (an estimated 1 million acres in the early 1960s), completion of the Aswan High Dam, by eliminating the annual flood, finally destroyed the basis for basin irrigation.

The immediate impetus for the transformation of the traditional system of water management was provided by the introduction of long-staple cotton in the early nineteenth century. With the personal encouragement of the Viceroy, Muhammed Ali, Egypt began exporting cotton to Europe in 1821.[22] Commercial ties were particularly strong with Great Britain which by the middle of the century was taking over half of Egypt's cotton exports. These ties were greatly reinforced by the American Civil War which both drove up the price of cotton and forced European textile manufacturers to seek alternative sources of supply. As a summer crop, however, cotton could not be grown within the traditional basin system. Thus expansion of the cotton acreage was inextricably linked with "development" of the low water flow of the Nile. Initially, this was accomplished through the deepening of existing summer irrigation canals and the construction of barrages which forced a flow of water into the summer canals by raising the level of the water while at the same time allowing free passage to the Nile flood. However, maintenance of the summer canals, many of which were poorly surveyed, imposed a tremendous burden on the country's manpower resources; moreover the Rosetta Barrage was eventually written off as a failure after the foundations sank and floods damaged the central gates. Thus it was not until after the British occupation, the subsequent repair of the Delta Barrage and excavation of abandoned summer canals, that the summer discharge of the Nile was effectively regulated and the transition to perennial irrigation finally accomplished in Lower Egypt.

Advances in construction and engineering techniques during the latter half of the nineteenth century, familiar to the British as a result of their experience in India, provided the opportunity for a more comprehensive approach to Nile development. For the first time in the modern era, serious consideration was given to the feasibility of redistributing the flow of the Nile through time, conserving the annual flood in a series of reservoirs for use during the following summer. The first such dam was completed at

Aswan in 1902; additional annual storage reservoirs were constructed on the Blue Nile at Sennar (1925) and on the White Nile at Gebel Aulia (1937). Collectively, these and related irrigation structures allowed for the gradual conversion of extensive areas in Upper Egypt from basin to perennial irrigation.

The evolving pattern of water management in the Nile Valley reflects the preoccupation with the annual and seasonal variations in Nile discharge. Thus the structural improvements in the irrigation system in the late nineteenth and first half of the twentieth century reveal the particular concern over low flow conditions—both during the flood season (of crucial importance in the basin irrigated lands) and during the non-flood season (of greater importance in the perennially irrigated areas). British engineers sought to "buffer" the impact of a low flood by constructing siphon canals linking independent basin systems.[23] While such improvements allowed for the most efficient use of the available supply in a poor year, the construction of barrages and reservoirs ensured a measure of independence from low discharge conditions during the non-flood season. Yet such "improvements" could not provide complete security against the vagaries of the Nile, providing neither protection against the devastating floods nor against the Biblical nightmare of a succession of abnormally low floods.

In these circumstances, engineers argued that a broader management basis than that of the annual flood was necessary to fully realize the potential of the Nile Basin. "Mean years are of no value since the surplus of one year is not available for the next...Each year must stand on its own base and there will never be any stable development of a tract of country depending upon irrigation unless all the possibilities of drought and deficiency are put beyond the power of recurrence."[24] Willcocks' comments may be regarded as one of the first expressions of the need to store water not only from one season to the next but from year to year, a concept later elaborated and defined for the Nile Basin by Hurst as century storage.[25] Although Willcocks and Hurst both favored the use of the equatorial lakes to provide century storage, this approach was realized with the completion of the Aswan High Dam, the primary purposes of which are to provide complete flood protection for Egypt and to eliminate uncertainty by storing more water than is needed in a single year.

Thus while cotton provided the initial motivation for abandonment of the traditional basin system of water management, improvements in engineering techniques and construction capabilities have provided the opportunity to overcome the physical constraints imposed by seasonal and annual fluctuations in streamflow. The Aswan High Dam merely represents the latest stage in the evolving effort to control the Nile's regime and by redistributing the flow over an extended period of time to provide a buffer against uncertainty.

EXISTING TRADITIONAL RESOURCE-USING SYSTEMS

Changes in the philosophical and technological bases of water management have not been restricted to the Nile Valley. Traditionally, water resource development has been for immediate agricultural and domestic needs and has relied upon local surface and groundwater sources; today's emphasis is upon the control and use of water to meet a wider range of human needs. Although political boundaries and disputes have frequently frustrated attempts at integrated river basin development, multi-purpose water development projects have been completed in virtually every major drainage basin in the Middle East. Multi-purpose water development has come to be regarded as essential to the orderly process of social and economic development, contributing not only to an increase in the cultivable area but to the generation of hydroelectric power for industrialization, to the elimination of disease, and to the enhancement of living standards through improved rural and urban water supply systems. In broad terms, the shift to multiple-purpose development corresponds to the American experience. Such an observation should not be surprising for, as Gilbert White has noted, the United States has actively encouraged the diffusion of its skills and techniques of water management to developing nations on a broad scale:[26]

> Since its dam design and construction methods were transferred by Cooper and his associated to the Dnieper in the 1930's, its techniques have been spread through the activities of the Bureau of Reclamation, university centers, construction companies, and consulting engineers. Bilateral aid programs have enforced the diffusion process. In its proposal for a Water for Peace program (as announced in 1966) the United States appeared to be seeking in a more explicit way to dominate the style of thinking about water management in other countries.

The attempt to make more effective use of the region's surface waters have resulted in the disappearance or transformation of many small-scale irrigation systems. Even where locally constructed and controlled systems have not been incorporated into large-scale, multiple purpose projects, they have frequently been "modernized" with permanent diversion structures and concrete-lined distribution canals. The hand-excavated, mud-lined channels, offtaking from rock and rubble weirs that must be reconstructed after each flood season, often winding tortuously across hillsides to command a few irrigable acres, are therefore a less common feature of today's irrigation landscape.

Similar changes are occurring in the methods used to apply water to the soil, although surface methods of application (whereby water is spread across the field by gravity flow) continue to predominate. Surface irrigation usually involves the use of earth embankments ("flood irrigation") or furrows ("furrow irrigation") to direct the flow of water over the soil, but many local variants are to be found within the region. Since the purpose of irrigation is to replenish the moisture lost from the root zone as a result of evaporation, transpiration and percolation, any method of application is satisfactory *provided* it fulfills this function without wastage of water or soil. While no method of application can be 100% efficient, surface irrigation will be particularly wasteful wherever farmers have little control over the water being applied. In the worst instances of "wild flooding" water is simply allowed to flow unchecked across a field.[27] Without careful levelling, some areas remain unirrigated while other areas are inundated. The uncontrolled flow of water in the direction of greatest slope means that a large proportion of the water delivered to the field never infiltrates the soil but runs-off into the nearest drainage channel.[28] If a farmer attempts to compensate for underwatering of crops by increasing the head of water applied, the dangers of soil erosion and gullying are greatly increased. By no means do all Middle Eastern farmers engage in the "wild flooding" practices described above; indeed in the Nile Valley and in the highlands of Yemen, careful levelling of basins and construction of terraces ensured a higher level of control. Nevertheless, in most of the newer irrigation projects, there is a deliberate effort to persuade farmers to adopt sprinkler and subsurface systems that allow greater control over the timing and application of irrigation water.

While the pace of change has undoubtedly accelerated in the last two decades, traditional methods of water management are still to be found within the region. In Iran, for example, the *qanat* represents an extremely sophisticated technique for the development of groundwater that may well have been in use as early as the first millenium B.C. The physical basis for the *qanat* is a combination of mountainous terrain and adjacent sedimentary basins where flood run-off will provide recharge to the groundwater aquifers in the alluvial fans bordering the upland region (Figure 9). Once the presence of groundwater has been proven (through the excavation of a shaft referred to as the mother well), a gently sloping tunnel is dug back into the hillside from a designated outlet point towards the mother well.[29] To assist in tunnel construction, a series of vertical shafts are sunk that provide access to workers and allow for the removal of dirt and debris; the openings to these shafts, surrounded by spoil heaps, provide the only surface indication of a *qanat* and are a highly visible feature of the Iranian landscape when viewed from the air.[30] When the tunnel reaches the mother well, it is frequently extended still further into the hillside in order to maximize the amount of infiltrated groundwater that is collected. In some instances, a large *qanat* system may be fed by several tributary *qanats*. While excavation is laborious and time-consuming, the great merit of the *qanat* is that a reliable supply of water is made available by gravity flow over an extended period with little evaporation loss. Labor and energy inputs are minimized except for routine maintenance.

Local regulations governing the ownership and distribution of water from wells, springs and *qanats* are often extremely complicated.[31] The basis for all such water codes is to be found in established customs and uses as modified by religious beliefs and laws. Since the water codes essentially attempt to balance available resources with local needs, it is perhaps not surprising that the scarcer the water, the more elaborate and detailed the regulations governing its allocation.[32] The right to use water, for example, often appears to have originated with families who contributed to the construction of the irrigation system. A register is usually maintained by village officials in which all transactions relating to water rights are carefully recorded. Distribution of water to title holders (or renters of water) is usually on a rotation basis, the length of the rotation cycle being adjusted to the available supply and the number of users. Caponera describes how water was distributed in Wadi Yanbo, Saudi Arabia:[33]

> Each person entitled to water rights receives the total flow during his turn independently of the area which has to be irrigated or the volume of the flow. The rotation turn varies from spring to spring. At Ain Jadid it is equivalent to 64 *wajabah* (12 hours per day or night divided into hours or *jsa-ah*) i.e., 32 days. The time unit is calculated by a receptacle pierced at the bottom with holes, which, when placed in the water, takes one hour to become immersed.

Unfortunately, traditional methods of utilizing groundwater have been affected by the spread of modern well drilling and pumping technologies. Beaumont, for example, described the situation in the Varamin Plain, located on the margin of the Dasht-i-Kavir some 25 miles southeast of Tehran, where as much as 40% of all irrigation needs were

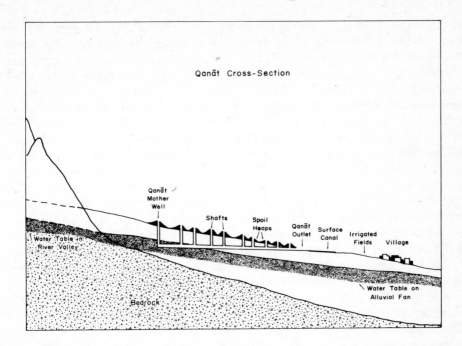

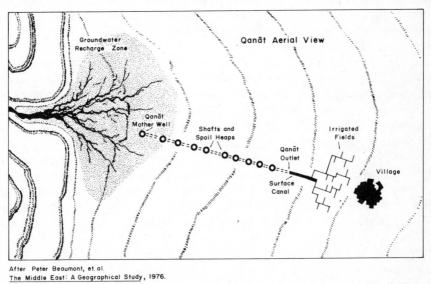

After Peter Beaumont, et. al.
The Middle East: A Geographical Study, 1976.

Fig. 9. The Qanat system of groundwater development.

previously met by *qanats*.[34] Beginning in the mid-1950s, a large number of deep pump wells were installed. As a result, there occurred a rapid decline in the water table and a marked reduction in the discharge of many *qanats*. In some instances the flow of *qanats* ceased completely causing considerable social and economic disruption.[35] The flow of a *qanat* cannot be regulated according to seasonal irrigation needs. For this reason consultants for one major water development project in Iran recommended that *qanats* should be replaced by pump wells. "Unfortunately, little attempt was made to enlist the cooperation of the peasants in the early stages or to tell them the purposes and details of the plan. As a result, the peasant farmers tended to regard the development authority as akin to a new landowner and a widespread resistance to change was generated."[36]

In that instance, the introduction of pump wells was actively resisted. Elsewhere, farmers dependent upon hand-dug wells for their water supply have been less reluctant to adopt modern drilling and pumping technologies. In the Jordan Valley, for example, the successful boring of a well on unreclaimed land near Jericho in the early 1950s triggered a wave of well drilling activity.[37] Ultimately a serious overdraft situation was created with rates of withdrawal greatly in excess of recharge. Moreover, the depletion of groundwater resources was accompanied by a serious deterioration in water quality, the existence of marked depression cones in the areas of maximum withdrawal leading to the intrusion of saline groundwater from underlying and bordering formations. In this situation the government was forced to intervene and restrict private drilling of new wells and, when this proved inadequate, to construct two small reservoirs on nearby wadis to store flood flow for artificial groundwater recharge. Similar cases of groundwater depletion and degradation, where the possibility of low but sustained increases in productivity have been sacrificed for spectacular but short-term gains, could be cited for most parts of the region. Such examples of resource mismanagement illustrate how disruptive water development can be in the long-term when the full range of social, economic and environmental impacts are not clearly identified and taken into account in advance of project implementation. Moreover, it is evident that the low level of stress associated with traditional patterns of resource husbandry may be as much a function of available technology as it is a matter of a conscious, conservation ethic. While most farmers possess a detailed knowledge of their immediate environment (soil, vegetation, water) when operating within a different technological framework there exists an initial failure to identify spatial and ecological linkages.

Irrigation is not the only system of resource use that is experiencing marked and perhaps irreversible change. As noted earlier, nomadic pastoralism represents a highly distinctive way of life in the Middle East. It has flourished along the margins of the cultivated area by bringing into productive use the resources of an ecological zone that, given the available level of technology, would have otherwise remained undeveloped.[38] Spatial and temporal variations in grazing conditions provide the ecological "compulsion" for the nomadic system of resource use. In a fluctuating environment, the key to effective use of the resource base (and indeed to survival) lies in the mobility provided by livestock and in an astute knowledge of water and pasture conditions. Yet nomadism is not an aimless wandering in search of water and pasture; it is rather a regular pattern of movement that is closely tied to the location of productive, though seasonally restricted, pastures.

Johnson distinguishes in this respect two major categories of nomadic movement in the Middle East.[39] In Iran, tribes such as the Lur and Bakhtiari exemplify *vertical nomadism* where herding takes advantage of altitudinal variations in the availability of pasture. In spring the nomads and their herds follow the retreating snowline from winter grazing grounds in the foothills of the Zagros Mountains to higher altitudes where snow-melt and cooler temperatures ensure productive summer pastures. On the return migra-tion in the fall, and before the winter rains revive the pastures at lower altitudes, herds are grazed on the stubble of harvested fields. In vertical nomadism, the livestock herded tend to be sheep and goats with camels and donkeys for transportation. Most herders also have strong links with the agricultural communities through whose territory they migrate; these may involve actual ownership of land, social and kinship ties, or simply an exchange of products.

In the Arabian peninsula, the movements of such tribes as the Ruwala, the Mutair, and the Murrah reveal a similar seasonality but are related to *horizontal* variations in the availability of water and pasture. Here the climatic regime, with the alternation of winter rainfall and summer drought, allows for a pattern of movement characterized by a cluster-ing around permanent wells and springs during the summer and migration after the first winter rainfall has revitalized desert pastures. Such a shift also allows for the conservation and regeneration of the overgrazed pastures surrounding the summer encampments. As noted by Johnson, while the overall regularity of the seasonal regime (combined with a tribal sense of territoriality) ensures that the same general area is grazed in sequence each year, the extreme variability of winter rainfall requires a degree of flexibility at the level of the individual tent or herding unit.[40]

> Thus, while the nomadic regime of any herder may mean that his herds always graze in a certain part of the tribal territory at a particular period of the year, the precise location that is grazed within this traditional zone may well vary widely from year to year depend-ing upon the distribution and quality of the season's precipitation.

Within a broad framework of ecological rationality, nomadism may reveal marked variations in structure. For example, while the particular combination of herd animals will depend in part on individual preferences (though this itself will be constrained by prevailing cultural and societal norms), it will also take account of the very different tolerances of livestock in relation to the availability and quality of water and grazing resources. In better watered areas, sheep (which require more frequent watering and are more selective in their grazing requirements) are likely to be the dominant element in nomads' herds. As grazing conditions deteriorate, the proportion of goats and camels will increase. Taking advantage of different livestock characteristics may allow a more intensive use of pasture resources. Barth, for example, has described how the foothills of the Zagros were previously grazed during winter by sheep-raising Kurdish nomads.[41] As these groups vacated the area in the spring, camel-herding tribes from central Arabia moved in to take advantage of pastures that were too degraded to support sheep. Other differences in the form of nomadism are likely to relate to the degree of dependency upon livestock and relationships with sedentary communities. Thus no pastoral economy can stand alone and nomads must in one way or another acquire grain and other products of settled agriculture. While raiding and the extraction of tribute are frequently cited to illustrate the antipathy that exists between the desert and the sown, other nomadic groups may engage in trade or even in agriculture (rental or ownership of land, employ-ment as agricultural laborers, etc.). In this respect as Johnson points out "more often than not the nomad and the sedentary are engaged in a reasonably symbiotic relationship in which the exchange of animal products for dates and grain play a prime role."[42]

The overall rationality of the nomadic adaptation is well illustrated by the herders of the Jabal al Akhdar in Cyrenaica.[43] Tribal territories in the Jabal al Akhdar comprise north to south strips extending from the Mediterranean coast across the better watered portion of the upland into the desert interior. Lower-level segments of each tribe utilize particular portions of the tribal territory, each segment specializing in the production of those animals and grains best suited to its particular zone. Goats and cattle are herded along the coast, sheep on the upland terraces, with camels becoming an increasingly important element in herd composition toward the desert interior. Similarly the sheep and goat herders optimize the potentialities of their niche by planting wheat and barley, while herders on the drier dip slope engage in more speculative cropping in the ephemeral wadis draining towards the interior. In such a manner, the available resources along the ecological gradient from coast to desert are fully used. Deficiencies at the section level are overcome through trade and exchange while ties of kinship and marriage create patterns of obligation and cooperation that can be activated in time of need. In this context, nomadism "can be visualized in ecosystem terms with each tribal component adjusted to the resources of a particular ecological niche but with all the components of the system linked to each other by social and kin relationships for purpose of mutual support."[44]

While nomadism has been depicted as a rational adjustment, it remains an extremely precarious way of life. Thus the equilibrium between the numbers of nomads and livestock and the water and grazing resources on which they depend is easily disrupted. It is precisely the conditions of uncertainty that place a premium on diversifying patterns of livelihood and on the development of social institutions and arrangements that favor a sharing of resources and a minimizing of risk so well exemplified in the Jabal al Akhdar. Similar patterns of adaptation are evident amongst Al Murrah, one of the great camel herding tribes of Arabia, whose annual migrations may extend over 1200 miles penetrating the Rub al Khali.[45] Yet the Murrah also own sheep and goats which are moved over far shorter distances between the wells that they own. Moreover, the Murrah make a conscious effort to avoid overgrazing those portions of their grazing grounds lying within the Rub al Khali. Rainfall, though intermittent and sparse, is sufficient to maintain adapted vegetation in the Rub al Khali for periods of three to four years. Every effort is made to conserve this resource for use in periods of vicissitude by taking advantage of the shorter lived grasses available elsewhere. Amongst other groups there is likely to be an emphasis not only on herd diversification but on increasing herd size as a means of providing security against a series of unfavorable years. While in the short-term, such pressures may result in a considerable increase in livestock numbers, this will be offset in the long-term by losses and/or sales during periods of drought.

REGION IN TRANSITION

In analyzing the collapse of nomadic pastoralism in North Africa, Johnson suggests that "both the pastoralist's perception of resource use and the technological and political systems that support nomadic existence have been challenged."[46] In one sense, pastoral nomadism represents a system of resource use that is adjusted at a given technological level to a precarious and unstable environment. In this context, technological changes that provide a buffer against the vagaries of an uncertain environment are likely to diffuse rapidly, significantly altering the resource potential of those regions that have traditionally been the preserve of the nomad. Yet, as Johnson emphasizes, nomadism also represents a distinctive cultural system, with values that reflect and reinforce the way in which resources are appraised and utilized, and a formidable political system, with an organizational structure capable of dominating the sedentary population. In this context, the emergence (initially under colonial rule) of strong, highly centralized government entities, together with the penetration of a value system emphasizing monetary and material incentives and rewards, have produced as profound a change in the nomadic lifestyle as has the advent of new technologies.

The most visible alteration in the nomadic way of life have undoubtedly resulted from the diffusion of alien technologies. Modern forms of transportation have contributed to the demise of the caravan and with it the opportunity to provide "protection," guides, and baggage animals; simultaneously, mechanization has eroded the major market for draft animals as farmers turn to diesel pumps and tractors. "No longer useful in caravan traffic, often replaced by a truck or jeep in the movement of the bedouin family's household baggage, the camel is being abandoned as a primary subsistence animal by all except the inhabitants of the most marginal areas."[47]

Those technologies that have tended to undermine the nomadic economy by displacing traditional functions have been described as "antinomad," to which may be added the military technologies that have altered the balance of power between central governments and tribal confederations.[48] Yet other technological changes have had (at least in the short-term) a more positive impact on pastoralism. In Saudi Arabia, for example, which is usually cited as the last remaining stronghold of traditional nomadic pastoralism, even Al Murrah have begun to follow the example of other bedouin tribes in emphasizing the commercial herding of sheep and goats in place of the subsistence herding of camels. This change in the structure and orientation of pastoralism is directly related to the growing demand for quality livestock products in urban markets and to the technological changes that have effectively relaxed some of the ecological constraints on herding activity. Thus government drilling of deep wells tapping hitherto inaccessible aquifers has opened up large areas previously utilizable only by camels, while the use of trucks allows sheep and goats to be moved easily and frequently from well to well and from pasture to pasture. As stated by Cole:[49]

> The change from camels to sheep and goats has been spontaneous among the Bedouin and not the result of any governmental or other outside encouragement. Because of the very nature of their acculturation as pastoralists, it is not surprising that the Bedouin have automatically responded to changing conditions in Saudi Arabia by introducing change themselves in the area of activity they not only know best but regard as their special domain.

As a result, the herding of sheep and goats in the Arabian peninsula is no longer relegated to lower status, politically subservient tribal groups. Whether the Bedouin can successfully make the transition from subsistence-oriented camel herding to commercially-oriented sheep and goat herding remains unclear. It is, however, a spontaneous change that takes advantage of the specialized skills and knowledge of the nomad. "The Bedouin...know the capacity of the desert. Now that the herding of sheep and goats appears to accommodate the demands of the modernized urban society, they are willing and eager to accommodate themselves accordingly. . .they do not now want to lose the desert environment that has produced so successfully for them throughout many thousands of years."[50] As Cole observes, can we afford to lose the skills that have exploited the desert environment so effectively? Technology has created the opportunity for a more productive use of the resource base. In the long-term, however, the ability to sustain larger numbers of sheep and goats (resulting from improvements in veterinary services as well as water supply) must be matched by a greater emphasis on range conservation, irrigated pastures, and marketing infrastructure, if the increase in productivity is to be sustained. In this respect, the severe overgrazing already apparent in the vicinity of many wells in interior Arabia must be a matter of considerable concern.

In an age of rapid scientific and technological change, where even the most isolated community is exposed to regional, national, and even international influences through communication networks, it is hardly surprising that the nomadic way of using the resources of a marginal and unstable environment, together with the values associated with that way of life, should have been profoundly modified. Technology has produced immediate and obvious changes in the character and orientation of nomadic pastoralism. While many tribes continue to engage in some form of pastoralism, the full-scale migrations of peoples, their possessions and livestock, is now largely a matter of historical record. Yet equally significant in terms of the demise of traditional nomadism, have been changes in the economic, social, and political framework within which tribal groups have had to operate. Nomads no longer enjoy a position of social and political pre-eminence; indeed, they are often at a disadvantage, economically, in their relationship with the sedentary agricultural population they previously dominated. "Unable to subsist solely successfully on the produce of their herds or to enter economically into a free trade market vis a vis their sedentary contacts, a drift towards sedentary life has been inevitable in most nomadic communities."[51] Sedentarization will inevitably take different forms. Initially there may be a shift to more restricted forms of nomadism where herds are moved over shorter distances and cropping is given greater emphasis. In the long-term, the problems of maintaining access to pasture and water and of finding reliable herders often make this a transitional stage and a prelude to full sedentarization.[52] In other instances, nomads, along with other rural populations, have sought to improve their economic position by migrating to the major urban centers where they may be found in occupations as diverse as taxi-drivers and surveyors. In some cases the break with nomadic traditions has been complete; in other cases, tribal ties have been maintained through marriage, remittance of earnings, or even the investment of accumulated wealth in livestock managed by relatives or herdsmen.

At the same time as the nomad has been forced to adjust to changes in his economic relationship with the outside world, his freedom to use desert grazing areas has been severely restricted. At a macro-scale, the imposition of political boundaries has on occasion disrupted the migratory regime of nomadic tribes. Even where nomadic migrations can be accommodated within national boundaries, the steady expansion of the agricultural frontier, frequently promoted by the central government and accompanied by restrictions on migration routes, grazing areas, and watering points, has undermined the ecological rationality of nomadic pastoralism.

The consequence everywhere was interference in the normal phasing of the pastoral migration, greatly restricting the scope of pastoral movements and, at least in the case of herders
of sheep and goats, forcing them to utilize, for extended periods of time, resources of a
marginal nature. Decimation of the herds in drought years with resulting improverishment
of the nomadic way of life was inevitable.[53]

Accompanying such government restrictions have been more positive inducements
towards sedentarization. Thus in such nations as Iran, Saudi Arabia and Libya, the
revenue from oil development has provided the opportunity for major development
programs encompassing economic and social objectives. The latter, particularly the
construction of schools, health clinics, public housing, rural electrication, improved
sanitation, water supply and veterinary facilities, have had a marked impact on rural
and nomadic populations.[54]

Thus, not only are governments generally eager to bring the benefits of modernization
directly to their citizens but they are also convinced that selective adoption of western
values and the conversion of nomads into farmers will make them better citizens and more
productive contributors to the national economy. In the present context governments
have both the lure of financially rewarding employment and services outside the nomadic
sector and the political and economic muscle to guide development into channels that suit
national goals. The end-product has been the sedentarization of an increasing proportion
of nomadic society.

While the dominant process affecting nomadism today is sedentarization, it must
be recognized that there continue to be major differences in the way that people respond
to changes in their operational environment. Decisions, whether relating to herd composition, agricultural activities, or urban employment will reflect the nomad's own
appraisal of the opportunities available to him, the means at his disposal, and the likely
returns from alternative courses of action, although any final decision will be made within
the context of prevailing cultural norms and values. At a very different scale, there have
been similar differences in the manner and speed with which central governments have
sought to integrate the nomadic community into the body politic. Where the nomad
has been viewed as an anachronism in a modern state or as posing the threat of a state
within a state, governments have proceeded more severely. In Iran during the 1920s
and 1930s, for example, nomadic tribes were dealt with severely, enforced relocation
in villages far removed from tribal territories resulting in severe social and economic
dislocation. Elsewhere, governments have sought to encourage sedentarization while
simultaneously retaining tribal identities and values by redirecting nomadic loyalties
and energies into the military structure of the state. Thus in Saudi Arabia, Al Murrah
tribesmen were encouraged to enroll in the elite National Guard, extending to the state
protection traditionally provided at a local level to the sedentary population.

Elements that have had the greatest impact on the nomadic community have been
discussed in some detail since essentially the same forces have profoundly modified
other traditional methods of resource use. Thus it is not only the nomad's perception
of the resource base that has been altered; the technological, political and economic
bases of other traditional lifestyles have been similarly challenged. Johnson related
the changes that have undermined nomadism to the scale within which social and economic interactions take place. Such an assessment can be applied with equal force to

the position of the village farmer. The intervention of a strong central government anxious to promote economic development and social well-being, the shift from an emphasis on self-sufficiency to involvement in a wider cash economy, the rapid diffusion and adoption of a wide range of modern technologies, the exposure to alien value systems, all represent forces that impact local communities but which they cannot control. Flannery places these forces in a broader context, characterizing the process of centralization in terms of the growing linkages within a society between various lower-order entities (the local village system) and higher-order (or "governmental") controls.[55] Thus, in the Nile Valley at the beginning of the 19th century, irrigation was essentially a local responsibility; water management and allocation was handled by each community in its own way although constrained by those local institutions and customs that had evolved over centuries of basin irrigation. Construction and maintenance of the basins and feeder canals were carried out by the villagers in the way in which all public tasks were undertaken—communally. The nineteenth century, however, witnessed what Flannery describes as linearization, i.e., a situation where the lower-order controls over a critical variable (water) are increasingly subverted or even by-passed by higher-order controls, the government directly regulating and controlling not only water allocation but also land use practices. The villager finds that the price of development has been a loss of autonomy. Berger notes the long-term social dislocation that may result from linearization:[56]

> A prominent Egyptian geographer, Dr. Huzzayin, has argued that perennial irrigation has affected the very nature of the Egyptian village and the relations among its inhabitants. When the Nile at flood-time was the sole source of water...the villagers had to build up a hill on which to place their settlement in order to keep it above the water level. They also worked together to build the dykes and basins, and in general engaged in a cooperative life based on their common needs. With perennial irrigation, villages did not have to be elevated and the work of maintaining the system was done through a central administration. The real purpose and motive of solidarity, collaboration and cooperation had vanished...Thus Egypt had to face one of the most serious problems in its modern history, that of the decaying and somewhat disrupted large village systems.

What factors or groups of factors (sometimes referred to by ethnographers as "prime movers" and by Flannery as "socioenvironmental stresses") serve to trigger the process of centralization? "Warfare, population pressure, the demands of large-scale trade, or any combination of these (and other) socioenvironmental conditions...may provide the adaptive milieu in which various evolutionary mechanisms are triggered."[57] Boserup has suggested that it is population pressure that exerts "causal" pressure for the adoption of more advanced agricultural technologies.[58] Such explanation does not seem convincing in the context of the Nile Valley during the 19th century.[59] It is noteworthy, however, that the process of linearization extended *beyond* the national level, for with the integration of Egypt within a wider political-economic system, local systems become increasingly subject to distant events, interests, and processes. Thus, international considerations, and particularly the demands of large-scale trade, replace local interests. The subsistence economy under which the villagers had lived for centuries is replaced by an export-oriented economy; an imposed development which promotes the introduction of more advanced irrigation technologies. This sets the stage for what Rappaport calls a "systemic pathology" for linearization effectively destroys the intervening controls which buffer one subsystem from perturbations in another.[60] The further stresses induced as a result of these perturbations are likely to encourage still further centralization; the process of centralization once triggered is thus one with many positive feedback loops. The drastic fall in the price of cotton following the end of the American Civil War contributing to the bankruptcy of the Egyptian state and ultimately to direct British intervention is a vivid illustration of such a "pathology."

CONCLUDING ASSESSMENT

This chapter attempted to address itself to a number of themes relating to resource management in the Middle East. The first theme has been the high degree of risk and uncertainty encountered in these arid and semi-arid lands. A second theme has been the skillful manner in which different societies have adapted to the prevailing conditions of scarcity and variability in the moisture supply. Traditional patterns of resource management, such as those described in this chapter, often associated with distinctive cultural values that will in turn reflect and reinforce the way in which resources are appraised and used, represent those adjustments that have proved viable and successful over the long-term. Although this chapter has emphasized successful resource management strategies, we have just as much to learn from past failures. As noted by White:[61]

> Man's decision to avoid, use, develop or withdraw from arid lands may be thought of in terms of a slow intricate process in which he assesses the resources with which he has to deal, applies the technology and organization at his command to using them, winnows out the measures that seem inefficient on economic grounds, takes account of effects upon other areas, and progressively adjusts his institutions to advancing uses that seem desirable. But the results are not always happy; sometimes they are tragic and are written in abandoned projects or traces of forgotten farming. . .

Jacobsen and Adams have documented cycles of irrigation, salinization, and land abandonment over a period of 6,000 years in Mesopotamia, while accelerated soil erosion due to deforestation and exploitive land use practices has been a problem throughout the region since Classical times.[62] The history of the Middle East is filled with examples of the way in which human modification of the natural environment can generate positive feedback, disrupting the dynamic equilibrium existing prior to intervention.

Thus it is not only contemporary technological man who has failed, all too frequently, to recognize that the balance between water, soil and vegetation in Middle Eastern lands is a delicate one and that the consequences of ill-advised adjustments will be marked and rapid degradation of the resource base. Nor, by the same token, should it be implied that modern technologies of resource development are inherently maladaptive. What is abundantly clear, however, is that technological advances have greatly enhanced our capacity for such disruptive intervention. Moreover, there exists, at least in the West, a deeply-entrenched confidence in our ability to "manage" nature, to apply our unique organizational and scientific talents to the development of resources and to the control of environmental processes in such a way as to improve the human condition. This view of the world and of our place in the "web of life" emphasizes the role of technology. To use O'Riordan's evocative phrase, it is the ideology of "technocentrism," a set of beliefs, attitudes and actions that "is almost arrogant in its assumption that man is supremely able to understand and control events to suit his purpose."[63] Yet as White correctly emphasizes:[64]

> One of the dangerous myths running through much of the work done with water resources in the arid zone is that the mere application of modern technology will in itself be certain to be beneficial. Unless properly designed to suit the local environment and culture, the new efforts can bring resource destruction and economic distress, as has been seen from the rapid over-drafts on aquifers by power pumps and the waterlogging of fertile lands by new irrigation works.

What is required is the sensitive application of available technologies, capital, and managerial skills to meeting human needs and aspirations. This involves not only the identification of the full range of social, economic and ecological impacts of any development proposal, but the questioning of existing priorities and the appraisal of alternative investment options. "To what extent is the capital going into high concrete dams, deep wells and afforestation being wisely spent to serve the ends of national development and stability?"[65]

Yet it must be recognized that the western technocentric view of nature has deeply influenced patterns of resource use in the Middle East as in other developing regions. The colonial-commercial expansion of the west from the fifteenth century onwards subjected large portions of the globe to what Carl Sauer termed "destructive exploitation," a process that all too often resulted in the permanent degradation of the resource base and to the destruction of local economies and cultures.[66] Thus Sauer was particularly disturbed by the way in which local communities became functionally integrated into wider economic systems. The transfer of resources "from place of origin to place of demand tended to set up growing disturbance of whatever ecological equilibrium had been maintained by the older-self-sustaining rural communities."[67] In the latter half of the 20th century, the influence of the technocentric view in the non-western world is no less evident if perhaps more subtly expressed. In many developing countries, decisions about the development and allocation of resources are increasingly being made by professional elites educated and trained in western institutions. Yet it is this group, as O'Riordan points out, that more than any other espouses the technocentric view and regard the natural environment as "neutral stuff" to be developed through the application of rational and value-free scientific and managerial techniques. The extent to which such professional attitudes and values have been assimilated remain unclear, although the initial impression is not encouraging. Thus it may well be that the future problems will arise not from the direct impact of an expansive and aggressive western colonial or neo-colonial economic culture, nor from the direct transfer of technologies from temperate to nontemperate latitudes, but from acceptance of the western ideology of technocentrism. The overall result, reinforced by the understandable desire to appear progressive and modern, is to bring further pressure to bear on traditional patterns of livelihood. "We present and recommend to the world a blueprint of what works well with us at the moment, heedless that we may be destroying wise and durable native systems of living with the land."[68]

NOTES

[1] Ian R. Manners, "The Political Dimension: Colonialism to Nationalism," in Alice Taylor, ed., *Focus on the Middle East* (New York: Praeger, 1971), pp. 3–8. For other commentaries on the nature and appropriate delineation of a Middle East region see Roderick H. Davidson, "Where is the Middle East?" *Foreign Affairs*, Vol. 38 (1960), pp. 665–675; W. B. Fisher, "Unity and Diversity in the Middle East," *Geographical Review*, Vol. 37 (1947), pp. 414–435; Nikki R. Keddie, "Is There a Middle East?" *International Journal of Middle East Studies*, Vol. 4 (1973), pp. 255–271.

[2] C. G. Smith, "The Emergence of the Middle East," *Journal of Contemporary History*, Vol. 3 (1968), pp. 3–17.

[3] Bernard Lewis, *The Middle East and the West* (New York: Harper Torchbook, 1966), p. 94.

[4] Only along the northern slopes of the Pontic and Elburz ranges and the narrow coastal plains fronting the Black and Caspian Seas (where mid-latitude cyclonic disturbances are likely to influence weather patterns throughout the year) and in the highlands of Yemen (which are subject to the influence of the monsoonal circulation system) is summer rainfall significant.

[5] Gilbert F. White, "The World's Arid Areas," in E. S. Hills, ed., *Arid Lands: A Geographical Appraisal* (London: Methuen, 1966), p. 25.

[6] C. G. Smith, "Water Resources and Irrigation Development in the Middle East," *Geography*, Vol. 55 (1970), pp. 407–425.

[7] Marion Clawson, Hans H. Landsberg and Lyle T. Alexander, *The Agricultural Potential of the Middle East* (New York: American Elsevier, 1971), pp. 209–210.

[8] Sir William Willcocks and J. I. Craig, *Egyptian Irrigation* (London: E. & F.N. Spon Ltd., 1913), p. 312.

[9] Willcocks and Craig, op. cit., note 8, p. 533.

[10] See, for example, Marvin W. Mikesell, "The Deforestation of Mount Lebanon," *Geographical Review*, Vol. 59 (1969), pp. 1–28. Butzer provides an excellent analyses of the processes and extent of accelerated soil erosion in the Middle East; see Karl W. Butzer, "Accelerated Soil Erosion: A Problem of Man-Land Relationships," in Ian R. Manners and Marvin W. Mikesell, eds., *Perspectives on Environment* (Washington, D.C.: Association of American Geographers, 1974), pp. 57–78.

[11] Ian R. Manners, "The Desert and the Sown: An Ecological Appraisal," *Focus*, Vol. 22 (1971), pp. 1–5.

[12] In view of the difficulties inherent in establishing the actual age of alluvial soils, it is important to reiterate Butzer's warning against attributing all denuded mountain slopes in this region to the impact of human activities. (See Butzer, op. cit., note 10, p. 67). Moreover, the effectiveness of cultivators in constructing terraces to conserve soil and water should be noted.

[13] C. C. Wallen and G. Perrin de Brichambaut, *A Study of Agroclimatology in Semi-Arid and Arid Zones of the Near East* (Rome: FAO, UNESCO, WMO, 1962).

[14] Ian R. Manners, "Problems of Water Resource Management in a Semi-Arid Environment: The Case of Irrigation Agriculture in the Central Jordan Rift Valley," in Brian S. Hoyle, ed., *Spatial Aspects of Development* (London: John Wiley, 1974), pp. 98–101.

[15] Wallen and de Brichambaut, op. cit., note 13, p. 96. This threshold value must be seen for what it is, a theoretical value that does not take into account such factors as soil characteristics, crop varieties, technological developments, human perceptions or even the pressure of population on the land.

[16] Douglas L. Johnson, *The Nature of Nomadism: A Comparative Study of Pastoral Migrations in Southwestern Asia and Northern Africa*, Research Paper No. 118 (Chicago: University of Chicago, Department of Geography, 1969), p. 17.

[17] Johnson, op. cit., note 16, p. 6.

[18] Johnson, op. cit., note 16, p. 7.

[19] For an excellent analysis of the origins of irrigation agriculture in the Nile Valley, see Karl W. Butzer, *Early Hydraulic Civilization in Egypt: A Study in Cultural Ecology* (Chicago: University of Chicago Press, 1976). Butzer demonstrates that the "valley bottomlands have been a center of settlement from time immemorial" (p. 15), thereby undermining the conventional view that settlement only shifted from the margins of the flood plain after irrigation techniques had been developed.

Butzer also shows how technological limitations (particularly the difficulty of raising water from low-water channels to adjacent fields) restricted land use in the Dynastic period to "a simple pattern of winter agriculture, largely confined to the flood basins, with their crude but effective system of annual flood irrigation." (p. 50)

[20] William Willcocks, *Egyptian Irrigation* (London: E. & F.N. Spon Ltd., 1889), pp. 36–37.

[21] Willcocks, op. cit., note 20, pp. 49–50.

[22] For an outstanding account of the introduction of cotton and the subsequent impact of this cash crop on Egyptian economy and society, see E. R. J. Owen, *Cotton and the Egyptian Economy*, 1820–1914 (Oxford: Clarendon Press, 1969). Owen suggests that the attraction of cotton, from Muhammed Ali's point of view, lay in the fact that it was an ideal product for a government monopoly, that its high cash value offered the prospect of revenue for ambitious modernization programs at a time when Egypt's major export, wheat, was being outcompeted in European markets by higher quality Black Sea grain, and that its cultivation could be easily accommodated within the existing structure of agricultural administration.

[23] J. C. Ross, *Notes on the Distribution of Water in Upper Egypt* (Cairo: Ministry of Public Works, 1892).

[24] Sir William Willcocks, *The Nile Reservoir at Aswan and After* (London: E. & F.N. Spon Ltd., 1903), p. ii.

[25] H. E. Hurst, "Long-Term Storage Capacity of Reservoirs," *Transactions of the American Society of Civil Engineers*, Vol. 116 (1951), p. 770.

[26] Gilbert F. White, *Strategies of American Water Management* (Ann Arbor: University of Michigan Press, 1969), p. 8.

[27] Manners, op. cit., note 14, pp. 109–111.

[28] Since many farmers in the Middle East are dependent upon groundwater, it is perhaps a little misleading to say that seepage through unlined canals or run-off from fields is water "lost" or "wasted." Such water may be an important component in groundwater recharge. However, in a narrower context, such "losses" mean very low physical irrigation efficiencies with a large proportion of the water diverted for irrigation failing to be used productively.

[29] Peter Beaumont, "Qanat systems in Iran," *Bulletin of International Association of Hydrologists*, Vol. 16 (1971), pp. 39–59; Peter Beaumont et al., *The Middle East: A Geographical Study* (London: John Wiley, 1976), pp. 88–92.

[30] In the vicinity of Kerman some qanats extend for 20 miles or more but most appear to be between ½ and 3 miles in length. Depth to groundwater also varies, although instances of qanats tapping groundwater at depths of over 250 feet have been noted. Beaumont et al., op. cit., note 29, p. 91.

[31] Local codes are still strictly observed in parts of the Arabian peninsula, notably Oman and Yemen. Two excellent studies of such codes are A.M.A. Maktari, *Water Rights and Irrigation Practices in Lahj: A Study of the Application of Customary and Shari'ah Law in South-West Arabia* (Cambridge: Cambridge University Press, 1971) and J. C. Wilkinson, *Water and Tribal Settlement in South-East Arabia: A Study of the Aflaj of Oman* (Oxford: Clarendon Press, 1977).

[32] Dante A. Caponera, *Water Laws in Moslem Countries*, FAO Development Paper No. 43 (Rome: FAO, 1954), p. 47.

[33] Caponera, op. cit., note 32, p. 76.

[34] Peter Beaumont, "Qanats on the Varamin Plain, Iran," *Transactions*, Institute of British Geographers, No. 45 (1968), pp. 169–179.

[35] The situation in the Varamin Plain appears to have been exacerbated by a period of abnormally low rainfall and reduced groundwater recharge. Ultimately government intervention became necessary to restrict private well drilling.

[36] Beaumont et al., op. cit., note 29, p. 92.

[37] Manners, op. cit., note 14, pp. 97–98.

[38] Douglas L. Johnson, "Changing Patterns of Pastoral Nomadism in North Africa," in Brian S. Hoyle, ed., *Spatial Aspects of Development* (London: John Wiley, 1974), p. 147.

[39] Johnson, op. cit., note 16, pp. 166–184. This research paper also contains excellent case studies of the major nomadic groups in the Middle East.

[40] Johnson, op. cit., note 16, p. 16.

[41] Frederick Barth, *Principles of Social Organization in Southern Kurdistan* (Oslo: Oslo University Press, 1953), p. 13.

[42] Johnson, op. cit., note 16, p. 12.

[43] Douglas L. Johnson, *Jabal al-Akhdar, Cyrenaica*, Research Paper No. 148 (Chicago: University of Chicago, Department of Geography, 1973).

[44] Johnson, op. cit., note 43, p. 49.

[45] Donald Cole, *Nomads of the Nomads: The Al Murrah Bedouin of the Empty Quarter* (Chicago: Aldine, 1975).

[46] Johnson, op. cit., note 38, p. 156.

[47] Johnson, op. cit., note 38, p. 159.

[48] Paul Ward English, "Urbanites, Peasants, and Nomads: The Middle Eastern Ecological Trilogy," *Journal of Geography*, Vol. 66 (1967), p. 59.

[49] Cole, op. cit., note 45, p. 160.

[50] Cole, op. cit., note 45, p. 163.

[51] Johnson, op. cit., note 38, p. 157.

[52] Johnson, op. cit., note 38, p. 162.

[53] Johnson, op. cit., note 38, p. 159.

[54] Johnson, op. cit., note 38, p. 160.

[55] Kent V. Flannery, "The Cultural Evolution of Civilizations," *Annual Review of Ecology and Systematics*, Vol. 3 (1972), pp. 399–426.

[56] Morroe Berger, *The Arab World Today* (Garden City, N.Y.: Anchor Books, 1964), p. 413.

[57] Flannery, op. cit., note 55, p. 412.

[58] Esther Boserup, *The Conditions of Agricultural Growth* (Chicago: Aldine, 1965).

[59] It is curious that Boserup does not include Egypt in her analysis. It would appear that labor shortage rather than labor surplus plagued agricultural development throughout the 19th century. Plans for the large-scale importation of labor from India, Italy, and China were discussed as late as 1871. It was not until the 1930s that the growth of population began to create serious pressure on the land; see Wendell Cleland, *The Population Problem in Egypt* (Lancaster, 1936).

[60] Roy A. Rappaport, "Sanctity and Adaptation," paper presented at the Wenner-Gren Symposium on the Moral and Esthetic Structure of Human Adaptation, New York, 1969.

[61] White, op. cit., note 5, p. 16.

[62] Thorkild Jacobsen and Robert M. Adams, "Salt and Silt in Ancient Mesopotamian Agriculture," *Science*, Vol. 128 (1958), pp. 1251–1258.

[63] T. O'Riordan, *Environmentalism* (London: Pion, 1976), p. 1.

[64] Gilbert F. White, "Alternative Uses of Limited Water Supplies," *Arid Zone Research*, No. 18 (1960), p. 419.

[65] White, op. cit., note 5, p. 30.

[66] This theme in the work of Carl Sauer is extremely well described in William W. Speth, "Carl Ortwin Sauer on Destructive Exploitation," *Biological Conservation*, Vol. 11 (1977), pp. 145–160.

[67] Carl O. Sauer, "The Agency of Man on the Earth," in William L. Thomas, Jr. ed., *Man's Role in Changing the Face of the Earth* (Chicago: University of Chicago Press, 1956), p. 55.

[68] Sauer, op. cit., note 67, p. 60.

Chapter 4

South Asia

Brian J. Murton

South Asia, bounded by the immense Himalayan ranges to the north, by the mountains along the border with Burma, and by the rugged topography of Iran and Afghanistan to the west, is a clearly discernible region, in which the one great factor underlying all life is the rhythm of the monsoonal year. The peoples of the area are predominantly agrarian, and despite differences in degree, the fundamental lineaments of life are similar, being controlled by a seasonal cycle in which the bulk of the rainfall comes in the warmer half of the year. There is also—away from the mountains—a certain sameness in the regimes of temperatures; but, though we commonly think of the area as tropical, it must be remembered that half of the area and over half of the population are north of the Tropic of Cancer. Fortunately the Himalayan mountain wall insulates the lowlands from the continental extremes of central Asia, so that all south the Himalayas is essentially tropical.

Hinduism gives, or until very recently has given, a certain common tone to most of the area. For millenia the area has been virtually a cul-de-sac into which peoples and cultures have infiltrated or have been driven, retaining many of their ancient rules of life and yet ceaselessly reacting upon one another, and for the most part, if not welded together, at least held together in the iron clasp of the caste system, a unique solution to the problems of plural society. The contemporary political framework is such that India, the giant in population and area, lies surrounded by several smaller political units (Figure 10). Bangladesh and Pakistan flank India on the east and west respectively, and to the north lies the landlocked states of Nepal and Bhutan. Off the southern tip of the Indian triangle lies the island state of Sri Lanka. These countries, with the exception of Nepal, had a common political, economic, and social history during the nineteenth and twentieth centuries when they were under British rule.

At the time the British established their ascendancy over the area, more than 5,000

Fig. 10. Political divisions of South Asia.

years of interaction between man and an at-times capricious environment had led to the evolution of a number of resource-use systems characterized by a range of techniques and management practices. Under traditional management conditions there was near total dependence on local biologic productivity to sustain life.[1] It is to the ways in which South Asians have evaluated and appraised this biologic productivity, and have directed it to their own ends on a sustaining basis through the use of particular resource management techniques and practices, that this chapter is directed.[2]

THE RESOURCE BASE

The biophysical setting of South Asia may be described in a number of ways, but in human terms, bioclimatic systems are of the greatest importance because most people in the region continue to rely on natural energy (solar radiation) and natural water (rain-fall) as the basis of their subsistence.[3] Apart from the mountain rimlands, limited areas of hilly terrain in the peninsular, and small portions of plateau and plain which are deeply dissected, most of South Asia (approximately 66%) is topographically usable. The soils of this vast lowland area (nearly 2 million of South Asia's 3.2 million square kilometers), while not of exceptional fertility, offer no major handicaps to cultivation. Some 30 to 35% of the area consists of alluvial gravels, sands, silts, clays, or wind-blown sands. About 320,000 square kilometers, primarily in the northwestern and central parts of the penin-sular are covered with dark brown and black clayey soils, known as *regur* or black cotton soils. The remainder of South Asia, especially where rainfall is over 150 centimeters, has lateritic soils which vary from deep and clayey soils found in lowland areas, to light red and yellow gravelly or loamy soils of hills and lower slopes.

But it is climate that influences most the use of South Asia by man, especially the amounts of radiant energy from the sun and water available for plant growth. The a-mount of energy available determines the potential limits of productivity over the sur-face of South Asia; the actual amount of productivity, however, depends upon the presence of water and how it is utilized.[4] From a comparison of energy converted to water equivalents (potential evapotranspiration) with available moisture a clear picture can be obtained of the bioclimate of a place. It is further possible to reduce the great variety of individual water balances of South Asia to three environmental activity bud-gets: *low-work environmental budgets* which are characterized by very short periods during which biological growth, chemical changes, leaching, or erosion are active; *high-work environmental budgets* characterized by high energy and moisture endowments throughout the year which drive biological and chemical activity at high rates; and *seasonal-work environmental budgets* which have at least one extended period of en-vironmental budgets which have at least one extended period of environmental work.[5] These different work patterns of environments at different places in South Asia have presented different opportunities and problems for man, as many aspects of human living have involved responding to particular environmental conditions.

Low-Work Environments

In South Asia these conditions prevail in most of Pakistan, and in the Indian states of Rajasthan, western and southwestern Punjab and Haryana, western Gujarat, and along the less of the Western Ghats in Maharashtra and Karnataka (Figure 11). In all of these areas energy conditions are favorable throughout the year, but rainfall is low, even during the Southwest Monsoon period (normally June through September). However, seasonal rainfall does trigger considerable environmental activity, especially in peninsular India, where unfortunately the effects of relatively high rainfall during the Southwest Monsoon are offset by equally high potential evapotranspiration.

Obviously, such environments would be unable to sustain large populations if the people had to depend on local resources. Bringing in outside resources or reorganizing available ones can, however, provide opportunities for large numbers of people to thrive there. Irrigation represents one such reorganization of considerable antiquity in South Asia. As we shall see, the use of water from natural streams has permitted South Asians to use the generally high potential energy of the low-work environment area, through in-creasing evapotranspiration, and thus enhancing biological growth.

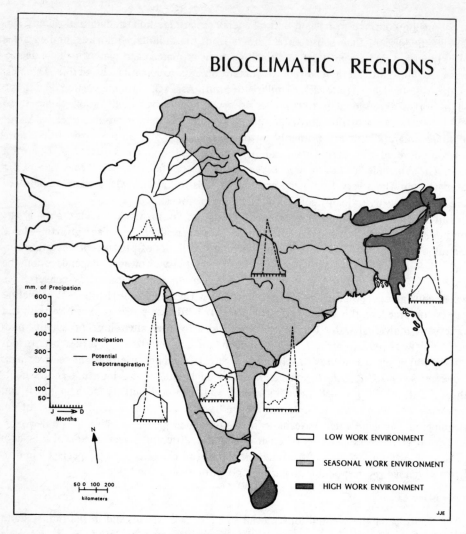

Fig. 11. Bioclimatic regions.

Seasonal-Work Environments

Bioclimates which have at least one period of environmental activity dominate much of the rest of South Asia (Figure 11). Most of the Ganga valley and peninsular India are characterized by a period of adequate rainfall for productive plant growth during the Southwest Monsoon. Along the southeastern coast of the peninsular rainfall comes primarily during the Northeast Monsoon (especially in October, November, and December). In contrast to seasonality in lowland South Asia, in the northern mountains the dormant season results from low temperatures which freeze surplus water and make vegetation growth impossible.

In environments with such seasonal sequences there is a growth phase during the summer rains and a dormant or storage phase during the dry and/or cold season. Such a sequence means that products of the growing season mature more or less simultaneously. The major crops grown in these environments, mainly grains, may be easily kept through the dry season, and people can consume stored production throughout the year. Moreover, the sequence of environmental work has made management easier. People have adapted their activities to those of the season: a time to plant, a time to cultivate and protect crops, a time to harvest, and a time to rest and prepare for the next cycle.

High-Work Environments

In South Asia high-work environments are found in parts of Assam, West Bengal, the hill states and territories of eastern India, as well as in eastern Bangladesh and the southern part of Sri Lanka (Figure 11). High energy endowments throughout the year characterize these areas and although there is seasonal rainfall, the period of inadequate moisture is short and deficits are small compared to the moisture excesses which normally prevail.

It would seem reasonable that the abundance of biological resources in these areas of high energy and moisture endowments would attract human settlement. In most such environments in South Asia, however, population densities were low and remain so today. Most South Asians continue to reside in the seasonal-work environmental areas where there is an orderly and manageable cycle of production and dormancy.

EVOLUTION OF A TRADITION

Origin and Development

While there is evidence that early man occupied part of South Asia continuously from at least 500,000 years ago, the resource complexes of the immediate pre-British period had their roots in events which began to influence the region after 10,000 years before the present.[6] From this time onwards two traditions began to develop in the region: a peasant village tradition with associated urban centers, which reflected the interests of the vast majority of South Asians; and a tribal tradition, which was primarily that of non-Hinduized people.

The peasant village tradition appears to have grown out of the diffusion of settled life into the area from the west, probably after 4,000 B.C. In West Asia a primary village phase of development can be dated to 8,000 to 6,500 B.C., with wheat, barley, leguminous plants, sheep and goats as the economic basis of life. From this time food production diffused westwards, to the south, and to the east, reaching southern Afghanistan by about 3,000 B.C. In the hill country of western Pakistan sites show evidence that three distinct socio-economic entities—hunting and gathering, pastoralism, and farming—co-existed by about 2,500 B.C.

The next phase of settled life in South Asia is dominated by the urban Harappan civilization which arose in the lower Indus River Valley after 2,300 B.C. and spread over all the Indus Valley, the Indian Punjab as far east as Delhi, and into southern Gujarat. The resource base of this civilization was primarily West Asian in origin: wheat, barley, sheep, goats, and cattle. However, in its latter phases in Gujarat there is evidence of humped Indian cattle, domestic buffalo, rice, and peal millet, all of South or Southeast Asian origin.

At the same time several other regional food producing complexes emerged in eastern, central, and southern India. In the eastern Ganga Valley a rice-based system with strong Southeast Asian affinities developed after 1,500 B.C. In southern India a pastoral- and millet- and pulse-based dry farming economy gradually evolved after 2,300–1,800 B.C. and the rice system of eastern India spread along the southeastern coast in the latter half of the first millenium B.C. A wheat- and pulse-based system which originated in central India after 2,000 B.C. shifted eastwards into the central Ganga Valley after 1,500 B.C., and here a mixed wheat, rice, and bulrush millet economy developed.[7] After about 1,000 B.C. the whole of the western and central Ganga Valley was the preserve of a pastoral-agricultural peasant economy, which was gradually diffusing eastwards. Thus at the end of the first millenium B.C. the major lineaments of the traditional resource complexes of South Asia were all in place. The resource complexes which had evolved were adaptations to the varied environments of the region. Most involved crops, livestock, and techniques from outside the region; but indigenous plants and animals were domesticated as well. In like manner, many of the management and conservation practices were commonly found in other parts of the Old World where similar crops were grown. But certain practices of distinctly South Asian origin emerged.

By the beginning of the nineteenth century when South Asia came under British rule, peasant village resource complexes had come to dominate most of the lowlands of the region, although detailed analyses have shown that a considerable part of the region was still forested in 1800 (Figure 12).[8] The exact character of both peasant village and tribal resource complexes varied greatly over the face of South Asia. Different crops, and the degree to which pastoral and fishing activities were important, were the major factors in distinguishing different types of peasant resource complexes (Figure 13). Rice was the major crop, indeed often the only crop, grown in areas of over 125 centimeters of rainfall. In Assam, Bengal, Orissa, and on the coasts of the peninsular, rice was cultivated to the virtual exclusion of anything else.[9] In the central Ganga Valley it was a significant crop, and it dominated the lower Indus Valley. Wheat was important in the central Ganga region, and was the staple in the western Ganga Valley and Punjab region. Barley was grown in association with wheat, and in places in the foothills of the Himalayas was the most important crop. Sorghum and millets were grown in these areas as well, but they dominated the drier parts of the peninsular and northern India. Sorghum (*jowar*) was the food staple in the northwestern peninsular, pearl millet (*bajra*) in the dry zone along the margins of the Thar Desert, and finger millet (*ragi*) in the southern and central parts of the interior of the peninsular.

But this is a great simplification of the crop pattern, because crops very rarely occurred in monoculture situations. In fact, considerable crop diversity was the general rule, with the exception of some of the rice areas. Furthermore, in many parts of the region pastoralism was a very important subsidiary, or even dominant, activity. Throughout the sorghum-millet zone the grazing of cattle, sheep, and goats was common, and in the more arid western and mountain fringes of South Asia, pastoralism provided the

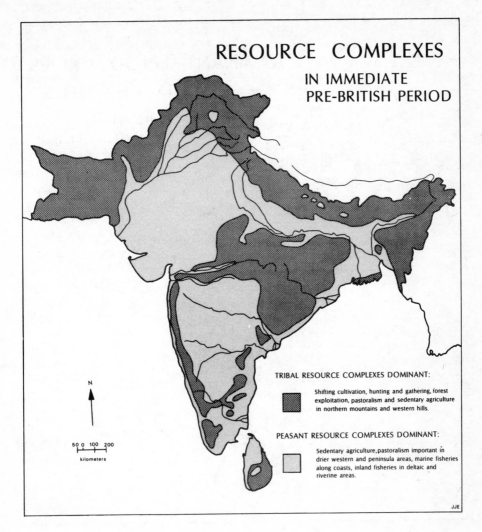

RESOURCE COMPLEXES
IN IMMEDIATE PRE-BRITISH PERIOD

N

50 0 100 200
kilometers

TRIBAL RESOURCE COMPLEXES DOMINANT:

Shifting cultivation, hunting and gathering, forest exploitation, pastoralism and sedentary agriculture in northern mountains and western hills.

PEASANT RESOURCE COMPLEXES DOMINANT:

Sedentary agriculture, pastoralism important in drier western and peninsula areas, marine fisheries along coasts, inland fisheries in deltaic and riverine areas.

JJE

Fig. 12. Resource complexes in the immediate pre-British period.

basis of subsistence for a considerable proportion of the population. Most of this pastoral activity was intimately linked to village economies, and in many places symbiotic relationships between agriculturalist and pastoralist had developed. In the coastal zone, estuaries, riverine, and delta areas of South Asia, a relatively insignificant fisheries component added a further dimension to the peasant resource complex. In most places this was weakly integrated with the mainstream of South Asian life, and only in the water environment of the Ganga-Brahmaputra delta, and along parts of the peninsular coasts, did fishing assume local importance, and did fish have much place in the diet.

The tribal resource complex, dominated by shifting cultivation practices, was located in the forested hill regions of central and eastern north India, and was found in the hills of the western and eastern fringes of the peninsular (Figure 12). This complex was also

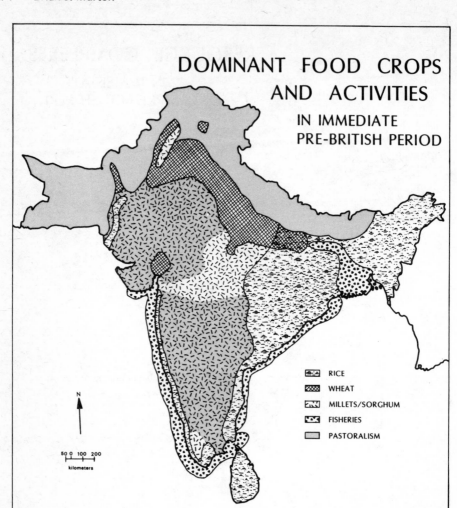

DOMINANT FOOD CROPS AND ACTIVITIES IN IMMEDIATE PRE-BRITISH PERIOD

N

50 0 100 200
kilometers

RICE
WHEAT
MILLETS/SORGHUM
FISHERIES
PASTORALISM

JJE

Fig. 13. Dominant food crops and activities in the immediate pre-British period.

found in forested lowland areas, such as the Tarai and the Brahmaputra valley. Rice was the dominant crop of this complex in eastern South Asia, but sorghum and millets were important elsewhere. Minute numbers of hunters and gatherers inhabited some of the more inaccessible hill regions, and both tribal and peasant peoples were involved in exploiting forest products to some extent everywhere.

Traditional Conservation Context

The resource complexes of the immediate pre-British period had two outstanding conservation characteristics. First, the resource complexes of South Asia were characterized by extreme diversity. Within the bounds of village territories and local regions were found wet land, dry land, garden land, orchards, waste land, and even forest land. With the exception of the few intensively cultivated areas, cultivated land was fragmented and discontinuous. Furthermore, village territories typically had zonal arrangements of land around them: the land immediately around the settlement site was manured, irrigated, and also had greater labor input and care, whereas outlying land was less manured or not manured at all and in consequence was less productive.[10] This outlying area was often subdivided into intermediate land and outlying (peripheral) land. Pasture, waste, and forest lands were usually located in the outlying zone.

Within areas under cultivation crop patterns mirrored variations in soil-water distribution.[11] In northern India, for example, the presence of millets suggested a relatively low water table where regular irrigation would be difficult to maintain. Millets themselves reflected differences in soil quality: sorghum (jowar) was grown on "good" dry land soil, pearl millet (bajra) on inferior. Wheat was grown only on the best soils where good irrigation facilities could supplement rainfall. Rice was found in low areas where drainage was poor, and where the soils tended toward sodic-alkalinity.

Within this mosaic of crop-environment relationships, there was also varietal diversity. Rice had undergone considerable genetic diversification and over 4,000 varieties were recorded in South Asia in 1900.[12] In one district in Orissa over 1,000 varieties had been collected, and even in areas where rice was not the major crop numerous varieties were grown: in Salem and Coimbatore Districts of Madras Presidency (millet areas) 22 and 13 varieties of rice were grown in the mid-19th century.[13] The same type of varietal diversity existed in the wheat-growing areas, and through the millet-sorghum zone.[14]

Second, the South Asian resource complexes of the pre-British period lacked complexity. Complexity in a systems context refers not only to size but to the degree of interconnection among components of a system which ties them together into an interdependent web of causal pathways. To be sure there was trade and movement of people from one part of the region to another.[15] But perhaps the outstanding characteristic of pre-British South Asia was the segmentary nature of society and economy. Current anthropological writings stress the idea that traditional social organization in South Asia has been contained within a territorial setting of rather small scale.[16] Likewise, recent analyses of the political organization of the pre-British period convincingly demonstrate that Indian states, as formal and concrete systems, were characterized by the following salient attributes: they were custodial, tributary, locally based, and oriented toward rural networks.[17]

Thus an identifiable spatial characteristic of pre-British South Asia was the existence of economically self-sufficient local regions.[18] This mosaic of small territories, based upon locally available knowledge of resource characteristics and locally available energy and materials for resources management, is a classic example of the principles underlying traditional resource systems. Available energy sources (human and animal muscle) and the nature of the technology, in conjunction with social norms, effectively limited the scale of resource use to the locality. Most things needed by a population were produced locally and there was virtually no specialization of the production of any important subsistence products.

EXISTING TRADITIONAL RESOURCE-USING SYSTEMS

Contemporary Resource Complexes

Over the past 200 years South Asia's resource complexes have been transformed and expanded. In the first place, the peasant resource complex has greatly increased in area at the expense of forest, much of which was formerly the domain of the tribal resource complex. Forest and areas of shifting cultivation, have been displaced by plantations in the foothills of the Himalayas, in the hill regions in southern India, and in Sri Lanka. The cropping pattern within the peasant complex has retained its traditional outline, but within these broad constraints, a number of introduced crops and greatly improved varieties have led to changes in the agricultural landscape. The introduction of modern scientific knowledge, modern technology, and extra-local energy sources have added another dimension to all cropping systems, but especially to the wheat-growing areas of northwestern India and Pakistan, some of the rice areas of eastern and peninsular India, and to areas in which cash cropping has become important.

Along with the introduction of modern science and technology have come many of the standard conservation practices found in the western world. All of these have transformed aspects of the resource complexes of South Asia, and today many farmers do rely upon information from scientific and educational institutions, and upon supplies of fuels, chemicals, equipment, and other inputs from outside the local community. Of course, the great bulk of South Asian resource managers continue to rely heavily upon traditional conservation practices. Their main energy sources continue to be human and animal muscle, augmented by gravity whenever possible. But everywhere today elements of modern science and technology have either blended into, or stand in stark contrast to, traditional practices.

The elements of the biophysical resource base of South Asia—climate, water, slope, soil, space, time, plants, and animals—constitute resource elements for people anywhere. To use and conserve these elements, South Asian resource managers relied on individual or local group knowledge of resource characteristics, and upon a technology based upon locally available energy and materials.[19] Today, while there is little question that major changes have occurred, traditional systems of agricultural knowledge and of technologies and practices remain important to most South Asia resource managers.

The Conservation Context: Systems of Knowledge

Specific techniques, practices, and technologies are but the surface manifestations, the observable behavioral realities, of an underlying cognitive system of knowledge about resources. No systematic accounting of this knowledge has been compiled for South Asia, yet relevant material is described in a number of places, and can be used as a general guide to folk systems of resource knowledge.[20]

General premises. South Asian folk science is rooted in indigenous religious beliefs and cosmography, and is closely tied to the spiritual fabric of traditional society. The general premises that underlie the folk agricultural science of South Asia include several sets of interlocking principles derived from South Asian world view. The basic concepts which allow people to share similar sets of evaluations and strategies, as well as comparable outlooks towards the future, are: *samsara*, the belief in rebirth; *karma*, the belief that actions in one life determine fortune and status in the next; *dharma*, the definition of what one's behavior must be in the life status to which one's karma has brought one; *moksha*, salvation by release from the wheel of eternal rebirths through the ideal of perfect asceticism, of absolute wantlessness; *ahimsa*, the belief in the sacredness of all life.[21] The Universe is viewed as consisting of places, each of which may contain gods, men, animals, plants, and things in varying mixtures and proportions. In this view there is no separation of Man and Nature and the Supernatural: all have a place, all have a role; all are equally "real." Perhaps a more important general principle is that within each location all phenomena (people, animals, plants, gods, things) are arranged in hierarchical order.[22] This notion of hierarchy is of critical importance in comprehending systems of knowledge about resources because ranking is a feature of many aspects of resource use: land categories are ranked; soil types are ranked; crops, even varieties, are ranked. In addition, resource-users themselves are ranked, both in terms of socio-ritual status (*jati* or caste) and in terms of the control and use of land. *Jati*, locally at least, are also occupational groupings. Thus there are farming *jati*, service *jati*, artisan *jati*, laboring *jati*, pastoral *jati*, trading *jati*, fishing *jati*. Farming *jati* usually rank high whereas laborers and fishermen are low. But village and local dominance of resources is also a question of the possession of land.[23] The system of such interest groups relating to the control of land is neither simple nor uniform throughout South Asia, but it is central to the way in which scarce resources, e.g., irrigation water, are allocated.[24]

South Asians also segment the continuum of nature: the year is divided into seasons; landscapes are categorized; soils are divided into classes; crop varieties are distinguished. But the South Asian mind does not only segment phenomena but arranges them in opposite pairs. Binary opposites are reflected in numerous aspects of South Asian life: in southern India most *jati* are grouped into either right or left divisions; in the ascribing of heating or cooling attributes to natural phenomena; in the polarization of the year into two major family feast periods; in terms of basic geographical polarities, such as north and south, east and west, lowland and upland, center and periphery; and in terms of opposed landscape types.[25] Many of these opposites are mediated by a third term, which reconcile their bipolar tendencies. Furthermore, South Asians recognize a few basic substances or elements that underlie the multiplicity of phenomena: earth, water, fire, wind, and sky.[26] Each substance is identified with a distinctive quality and each is also a process or the embodiment of a principle for action. Each is identified with a range of other phenomena, so that nature is made intelligible and coherent.

Of equal importance is South Asian understanding of time. Time moves in cycles within cycles—days within astral periods within months within seasons within years within eras of approximately 300 million years.[27] Another characteristic of South Asian time is that it had no beginning or ending: there is only endless repetition of cycles. Finally, nothing is more indicative of the all-encompassing nature of time than that the gods, no less than men, are part of the eternal cycle. There is no dividing line between the human and the divine: there is a continuum between man and nature and between man and the gods, because all are bound in the movement of time.

Co-ordination of resource-use activities. They key operation which ties together the events in the chain which linked environment with resource potential is cognition, especially appraisals of the environment, which, along with overt resource behaviors, constitute part of the South Asian definition of proper resource-use practices. The co-ordination of resource-use activities has both temporal and spatial aspects. Systems of dividing time are common to all parts of South Asia. Three methods of computing yearly cycles are in use (solar, lunar, *fasli* or revenue year), but in terms of resource use the solar year which begins in mid-April is the most important as its beginning more or less coincides with the thundershowers of April which herald the coming monsoon, the beginning of the agricultural season.

The exact number and dates of seasons in the year varies from place to place, but there are usually six, of two months each. As important as recognized seasons are sowing periods, which are highly localized, reflecting appraisals of the moisture environment in relationship to particular crops. But perhaps the most important devices for regulating the timing of agricultural operations are astral periods (*nakshatra*). These are formulated in terms of the relationships of the sun, the twelve signs of the zodiac and twenty-seven stars. There are twenty-seven periods, to each of which are assigned agricultural operations and tasks. If time is organized into years, months, seasons, and astral periods, space is organized into a number of land-soil-crop associations. Throughout South Asia certain crops or crop associations are related to certain land and soil types. These interrelationships are models which farmers use to guide them in their agricultural activities: indeed, they are culturally prescribed ways of doing things.

However, South Asian resource knowledge is not confined to a sum of unconnected parts. Resource appraisal, as well as resource-use, requires that terms be linked in webs of associations: sorghum intersects with certain land types, soil/water conditions, insect pests; rice with others; wheat with yet others. Different seasons intersect with the availability of different forage plants, different weather conditions intersect with different diseases, and different terrains with different plant associations. Thousands of these simple linkages constitute the building blocks of South Asian resource strategy: the ways in which resources are combined and timed.

Resource predictability. Time and space are organized into sequences and segments, linked into webs of association. A wealth of knowledge associated with these, makes the somewhat limited and unpredictable resources of South Asia less limited and more predictable. This accumulation of experience is formalized in the form of folk songs, sayings, and proverbs.[28] The months of the year, the seasons, and especially the astral periods, all have associated with them a vast array of pithy statements about every aspect of tillage and agricultural operations. Agricultural operations are guided by such statements, especially those relating to rainfall and the appropriate timing of cultivation practices. Much of this information about rainfall is contained in agricultural almanacs which predict in detail the expectation of rainfall based upon the position of the stars in relationship to the moon. Indian farmers have also developed devices to make their uncertain environment determinate and knowable, most of which involve a belief in the use of natural phenomena to predict the occurrence or non-occurrence of rainfall. Land and soil types also have sayings and proverbs associated with them, as do most agricultural practices, crops, and livestock. Proverbs also allude to the knowledge of agriculture held by some *jati* and the lack of it by others.

Categories of resource discrimination. The principal categories of resource discrimination in South Asia include soil, slope, water, climate, time, space, plants, animals, and fish, all aspects of environmental elements. Such terminological domains are further elaborated in taxonomies. South Asians have classifications of landscape morphology, land types, soils, vegetation, crops, macroclimatic and microclimatic resources. These are related to the general principles discussed earlier, and although each can be isolated and reviewed separately, in reality they make up a complex of intersecting, interconnected entities and events.

Resource classifications reflect local characteristics of the biophysical environment. Throughout the region land is initially classified as either wet or dry. This distinction between wet (irrigated) and dry (rainfed) land is of major importance because distinctive types of management and conservation practices are related to wet and dry land. In the Ganga Valley and delta areas land is further classified in terms of elevation above water level. Soils are most often initially classified according to their color (e.g., red or black), and then in terms of very fine textural discriminations, as well as distance from settlement sites. Crop varieties are classified in terms of obvious seed color, height, seedhead shape, duration, taste, and other visible characteristics.

In summary, considerable empirical knowledge of the physical world and taxonomies of a fair degree of sophistication exist. This resource knowledge is tied to the fundamental paradigms of knowledge in South Asian society through a set of general principles. These paradigms ultimately cross the boundary between science and religion, even if day-to-day forces in the environment do not. In fact, to dichotomize between science and religion is undoubtedly erroneous in South Asia: a simple pragmatic solution to a problem may well be an appropriate ceremony or prayer.

The Conservation Context: Technologies, Techniques, Practices

To survey the vast array of traditional technologies, techniques, and practices of a resource conserving nature would require more space than is available here. What I do is an inventory, through the use of tables constructed from a diversity of source materials, of the form of management practice, the resource complex in which it is found, whether it is located on irrigated or rainfed land, and examples of specific areas in South Asia where the form is located.[29]

Soil management. An impressive array of soil management techniques is employed by South Asian farmers (Table 6). These techniques can be divided into three major groupings—soil fertility practices, tillage practices, and field forms. Soil fertility is maintained or improved by a variety of animal, green, and human manures, usually produced within the farm area. Cattle dung remains the preferred manure, but in many places by the early nineteenth century a shortage of firewood meant that it was more often than not used as a fuel for cooking.

A striking feature of soil fertility maintenance and enhancement practices is that most of them are only applied to irrigated land. Only the penning of sheep and goats, the use of ash (shifting cultivation), fallowing, crop mixing, the use of leguminous crops, and crop rotation are found on rainfed land. Furthermore, much of the manure of one type or another, in millet-growing areas, as well as in wheat and rice staple areas, is applied to land destined for cash crops such as sugarcane, vegetables, tobacco, and betel, rather than for staple food grains.

Table 6. Soil Management

Form	Land type[a]	Resource complex-crop[b]	Location[c]
Soil Fertility			
Animal Manure			
Cattle dung	I	P–R, W, M	Everywhere
Sheep dung	I, R	P–R, W, M	Everywhere
Goat dung	I, R	P–R, W, M	Everywhere
Horse dung	I	P–W	P, Ba
Camel dung	I	P–W	P, Ba
Donkey dung	I	P–W	P, Ba
Bat dung	K	P–M	Ka
Human manure	I	P–R, W, M	Small amounts everywhere
Green manure			
Ploughed crops	I	P–R, M	Ka, G, M, WB, BD, O
Leaves, branches	I	P–R, M, W	T, Ka, M, Ke, WB, BD
Village debris	I	P–M, W	Ka, P, S
Household refuse	I	P–R, W, M	Everywhere
Ash	I	P–R, W, M, T–SC	M, Ka, Ke, T, AP, O, MP, A, BD, N, MR, S, SL
Oil seed waste	I	P–R, W, M	G, UP, M, P, WB, BD, T, O
Fallowing	I, R	P–R, W, M, T–SC	Known everywhere
Texture improvement			
and soil transfer	I	P–R, W, M	M, Ka, Ke, T, G, MP, O, WB, BD, P
Crop mixing	I, R	P–W, M, T–SC	Everywhere
Leguminous crops	I, R	P–R, W, M, T–SC	Everywhere
Crop rotation	I, R	P–R, W, M	Known everywhere, but was restricted
Natural silting	I	P–R, W	A, BD, WB, Bi, UP, S, O
Fish	I		Coastal areas of G and S
Flushing soil	I		O, AP
Tillage			
Ploughing			
Light ploughs	I, R	P–R, W, M	Everywhere
Heavy ploughs	R	P–M	Ma, Ka, AP
Multiple ploughing	I, R	P–R, W, M	Everywhere
Wet ploughing	I	P–R, W	Everywhere
Dry ploughing	I, R	P–R, W, M	
Hoeing	R	P–R, W, M, T–SC	Ma, Ka, Ke, T, AP, O, WB, BD, A, Bi, MP, MR, SL
Harrowing	I, R	P–R, W, M	Everywhere, but very important in Ma, Ka, AP
Clod breaking	I, R	P–R, W, M	Everywhere
Puddling	I	P–R	Everywhere
Heating soil	R	T–SC	Ma, Ka, Ke, T, AP, O, WB, BD, A, Bi, MP
Field Forms			
Embankments against			
salt water	I	P–R	Ke, WB, BD, S
Bunding	I, R	P–R, W, M	Everywhere, but especially important in Ba, MP, Ma, MB, Bi
Levelling	I	P–R, W, M	Everywhere
Mounding	I	P–R	Ke

Various tillage practices affect tilth for better or for worse. Most land receives multiple ploughings, usually at intervals of a week or two (Figure 14). Although ploughings are shallow this does result in extremely fine tilth in the top four to eight inches. Hoes are used throughout the region to break up clods left after ploughing. Harrowing using a variety of harrow-type implements is widespread, but it is especially important in the black soil parts of peninsular India, where it often supplants ploughing. Clod-breaking, either by hoeing by pulling beams across the fields, or by using hammers or mallets, is universal, as is puddling in rice-growing areas. The heating of the top four to eight inches of the soil which kills insect pects is a by-product of burning in shifting cultivation areas. Certain kinds of field forms are important soil-management practices in Kerala, West Bengal, Bangladesh, and Orissa.

Slope management. Slope management is closely related to soil management and water management, especially where erosion control and irrigation are practiced. Terracing is perhaps the most widespread and best-known form of slope control in South Asia (Table 7). It is possible to distinguish many different types of terraces, and in South Asia terrace forms fall into the following categories: silt-trap dams; crude stone walls across sloping surfaces; stone-walled terraces for both dry and irrigated crops; series of irrigated fields below water sources (Figure 15). Field levelling is a widespread slope management technique found in association with terracing. It is especially important in irrigated areas where it is an aspect of water control as well. Planted vegetation, usually hedges, is in use in several parts of South Asia where terrain is either rolling or sloping, often in association with low piled rock walls, which creates very distinctive, almost "bocage" type landscapes.

Water management. Management of water resources includes some of the oldest and most widespread of traditional practices. This stems in part from the fluid nature of water which permits the use of gravity to perform such work functions as collection, transfer, and application. Most South Asian systems simply interrupt and reorganize the overland portion of the hydrologic cycle to secure a supply of irrigation water (Table 8)

Water storage is quite complex as it involves artificial devices (tanks) for true water storage, rather than simply diversion (Figure 16). Water from wells, rivers, and tanks is raised or transferred by a variety of lifting devices, and water is diverted from streams through the construction of embankments in their beds. Water delivery systems almost universally depend upon gravity flow through open canals, though underground channels (*kariz*) are common in Baluchistan. Once at the fields most water is applied through surface flooding, although where water is scarce it is applied by hand from pots. Various forms of bunding controls the flow of water through fields (Figure 17).

Fig. 14. Ploughing dry fields; sheep pens can be seen in background.

Table 7. Slope Management

Form	Land type	Resource complex-crop	Location
Terracing	I	P–R, W, M	SL, T, Ke, Ka, Ma, MP, WB, BD, A, MR, Na, Ne, Bi, K
Field Levelling	I	P–R, W, M	Everywhere
Silt-trap dams	I	P–W, M	Ka, Ba
Planted Vegetation	R	P–M, W	T, Ka, G, NW

Key to symbols: See Table 6.
Source: See note 29.

Fig. 15. Terraces.

Table 8. Water Management

Form	Land type	Resource complex-crop	Location
Storage			
Large tanks	I	P–R, M	Ka, Ta, R, MP
Small tanks	I	P–R, W	T, WB, BD, Bi, Up, P
Permanent wells	I	P–R, W, M	Everywhere
Temporary wells	I	P–R, W, M	Everywhere
Lifting Devices			
Baskets	I	P–R, W, M	Everywhere
Lever lifts	I	P–R, W, M	Everywhere
Cattle lifts	I	P–R, W, M	Everywhere
Persian wheels	I	P–R, W	P, S, UP, R, G, Ke
Diversion Devices			
Embankments in river beds	I	P–R, M	Everywhere
Delivery Systems			
Natural inundation canals	I	P–R, W	S, P
Excavated inundation canals	I	P–R, W	S, P, UP
Channels			
From diverted streams	I	P–R, W, M	Everywhere
From tanks	I	P–R, W, M	Everywhere
From wells	I	P–R, W, M	Everywhere
Kariz	I	P–W	Ba
Application Practices			
Surface flooding	I	P–R, W, M	Everywhere
Hand sprinkling	I	P–R, W, M	Everywhere
Single bunds around fields	I	P–R, W, M	Everywhere
Multiple bunds in fields	I	P–R, W, M	Everywhere, but notable in T, Ka, Bi, S
Drainage Systems			
Downslope terrace draining	I	P–R	WB, BD, A, Bi
Bailing	I	P–R	Ke
Ditches	I	P–R	Ke
Flood Prevention			
Embankments along rivers	I	P–R	S, WD, BD, O, Bi
Dams to keep out salt water and storm surges	I	P–R	S, WB, BD

Key to symbols: See Table 6.
Source: See note 29.

Numerous devices are used to measure the allocation of water: graduated stakes, graduated sundials, the position of moon and stars, pots from which water drops through a hole. It is usual to have a designated official supervise the actual apportioning of the water, although in some areas landholders construct, maintain, and control, water allocation to tenants. Elsewhere, farmers usually build, maintain, and repair small-scale facilities themselves, but large works which were constructed and repaired with state or religious institutional support, are now maintained by government departments. Medium-sized facilities—most often large tanks, diversion devices, *kariz*, and less often wells—are built and maintained by one or several village communities, or by the government.

Fig. 16. Irrigation tank during dry season; soil has been removed from the tank-bed to enrich nearby fields.

Fig. 17. Major and minor field bunds for careful control of water.

Drainage systems also exist: downslope systems in terraced ricefields; water lifts; and ditch systems. Flood prevention systems— levees along rivers and embankments and dams across tidal estuaries to keep out salt water—are found in low-lying delta areas of the major river systems.

Microclimatic management. Traditional farmers in South Asia are not able to cope with enormous energy fluxes and mass transfers involved in macro- or meso-scale climates but they have achieved considerable control over individual plant or small plot microclimates (Table 9). Perhaps the most basic way of modifying microclimates is the management of the amount of sunlight entering the soil-plant system. Shade management is widespread: shade reduction through forest clearance; plant spacing; shade enhancement; mixed cropping. The intensity of solar radiation received at the surface is also changed through the use of raised ridges and walls. Heat and moisture fluxes are controlled by tillage practices and, to a much more limited extent, by mulching. Tillage practices serve the multiple purposes of increasing precipitation absorption, reducing heat flows between surface and subsoil, controlling weeds, and improving root and tuber development. Tillage methods produce a fine surface tilth, a "dry soil mulch." The harrowing and hand pulling of weeds reduces transpiration losses. Windbreaks of one type or another are also used in several parts of the region.

Space management. Although South Asian farmers live and work in a relatively small world, distances and spatial arrangements enter into their decisions (Table 10). South Asia has had numerous large cities and smaller towns with permanent markets for nearly three millenia, and in addition there was a well-developed network of fairs and periodic markets. Within local regions virtually every village has access to a periodic market, and commonly a fair at an important temple or shrine. The actual effect of markets on agricultural production and land use in South Asia before the early 19th century is unclear, although cash crops were cultivated in many places.[30]

Distances and distribution of fields in relation to farmstead is also important. Location is an attribute of land at the village level, just as is soil quality and water availability. This is reflected in decreasing land use intensity from the settlement site, a question already commented upon. Another aspect of farmstead-field distance is the fragmentation of land holdings. Farmers prefer to have fields located in all zones around a settlement site, so they can share in all types of production, thus minimizing the risk of total crop failure. Space also is managed at the plot level, where mixed cropping, which includes multistoried cropping, enables maximum use to be made of both horizontal and vertical space.

Plant-vegetation management. A variety of techniques is employed to maintain or enhance crop, orchard, forest, and pasture production (Table 11). This includes choice of appropriate crop, especially in relationship to local soil characteristics, and choice of variety in relationship to season, soil, and distance from settlement site. Seed selection is known everywhere, but usually only practiced by larger farmers. Selection is done on the basis of size and color of the grain. Grafting of fruit trees, introduced from West and Central Asia in the sixteenth century, has become widespread.

A range of planting methods, each with its own conservation rationale, is in use. Of particular note is the practice of drilling seed, especially millets in peninsular India and wheat in Punjab and western Uttar Pradesh. When crops are growing and maturing they are protected from bird, animal, and human predation with hedges, fences, planted

Table 9. Microclimatic Management

Form	Land type	Resource complex-crop	Location
Shade Management			
Shade reduction	R	T–SC	Ma, Ka, Ke, T, AP, O, MP, A, BD, WB, Na, MR
Plant spacing–transplantation	I	P–R	Ke, T, AP, O, WB, BD, Bi, A, S
Plant spacing–thinning	I, R	P–R, W, M	Everywhere
Shade enhancement	R	T–SC	Ma, Ke, Ka, T, AP, O, MP, A, BD, WB, Na, MR
Mixed cropping	I, R		Everywhere
Surface Geometry Management			
Stone walls	R	P–M, W	Widespread
Earth bunds	R	P–M, W	Ma, Ka, AP, Ba
Tillage Systems			
Multiple ploughing	I, R	P–R, W, M	Everywhere
Shallow ploughing	I, R	P–R, W, M	Everywhere
Clod crushing	I, R	P–R, W, M	Everywhere
Harrowing	R	P–W, M	Everywhere
Weeding	I, R	P–R, W, M	Everywhere
Mulches	I, R	P–R	Ma, WB, BD
Wind Management			
Hedges	I, R	P–W, M	T, Ka, G, P
Tree rows	I	P–W	NW
Fences	I	P–W	P, UP

Key to symbols: See Table 6.
Source: See note 29.

Table 10. Space Management

Form	Land type	Resource complex-crop	Location
Distance			
Farmstead to market			
Periodic	I, R	P–R, W, M	Everywhere
Permanent	I, R	P–R, W, M	Everywhere
Farmstead to fields			
Decreasing intensity of use	I, R	P–R, W, M	Everywhere
Farm fragmentation	I, R	P–R, W, M	Everywhere
Spatial Arrangement of Crops in Fields			
Rotation	I, R	P–R, W, M	Everywhere though restricted use
Crop mixing	I, R	P–R, W, M, T–SC	Everywhere

Key to symbols: See Table 6.
Source: See note 29.

Table 11. Plant–Vegetation Management

Form	Land type	Resource complex-crop	Location
Crop Selection	I, R	P–R, W, M	Everywhere
Crop-soil Association	I, R	P–R, W, M	Everywhere
Variety Selection	I, R	P–R, W, M	Everywhere
Seed Selection	I, R	P–R, W, M	Know everywhere
Yield Improvement			
Grafting trees	I	P–R, W, M	Everywhere after sixteenth century
Planting Methods			
Seed drilling	I, R	P–M, W	Ma, Ka, AP, P, UP
Broadcasting	I, R	P–R, W, M	Everywhere
Sprouted seed	I	P–R	Everywhere
Transplanting	I	P–R	Everywhere
Dibbling	R	T–SC	Ma, Ka, Ke, T, AP, O, WB, A, Na, Mr, Bi
Predation Management			
Crop watching	I, R	P–R, W, M, T–SC	Everywhere
Hedging and fencing	I, R	P–W, M	T, Ka, Ke, G, P, UP, NW
Storage			
Above ground	I, R	P–R, W	Ka, T, AP, O, BD, WB, A, Bi, UP
Underground	I, R	P–M, W	P, R, Ma, Ka, AP
Forest Management			
Forest regeneration	R	T–SC	Ma, Ka, Ke, T, AP, O, MP, WB, A, Na, MR, Bi
"Royal trees"	R	P–M, T–SC	Everywhere
Licensing of gathering rights	R	P–R, M, W, T–SC	Everywhere
Pasture Management			
Lateral seasonal movement	R	P–W, M	Ba, R, K, Ne, Ma, Ka, AP, T
Vertical seasonal movement	R	P–W, M	K, N, NW
Symbiotic arrangement with farmers	R	P–W, M	Ba, P, R, UP, MP, G, Ma, Ka, AP, T
Fodder storage	I, R	P–R, W, M	Everywhere

Key to symbols: See Table 6.
Source: See note 29.

crops, scarecrows, noise-making devices, and traps. Grain is stored for use during the dry season in different types of granaries.

In pre-British times South Asian resource users managed their forest lands to a limited extent. In shifting cultivation areas forest was permitted to regenerate, but elsewhere the forest was the enemy of the cultivator and was constantly under attack. But forests did provide lumber, firewood, gum, honey, fragrant woods, flowers, and animal products. They also served as important grazing grounds for cattle during the dry season when little fodder was naturally available in cultivated areas. The cutting of timber and the gathering of forest products was usually licensed by local overlords, and on occasion there were restrictions placed on how much could be taken. However, most of the licensed contractors had little conservation sense, and frequently completed gutted forests of valuable timber and other products, to make quick profit. Certain trees, the timber of which had a recognized value, were proclaimed "royal trees" by the rulers of territories in which they flourished, but with this exception the forests were open to all.

In western South Asia, the northern mountains, and in peninsular India, natural pasture is managed through a variety of practices. Most common is the movement of livestock, especially sheep and goats, to seasonal pastures. In the Himalayan region grasslands situated at altitudes of 3,000 to 4,000 meters are utilized during the summer, and during the winter the flocks are moved down into the valleys or even out onto the northern plains. In Baluchistan, Sind, Rajasthan, and throughout peninsular India sheep and goats are moved seasonally. Fodder is cut and stored in areas like Baluchistan where snow and rain during the winter created difficult conditions.

Animal management. Livestock provide the main agricultural energy source in South Asia and are carefully managed in many areas (Table 12). The raising of distinctive cattle, buffalo, sheep, goat, and camel breeds is carried out to the limit of indigenous scientific knowledge, and the best animals are striking examples of their kind. Cattle, buffalos and camels are the major provides of energy for agriculture, but they also are sources of milk, hides, dung, and even meat. Sheep and goats provide wool, hair, meat, milk, and dung.

The forests, jungles, and marshes of South Asia formerly were inhabited by an enormous variety of mammals, reptiles, and birds. Many of these were protected by general religious sanctions against killing, but often such sanctions were offset by just as powerful hunting traditions, especially among the princely elites, who often had loosely established game preserves. Game seasons were observed, but generally speaking, predators were the enemy of peasant farmers and were killed without mercy when necessary.

Fisheries management. Fishing in South Asia formerly was a relatively minor aspect of resource use and traditional technologies and practices were poorly developed. Ocean fishing was confined to a narrow belt of five to seven miles. Vast stretches of inland water remained partially or completely untouched, and there was no fish culture. Adequate conservation practices were not followed to any great extent, although fishing seasons, and even closed seasons, were observed (Table 13). Nets were the most common method of capture, but fishtraps of considerable size were used in the marine fisheries of Gujarat and the fresh water fisheries of Bengal. It has been estimated that less than half the catch was eaten fresh, and drying and salting were commonly used as preservation methods. Pearl oyster beds were exploited through diving in Gujarat and the Palk Strait area of Tamil Nadu.

The Conservation Context: Assessment

The systems of agricultural knowledge and of technologies and practices which continue to survive in South Asia, were essential mechanisms in maintaining long-term stability in the traditional resource complexes of the region. In pre-British times the raison-d'etre of man-resource relations can be conceived of as the maintenance of ecological stability. Not that South Asians had achieved a perfect equilibrium with nature in their management of their natural ecological systems, but before the nineteenth century a relationship between man and nature which protected and conserved human survival, as well as the delicate and interdependent equilibrium of agro-ecosystems, was in existence in the region.

Table 12. Animal Management

Form	Land type	Resource complex-crop	Location
Domestic Animal Management			
Cattle breeding	R	P–M, W	P, S, G, AP, MP, Ma, UP, R, Bi, Ka, T
Buffalo breeding	I, R	P–R, M, W	P, UP, Bi, G, MP
Sheep and goat breeding	R	P–M, W	K, Ne, S, Ba, R, G, MP, P, UP, Bi, Ma, AP, Ka, T
Camel breeding	I, R	P–W	P, S, Ba
Cattle utilization			
Agriculture	I, R	P–R, W, M	Everywhere
Milk	I, R	P–R, W, M	Everywhere
Carriage	I, R	P–R, W, M	Everywhere
Hides	I, R	P–R, W, M	Everywhere
Dung	I, R	P–R, W, M	Everywhere
Meat	I, R	P–R, W, M	Everywhere among Harijans and non Hindu peoples
Buffalo utilization			
Agriculture	I	P–R	BD, WB, O
Milk	I, R	P–R, W, M	Everywhere
Carriage	I, R	P–R, W, M	Everywhere
Hides	I, R	P–R, W, M	Everywhere
Dung	I, R	P–R, W, M	Everywhere
Meat	I, R	P–R, W, M	Everywhere among Harijans and non Hindu peoples
Sheep and goat utilization			
Wool and hair	R	P–W, M	K, Ne, NW, S, Ba, R, G, MP, P, UP, Ma, AP, Ka, T
Meat	R	P–W, M	K, Ne, NW, S, Ba, R, G, MP, P, UP, Ma, AP, Ka, T
Milk	R	P–W, M	K, Ne, NW, S, Ba, R, G, MP, P, UP, Ma, AP, Ka, T
Dung	R	P–W, M	K, Ne, MW, A, Ba, R, T, MP, P, UP, Ma, AP, Ka, T
Camel utilization			
Agriculture	I	P–W	P, S, Ba
Carriage	I, R	P–W	P, S, R, Ba
Wild Animal Management			
Sanctions vs. killing	I, R	P–R, W, M	Everywhere but little observed
Game preserves	I, R	P–R, W, M	Small preserves for ruling princes everywhere
Game seasons	I, R	P–R, W, M	Everywhere for birdlife and major game animals

Key to symbols: See Table 6.
Source: See note 29.

Most of the specific practices which scientific understanding would state are of considerable conservation value have not been purposefully adopted, but rather can be described as incidental. They were largely unconscious on the part of the farmer, and in this sense, South Asians farmed better than they knew. Clearly the traditional resource complexes of South Asia had a considerable built-in conservation capacity.

Table 13. Fisheries Management

Form	Resource complex	Location
Freshwater		
Seasons		
June–Sept.	P–R	Ma, Ke, WB, BD
Dec.–April	P–R	WB, BD
Mar.–May	P–R, W	Bi, UP
Closed seasons	P–R	WB, BD
Methods		
Nets	P–R	WB, BD, Bi
Lines	P–R, W	UP, Bi
Traps	P–R	WB, BD
Preservation		
Drying	P–R	WB, BD
Marine		
Seasons		
Oct.–May	P–R	G, Ma, Ke, T, AP, O, WB, BD
Methods		
Nets	P–R	G, Ma, Ke, T, AP, O, WB, BD
Lines	P–R	Everywhere, but limited use
Traps	P–R	G
Diving	P–R	G, T
Preservation		
Salting	P–R	G, Ma, Ke
Drying	P–R	G, Ke, T

Key to symbols: See Table 6.
Source: See note 29.

South Asia is today the theater of an indescribably complex interaction between the forces of modern science and technology (with its own metamorphosing mental outlook) and of an age-old metaphysical tradition. Despite the beginnings during the colonial period, and the efforts of the last 30 years, in the villages custom is a king not yet and not easily dethroned. That the countries of South Asia will reain predominantly agrarian for many decades is self-evident. Yet at the same time changes have taken place which have markedly affected resource conservation knowledge and practice.

REGION IN TRANSITION

The Nature of Transition

Over the past 200 years South Asian resource complexes have undergone a major transformation in structure, function, general characteristics, and areal extent. Population growth has been a major cause of change, because population pressure has compelled changes in farming methods and land use.[31] The imposition of British rule and law and order in the early 19th century resulted in the construction of public works—the great road railway, and canal systems which stood as the symbol of modernity in British India. During the three decades since Independence public works schemes have continued to modify the landscape of the region.

Management frameworks have also changed. The British, for the first time, brought most of the area under the control and management of a single ruling power, and although this is no longer the case, several of the national management units are large. The British also brought to South Asia their own conceptions of land, land tenure, land revenue, and land classification and set in progress a vast, often hidden, transformation of the agrarian economy. In conjunction with this, the British transformed rural agrarian social structure, partly as a result of the new land systems introduced and partly as a result of the spread of commercial agriculture. These helped to elaborate a hierarchy or rights to land which established more securely than ever the power of landholders. British investment in plantations (mainly coffee and tea) opened up previously forested areas, and added a further dimension to South Asia's resource complexes.

The British also had a major impact upon South Asian understanding of science and technology, negligible at first, but significant after 1870 when agricultural and forestry departments were established. In the early 20th century educational and research programs came into being, and since Independence, these have been expanded enormously. All development since Independence has taken place within the context of five-year plans, ten-year plans, or five-year plans complemented by longer-term "perspective planning" of about the order of 15 years. Each country has created its own form of central planning and government control to promote development, and although the precise details vary, all have undergone somewhat similar resource development experiences.[32]

The impact of this transformation upon the resource complexes of South Asia has occurred at two scales of resolution: the most general involve overall ecological modification, changes in the institutional framework of management, and changes in systems of knowledge; the most numerous are associated with specific technologies and practices. Modifications to the general ecological structure of South Asia have in the most part been inadvertent, while the utilization of new knowledge, as well as technologies and practices, and the dropping of old ideas and techniques, has more often than not been conscious and intentional.

Ecological Modification

The clearing of forest for cultivation, and for fuel for locomotives in the 19th century, plus the expansion of permanent cultivation onto land previously under various forms of rotating fallow systems, reduced the diversity of the overall ecological systems of South Asia, in addition to changing the relative importance of different systems of resource management. The diversity in traditional resource management systems, plus their small scale, must be viewed as extremely important mechanisms in the maintenance of agro-ecosystem stability in South Asia in the past. In addition, in some parts of South Asia the occupation of forest and fallow land has changed conservation practices: pasturage for livestock has been reduced, creating the so-called cattle problem; firewood has come to be in short supply and animal dung has come to be used for fuel instead of manure; fallowing is no longer possible to permit poor quality soils to recuperate from cropping. A concomitant aspect of decreasing diversity has been the gradual reduction in numbers of crops cultivated, and after the 1920s the beginnings of reduction in the numbers of varieties cultivated. Large-scale irrigation projects have contributed to reduction of agro-ecosystem diversity, in that they have encouraged cultivators to concentrate on a few "valuable" crops—sugarcane, cotton, wheat, barley, rice—which have high market value. Thus large areas have become devoted to a smaller range of crops and varieties, whereas before the 19th century cropping patterns broadly reflected the heterogeneity and micro-scale differences in soil-water distribution. Agriculture today is no longer carried out at the local scale. In fact, the development of improved communications has linked those areas which produce cash crops to the outside world: these agro-ecosystems have become more complex, more interconnected, more interdependent, and hence more vulnerable to non-local effects and influences.

Institutional Framework

Throughout South Asia the institutional framework for the management of resources has been totally transformed. These changes began to occur during the British period with the creation of a new administrative and bureaucratic structure, with the tentative beginnings of resource policies, including education, research, and extension, and with the far-reaching changes in social organization set in motion by land revenue and tenure policies. Since 1947 events have further changed the institutional framework of South Asia's resource complexes. British India has become a number of independent countries, all with somewhat similar resource problems. All have experimented with formal developmental planning set within central and local-level planning contexts. Much of the administrative and bureaucratic structure inherited from the British remains, however, and the major trend of the concentration of the rural resources in fewer and fewer hands, which started during the British period has, if anything, increased, despite land reform and social legislation programs in all parts of the region.

Systems of Knowledge

Major changes also have been to manifest themselves with regard to the South Asian resource-user's knowledge and understanding of his environment. More than 100 years of contact with western scientific ideas and the acceptance of many of the basic premises of western science by educated elites at least, has led to apparent widespread changes in beliefs about the natural world. Each of the countries of South Asia has begun to develop a sophisticated scientific and technological community, involved in the education process and basic research. These are the people and institutions which are attempting to change existing resource technologies and practices into something new, and that new something is a rational, or at least rationalistic, scientific system of resource management.

That the folk system of knowledge has survived to the extent that it has is fortunate, because it is beginning to be recognized that indigenous knowledge has something to contribute to efforts to develop resource systems. To date, in its arrogance and ethnocentricity, Western science has only too often pushed aside the wealth of folk knowledge and experience that is embodied in traditional resource complexes. But in an age of potential shortages of energy to fuel the new agro-technologies it has become doubly important to have some understanding of traditional resource knowledge systems. In particular, it is being recognized that resource complexes which have existed for so long as those of South Asia represent at least partially successful solutions to specific sets of man–environment situations, and that the systems of knowledge associated with these complexes may contain valuable information.

Technologies and Practices

Throughout most of South Asia the multitude of management practices which existed in the nineteenth century are still known, even if some are today little used in some areas. Soil management practices to maintain soil fertility have been changed as much as any practice. In areas where irrigation water is available and high-yielding hybrid seed varieties have been introduced, large amounts of inorganic fertilizer are in use today. Cattle dung, traditionally the preferred manure, has all but disappeared from use over much of South Asia, because it is used as fuel in the absence of firewood. A partial solution to this problem may well be the introduction of biogas plants, which treat dung to provide both cooking fuel and fertilizer. Other forms of manuring are also carried out to a much more limited extent than formerly. Certain other practices are still maintained: crop mixing, the use of leguminous crops, crop rotation. All such practices are still mainly carried out on irrigated land, although there is now more attention to food crops. As far as tillage practices are concerned, traditional tools and practices continue to dominate, despite the introduction of steel ploughs in many areas, and the widespread use of tractors in the wheat-growing area. Scientific evidence has accumulated to indicate that traditional shallow tilth practices are perhaps better suited to the shallow sandy soils found over much of South Asia than deep ploughing. Multiple ploughing, a dry-farming technique, seems to be less prevalent than formerly.

Slope management practices, especially terracing, have been greatly extended throughout the region. Soil erosion has been acknowledged as a major problem and western science has been integrated quite successfully with traditional techniques in this regard. One practice which seems to have declined is that of planting hedgerows to control erosion, reduce wind damage, and to better manage livestock.

All the traditional forms of water management are still in existence in the region. However, modern technology has affected every aspect of these activities. Today modern machinery is used to excavate tanks and dig wells and channels. Gasoline, diesel, and especially electrical pumps have become the common means of lifting water in many areas. The large-scale dam and reservoir, essentially a temperate latitude device, has been added to the list of water management practices. In fact, some of the most spectacular water management accomplishments relate to the building and use of large-scale multipurpose dams, but problems have also arisen: displacement of population, rapid siltation, health problems, lack of depositional material in the water below the dams.

The building of large-scale canal systems, one of the major accomplishments of the British, has been continued since 1947. During British times, and since, canals have had numerous adverse effects on the environment. In the first place, the introduction of flush irrigation from canals contributed to the decay of the careful water application practices characteristic of areas of well irrigation. In many parts of Pakistan and northern India, salinity, alkalinity, the creation of swamps and hardpans have been results of the extension of the canal system. This has come about through overuse of water, the raising of the water table, and the obstruction of natural drainage lines. Before the mid-nineteenth century in northern India there was a long established and sophisticated pattern of farming in which well irrigation played a large part. Only suitable soils were irrigated, and because lift irrigation required much labor and livestock, the water, along with manure, was carefully applied to the fields. Canal irrigation changed this. Many areas, where careful rotation had formerly been used, were now continuously cropped. The land deteriorated as an environmentally unstable condition was created and old conservation methods disappeared: another example of the unthinking substitution of temperate for tropical zone technology.

Flood prevention practices, especially in deltaic and coastal regions, also seems to have become woefully inadequate. Part of the problem is that ever-increasing numbers of people inhabit the low-lying fringes of river deltas around the Bay of Bengal and the beds of rivers, and when tropical cyclones and even normal flooding occurs traditional methods of adjustment do not suffice.

Today the accessibility of most villages has improved, as a result of road or cart track construction under community development programs. There has also been an increase in the number of rural shops, a marked improvement in transportation and communications, and consequently the average villager is more intimately linked to the outside world, and perhaps more vulnerable to it, than ever before. Within the village, land use continues to display a decrease in intensity with increasing distance from the settlement site, but farm fragmentation has increased and has become a major problem in many areas, especially where it is associated with small size of holding. Crop mixing persists everywhere. In many areas, especially where water, hybrid seeds, fertilizer, and pesticides are readily available, crop rotation in association with multiple cropping has increased.

There have also been marked changes in certain plant management practices. Crop selection, variety selection, and seed selection practices have been vastly modified, and there have been great improvements in the yields of many crops. Scientific soil survey methods have added a new dimension to the traditional practice of carefully associating crops and soil types. Improved planting methods, such as transplantation, and especially the traditional seed drill, reinforced by scientific knowledge, have spread over a wider area.

Predator management practices remain the same, but pesticides and poisons have been added to the farmers' arsenal, often with deleterious effects to the environment. Traditional storage techniques have been replaced to a certain extent by the use of gunny sacks and warehouses. Certainly predators, especially rats, and poor storage facilities contribute to 10 to 25% estimated loss of foodgrain after harvest.

Although fairly efficient forestry operations exist in all of the South Asian countries, continuing pressure from man and his animals makes conservation efforts difficult. In many areas rapidly growing exotic trees (ironwoods and eucalypts) have been planted, rather than indigenous species.

The spread of cultivation has also created a huge shortage of suitable pasture for cattle, sheep, and goats. A major problem facing South Asia is the provision of sufficient fodder for work animals. As animal energy will remain the principal energy source for farming operations in the foreseeable future, this is a matter of some concern. In addition, while numerous excellent work cattle breeds exist, little has been done on a scientific level to improve work capacity, although work is in progress to improve milk cows. The spread of agriculture over the past century has also led to a disastrous reduction in South Asia's wild animal population. All countries have National Parks, Game Preserves, and Zoos, and many animals (for example, the tiger and the Indian lion) are protected species. Nonetheless, the existing numbers of animals of many species make their future survival prospects less than hopeful—another byproduct of population growth and agricultural expansion. Freshwater fisheries have received little attention, other than in Bangladesh, and traditional techniques remain supreme. There has been considerable research and development of marine fisheries, especially in Kerala, and fish catches have increased considerably. However, problems of scale of operation, of marketing, storage, and distribution continue to plague the further expansion of fishing.

CONCLUDING REGIONAL ASSESSMENT

At the time when the West began to intrude into South Asia a system of knowledge and a vast array of practices, most of a resource conserving nature, existed in the region. A detailed examination of this knowledge and practices indicates that while much of it was common to the whole region, there were certain areas in South Asia in which existed "packages" of knowledge and practices which were associated with careful, sustaining, and highly productive management of resources. That different levels of resource use proficiency existed was noted a number of times by nineteenth century observers, who ascribed the variation to: different physical, economic, and political conditions; the fact that knowledge about techniques and practices was not the same everywhere; and, the fact that certain castes were bad at, and others good at, cultivation.

Over the past century, and especially over the last 30 years, many specific practices have been modified or selectively replaced by elements of modern technology. This is most marked with regard to water management practices, soil fertility management practices, and crop management practices, because it is these which have been most effected by modern package programs. However, such adoptions have been highly selective, and even in the most advanced areas, farmers neglect parts of the modern package.[33] What has occurred to some extent everywhere has been an integration of traditional and modern technologies and practices, the dimensions of which are only now beginning to emerge and which are poorly understood. Likewise, the way in which farmers integrate modern scientific with traditional systems of knowledge is little understood, yet is obviously done. Perhaps one major development strategy in the future might be that of making farmers aware of the full value of many of their incidental conservation practices.

That traditional technologies and practices have been maintained as extensively as they have is the outcome of several sets of interrelated factors. In the first place, many farmers are too poor, or have no access to information, to adopt new methods. On the other hand, even among wealthy farmers selective adoption suggests that factors such as traditional ecological awareness, the sheer force of custom, and the ability of good farmers to weight the pros and cons of new methods against known ways, play an important role in maintaining traditional practices.

The reduction of environmental diversity and the increasing complexity of agro-eco-systems in South Asia, could with considerable effort be ameliorated. In fact, soil and forest conservation have been directed toward this end. Fundamentally, the planting of woodlots and orchards, plus the establishment of permanent pasture land, all of which were important aspects, albeit inadvertent, of the traditional conservation system, would be of major importance. In this regard, modern scientific understanding of problems arising from ecological modification could well be integrated with traditional comprehension. Furthermore, with forethought and planning it is possible to maintain crop and varietal diversity as South Asian resource managers understand such principles. More emphasis could also be placed on local-scale improvements in such things as irrigation systems and supplies of energy rather than on items from outside localities.

Today modern scientific information has become available to the managers of South Asia's biological resources, and this has led to changes in the comprehension of environmental events and processes. Certainly, the western view of man as separate from nature, and capable of large-scale manipulation and modification of nature, has partially led to a less balanced concept of man and environmental interrelationships. But this is a matter that can be modified by education, especially through the integration of South Asian and western ecological ideas. In a similar fashion much of South Asia's traditional resource knowledge could, through research and education, be related to scientific understandings of environmental patterns and processes. This would require enormous effort, but it might result in new insights which would be intelligible to the mass of South Asia's people.

Many of the more useful traditional practices which have all but lapsed could be revived, although perhaps in modified form. For example, if animal manure is used in bio-gas plants, the residue is available as manure. Many tillage and planting practices could also be revived, and some, such as the use of seed drills, could be expanded. Water application practices, many of which have become sloppy, could also be returned to their previously high standard. The primary agricultural energy source is draft animals (about 70%), and while there are good quality work breeds, much can be done to improve them, and use them to replace poor quality stock. Such lapsed practices, and those that survive almost untouched, can all be improved. In fact, there are few practices in South Asia, traditional and modern, incapable of further development. The emergence of E. G. Schumacher's "intermediate" or "appropriate" technology approach to resource development is leading to a re-evaluation in South Asia of the potential worth of traditional technology and practices.[34] There are now a number of institutions in South Asia whose primary task is to improve local technology through the application of modern knowledge and materials. The close scrutiny that these groups are giving to existing packages of traditional technologies and practices will permit the conscious retention of the useful, and their further improvement. It has been recognized, belatedly in many cases, that resource management systems need to be evaluated carefully before they are replaced: modern methods have had unexpected and undesirable side effects. Furthermore, modern methods are dependent upon fossil fuels which are becoming scarce and expensive. The best traditional technologies and practices, augmented by modern knowledge, would utilize locally available energy and material. As long as the low energy, small farm environment of South Asia endures, traditional technology and practices can offer valuable alternatives to modern-day resource managers.

NOTES

[1]It deserves to be noted, however, that South Asians mined a variety of minerals (especially gold, copper, and iron), quarried stone, and were engaged in manufacturing a wide range of products, including cotton and silk cloth, jewelery, salt, iron and steel.

[2]See Walter Firey, *Man, Mind, and Land. A Theory of Resource Use* (Glencoe, Ill.: Free Press, 1960), pp. 13-44.

[3]For a comprehensive discussion of terrain, soils, vegetation, and climate see Oscar H. K. Spate and Anthony T. Learmonth, *India and Pakistan* (London: Methuen, 1967).

[4]See Jen-hu Chang, *Climate and Agriculture. An Ecological Survey* (Chicago: Aldine, 1969), pp. 118-224 for comprehensive treatment of the relationships of radiation and water. The available energy moving through the biosystem can be converted into a water equivalent, evapotranspiration. If it is assumed that there is an unlimited amount of water available, the maximum amount of evapotranspiration that can occur at any place depends on the amount of energy received from the sun: This maximum is referred to as potential evapotranspiration. Once potential evapotranspiration has been calculated it can be compared to available moisture and a balance derived between the income of water from rainfall and that which is needed for potential biosystem productivity.

[5]Robert A. Harper and Theodore H. Schmudde, *Between Two Worlds. An Introduction to Geography* (Boston: Houghton Mifflin, 1978), pp. 52-91 contains an overview of environmental activity budgets and the concept of environmental work.

[6]The best up-to-date account of the pre-history of South Asia is Walter A. Fairservis, *The Roots of Ancient India: The Archaeology of Early Indian Civilization* (Chicago: University of Chicago Press, 1975).

[7]Clarence Maloney, "Archaeology in South India: Accomplishments and Prospects," in Burton Stein, ed., *Essays on South India* (Honolulu: University Press of Hawaii, Asian Studies at Hawaii, No. 15, 1975), pp. 1-40.

[8]This process is documented in numerous studies, e.g., Irfan Habib, *The Agrarian System of Mughal India* (New York: Asia Publishing House, 1963); Burton Stein, "Brahman and Peasant in Early South Indian History," *The Adyar Library Bulletin* (Madras), Vol. 31-32 (1967-1968), pp. 235-237; R. L. Singh, "Evolution of Clan Territorial Units Through Land Occupance in the Middle Gange Valley," *The National Geographic Journal of India*, Vol. 20 (1974), pp. 1-19.

[9]Habib, op. cit., note 8, p. 36.

[10]Hiroshi Ishida, *A Cultural Geography of the Great Plains of India: Essays, Techniques, and Interim Reports-cum-Methods* (Hiroshima: Department of Geography, University of Hiroshima, Special Publication No. 3, 1972), pp. 47-48.

[11]Elizabeth Whitcombe, "The Physical Consequences of Canal-Irrigation in North India: Some Nineteenth Century Antecedents," in J. G. Nelson and R. C. Scace, eds., *Impact of Technology on Environment: Some Global Examples* (London, Ontario: University of Western Ontario, Studies in Land Use History and Landscape Change, No. 6, 1974), p. 142.

[12]N. G. Mukherji, *Handbook of Indian Agriculture* (Calcutta: Thacker, Spink, & Co., 1901), p. 167.

[13]R. L. M. Ghose, M. B. Ghatge and V. Subrahmanyan, *Rice in India* (New Delhi: Indian Council of Agricultural Research, 1967), p. 13-14; R. Ratman, *Agricultural Development in Madras State Prior to 1900* (Madras: New Century Book House, 1960), p. 71 and pp. 402-403.

[14]*Punjab Wheat: Its Varieties, Distribution, and Husbandry* (Lahore: Punjab Government Press, 1884); V. T. Subbiah Mudaliar, *South Indian Field Crops* (Madras: Central Art Press, 1960), pp. 40-73; C. Hayavadana Rao, *Mysore Gazetteer. Vol. III. Economic* (Bangalore: The Government Press, 1929), pp. 59-74.

[15]Habib, op. cit., note 8, pp. 61-89; Burton Stein, "Coromandel Trade in Medieval India," in John H. Parker, ed., *Merchants and Scholars* (Minneapolis: University of Minnesota Press, 1965), pp. 47-62; Burton Stein, "Circulation and the Historical Geography of Tamil Country," *Journal of Asian Studies*, Vol. 37 (1977), pp. 7-26.

[16]Louis Dumont, *Homo Hierarchus: The Caste System and its Implications* (Chicago: University of Chicago Press, 1970), p. 154.

[17]Burton Stein, "The State and the Agrarian Order," in Burton Stein, ed., *Essays on South India* (Honolulu: University Press of Hawaii, Asian Studies at Hawaii, No. 15, 1975), p. 76.

[18]Richard G. Fox, *Kin, Clan, Raja, and Rule: State-Hinterland Relations in Pre-Industrial India* (Berkeley: University of California Press, 1971), p. 9.

[19]Gene C. Wilken, "Some Aspects of Resource Management by Traditional Farmers," in Huntley H. Biggs and Ronald L. Tinnermeier, eds., *Small Farm Agricultural Development Problems* (Fort Collins: Colorado State University, 1974), pp. 47-60 contains a comprehensive discussion of the constituent elements of traditional resource systems.

[20]Such sources include the periodicals *Man in India* and *Folklore*, various agricultural journals, such as the *Madras Agricultural Journal*, e.g., C. Balasubramanian and R. Gopalkrishnan, "Agricultural Folklore in Malabar," *Madras Agricultural Journal*, Vol. 40 (1953), pp. 55-59; the District Gazetteers of British India (see Henry Scholberg, *The District Gazetteers of British India: A Bibliography* (Zug, Switzerland: InterDocumentation Co., 1970), books such as George A. Grierson, *Bihar Peasant Life* (Calcutta: Bengal Secretariat Press, 1885), and numerous books, monographs, and articles dealing with religion and philosophy.

[21]See Morris D. Morris, "Values as an Obstacle to Economic Growth in South Asia: An Historical Survey," *Journal of Economic History*, Vol. 27 (1967), pp. 588-607.

[22]Alan Beals, *Village Life in South India. Cultural Design and Environmental Variation* (Chicago: Aldine, 1974), p. 29.

[23]Morris, op. cit., note 21, p. 605.

[24]Good examples of research which demonstrates this diversity are Robert E. Frykenberg, ed., *Land Control and Social Structure in Indian History* (Madison: University of Wisconsin Press, 1969) and Robert E. Frykenberg, ed., *Land Tenure and Peasant in South Asia* (New Delhi: Orient Longman, 1977).

[25]Brenda E. F. Beck, "The Right-Left Division of South Indian Society," *The Journal of Asian Studies*, Vol. 29 (1970), pp. 779-798; Brenda E. F. Beck, "Colour and Heat in South Indian Ritual," *Man*, Vol. 4 (1969), pp. 553-572; Brenda E. F. Beck, *Peasant Society in Konku: A Study of Right and Left Subcastes in South India* (Vancouver: University of British Columbia Press, 1972), pp. 52-56.

[26]A. K. Ramanujan, "Form in Classical Tamil Poetry," paper presented at meeting of Society for South Indian Studies, Austin, University of Texas, 1968.

[27]Ainslie T. Embree, "Tradition and Modernization in India: Synthesis or Encapsulization," in W. Morehouse, ed., *Science and the Human Condition in India and Pakistan* (N.Y.: Rockefeller University Press, 1968), pp. 29-38.

[28]C. E. Gover, *The Folk Songs of Southern India* (Madras: Higginbottom & Co., 1871); S. S. Gupta, eds., *Rain in Indian Life and Lore* (Calcutta: Indian Publications, 1963); C. Balasubramanian and R. Gopalkrishnan, "Agricultural Folklore in Malabar," *The Madras Agricultural Journal*, Vol. 40 (1953), pp. 55-59; C. Balasubramanian and M. B. V. Narasinga Rao, "Meteorology and Agriculture," *The Madras Agricultural Journal*, Vol. 37 (1950), pp. 239-241.

[29]The most valuable sources are the district gazetteer series which are described comprehensively in Scholberg, op. cit., note 20. These were used extensively in the compilation of the information presented in the tables. Forty-five gazetteers selected from all parts of British India were reviewed to give a representative view of resource and crop complexes. In addition, two reports proved to be invaluable for their descriptions of South Asian agricultural techniques and practices: J. A. Voelcker, *Report on the Improvement of Indian Agriculture* (London: Eyre & Spottiswoode, 1893), and Great Britain, Royal Commission on Agriculture in India: *Report of the Royal Commission on Agriculture in India* (London: His Majesty's Stationary Office, 1928).

[30]Habib, op. cit., note 8, pp. 39-47 lists cotton in Maharashtra, sugar in Bengal, indigo in central Uttar Pradesh, Gujarat, and Sind, opium poppies in Bihar and Madhya Pradesh, pepper in Bengal and Kerala, and betel everywhere.

[31]For a discussion of the agricultural response to population growth see Ester Boserup, *The Conditions of Agricultural Growth: The Economics of Agrarian Change Under Population Pressure* (London: Allen & Unwin, 1965); Harold C. Brookfield, "Intensification and Disintensification in Pacific Agriculture," *Pacific Viewpoint*, Vol. 13 (1972), pp. 30-48; David B. Grigg, "Population Pressure and Agricultural Change," *Progress in Geography*, Vol. 8 (1976), pp. 133-176.

[32]Michael Lipton, *Why Poor People Stay Poor: A Study of Urban Bias in World Development* (London: Maurice Temple Smith Ltd., 1977) contains an excellent general account of the development experience of the Third World since 1945. Many of his examples are drawn from South Asia. Lawrence A. Veit, *India's Second Revolution: The Dimensions of Development* (New York: McGraw-Hill, 1976) deals very adequately with India's problems and prospects.

[33]Francine R. Frankel, *India's Green Revolution: Economic Gains and Political Costs* (Princeton, N.J.: Princeton University Press, 1971); Benjamin H. Farmer, ed., *Green Revolution? Technology and Change in Rice-Growing Areas of Tamil Nadu and Sri Lanka* (Boulder, Colorado: Westview Press, 1977).

[34]E. F. Schumacher, *Small is Beautiful* (London: Blond & Briggs, 1973); M. K. Garg, "Problems of Developing Appropriate Technologies in India," *Appropriate Technology*, Vol. 1 (1974), pp. 16-18.

Chapter 5

East Asia

Joseph Whitney

The countries of China, Korea and Japan which comprise the East Asian region today contain some seven percent of the world's cultivated area but support some 25% of its population. This high ratio of population to cultivated land, which is the hallmark of the East Asian traditional resource management system, is not a modern development but one that has existed over the centuries. It has permitted densities and levels of urbanization to exist there that were not equalled or exceeded in the rest of the world until the advent of the industrial revolution.

These high population densities and food surpluses needed to support large urban centres were purchased at the cost of prodigious inputs of labor and the almost complete transformation of natural ecosystems to serve the needs of lowland agriculture. Although such transformation often resulted in deforestation, severe soil erosion, floods and droughts, one of the main organizational achievements of East Asian societies was that they were able to maintain their resource system and population in a state of unstable equilibrium with the environment over long periods of time without any widespread eco-catastrophe occurring.[1]

This achievement resulted from a common cultural heritage throughout the region that gave those who gained a livelihood from the environment a rather accurate ethno-scientific understanding of the flows of energy, water and minerals passing through natural and man-made ecological systems and the ways in which those flows could be manipulated on a long term basis without seriously affecting the harmonious man-nature relationship. There was also a clear recognition of the fact, only recently appreciated in the West, that most so-called natural hazards have their origins in man himself through unwise locational choice, greedy resource management practices or from poor government or social organization that neglects the maintenance of irrigation systems or flood control works.[2]

Because of China's dominant role in the cultural and resource management traditions of East Asia, the discussion that follows will be illustrated primarily from Chinese examples. Except where noted in the text, it is to be assumed that such resource management practices were common to both Korea and Japan.

THE RESOURCE BASE

The East Asian region is defined by certain physical and cultural attributes. Physically it comprises the collision zone of three great tectonic plates: the Pacific, the Eurasian and the Indian. During the last 300 million years or so, the collision of these plates has produced most of the major relief forms of East Asia and has distinguished it from the rest of the Eurasian continent as a distinct geomorphological entity. The checkerboard pattern that has arisen from the collision of the plates has had a profound impact on East Asian society and resource management giving rise to a strong sense of regionalism and the relative isolation of different economic areas.[3]

A further feature that has affected the setting of East Asian civilization is the thick mantle of fine yellow wind and water-borne dust called loess, that covers much of North China to a depth of hundreds of feet in many places.[4] The soil produced from the loess, if properly farmed and watered, is highly productive and provided the resource base for the development of early Chinese civilization.[5] Under poor farming practices and when the vegetation covering is removed, however, it is easily eroded and much of the landscape of Kansu, Shensi, and Shansi and the uplands parts of Honan have been carved into fantastic networks of gorges and gullies by this kind of erosion. A more serious problem has been that caused by the eroded material being washed into the river systems of North China. The silt-laden waters cause the river to raise its bed year by year. Dikes and levees then have to be heightened to compensate for the decreased volume of the channel, and the rivers eventually flow in courses that are many feet above the level of the surrounding lowlands. When the dikes have broken and flooding occurs, the ground becomes waterlogged for long periods of time since the water cannot flow back into the river channels again under gravity. Thus, to the problem of flooding is added the damage done to crops from long periods of waterlogged soils—in many respects a more severe problem than the flood itself. Because of these characteristics, the rivers of the North China plain have frequently affected major crop growing and populated areas, and have disrupted the Grand Canal—the essential supply link for the grain deficient cities of the North.[6]

The peninsula of Korea is essentially a continuation of the checkerboard pattern of China. It comprises part of a single "block" that has been upthrust on its eastern edge and tilted towards the west. This has resulted in longer rivers flowing towards the west and broader alluvial valleys developing there than on the eastern precipitous coastline.[7]

The rapid uplift of the Japanese islands and their constantly changing and unstable crust has produced a landscape characterized by marked and abrupt changes of slope and elevation. Rivers are short, swift, and braided. Only around Tokyo, Nagoya, and Osaka do narrow alluvial plains separate the sea from the mountains by more than a few miles. Even in the lowland regions, the rapid uplift of coastal plains has caused the older alluvium to be elevated above the present stream levels and it now forms board terraces of infertile soil known as diluvium, which, until recently, have been little used for agriculture.[8]

The region of East Asia also forms a distinct cultural area whose society, written language, agriculture, and government have been profoundly influenced by Han civilization—a culture that originated in the middle part of the Yellow River basin and gradually spread until it occupies most of the contemporary territory of China.[9]

THE ENVIRONMENTAL SETTING: POTENTIAL AND HAZARDS

Over the millennia, climate and landforms have interacted to produce distinct patterns of soils, plant associations and plant productivity. The natural ecosystems, before man disrupted them, had achieved equilibrium with their climatic, nutrient and moisture environment and had developed special mechanisms to deal with such hazards as flood, drought, insect pests, and disease.

The primary determinants of the climate of East Asia, the most important abiotic component of any ecosystem, can be summarized briefly. A high pressure system in winter builds up over East Siberia producing cool dry weather over most of the area except where the outwardly spiralling winds cross water bodies, such as the sea of Japan, and bring some of the heaviest snowfalls in the world to western Japan. In summer, the low pressure that replaces the high over eastern Asia causes warm moist conditions to be experienced in all coastal areas. But inland, the air dries out and rainfall declines rapidly to the northwest.

However, neither rainfall nor temperature are particularly good indicators, in themselves, of the resource potential of a climate. Provided that nutrients are available, the major determinant of plant growth is the amount of solar energy available for photosynthesis and the availability of water to satisfy the transpiration requirements for optimal growth. If the moisture required for such optimal growth is lacking, a condition of moisture stress or drought exists that will cause plants to grow more slowly or wilt completely. In these latter areas the predominant biome is usually shrub or grassland and since the movement of moisture in the soils is upwards and since most of the plant mass is underground in the form of bulbs and roots, the soils here tend to be rich in organic matter and nutrients (Figure 18). If on the other hand, moisture is in excess of what can be transpired, run off occurs and forest biomes become predominant. In these regions, particularly where there are high summer temperatures, very different soils develop. Since most of the mass of vegetation is above ground, the plant litter which falls is rapidly decomposed and leached by the heavy rain. Hence, the soils are acidic and infertile and the greater part of the nutrient stock is tied up in the vegetation rather than in the soil itself. Hence, when destruction of that vegetation takes place, the fertility goes with it.

The productivity of the natural biomes growing under different energy and moisture regimes gives some indication of what ecosystems in a state of equilibrium with their environment will yield and provides some measure against which the productivity of traditional farming systems can be judged. The productivity of biomes ranges from 4 metric tons per hectare per year (4 mt. $ha^{-1} yr^{-1}$) [1.6 tons per acre per year] in the north, to over 37 mt. $ha^{-1} yr^{-1}$ [14.8 tons per acre per year] in Hainan Island in the South (Figure 19).[10]

While the climatic environment provides potential for plant growth, there are also

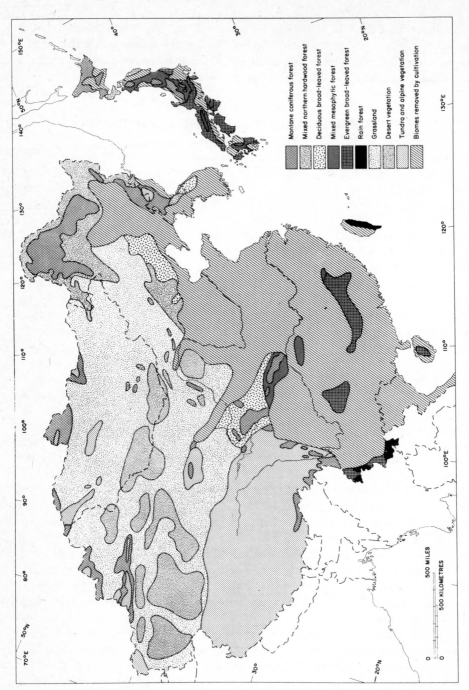

Legend (top-right of map):

Montane coniferous forest
Mixed northern hardwood forest
Deciduous broad-leaved forest
Mixed mesophytic forest
Evergreen broad-leaved forest
Rain forest
Grassland
Desert vegetation
Tundra and alpine vegetation
Biomes removed by cultivation

500 MILES

500 KILOMETRES

Fig. 18. The Biomes of East Asia.

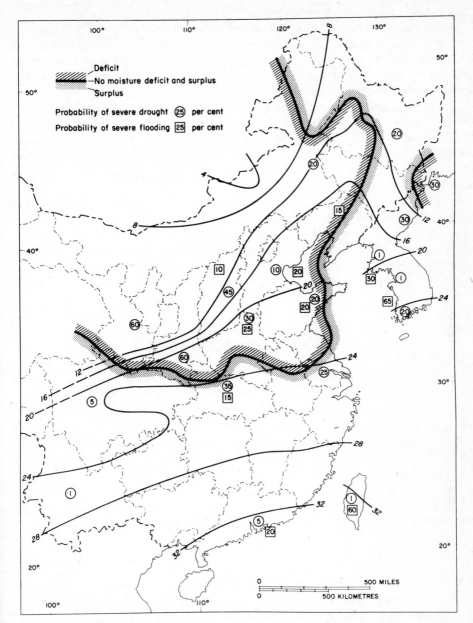

Fig. 19. Moisture stress and the annual net productivity of biomes (tonnes ha^{-1}yr^{-1} dry weight).

natural ecosystems have developed devices for coping with these hazards, but in man-modified ecosystems, such as agriculture, most of these devices have been destroyed and man himself has to substitute for them.

The line separating areas that experience moisture stress from those which do not is crucial for man and crops (Figure 19). Apart from a very small area in northeastern

Korea, the major area experiencing such stress lies in north and northwest China.

From the point of view of agriculture and man, it is not moisture stress alone that is a hazard, but the frequency and intensity of its occurrence. Hence, on the map the circled values indicate the probability (number of years in one hundred) when a serious shortfall in crop production will result from moisture stress.[11] In the more easterly parts of North China, serious drought will occur in one out of five years; further west, in the Huang Ho basin and the loess region, the situation deteriorates, and six out of ten years will experience potential famine conditions unless irrigation is practiced. Although the possibility of drought, due to lack of rainfall, does occur in other parts of East Asia, there is usually sufficient soil moisture available to tide crops over the worst of the dry period.

Severe flooding (as indicated by the probabilities in the square boxes) also occurs in the area. This is especially serious in coastal areas subject to typhoon activity. However, the greatest damage to crops and man occurs in parts of North China also subject to drought. It is particularly severe here, because, as indicated earlier, rivers flow above the plain and the poor drainage results in extensive waterlogging. Indeed, the combination of drought and flood in this area makes the changes of a good farming year occurring less than 50% of the time.[12]

THE EVOLUTION OF THREE RESOURCE TRADITIONS

Three major, man-made ecosystems have been created in East Asia as ways of balancing populations against the carrying capacity of land and climate: shifting agriculture; peasant gardening with a wet-field and a dry-field variety; and nomadic herding.[13] Not only are there many variations within each system, but contained in each area, may be smaller portions of the others. Although the three systems have many different characteristics, they all represent attempts by man to channel the flows of solar energy, moisture, and nutrients into food crops rather than into plants of no human value. Each system, too, attempts to balance crop productivity with the demographic and cultural demands that the society makes. Arrangements also have to be made to deal with the problem of fluctuations in the moisture, nutrient, and pest environment.

Shifting Cultivation

Shifting cultivation societies once made up most of the oriental world and, indeed, much of the other continents as well. They represented one of the most advanced cultures of their day, replacing as they did the more primitive and declining hunting and collecting societies. In Asia, today, they are confined to the southwest of China, upland areas of the southeast, and scattered parts of the highlands of Korea and remote parts of Japan. In China, shifting agriculture is practiced primarily by minority groups such as Miao, Yeo and Lolo who have been forced into less favorable farming land of the southwest by the advancing Han people practicing peasant-garden cultivation.

Shifting cultivation in East Asia is man's labor-saving response to an environment where soil fertility is low and where most of the nutrients are tied up in the woody tissues of forest vegetation.[14] It is an environment, too, of heavy rains and high temperatures that leach exposed soil of its nutrients and degrade the structure so that air, moisture and nutrients cannot circulate freely throughout it.

The strategy used by shifting cultivators is to use fire to release the nutrients stored in trees and to make them available for a few years for crops which are planted in forest clearings. At the end of two or three years most crops have extracted all the soil nutrients and yields fall quickly. There are other reasons for abandoning the land besides declining fertility. The growth of new vegetation increasingly cuts off light from crops, and plant diseases and pests invade the area. New fields are cleared and the abandoned fields are left to forest fallow so that the nutrients that have been dissipated through cultivation, are gradually accumulated again (Figure 20).

Because of the need to put large areas into forest fallow for a couple of decades, the overall carrying capacity of the shifting cultivation system in East Asia is low, varying between ten and a hundred persons per square mile (4 to 40 persons km^{-2}). However, moderately high densities of up to 200 to 300 people can be supported per square mile of cultivated land (78 to 117 persons km^{-2}).

When shifting cultivators practice a system where population pressure does not shorten the period of rotation, little environmental destruction results.[15]

The Peasant-Gardening Ecosystem

Almost a billion people in East Asia, or one-quarter of the world's population, are supported by the peasant-gardening ecosystem. The high, and ever increasing, levels of crop yields, produced century after century, and the rural and urban populations more dense than any found in the world before the industrial revolution, have created a profound transformation of the natural landscape.

In the peasant-garden system certain management techniques were used to save both space and time so that more crops can be grown. Landscapes were also realigned so that flows of moisture, energy, and nutrients were continuously channeled into a relatively small area of cultivated land.

The principal characteristics of the system were as follows:

(1) The permanent use of the same plot of land for crop production. The lack of fallow land was a primary cause for the relatively few draft animals.[16]

(2) Wherever possible, irrigation was practiced not only to satisfy the transpirational needs of rice, the most productive of all grain crops known to traditional East Asia, but to iron out the lesser annual and season fluctuations of precipitation. Irrigation also cools down ambient air and root temperatures thus reducing carbohydrate loss and enhancing higher growth rates. Nutrient-rich waters fed to fields through stream and irrigation systems help maintain the fertility of paddy soils.[17]

(3) In many wet-field areas where there is an approximate simulation of natural vegetation systems that gave them higher productivity and resistance to pests and disease (multiple-cropping, intercropping, nursery beds).[18]

(4) Labor intensive composting and fertilization techniques, closely linked to pig raising and aquaculture speed up the rate of decomposition and return nutrients more rapidly and with fewer losses to the soil for further crop growth.[19]

(5) The integrated spatial management of the nutrient sources of hillsides and water bodies adjunct to the cultivated lands and the channeling of these nutrients into the

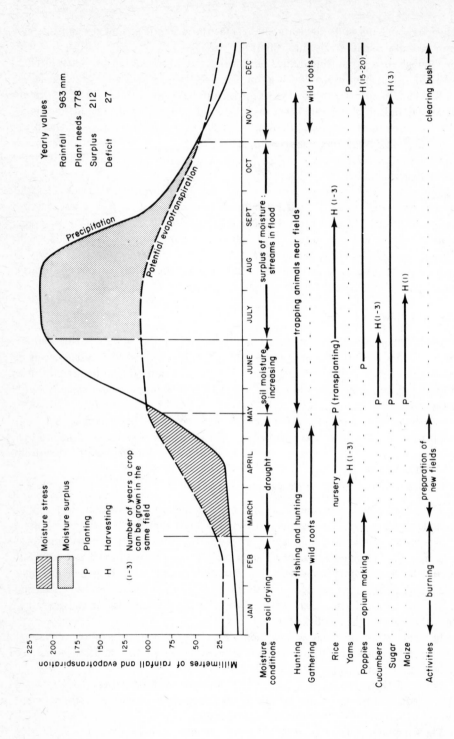

Fig. 20. The yearly cycle of work in shifting agriculture.

fields through the burning of hillsides, and the collection of wood and grass for fuel, fodder and fertilizer. Fertile muds and aquatic weeds from channels and irrigation ponds are also applied. The major "leaks" in this integrated nutrient system are through exports to urban centres. These were "plugged" through a massive system of spatial nutrient cycling in the form of the nightsoil trade. Where there were net exports of nutrients, fertility migration occurred (Figure 21).[20]

The hillsides, apart from playing the important role of supplying nutrients, also provided fuel and grazing lands for those farm animals that could not be fed entirely from the non-edible parts of the farm crops and were thus vital adjuncts to the maintenance of the lowland farm systems. The intensive use of the upland areas, however, was not conducive to forest growth, and their overuse contributed seriously to problems of soil erosion and flooding. One of the many benefits of the increased use of commercial fertilizers in East Asia since the 14th century, and the more recent use of fossil fuels, has been the fact that much of the pressure has been taken off the hill lands and has allowed programs of reforestation to succeed.[21]

The solution to the problem of low fertility of soils in the shifting agriculture system was to trade time for space by allowing the regrowth of natural vegetation over a long period to do the work of nutrient regeneration, and to move cultivation to some other area while that work was being done. The solution to the problem in the peasant–gardening system was to save both time and space by realigning the landscape so that flows of moisture, energy and nutrients were continuously fed from uncultivated areas to farm fields.

But this saving of space and time could only by purchased through the prodigious application of human labor. For not only did the infrastructure of heavy agriculture—the terraces, graded fields, irrigation systems—have to be constructed, but by profoundly modifying the natural ecosystem in the farmed areas and in the uplands, man seriously modified the free services of flood control, moisture retention and protection from pests and diseases that that system would have provided.[22] Further human effort was required, therefore, to replace these free services. A rough approximation of what these expenditures of labor were and what output of food energy resulted is given (Table 14).

It will be seen that, despite the high yields of the shifting system, its carrying capacity is about ten times lower than the dry-field and about twenty times less than the wet-field, since only 10% of the land is under crops at any one time. The price that the wet-field system pays for this intensive saving of space and time is an increase of work that is eight times greater than in shifting agriculture.

The most important thing about the peasant-gardening system, however, was the fact that it could generate sufficient surpluses to support large non-agricultural populations in urban centres.[23]

The Nomad-Herder Ecosystem

The carrying capacity of the nomad-herder ecosystem is easily the lowest of the three systems considered. In the late 19th century it is estimated that some five million people, or one percent of the population of East Asia, were minority group, nomadic herders. This small population, however, required for its support a land area of some 4 million

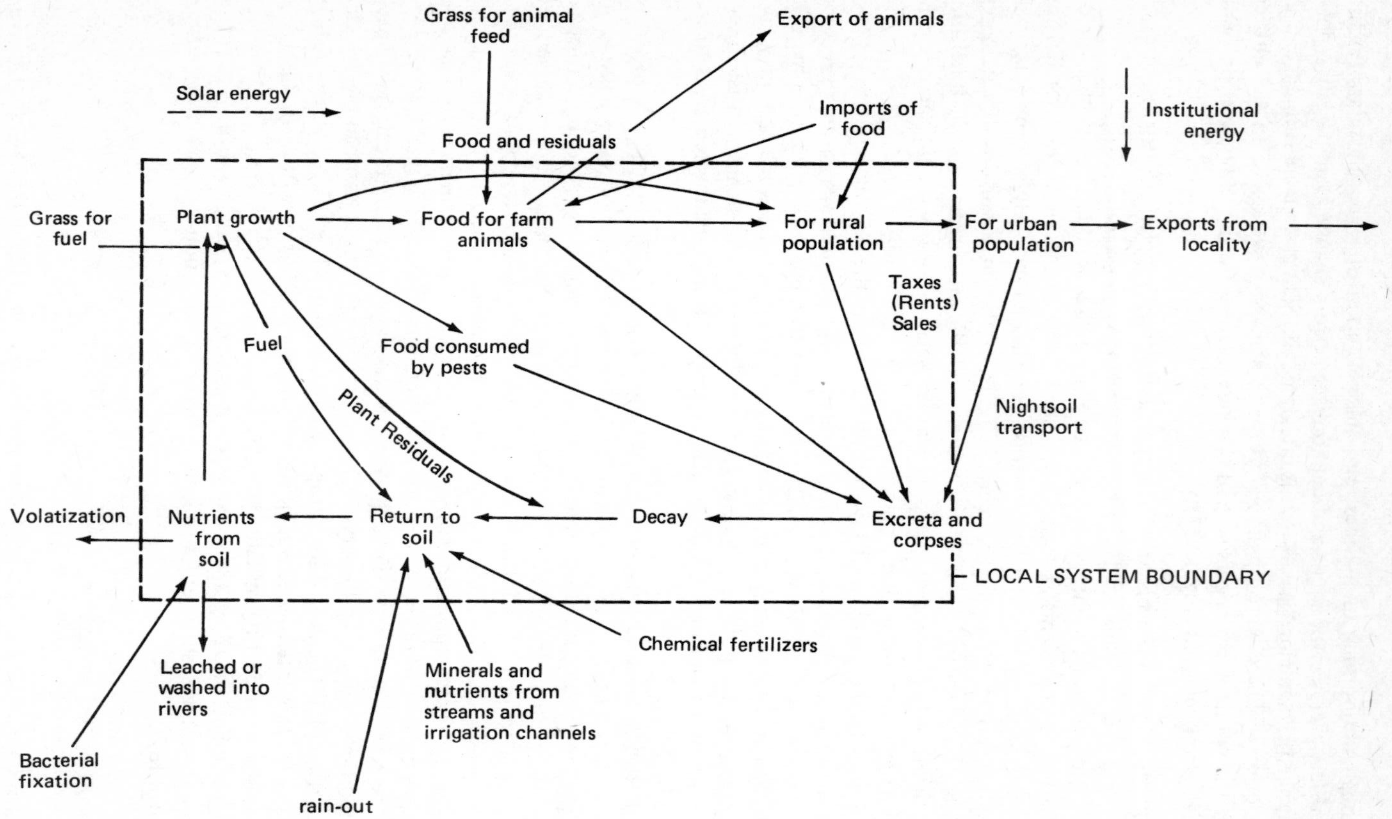

Fig. 21. The flow of nutrients in East Asian farming systems.

Table 14. Comparison of Energy Use and Production in Four
East Asian Farming Systems[a]

System	Farm work	Food yield	Ratio Work:yield	Theoretical pop. km^{-2}	Surplus non-farm population	Area to support city, 100,000 km^2
Wet field	168	964	1:5.7	1205	133	750
Dry field	62	456	1:7.3	570	51	2000
Shifting	20	400	1:20	(500)→50	nil	nil
Hong Kong[b]	1166	1525	1:1.25	1900	1650	60

Notes:
[a]In early 20th century. All valves are in millions of k.cal.km^{-2}.
[b]Data for 1971. Based on K. Newcombe, "Energy Use in the Hong Kong Food System," *Agro-Ecosystems, 2* (1976), pp. 253–276.

square kilometers (1.6 million square miles) or 40% of the region. Although small in total size, the nomadic populations of central Asia have played a role in East Asian history out of all proportion to their numbers.[24]

In the steppes, the basic problem of balancing population against food supplies is made more difficult by the fact that there is insufficient moisture to grow crops and man has to lengthen the food chain and depend on a variety of herbivores for his sustenance. The herbivores—sheep, goats, cattle, horses, camel, yak—depend, in their turn, on the abundance and spatial and seasonal distribution of grass. In the high steppe, in parts of Sinkiang, Tibet, and Chinghai, the abundance of grass is primarily dependent on the length of the growing season; on the low Mongolian steppe, the abundance is largely a function of moisture availability.[25]

It has been estimated that a nomadic family of four can be completely self-sufficient with a herd of 300 sheep equivalent (five sheep to one bovine).[26] In the moist parts of the steppe, the grasslands have a carrying capacity of about 50 sheep per square kilometer (128 sheep mile^{-2}) and, in the drier parts, about 27 (70 sheep mile^{-2}). Thus, in the former region, the herd of a single family would have to graze an area of some 6 square kilometers (2.3 sq. miles), and, in the drier parts, some 20 square kilometers (7.8 sq. miles). Population densities would, therefore, be about 0.6 per square kilometer (1.5 mile^{-2}) in the moist steppe and about 0.2 (0.5 mile^{-2}) in the dry areas. Because of these low densities and because of the fact that annual migrations over hundreds of kilometers occurred in search of new pastures, few permanent settlements developed.[27]

The high mobility of the steppe people made them formidable enemies for the peasant-gardening societies, since the latter were tied to fixed settlements, immobile lands, and grain storage facilities. The nomadic tribes, on the other hand, were practically impervious to conquest, since they had no fixed settlements and their fields and granaries were "on the hoof."[28]

DEVELOPMENTS IN TRADITIONAL RESOURCE-USING SYSTEMS

Each of the traditional resource-using systems described above has survived down to the present time, although each has changed in significant ways.

The system of shifting agriculture has suffered greatly where population pressures have risen or where the shifting cultivators have been pushed back into land with less and less carrying capacity. In these cases the forest fallow period becomes shortened, less plant cover remains to prevent soil erosion, and nutrient depletion accelerates, causing serious environmental degradation.[29]

Most shifting cultivators in China belong to ethnic minorities, living apart from Han populations, and having their own socio-political structures and controls. Because of the low carrying capacity of the land and the small agricultural surpluses, shifting cultivation has not stimulated the growth of urban centers—most farmers living in small settlements ranging from a dozen to a couple of hundred units.[30] Because of their very different ethnic, social and economic organization, the Chinese government over the centuries has never incorporated these groups into its regular administrative structure. Today, most of these tribes are organized into autonomous counties, districts and provinces. In 1953, some 15 million people or 2.5% of China's population are estimated to be shifting cultivators.[31]

The nomadic-herder system has also suffered greatly with the passage of time. In the 19th and 20th centuries, for example, as Chinese farmers, backed by railways and by the political and military power of a government anxious to colonize, began to penetrate the steppe, the great territorial range necessary to make the nomad ecosystem function effectively was decreased and nomadism, as a way of life, has been declining in most parts of Asia since that time.[32]

The wide ranging movements necessary for the successful functioning of the nomadic system have also been curtailed by the "hardening" of international boundaries across which the herders made their annual crossings and by the attempts of governments to collectivize the herders and relegate their activities to more circumscribed territorial boundaries.[33]

Of the three ecosystems, only one, the peasant-gardening, could rise above the natural carrying capacity of the local environment and could initiate a cycle of events that can best be described as a kind of pre-modern take-off to sustained economic growth. Neither shifting agriculture nor the "fields on the hoof" had surpluses large enough to support large elite groups, let alone whole urban populations. Yet the peasant-gardening system, through ever intensifying techniques for saving space was, as mentioned above, able to support nearly one-half of the world's urban population.

Those areas that were able to mobilize their rural populations and extract their surpluses for the construction of water resource management projects and water transportation networks—the wet-field regions—achieved greater comparative political, social and economic advantage than areas that lacked this ability.[34] Such regions were characterized by high population densities, high yields, large cities, a denser urban network and a higher degree of commercialization of the economy (Figure 22).[35] As wealth accumulated, local elites financed further resource management projects, and all of these, through a process of circular causation, mutually reinforced each other to give such wet-field areas a permanent and increasing comparative advantage over all other regions.[36]

The close relationship between the wet-field type of peasant-gardening and urbanization can be clearly seen (Table 15). Not only does each square kilometer of cultivated land in the wet-field system support an urban population that is three to five times larger than in the dry-field system, but the density of large cities is also higher. This is

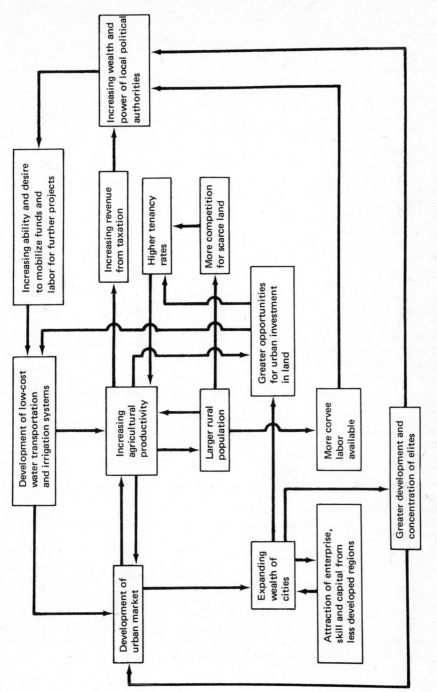

Fig. 22. The creation of developed areas in traditional East Asia.

113

Table 15. Urbanization in Wet and Dry Field Areas of East Asia in Mid-19th Century

Indices of population and cities	"Backward" dry-field areas N. China[a]	"Advanced" wet-field areas	
		S. China[b] (Developed)	Japan (Most developed)
Density of population per sq. km. of cultivated land[c]	414	788	621
Urban population supported per sq. km. of cultivated land[d]	19	60	96
Index of urban population density supported per sq. km. of cultivated land adjusted for population density (N. China = 100)[e]	100	180	339
Number of large cities per 100,000 sq. km. of cultivated land[f]	8	25	43
Index of number of large cities per 100,000 sq. km. adjusted for population density (N. China = 100)[g]	100	168	370
Number of small cities per 10,000 sq. km. of cultivated land[h]	256	592	360
Index of number of small cities per 10,000 sq. km. adjusted for population density (N. China = 100)[i]	100	121	93
Percent of total population in cities[j]	4.5	7.5	16.5
Percent of urban population in large cities[k]	36	59	55

Notes and sources:

[a]N. China refers to the provinces of Chihli, Shansi, Honan and Shantung.

[b]S. China refers to Fukien and Kwangtung.

[c]Data based on Dwight H. Perkins, *Agricultural Development in China, 1368-1968* (Chicago: Aldine, 1968), p. 212.

[d]Urban population from Rozman (*see note 35*) pp. 199 and 272.

[e]The influence of different densities of population on the levels of urbanization is removed by using the following index:

$$\text{Index of urban population density} = \frac{\dfrac{\text{wet-field urban density}}{\text{dry-field urban density}}}{\dfrac{\text{wet-field population density}}{\text{dry-field population density}}} \times 100$$

[f]These are the 1–3b level cities of Rozman's hierarchy (*see* pp. 109, 205, 239 and 272).

[g]This index is constructed in the same way as above in note *e*.

[h]These are the 4–7 level cities of Rozman (*see* references in note *f* above).

[i]Index constructed as described above.

[j]Rozman's data on pages cited above.

[k]Ibid.

Table 16. Representative Labor Requirements and Yields of Traditional, Transitional and Modern Peasant Gardening Resource Systems

System	Man-days per hectare of cultivated land	Yield (kg. man-day^{-1} ha^{-1})[c]
Traditional		
Dry farming	119[a]	4-6
Wet farming	347[b]	6-8
Contemporary		
Traditional	550[c]	2-4
Transitional	1200[d]	6-9
Modernized	102[e]	40-60

Notes and sources:

[a]Based on data for Hopei province in J. Lossing Buck, *Land Utilization in China* (Nanking: University of Nanking Press, 1937), Statistical Volume, Section vii, Table 9. The labor requirements are weighted for sown area data in Hsin-i Chang, *Chung-kuo nung-yeh kai-k'uang ku-chi* [An Estimate of China's Farms and Crops] (Nanking: 1933), Table 5.

[b]Based on data for Kuangtung province and calculated in the same manner as for note *a*.

[c]J. Whitney, *China, Development and Challenge*, 1979, in press.

[d]Ibid.

[e]Japan, Ministry of Agriculture and Forestry, *Statistical Yearbook* (Tokyo: 1975), p. 171.

due mainly to the smaller food surpluses of the latter areas and the higher transportation costs incurred in carrying food to the larger centres. Small urban centres, on the other hand, with lower support costs to maintain them are more equally distributed between the two areas.

Thus, long before the advent of the West and "modernization," there were already developed and underdeveloped regions of East Asia even within a single resource system such as peasant-gardening. By the 1930s the advanced areas of the peasant-garden system had reached productivity levels of over 50% of the natural biomes of the area, whereas the backward dry areas were able to attain only 20 to 30% of the natural systems' productivity.[37]

Three stages of development can be observed in the peasant-gardening system today: traditional, transitional, and modernized. The major factor that differentiates each is the labor input required for farming (Table 16).

Traditional Peasant-Gardening

This remains essentially the same as described earlier, except that, in the case of China, the small farms based on individual household ownership have been replaced by production teams of thirty to forty families and large communes embracing several square miles and populations running into the thousands.[38] Although there may be a few modern inputs such as mechanical pumping of irrigation water and some chemical fertilizers and pesticides, the major part of the farm work is still carried out in traditional ways and primarily with human labor. The latter, however, under the commune system can be mobilized more effectively to help cope with peak labor demands and to carry out winter-works projects.[39]

Table 17. Labor Requirements During Peak Demand Period[a]

Crop	Input	Man-days per hectare
First	Harvesting	19
	Carrying	7
	Threshing	16
	Drying	6
	Storage	4
Second	Ploughing	5
	Harrowing	7
	Transplanting	20
Total for peak period		84
Total for double rice crop		305

Note:

[a]Double rice-cropping area.

Source: Buck (*see Table 16, note a*).

In the northern and more arid part of China, such remaining traditional systems will probably still be limited to one major crop per year because they lack the ability to tap underground or distant surface sources of water. In the south, where water is available, inability to introduce multiple-cropping will be due primarily to the bottleneck of labor shortages at peak periods. Buck's survey of traditional Chinese agriculture carried out in the 1930s shows that in many areas potentially capable of growing two or three major crops per year, multiple cropping was not practiced because of peak-period labor shortage.[40]

Large labor inputs for the critical period from harvesting the first rice crop to planting the second were required (Table 17). Nearly 28% of the total man-days to cultivate the two rice crops was concentrated into a matter of 15 to 20 days. If the planting of the second crop were delayed, the growing season for the second crop would be reduced and hence yields lowered.

Undoubtedly, in many of the traditional areas, despite attempts to rationalize farm labor on a commune basis, a similar situation still exists, inhibiting the planting of second or third crops.

Transitional Peasant-Gardening

The transitional sector has greatly increased input of labor above those of the traditional or modern systems, and this may seem paradoxical until the nature of the modernization occurring in the transitional system is examined (Table 16). The key to the understanding of this phenomenon is found in the role that the introduction of mechanical irrigation plays, particularly in those areas where water must be pumped from deep underground aquifers.[41]

Irrigation triggers off the following labor demanding activities:

(1) The introduction of multiple-covering (crops raised successively during a single year from the same plot of land);

(2) Greatly increased demand for organic fertilizers to be collected from hillsides, irrigation channels, pig raising and estimated to occupy 45% of all labor activities compared to some 9 or 10% in the traditional system;[42]

(3) Moist fields, well supplied with nutrients, increase weeds, pests, and diseases which must be controlled;

(4) The infrastructure for storing and distributing water must be constructed and repaired.

Thus, the modernization of the traditional system that is now going on in China and which occurred in Japan half a century or so earlier, while saving labor through mechanization in such activities as mechanical irrigation, and cutting down on peak labor demand through the use of transplanting machines and mechanical threshing, generates a demand for even more labor. Hence, even in a transitional farming system, traditional activities for recycling nutrients are more important than those of chemical fertilization (Figure 23).

The nutrient budget for a small farm area in North China shows clearly the important role played by such adjunct hill-lands which provide over 80% of the gross nutrient supply in contrast to chemical fertilizers which supply over 13%.[43] If hillside sources were cut off, in this example, nutrients from chemical supplies would have to be increased six-fold. There is indeed a modest annual net gain to the available N, P, and K soil nutrients of 6, 21, and 3% respectively, largely derived from hillsides, thus allowing for another round of crop increased in the following year. However, in areas where adjunct hills are not available or where there is insufficient labor and/or enthusiasm to collect organic manures (applied at the rate of over 100 tonnes $ha^{-1} yr^{-1}$ [40 tons $acre^{-1} yr^{-1}$]), it can be expected that yields will be lower or that, if they are not, soil fertility reserves are being depleted. This process, judging from the available nutrients in the soils of the budget example, could be completed in a matter of a year or two.

REGION IN TRANSITION

As has been demonstrated above, the initial impact of the modernization of the traditional farming system is to intensify many of the traditional labor intensive farming practices while reducing or eliminating others, the net result being a greatly expanded demand for labor particularly in those dry farming regions where irrigation is introduced for the first time. The modernization of the traditional resource sector also affects the relationship between the lowland farming system and the upland adjuncts as described earlier. In the first place many upland areas that were formerly used for fuel and fodder can now be turned into terraced cultivated lands. Secondly, while still relatively unimportant in many areas, the pressure on the hillsides to produce nutrients for lowland farming is being reduced through alternative sources of organic or chemical fertilizers. Thirdly, the provision of electricity and other sources of fuel for domestic purposes reduces the demand made on the hillsides to provide energy for lowland use. It also means that more of the crop residues formerly used as fuel can be composted and returned to the land.

The net result of this reduction in the demand made on hillside resources has enabled

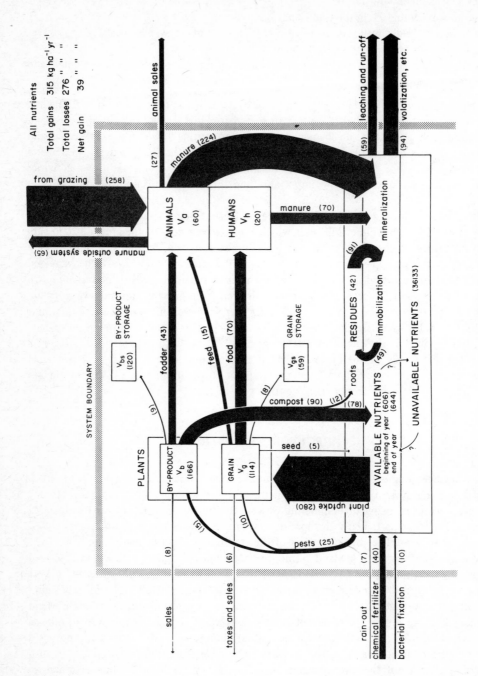

Fig. 23. The flow of nutrients in a transitional farming system.

118

Table 18. Increase of Part-Time Farming in Modern Peasant
Gardening in Japan

Household indices	1950[a]	1976[b]
Farm households as percent of total households	37	15
Percent of farm households		
fully dependent on farm income	50	13
partly dependent on farm income	50	87
who gain over 60% of income from farming	57	24
who gain over 60% of income from other sources	43	76
Percent of total Japanese households gaining over		
60% of income from farming	29	5

Sources:
[a]*Japan Statistical Yearbook, 1958*, p. 99.
[b]*Japan Statistical Yearbook, 1977*, p. 121.

reafforestation of the slopes to be accomplished, whereas in the traditional system even when it was perceived as being desirable it was often unfeasible for the reasons stated above.

The Modern Peasant-Gardening Resource System

While the traditional and transitional forms of peasant gardening result in an intensification of cultivation, labor inputs and the channeling of regional natural resources to the agricultural sector, the modernized form of the system as now practiced in Japan shows striking differences. In the first place, the labor requirement per unit of cultivated land for crop production is greatly reduced, amounting to one-tenth of the transitional system (Table 16). This, of course, is due to the fact that the modern sector is now heavily subsidized with fossil fuels in the form of energy, chemical fertilizers, pesticides, and herbicides.[44] This reduction in the demand for agricultural labor has had profound impacts on the whole fabric of Japanese rural life (Table 18).

By the 1970s those earning most of their income from farming comprised a mere 5% of the total population 66% of the farm households derived most of their income from sources other than farming. The primary reason for this is that the majority of farms are too small to provide an adequate income for farming families and that there are higher paying jobs in the urban-industrial economy.[45]

Dramatic changes have also occurred in farming land use. Whereas, in the traditional and transitional sectors, the trend is to greater intensity of land use through intercropping, multiple-cropping and transplanting, in the modern system of Japan the trend is toward a single crop grown once a year; thus in 1976, 93% of farm families practiced monoculture and between 1956 and 1976 the multiple-cropping index (sown area/cultivated area X 100) showed a decrease from 160 to 103%.[46]

These trends can be attributed to the fact that the crops that follow rice (whose production is subsidized by the Japanese government) in the multiple-cropping system such as wheat and barley can now be imported from abroad more cheaply than they can be produced at home.[47]

As labor costs in Japan rise, less and less attention is paid to the labor intensive practices of the traditional and transitional systems with the result that many environmental problems are being exacerbated. Instead of the recycling practiced in the traditional system, the modern one has devised a "once-through" path for its nutrients which does not utilize the waste organic products of crop and animal farming or of human wastes and thus creates pollution of land and water bodies.[48]

CONCLUDING REGIONAL ASSESSMENT

The traditional East Asian resource system, particularly its wet-field variety, had the capacity, as we have seen, not only to give employment to large numbers of people, but to produce further increments of food with each additional labor unit without appreciable diminishing marginal returns occurring.[49] This characteristic, called involution by Clifford Geertz, means that peasant gardening is the only productive system outside of the labor intensive industrial system developed at the beginning of the 19th century that is able to respond to a rapidly growing population associated with demographic transition (i.e., a population having high birth rates and falling death rates). Moreover, unlike the latter system, peasant gardening is not only able to provide economically efficient employment, but it is also able to feed, in addition to those in the agricultural sector, those in other parts of the economy as well.[50] Thus, for capital-short developing countries, experiencing the economic and social disruption caused by the period of demographic transition, the peasant-garden system enables a country to span this phase of its development with the minimum of dislocation since it continues to maintain a large and flourishing rural sector of society, conserving many of the traditional virtues and vices.[51]

In the case of China, between the 1930s and 1975, the peasant-gardening resource system was able to absorb some 135 million people into its labor force, and by the 1990s an additional 73 million workers can be accommodated.[52] At an earlier period, during the latter part of the 19th century the Japanese peasant-gardening system experienced a similar though less dramatic development.[53]

Although the peasant-garden system functioned on sound ecological principles, it was, nevertheless, in a condition of unstable equilibrium with its environment. As we have seen, the effectiveness of the system depended on the massive submission of all other resource systems to the needs of agriculture, through the diversion of their nutrients, energy and moisture for the needs of crops. As mere adjuncts to farming these other ecological systems suffered severe damage from vegetation and soil removal with the result that the free services of flood control and drought amelioration which they would have naturally provided were seriously curtailed.[54] However, through an untutored understanding of the basic ecological principles at work, the farmers of the peasant-garden system were able to combat a great many of these problems partly through the judicious imitation of natural ecosystems in such practices as inter-cropping, multiple-cropping, nutrient recycling, and predator pest control and partly through additional inputs of labor directly applied to combatting the environmental damage.[55]

The traditional peasant-gardening system has demonstrated its resilience in the face of environmental and social change over the centuries and this resilience was due not only to the massive labor inputs required to keep the system in equilibrium with its environment, but also to the care and understanding that generations of peasants developed in relation to their plants.[56]

The modern system of peasant gardening, while apparently as productive and less labor-demanding than its traditional counterpart is potentially much more fragile than the latter, since it relies heavily on inputs of fossil fuel sources of energy and nutrients.[57] While it is true that modern inputs have taken the farming pressure off adjunct ecological systems, urban-industrial developments present a large and ever-growing threat. Moreover, because monoculture is economically more efficient for the farmer to practice, most of the ecological farming practices of the traditional system have been lost, and the threat of diseases and pests is an ever potential and growing one that can be remedied only through the application of greater quantities of pesticides, herbicides and fertilizers—resulting in a further decline of environmental quality.[58]

The Future of the Past

Some of the principal practices and techniques of the traditional peasant-gardening system can be utilized in the transitional and modern variants without reducing yields provided that labor demands can be met (Table 19).

The table shows that throughout the greater part of the region the majority of the traditional practices are being continued in an even more intense form in the transitional system. Indeed, the Communist Chinese planning principle of "walking-on-two-legs" (the use and popularization of both traditional and modern methods to achieve economic development) is an indication that many traditional practices will be retained for some time to come despite the current frenetic efforts to modernize the economy.[59] Moreover, if additional employment cannot be found for the increasing labor force in the urban-industrial economy, and/or, if the undesirable effects of total reliance on fossil fuel farming should become widely apparent in the near future, it is quite possible that many of these practices would be carried on far into the future.

There are, however, some situations where modern technology cannot be replaced by labor without retarding yield increases.

Mechanical pumping. Particularly where deep ground water supplies are available even massive inputs of labor cannot pump the water up.

Cement lining of irrigation canals. In more arid regions, it is essential that there be no leakages from irrigation canals into the surrounding soils since this gives rise to salinization and hard-pan formation which is detrimental to agriculture.[60]

Mechanization to reduce peak load labor demand. As indicated earlier, there were many areas of the traditional resource system where multiple-cropping could not be practiced because the labor supply could not meet the demands for harvesting one crop and planting a second in a sufficiently short time. Thus, mechanization to replace labor at peak periods should be encouraged. This would include such devices as mechanical transplanters, threshing machines and small tractors for ploughing and harrowing.

Chemical fertilizers. For continued increases of crop yields there must be a blending of traditional and modern fertilization techniques. Chemical fertilizers with their high nutrient content in relation to weight can save a great deal of labor. Of greater importance is the fact that they can supply nutrients that might otherwise have to be supplied by

Table 19. A Selection of Techniques and Practices in the Traditional Resource System and Modern Applications

Technique or practice	Comment	System		
		Traditional	Transitional	Modern
Cropping				
Nursery beds (small plots to grow young plants)[a]	Saves time and space. Easy to control for low temperature, pests, and weeds.	◉	◉	◉
Black ash on nursery beds	Warms soil to increase germination of seeds.	⊛	◉	○◉ [b]
Inter-cropping (differrent crops planted in same field at staggered intervals)	More effective use of solar radiation for photosynthesis. Facilitates transfer of soluble plant nutrients.	⊛	◉	○○
Straw mulching dug into ridges of furrows	(1) Conserves moisture. (2) Allows aeration of soil (3) Ash elements in straw leached directly to crop roots. (4) Straw and soil constitute a compost.	⊛	◉	●○
Dwarf fruit trees	Ease of picking and pest control	⊛	⊛	◉
Multiple cropping	Two or more successive crops in same field.	⊛	◉	●○
Root-zone fertilization	Economizes on fertilizers. Prevents pollution of water bodies.	⊛	◉	●○
Ridging (after two crops of rice, soil banked into long ridges 1 meter wide to grow vegetables)	Permits ill-drained soils to be used during winter.	⊛	◉	○○
Close-deep furrowing	In areas of heavy intermittent rain prevents flooding of crops. Moisture and nutrients conserved in troughs.	⊛	◉	◉

Table 19 (cont'd.)

Technique or practice	Comment	System		
		Traditional	Transitional	Modern
Assymetrical ridging	Used in north-facing mountain areas to enable crops to receive maximum insolation.	⊙	◎	⊙○
Biological insect control	Natural predators control insect pests.	⊙	◎	○○
Landscape changes				
Terracing	(1) Increases cultivated area. (2) Retains runoff and prevents erosion. (3) Increases nutrient retention in the soil. (4) Permits irrigation.	⊙	◎	●○[c]
Trenching	The trenches retain moisture and nutrients washed off cultivated area for subsequent crop use.	⊙	⊙	○○
Embankment round fields	Conserves moisture and prevents nutrient loss during heavy rain.	◎	◎	○○
Ponds[d]	(1) Retain water for irrigation. (2) Act as nutrient sinks for surrounding fields. (3) Fertilized by waste materials from settlements. (4) Fertile mud applied to fields.	⊙	◎	●○
Fertilizing				
Urban sewage (nightsoil)[e]	Transported to surrounding agricultural lands.	⊙	◎	○○
Irrigation and stream mud	Mixed with organic material to form compost. Rich in plant nutrients.	⊙	◎	○○

Table 19 (cont'd.)

Technique or practice	Comment	System		
		Traditional	Transitional	Modern
Exchange of soil between rice fields and mulberry	Soil developed under each crop complements nutrient requirements of the other.	⊛	◉	✪?
Composting with canal mud, clover, human and animal manure, and ashes	Releases immobilized plant nutrients and provides them in soluble form for plant use.	⊛	◉	✪○
Green manure from hills		◉	◉	✪
Floor soil	The compacted soils used to construct floors when dampened over long periods of time produce nutrients in soluble form.	⊛	●	✪
Dried human and animal manure	Used in N. China. When pulverized the powder easily mixes with the soil providing soluble plant nutrients. Health hazards reduced.	◉	●	✪○
Chinese clover (medicago denticulata)	Used in inter-cropping or multiple-cropping with rice or barley followed by cotton. Increases nitrogen in soil.	⊛	◉	●○
Water hyacinths and lotus	Harvested for compost. Reduces nutrient wastes in canals and streams.	⊛	◉	✪○
Aquaculture[f]	(1) Fish provide high yield of protein per unit area. Cause rapid breakdown of organic materials fed to them.	⊛	◉	●○
	(2) Blue-green algae in rice fields convert atmospheric nitrogen into forms soluble by plants.	⊛	◉	✪[g]

Key to symbols:
⊛Important
⦿Very important
●Decreasing importance
◌Not important
◯Could be retained in modern system without reducing yield if sufficient labor available
Notes:
[a]See figure 24.
[b]Replaced by plastic covers.
[c]Except for tea and fruit (mandarin and orange in Japan).
[d]See Aquaculture below.
[e]See Figure 25.
[f]See Ponds above.
[g]Killed by herbicides.

---

adjunct hill lands and thus contribute to soil erosion. Nevertheless, traditional fertilization techniques should also be retained since they improve soil structure, help to retain moisture, and facilitate the aereation of soils. Moreover, the removal of nutrients from streams and other water bodies through aquatic weed harvesting and the dredging of mud reduces eutrophication problems and enhances water quality for other uses.[61]

In the modern system as practiced in Japan the traditional experience has for the most part been overthrown. The Japanese farmer, so financially involved with the farm machinery and chemical manufacturers, and, unable to afford the high price for farm labor, cannot afford to practice traditional techniques any longer.[62] Moreover, having lost most of the protective ecological devices of the traditional system, modern peasant gardening has now become even more dependent on the industrial sector in the fight

Fig. 24. Traditional peasant gardening rice cultivation scene, showing stages of cultivation from ploughing to harvesting (*Source: Kyoso* [1873]).

視聽自民圖

Fig. 25. Farmland around traditional Chinese city benefits from urban sewage.

against crop disease and pests. Lastly, it is likely that the experience and skills associated with the traditional resource system will die with the present generation of older farmers and will be difficult to acquire by their successors. Even if economic conditions became ripe for more labor intensive agriculture the experience required to employ that labor effectively would be lacking.

In the East Asian resource system, as in many other parts of the world, the past continues to live in the present and is likely to remain for some time to come. Not only does it survive but its many traditional practices continue to support over one-quarter of the world's population.

NOTES

[1] Yi-fu Tuan, "Discrepancies Between Environmental Attitudes and Behaviour: Examples from Europe and China," *The Canadian Geographer*, Vol. 12, No. 3 (1968), pp. 176–91; and Ping-ti Ho, *Studies on the Population of China 1368-1953* (Cambridge, Mass.: Harvard University Press, 1959), pp. 137–41.

[2] Derk Bodde, *China's Cultural Tradition* (N.Y.: Holt, Rinehart & Winston, 1957), pp. 37–39.

[3] Joseph E. Spencer and William L. Thomas, *Asia East by South* (N.Y.: John Wiley, 1971), pp. 120–72.

[4] George B. Cressey, *Land of the 500 Million* (N.Y.: McGraw-Hill, 1955), pp. 255–69.

[5] Owen L. Lattimore, *The Inner Asian Frontiers of China* (Boston: Beacon Press, 1962), pp. 279–374; and Ping-ti Ho, "The Loess and the Origin of Chinese Agriculture," *American Historical Review*, Vol. 75 (1969), pp. 1–36.

[6] Jung-pang Lo, "The Controversy over Grain Conveyance During the Reign of Qubilai Qaqan, 1260-1294," *Far Eastern Quarterly*, Vol. 13 (1954), pp. 263–85.

[7] Shannon McCune, *Korea's Heritage, A Regional and Social Geography* (Vermont: Charles Tuttle, 1956).

[8] Glenn T. Trewartha, *Japan: A Geography* (Madison: University of Wisconsin Press, 1965), pp. 25–38.

[9] Herold J. Wiens, *China's March Toward the Tropics* (Hamden, Conn.: Shoestring Press, 1954).

[10] The empirical work upon which these calculations are based is L. E. Rodin and N. I. Bazilevich, "Geographical Aspects of Biological Productivity," *Soviet Geography*, Vol. 12, No. 4 (1972), pp. 293–317.

[11] The probabilities are based on the study by Augustine Y. M. Yao, *Characteristics and Probabilities of Precipitation in China* (Washington, D.C.: U.S. Department of Commerce, 1969).

[12] Shan-yu Yao, "The Geographical Distribution of Floods and Droughts in Chinese History, 206 B.C.–A.D. 1911," *Far Eastern Quarterly*, Vol. 2 (1947), pp. 357–78.

[13] Joseph E. Spencer, *Oriental Asia: Themes Toward a Geography* (Englewood Cliffs, N.J.: Prentice-Hall, 1973), pp. 68–86.

[14] J. E. Spencer, *Shifting Cultivation in Southeastern Asia* (Berkeley, 1969).

[15] Spencer, op. cit., note 13.

[16] The relationship between population pressure, fallow land and farm animals is discussed in the seminal work by Ester Boserup, *The Conditions of Agricultural Growth: The Economics of Agrarian Change under Population Pressures* (Chicago: Aldine, 1965).

[17] F. H. King, *Farmers of Forty Centuries* (London: Jonathan Cape, 1949), pp. 238–65.

[18] Matthias U. Igbozurike, "Ecological Balance in Tropical Agriculture," *Geographical Review*, Vol. 61, No. 4 (Oct., 1971), pp. 495–529.

[19] Joseph B. R. Whitney, "Ecology and Environmental Control in China," in Michel Oksenburg, ed., *China's Developmental Experience* (N.Y.: Praeger, 1973), pp. 93–109; and D. D. Tapiador, et al., *Freshwater Fisheries and Aquaculture in China* (Rome: FAO, 1977).

[20] James Thorp, *Geography of the Soils of China* (Nanking: National Geological Survey of China, 1936), pp. 430–32.

[21] This point is discussed in Thomas C. Smith, *The Agrarian Origins of Modern Japan* (N.Y.: Atheneum, 1966), pp. 101–04; and in Edward A. Ackerman, *Japan's Natural Resources and their Relation to Japan's Economic Future* (Chicago: University of Chicago Press, 1953), pp. 330–53.

[22] Clifford Geertz, *Agricultural Involution* (Berkeley and Los Angeles: University of California Press, 1968), pp. 1–37.

[23] Joseph B. R. Whitney, *China: Area, Administration and Nation Building* (Chicago: University of Chicago Press, 1969), pp. 58–61.

[24] Owen Lattimore, *Studies in Frontier History* (London: Oxford University Press, 1962), pp. 469–91.

[25] Robert B. Ekvall, *Fields on the Hoof: Nexus of Tibetan Nomadic Pastoralism* (N.Y. and London: Holt, Rinehart & Winston, 1968), pp. 4–8.

[26] Ibid., pp. 18–19.

[27] Elizabeth E. Bason, "Types of Pastoral Nomadism in Central and Southwest Asia," *Southwestern Journal of Anthropology*, Vol. 10 (1954), pp. 44–68.

[28] Lattimore, op. cit., note 24, pp. 415–420.

[29] Spencer, op. cit., note 13, p. 72.

[30] Hugo A. Bernatzik, *Akha and Miao* (New Haven: Human Relations Area Files, 1970), pp. 460–492.

[31] Spencer and Thomas, op. cit., note 3, pp. 254–256.

[32] Isaiah Bowman, *The Pioneer Fringe* (N.Y.: American Geographical Society, 1931), pp. 267–95.

[33] Lattimore, op. cit., note 24, pp. 415–426.

[34] A full examination of this theme is found in Ch'ao-ting Ch'i, *Key Economic Areas in Chinese History* (London: George Allen & Unwin Ltd., 1936).

[35] Gilbert Rozman, *Urban Networks in Ch'ing China and Tokugawa Japan* (Princeton, N.J.: Princeton University Press, 1973), pp. 4–45.

[36] G. William Skinner, *The City in Late Imperial China* (Stanford, Calif.: Stanford University Press, 1977), pp. 211–351. Also Dwight H. Perkins, *Agricultural Development in China 1368–1968* (Chicago: Aldine, 1969), pp. 118–25.

[37] Joseph B. R. Whitney, "Temporal and Spatial Changes in the Flow and Storage of Energy and Nutrients in Chinese Farming Systems in Relation to Crop Yields," in Frank King, et al., eds., *China: Development and Challenge* (Hong Kong: Hong Kong University Press, 1979), Vol. 2 (in press).

[38] Gargi Dutt, *Rural Communes of China* (London: Asia Publishing House, 1967), pp. 1–63.

[39] Kenneth R. Walker, *Planning in Chinese Agriculture 1956–1962* (London: Frank Cass & Co. Ltd., 1965), pp. 1–19.

[40] John L. Buck, *Land Utilization in China* (Nanking: University of Nanking, 1937), pp. 295–303.

[41] Thomas G. Rawski, *Industrialization, Technology and Employment in the People's Republic of China* (Washington, D.C.: The World Bank, 1978), pp. 60–92.

[42] Ibid., p. 70; Buck, op. cit., note 40, Statistical Volume, Ch. VIII, Table 10.

[43] All calculations based on the elemental composition of the fertilizer, rather than compound weight.

[44] K. S. Sum, "Japanese Agriculture in Transition and its Trend," *Science Report of the Tohoku University*, 7th Series (Geography), Vol. 26, No. 2 (1976), pp. 183–203.

[45] Akira Ebato, *Postwar Japanese Agriculture* (Tokyo: International Society for Educational Information Press, 1973), pp. 97–103.

[46] Japan, Statistics and Information Department, Ministry of Agriculture and Fisheries, *Statistical Yearbook, 1975–76*, Table 4, p. 10, and Table 36, p. 125.

[47] Michael W. Donnelly, "Setting the Price of Rice: A Study in Political Decision-Making," in T. J. Pempel, ed., *Policymaking in Contemporary Japan* (Ithaca: Cornell University Press, 1977), pp. 143–200.

[48] Shigeto Tsuru, "Environmental Pollution Control in Japan," in S. Tsuru, ed., *Environmental Disruption: A Challenge to Social Scientists* (Tokyo: International Social Science Council, 1970), pp. 325–48.

[49] See Geertz, op. cit., note 22, and for a dissenting view, Mark Elvin, *The Pattern of the Chinese Past* (Stanford: Stanford University Press, 1973), pp. 285–316.

[50] Economically efficient in the sense that there are no significant diminishing marginal returns on additional labor invested.

[51] Smith, op. cit., note 21, pp. 87–107.

[52] J. B. R. Whitney, "Performance of Chinese Farming Regions," in North Ginsburg and C. K. Leung, eds., *Perspectives on the Geography of China* (Chicago: University of Chicago Press, forthcoming).

[53] Smith, op. cit., note 21, p. 107.

[54] Walter H. Mallory, *China: Land of Famine* (N.Y.: American Geographical Society, 1926).

[55] Rhoads Murphey, "Man and Nature in China," *Modern Asian Studies*, Vol. 1 (Oct., 1967), pp. 313–333.

[56] King, op. cit., note 17, gives the best account of the traditional East Asian farming system.

[57] For a discussion of this point see Ken Newcombe, "Energy Uses in the Hong Kong Food System," *Agro-Ecosystems*, Vol. 2 (1975), pp. 253–76.

[58] Ibid., pp. 270–274.

[59] Charles Hoffman, "The Maoist Economic Model," *Journal of Economic Issues*, Vol. 3, No. 2 (1971), pp. 12–27.

[60] Thomas R. Tregear, *A Geography of China* (Chicago: Aldine, 1965), pp. 37–38.

[61] King, op. cit., note 17, pp. 171–190.

[62] Susan George, *How the Other Half Dies* (N.Y.: Penguin Books, 1976), pp. 158–91.

Chapter 6

The Soviet Union

W. A. Douglas Jackson

The term "traditional," as pertaining to the use of Russia's agricultural resource, the essential focus of this essay, means prerevolutionary.[1] The revolution of 1917 nationalized resources and wiped out all vestiges of private farming in Russia. Collectivization, beginning in 1928, was for the mass of Russia's rural population the "real" revolution. It deprived them of their village farmlands and forced them into larger collective and state farms where they had even less decision-making power. Had traditional Russian land use been anything but backward, collectivization could be seen as a retreat from sound farming. But collectivization, and its associated agricultural goals, were carried through and implemented with such ruthlessness, that the consequences—at least during much of the 1930s—were little more than a disaster. If Russian agriculture by 1950 had regained the level of production of 1937 which was close to that of 1914, then it should suggest that—allowing for World War II's savage destruction—the use of Russia's land resources had literally gone from bad to worse. Perhaps the only bright spot in this entire dismal picture was the way in which the peasants and farmers tended their backyard gardens, the private plots.

THE RESOURCE BASE

Boundaries of the Region

European Russia, a vast lowland which possesses a considerable diversity of natural conditions, affords a suitable segment of Soviet earth space within which to consider the nature of the Soviet revolution in resource use and management. Excluding the Arctic islands, the territory extends through some 25° of latitude, from 45° to 70° north.

Physically it is bounded on the north by the Barents Sea and on the south by the piedmont of the Caucasus Mountains together with the adjacent Black and Caspian seas. Because of the region's great latitudinal extent, natural conditions, as different as the northern tundra and the interior continental desert, may be found.

Ordinarily the term "European Russia" is applied to that part of the Soviet Union that lies between the international boundary on the west—a boundary shared with Finland in the north and Bulgaria in the south—and the crest of the Ural Mountains and the Ural River on the east (Figure 26). In terms of ethnic identity, however, the region is not entirely Russian. Great Russians predominate and form the core of the Russian Soviet Federated Socialist Republic, the largest republic of the USSR, that stretches from Karelia in the northwest across European Russia and Siberia to the Pacific Ocean in the east. In addition to the Russians there are other Slavic peoples, such as Ukrainians and Belorussians. They are found to the south-southwest and west, respectively, of the Russians. Between the Ukraine and Romania live Moldavians, whose language like that of the Romanians, belongs to the Romance group. Along the Baltic littoral is the homeland of Estonians, Latvians, and Lithuanians, who enjoyed a brief period of independence between the two world wars. These varied ethnic groups occupy their own national or soviet socialist republics, which are constituent republics of the Soviet Union.

Inside the Russian Republic are numerous other non-Russian and non-Slavic peoples, whose occupance dates in most cases to very early times. Among these may be cited the Finnic peoples of Karelia and northern Russia, the Turco-Tatars in the vicinity of the middle Volga River, the Kalmyks (Mongols) near the Caspian Sea, and the diverse Caucasian peoples of the southern piedmont. Convenience only dictates the use of the term "European Russia" for a region so rich in cultures and history.

European Russia's Principle Biomes

Biomes are identified primarily on the basis of the plant life they support. The latter, of course, is closely associated with and dependent on other factors such as climate, soil conditions, and the lay of the land, and the fauna or native animal life. European Russia, because of its great north-south extent, is crossed by broad latitudinal belts that are characterized (in the most general terms) by differing plant communities. Russian geographers since the 19th century have known these belts or biomes as natural regions (Figure 27).

From north to south across the European Russian lowland, the following natural regions are found: (1) tundra, (2) taiga or subboreal evergreen forest, (3) temperate or mixed forest, (4) wooded or forest steppe, (5) steppe or grasslands, (6) semiarid steppe, and (7) desert. Along the southern coast of the Crimean peninsula is a zone that, because of its moderate climate, bears similarities to the Mediterranean coast. Though important to the Soviet Union because of its climatic uniqueness, it is a small area and therefore excluded from consideration here. In the upland regions, such as the Caucasus, Urals, and Carpathian mountains, the natural regions tend to have a vertical distribution.

The tundra is not extensive in European Russia, being confined to a narrow belt along the Barents Sea. A treeless expanse, its vegetation consists mainly of mosses and lichens. The mean temperature of the warmest month tends to fall below 50°F (10°C). The

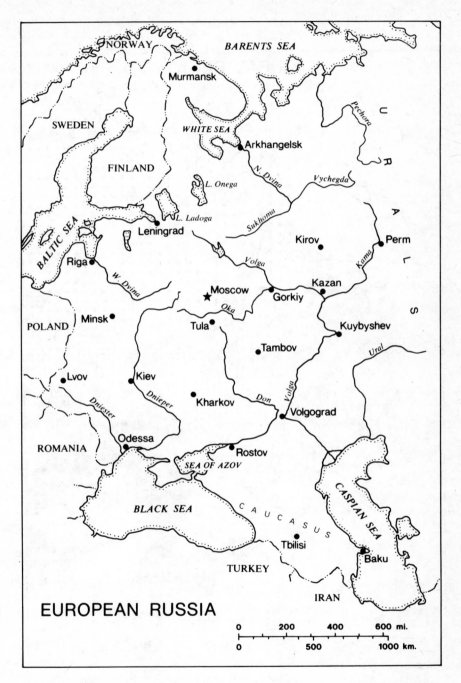

Fig. 26. European Russia, as shown within post-World War II boundaries.

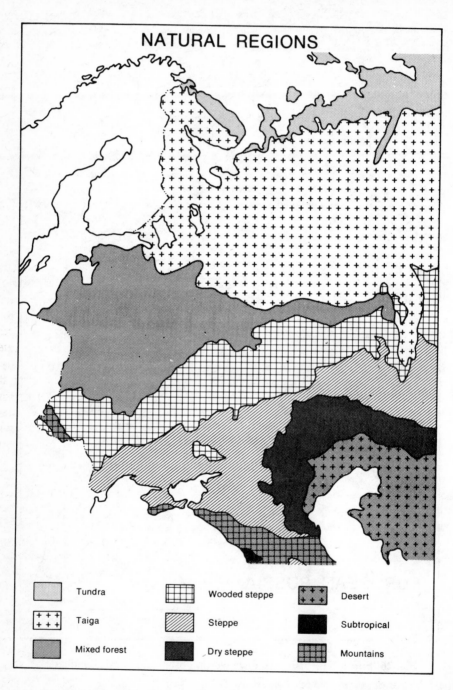

Fig. 27. Natural regions of European Russia, modified after L. S. Berg.

severity of the climate has supported the survival of permanent ground frost (permafrost), especially in the more easterly part of the tundra (Figure 27). Warm season melting, together with precipitation, lead to a peat or bog type soil but such areas are not widespread. Both wild and domestic reindeer are present, the tundra also being the traditional habitat of the polar bear, the arctic fox, the willow ptarmigan, the snowy owl, and other species.

The taiga lies to the south of the tundra. In the taiga the mean temperature of the warmest month rises to 50°F (10°C), with annual precipitation totalling about 20" (50 mm) or less (Figure 28). Spruce, larch, fir, and pine are the major evergreen species, with spruce predominating in the districts nearer the Urals. The Russians call the soils of the taiga *podzols* which, though in varying stages of development, are noted for their high acidity and low humus content (Figure 29). Bogs and poorly drained areas are widespread as are sandy soils, the residual of continental glaciation. There is no permafrost. Brown bear, marten, fox, elk, and hare were common.

The temperate or mixed forest zone to the south of the taiga is shaped like a triangle, its base extending roughly from the latitude of Leningrad to that of Kiev and its apex near Perm in the east. Throughout the triangle precipitation averages 20" (500 mm) or slightly above while mean temperatures of 50°F (20°C) range from three months along the northern edge to five months or more in the southwest. At the time of Slavic settlement in the 9th-10th centuries, stands of evergreens were common in the more northerly reaches of the zone, but toward the south the vegetation tended to become predominantly broadleaf deciduous—maple, elm, linden, ash, and others. Birch was and is common. Due to glacial deposition the terrain of the mixed forest zone is varied. Glacial hills, such as the Valday Hills—the source of the Volga northwest of Moscow—are interspersed with poorly drained depressions and extensive marshes (such as the Pripyat northwest of Kiev and the Meshchora east of Moscow). The soils, less acidic than the true podzols of the taiga, are called podzolic. Sandy areas are common; near Moscow they account for nearly 13% of the terrain.

The wooded or forest steppe is a zone of transition. It extends in a somewhat irregular and broken manner across Russia from south of Kiev toward the Urals. Its southern limit lies near the southern boundary of glaciation in European Russia. The original vegetative cover consisted of stands of deciduous forests with considerable areas of open grassland. In the north, and especially in the west, the forests consisted of oak on rich loamy soils. South of Moscow—and particularly south of the Oka—in the undulating .Central Russian Upland, associations of ash, linden, maple, and elm, with hornbeam, were prevalent (Figure 30). To the east of the Volga where the climate becomes drier as annual precipitation falls, birch-aspen groups predominate. Sub-humid conditions also contribute to the increase in soil alkalinity. For the most part, the soils of the wooded steppe, varying from a gray forest to a leached black earth have proven to be a rich agricultural resource.

The steppe is a wide treeless expanse which had a predominantly herbaceous vegetation at the time of agricultural colonization (17th-18th centuries). Because of the region's size, natural conditions vary. Annual precipitation ranges from 16" (400 mm) in the northwest to about 10" (250 mm) in the southeast, with the maximum occurring in the first half of summer. When it rains, the fall is in heavy downpours. The heat supply of the region tends to increase from north to south, but moisture is a problem (Figure 31).

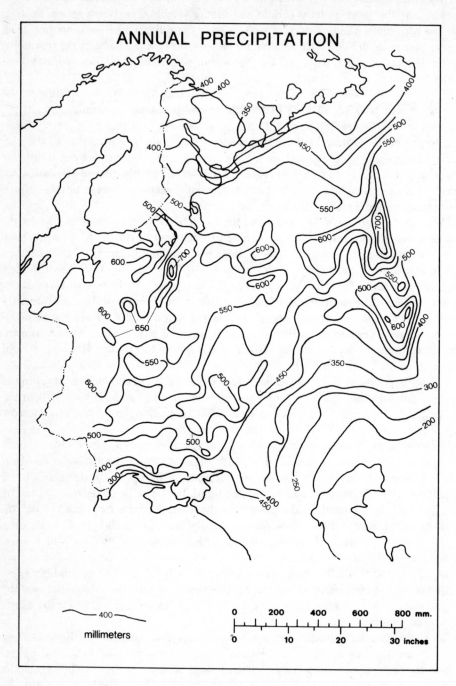

Fig. 28. Annual precipitation.

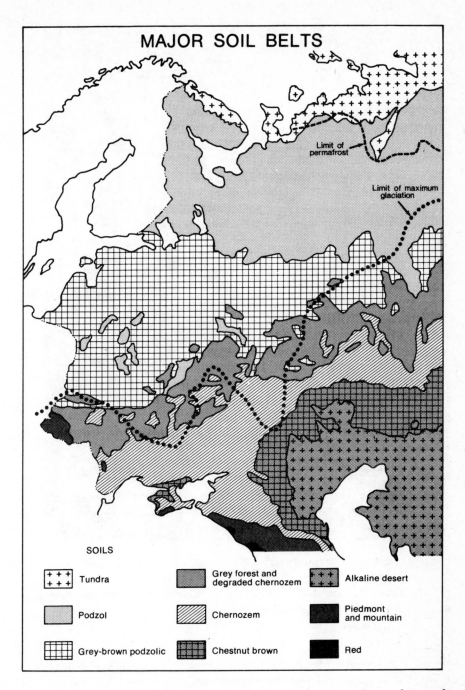

Fig. 29. Major soil belts of European Russia, showing southern limit of permafrost and southern extent of glaciation. Modified after a map compiled by the Institute of Soils, Academy of Sciences of the USSR.

Fig. 30. The forest at Yasnaya Polyana. The wooded estate of Leo Tolstoy, the famous Russian writer, at Yasnaya Polyana, south of Tulsa, was situated near the southern boundary of the deciduous forest. Its present stands of forest are suggestive of the original vegetation cover.

Drought is a common enough phenomenon, a condition which is intensified by the *sukhovey*, a hot dry wind that causes significant crop losses.[2] For the most part the soils are fertile; black and loamy where the grass sod was thick and deep shading into a chestnut brown where reduced precipitation permitted only a short grass prairie. The chernozem soils of the Ukraine are among the richest black soils in the world, having formed over a deep mantle of fine loess. Under repeated cultivation, the structure of

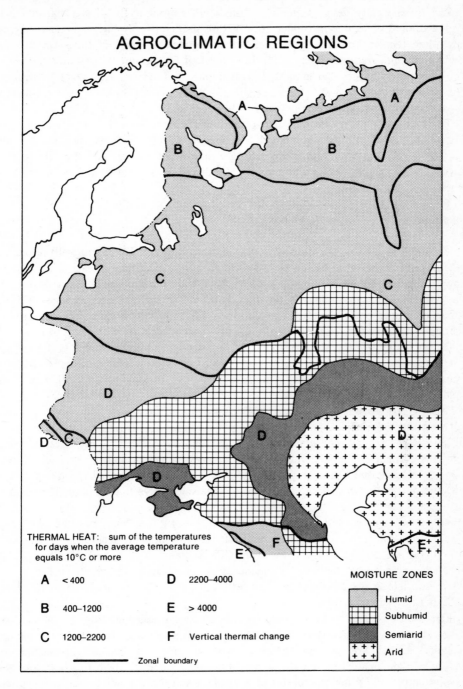

Fig. 31. Agroclimatic regions of European Russia. Modified after D. I. Shashko.

steppe soils tends to break down and, under the force of strong winds that sweep the treeless expanse, denudation and dust storms occur.

The semiarid and desert zones of southeastern European Russia are characterized by low annual precipitation (under 10" or 250 mm), relatively high summer temperatures, low relative humidity and, as elsewhere throughout much of European Russia, low winter temperatures. Precipitation is insufficient for farming. Irrigation is essential. The soils generally are high in salts, low in humus, and have a sparse vegetative cover. The presence of fresh water, however, has enabled native peoples to survive on the basis of a pastoral livestock economy.

The biomes or natural regions that constitute the framework for the study of agricultural resource utilization presented here include the mixed forest, wooded steppe, and steppe. Such a limitation seems arbitrary in view of the size and diversity of the Soviet Union, but the reader will understand that the need to be restrictive stems from practical considerations.

Implications for Traditional Resource Use

The traditional, i.e., the pre-Soviet, use of agricultural (and forest as well) resources in European Russia was colored by the socio-economic conditions of late tsarism. Serfdom, which had bound the peasantry to the land, had been abolished only in 1861. But, the economic and social life of the traditional village suffered little change. Still, as Russia embarked on the industrial revolution in the 1880s, there was some spillover into the agricultural sector. The rise of the factory system together with the growth in the urban population (in the Moscow region, St. Petersburg, and in the Donbas in the south), placed growing demands for foodstuffs on Russia's producers. However, Russia's peasant households had *also* continued to increase in number making modernization of their holdings a difficult task to entertain.[3]

The modern Russian state had its political origins in the forest (nonchernozem) belt between the Volga and Oka rivers some eight centuries ago. During the early centuries of Muscovite territorial consolidation, the population was confined to the forest. Merging with the original Finnic inhabitants, the Slavic peoples had cleared the land for cultivation. Both game and fish were plentiful. By the 16th century, however, the population pressure on the land had risen, all the more acute since harvests were poor. The poverty of the land together with the imposition of serfdom that bound the rural population to it, stimulated a movement of people southward. Despite the danger of attack from nomadic Turco-Tatars in the grasslands, the serfs fled first into the deciduous forests south of Moscow and down into the valley of the Oka. Subsequently, as the Turco-Tatar threat was reduced and then eliminated altogether, successive waves of migrants pushed southward until late in the 18th century they settled the Black Sea coast. Serfdom, however, quickly caught up with them.

Despite the general backwardness that characterized Russian farming as a whole up to 1900, the wooded steppe and steppe regions of European Russia came to be regarded as a "breadbasket." Not only did the latter satisfy the needs of the slowly expanding domestic market—mainly in the forest belt—but it also helped make Russia before the revolution of 1917 a major exporter of grain. Low soil fertility and a short growing season reduced the output of Russia's forest belt, but drought was the key problem of the grasslands. In the steppe some steps were taken to combat it on the larger private farms that existed, but for the bulk of the peasantry, the nature of the land holding system made virtually impossible the introduction or application of sound conservation measures, even if they were understood. Social and political unrest had been a feature of steppe history. Land pressure brought it again to the surface in the early 20th century and the plight of the peasantry made an essential contribution to the climate that undermined the tsarist regime and brought new elements to power.

EVOLUTION OF A TRADITION

Historical Roots

The destruction of a tradition. The revolution of 1917 that swept away many of the historic vestiges of feudal Russia, was one that contained implicit instructions to steer a new course and find a new framework for economic development. The program that was to bring about the socialization of the use and management of Russia's agricultural resource was not clearly outlined at first. Rather it emerged during the 1920s with a format that became more comprehensible in the 1930s. On the one hand, the new Soviet regime, as guardian of the people's resources, intended to break with past performance. On the other hand, it was pledged to modernization with industrialization as its immediate central concern. Remembering this commitment, one can understand why there was a determination to break with inefficient, small-scale peasant cultivation. The intensity of the commitment—industrialization at any cost—helps us comprehend, if not applaud, the flagrant disregard in practice, if not in scientific theory and law, many of the basic tenets of intelligent land utilization. The revolution in agriculture, i.e., the collectivization of farming, that began only in 1928–29 altered the rural landscape and the form of farm practice, but it failed—at least until the 1960s—to replace ill-advised traditional uses of land with those that were clearly superior. Increases in farm output occurred, of course, but the costs were devastating.

So, the Soviet regime drew little if anything from the past. Russia's scientists had accumulated a fund of knowledge about natural conditions, farming practices, and the like. But the distance between the center of learning and the village was and generally remained enormous. Russia's peasants, the bulk of the rural population before the revolution, were ignorant and destitute, but like peasant peoples everywhere they had a long-standing relationship with the land. When they could work it for themselves, they had a love as well. They lived and died by the land—it was their sustenance. What the Soviet revolution hoped to achieve, in the course of instituting its planned rural production process, has been the destruction of that traditional relationship. The regime, however, had little to offer in return.

Rural settlements and landholding structure before the revolution. The predominant form of rural settlement in pre-revolutionary Russia (as today) was the village. Through the *obshchina*, or commune, a village landholding organization, Russia's peasants had access to land. The *obshchina* (Figure 32) had been set up to handle and distribute to village inhabitants the lands that had been surrendered by the gentry and various other institutions at emancipation in 1861 (Table 20). The bulk of the peasantry thus

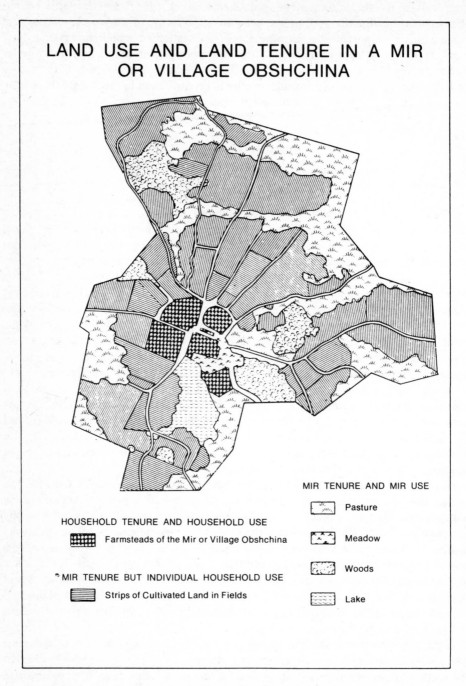

Fig. 32. Land use about the village of Pogost, Kostroma Province, northeast of Moscow. Adapted from N. V. Bochkov, et al., *Istoriya zemelnykh otnosheniy i zemleustroystva* (Moscow, 1956), p. 96.

Table 20. Ownership of Agricultural Lands in the 50
Provinces of European Russia, 1905

Category of land	Mill. dessiatines[a]	Mill. acres
Total land area	395.2	1,066.9
Agricultural area	280.0	755.9
Peasant communal lands[b]	138.8	374.7
Private lands, of which	101.7	274.6
Gentry estates	53.2	143.6
Large farms	35.3	95.4
Small farms	13.2	35.6
Institutional (state, church)	39.5	106.6

Notes:
[a] 1 dessiatine = 2.7 acres.
[b] Allotment lands.
Source: N. V. Bochkov *et al., Istoriya zemelnykh otnosheniy
i zemleustroystva* (Moscow, 1956), p. 70; I. V. Chernyshev,
Agrarnyy vopros v Rossii (1861-1917) (Kursk, 1927), pp. 15-
17, 22-23. The very real shortcomings in Russian statistics on
land holding are reflected in the way that various sources present
them. The lands included under the category *Institutional*
amounted ultimately to 154.7 des., but the larger figure represented lands other than agricultural. A recent useful study is
that by S. M. Dubrovskiy, *Selskoye khozyaystvo i krestyanstvo
Rossii v period imperializma* (Moscow, 1975), pp. 82-83.

participated in a communal land system, whereby they received in exchange for the pay-
ment of dues the use of village land. After the reforms of 1906 when all the financial
oblications of the village (and of the households) were abolished, and households were
encouraged to apply for individual, private land titles, communal land holding declined
somewhat. However, the pattern of land use and land management established in the
19th century, if not earlier, continued for the most part unchanged.

The gentry estates, on which a large segment of the peasantry had toiled as serfs
before emancipation in 1861, remained an important feature in the rural landscape,
but they were in decline both in numbers and in size. Between 1877 and 1905, the land
held by the gentry declined from approximately 73.1 to 53.2 million dessiatines (197.3
to 143.6 million acres). The gentry transferred increasing amounts of land to the village,
but the estates were being replaced in the rural scene by large commercial farms, whose
purpose was production for market or export. Rural Russia had, in addition, a number
of small private family farms.

Throughout rural Russia the size of the village settlement varied substantially. In the
mixed forest zone, the village was relatively small. At most it may have possessed some
300 inhabitants, their log houses or *izbis* strung out along a dirt road in linear fashion. In
the Baltic and western districts, villages seldom exceeded 100 persons and in some areas
where farming was especially poor they may have been substantially less.

In the grasslands, especially in the Ukraine, where rural densities were high (106.3
persons per square verst or 241.3 persons per square mile in Podolsk province), villages

Table 21. Size of Peasant Allotments, European Russia, 1905

Area		Households (%)	Land allotted (%)
Dessiatines[a]	Acres		
1.0–3.9	<10	15.7	3.5
4.0–7.9	11–21	34.6	19.0
8.0–19.9	22–53	39.2	41.8
>20	>54	10.5	38.7

Note:
[a]1 dessiatine = 2.7 acres
Source: P. I. Lyashchenko, *Istoriya narodnogo khozyaystva SSSR*, Vol. 2 (Moscow, 1952), p. 275.

were larger. Some even attained a size of several thousand inhabitants. Steppe villages were usually in river valleys to ensure a water supply.

Through the *obshchina* periodic repartition of peasant holdings or allotments took place. This was prompted by the growth in village population (from 1861–70 to 1891–1900, the rural population grew from 54.1 to 84.1 million). Where practiced—and it was not by any means a regular or universal phenomenon—repartition ensured that each village household had some land (other than the cottage garden) and at least a share of the better quality land. On the other hand, repartition tended to discourage land improvement, since the latter would only benefit a subsequent user. Repartition or not, the increase in the number of village households, despite the fact that the total amount of village land increased also, led to a decline in the average size of holding.[4] In 1905, 16% of the households had four dessiatines (10.8 acres) or less, amounting to 3.5% of the communal land. Almost 40% of the households had allotments ranging from 8.2 to 20 dessiatines (22 to 54 acres), totalling 42% of the communal land (Table 21). Some 7% of the households had no land at all. In the grasslands, peasant communal holdings were too small for efficient management. For both agronomic and economic reasons they should have been substantially larger. In the non-chernozem, holdings were larger, but because the soils were poor they could scarcely sustain peasant families.

Small size was one thing. Household lands were usually fractionalized. Some plots of land were scarcely large enough to turn a horse and plow around.[5] In 1905, from 60 to 80% of the allotments in the non-chernozem zone consisted of from 20 to 60 pieces of land (Table 22). Fragmentation was less in the grasslands, but the pattern was nevertheless a handicap. Some 80% of the households had allotments made up of ten or less pieces of land, but the latter were usually further from the village than in the mixed forest belt. Travel distance to the fields tended to be from three to seven miles, but at least 37% of the village families had to go seven miles or more to reach their fields.

The gentry estates by 1905 depended almost entirely on hired peasant labor. Three-fourths of the estates were at least 1,350 acres (500 dessiatines) in size. Their large size, however, did not necessarily imply the use of improved farming techniques. Like the peasant allotments, the gentry estates tended to adhere to traditional land use—the three-field system in the north and the long-term fallow system in the south.

Table 22. Fractionalization of Household Allotments, by Major Region, European Russia, 1905

Number of strips	Region (%)			
	North	Northwest	Center	South and southeast
Up to 5	–	1.7	.13.1	29.6
6 to 10	–	2.0	- 10.8	49.3
11 to 20	1.4	10.5	27.3	16.7
21 to 40	24.3	32.9	33.9	4.1
41 to 60	56.1	25.6	8.0	0.2
61 to 100	17.5	19.6	5.9	–
more than 100	0.7	7.7	1.0	0.1

Source: N. V. Bochkov *et al., Istoriya zemelnykh otnosheniy i zemleustroy-stva* (Moscow, 1956), p. 72.

With the decline of gentry economy, large commercial farms had become increasingly important.[6] From the latter part of the 19th century, such farms had employed more and more machinery, with output geared to market. Whatever technological or agronomic improvements were to find their way into Russia agriculture in the decades before the revolution, came largely through these large farms. In 1905 their average size was over 430 acres (160 dessiatines) but at least a fifth were over 1,350 acres (500 dessiatines) and some were considerably larger.

Because of the economic plight of the allotment peasants and the general backwardness of Russian farming, the tsarist regime was forced to accept a land reform program in 1906. Its architect was P. A. Stolypin, the prime minister. The Stolypin reforms were designed to accomplish two major goals: (a) the growth of private land tenure thus ultimately turning Russia's communal peasants into private land owners; and (b) the consolidation of the scattered peasant plots into compact farms. At the same time the burdensome payments that communal peasants had been forced to make for their land were abolished. Private property in farmland was now a possibility for millions of Russia's rural population. Between 1906 and 1916, it would appear that about half of the village population acquired private certificates, but only 10% of the communal holdings had been surveyed and consolidated into compact "farms."[7] It should not be assumed that all peasants wanted out of the commune. There is evidence to suggest that the *obshchina* had its supporters in the village, most likely among the lower or poorer peasants.

Traditional Use of the Land

In old Russia there were at least three different systems of land use. These were (1) slash-and-burn (*ognevoy*) or Swidden farming; (2) three-field (*trekhpolye*) rotation; and (3) long-term (*zalezhnaya* or *perelozhnaya*) fallowing (Figure 33). By the end of the 19th century a multiple cropping system had begun in the western districts of European Russia but it was not a widely practiced phenomenon.[8]

FARMING SYSTEMS IN TSARIST RUSSIA
CIRCA 1900

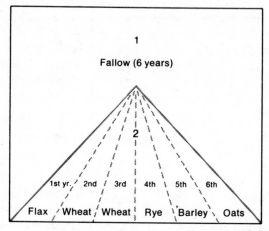

Two-field Rotation, with Zalezh (long-term) Fallow

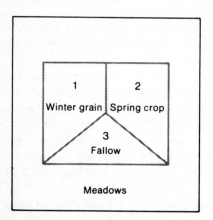

Three-field Rotation, with Meadowland

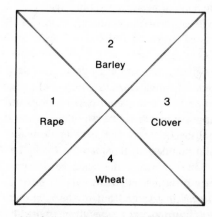

Norfolk or Multiple-field Rotation

Fig. 33. Farming systems in Tsarist Russia at the turn of the century. The *zalezh* system was widespread in the steppe, the three-field rotation in the forest belt and wooded steppe, but a multiple-cropping system had made its appearence in the western provinces of European Russia.

(1) Slash-and-burn was characteristic of the attack on forested land in early Muscovy. Population densities were low. Clearings were cropped for up to three years before being abandoned. As population grew, the periodic burning off of the forest was replaced by a two-field and subsequently a three-field rotation.

As long as densities remain low and land is plentiful, the slash-and-burn system is a useful one. Mineral nutrients stored in the vegetation are released into the soil upon being fired. Temperate and sub-boreal latitude forests, however, are generally slow growing. Should the population increase, forest soils (non-chernozem) can only be kept productive through extensive applications of lime and fertilizer. Neither of these were available in medieval Russia and peasant cultivators relied on the practice of fallowing.

(2) The three-field system, widely practiced in western Europe at an earlier time, came relatively late (through the principality of Lithuania) to Russia. By the 16th century the system was pretty much fastened on Russia's forest zone. Three-field rotation usually entailed one field in winter grain (rye—the best possible choice on acid soils), another in a spring crop (barley—for porridge (*kasha*), flax—for linen, and oats for feed for horses), and the third in fallow. Variations in crops varied from region to region, depending on local growing conditions.[9]

Once established, the three-field system tended to remain unchanged from generation to generation. The routine, reinforced by a growing population pressure on the land, afforded little opportunity for experimentation or innovation. It provided a subsistence. Its worst features were its excessive emphasis on grains and its unnecessary idling of a third of the land. Fallowing serves a good purpose where precipitation is irregular or light, because it permits the accumulation of moisture in the soil. In humid regions, however, moisture is not a requirement; fertilization is. Without a major role for livestock in the village economy, there was no way that the fertility of the soils could be enhanced. Where livestock played a role in the economy, as in the Baltic littoral, the three-field system had died out early in the 19th century. There livestock were fed grains and other crops, or were allowed to graze on improved pastures.

In the undulating Central Russian Upland to the south of Moscow, the extension of the three-field system that accompanied 17th century colonization contributed in time to serious soil erosion (Figure 34). Peasant holdings, often little more than strips, were apportioned in such a way as to ignore the contour. By the 19th century gulley formation had become a critical problem especially when, after 1861, the population increased, the allotments became increasingly fractionalized, and wooded areas were cut over.

Even though the Stolypin reforms encouraged the formation of compact private family farmsteads (*khutors* in the non-chernozem where the family lived on the land, *otrubs* in the grasslands where the family continued to live in the village). Three-field rotation remained a feature of Russian farming on *both* private and communal holdings until the 1920s.[10] It came to an end only with collectivization in the decade following 1928.

(3) The two-field system, found for the most part in the grasslands, entailed the cultivation of a piece of land over a period of years after which it was allowed to fallow or lie idle as cultivation was transferred to a second field.[11] The practice of allowing a field to lie idle over a period of years was designed to rebuild both soil structure and soil moisture. Where the practice was irregular and a field was idled for, say, 25 years, it was called *perelog*. However, in those districts—especially west of the Don River—where population

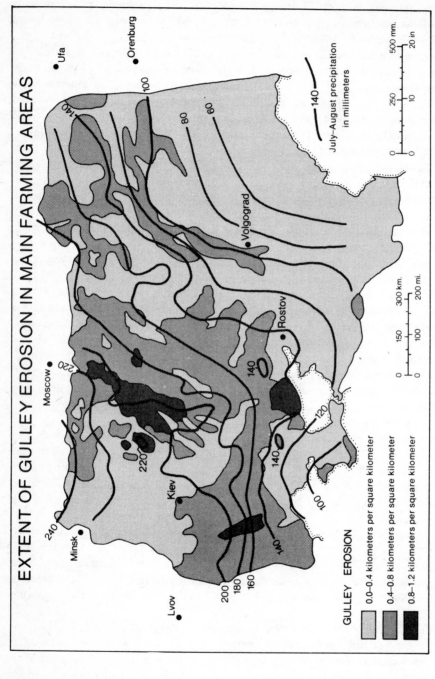

EXTENT OF GULLEY EROSION IN MAIN FARMING AREAS

GULLEY EROSION

0.0–0.4 kilometers per square kilometer

0.4–0.8 kilometers per square kilometer

0.8–1.2 kilometers per square kilometer

July–August precipitation in millimeters

Fig. 34. Extent of gully erosion in the wooded-steppe and steppe south of Moscow. The high incidence of gullying due south of Moscow occurred on the undulating Central Russian Upland. To the east of that lay the Oka-Don Depression, and to the east of the latter the Volga Heights.

densities grew and natural pastures were increasingly put to the plow, the system of idling or long-term fallowing became regularized (*zalezh*). A common practice was six years of cropping followed by an equal period of fallowing.

The principle of *zalezh* fallowing in subhumid regions is a good one, especially where fields are of significant size. In southern Russia, this principle could not be effectively employed where small peasant allotments prevailed. Moreover, the use of *zalezh* meant that a very large percentage of cropland was left unused for years. In the early decades of the 20th century at least a third of the land lay idle over long periods.[12] Its gradual reduction, however, did not necessarily mean a corresponding adoption of annual or short-term fallowing (*par*). Population pressure by the end of the 19th century, together with the growing demands of the export market, had simply led to an extension of cropping. Excessive cultivation severely depleted soil moisture and aggravated the drought problem. Dust storms became a regular feature, especially when the *sukhovey* blew. A useful system under certain conditions, zalezh farming was also a wasteful one when basic common sense could not be adhered to.

Tsarist Russia's agricultural economy was basically a grain economy; grains occupied almost 90% of the cropland. Consisting principally of rye (in the non-chernozem and wooded steppe) and wheat and barley (in the grasslands), grains were the basis of Russia's export trade. Despite low average yields per unit area, Russia led the world in the exports of grains and grain products.

Between 1900 and 1915, grain cultivation in the Russian Empire as a whole grew by almost 30 million acres (12.1 million ha.), due in large measure to the reduction of *zalezh* fallowing, natural pastures and wooded areas in European Russia, and the plowing of virgin lands in Siberia (Table 23). Peasant farms and allotments generally accounted for two-thirds of the total grain area and produced about half of Russia's output. Much of peasant output simply sustained the family. Estates and larger private farms, however, yielded three-fourths of the commercial grain and about 85% of the exports. The latter, too, were major producers of such market crops as sugar beets, sunflowers, and tobacco.

Table 23. Natural Pastures Plowed for More Intensive Use, 1901–15

Region	1901-10 area		1911-15 area	
	dessiatines[a]	acres[b]	dessiatines[a]	acres[b]
European Russia	17,622	47.6	17,626	47.7
Non-chernozem	(8,634)	(23.3)	(10,468)	(28.4)
Chernozem[c]	(8,988)	(24.3)	(7,158)	(19.3)
Asiatic Russia	8,443	22.8	10,751	29.0
Total empire	26,065	70.4	28,377	76.7

Notes:
[a]In millions; 1 dessiatine = 2.7 acres.
[b]In millions.
[c]Exclusive of southwestern districts.
Source: N. P. Oganovskiy, *Ocherki po ekonomicheskoy geografii*, 2nd ed. (Moscow, 1924), p. 189.

Table 24. Expansion in the Cultivation of Forage Grasses in European Russia, 1901–16

Region	1901		1912		1916	
	des.[a]	acres[b]	des.[a]	acres[b]	des.[a]	acres[b]
Non-chernozem	266	718	492	1,328	709	1,914
Chernozem	252	680	425	1,147	884	2,387

Notes:
[a]In tousands; 1 dessiatine = 2.7 acres.
[b]In thousands.
Source: N. P. Oganovskiy, *Ocherki po ekonomicheskoy geografii*, 2nd ed. (Moscow, 1924), p. 189.

Peasant farming for the most part operated at a low technical level. Inadequate use was made of manuring, especially in regions of acidic soils. Simple wooden implements were used to plow and cultivate the soil. Many peasant households (some 29% in 1905) were without workhorses. Even with population pressure, land use was far from intensive.

In Tsarist Russia livestock were raised mainly on meadows and pastures. Millions of acres of natural pastures were plowed for cropping between 1900 and 1914, but the loss was not offset by any significant increase in feed or forage crop production (Table 24). Little supplemental feed could be derived from cropland because (a) much of it was sown to grains for human consumption; and (b) where feed grains were produced, such as barley, large quantities were exported to western Europe. Except in the western districts of the Ukraine, grasses sown for feed for livestock were unimportant. Indeed, in 1911-15, legumes and grasses occupied no more than 2% of the cultivated area. Root crops for livestock were hardly planted at all. Whatever additional feed the peasants gave their livestock, especially during the long winters, consisted mainly of coarse by-products of field cropping.

Conservation Practices

The attitudes of Russia's peasant cultivators, despite the oppressive nature of historic social, economic and political institutions, had been significantly affected by the southern frontier. The frontier had never really been, as in the American experience, a frontier of freedom. But, the gradual elimination of the Turco-Tatar danger had afforded the peasants access to relatively abundant and fertile land.

The peasants had fled southward from settled Muscovy to escape the increasing burden of serfdom and the low productivity of the podzolic soils of the forest belt. Except for the burning off of the vegetation, the movement southward—into the wooded steppe and then into the steppe—did not necessarily alter traditional land practices. Farmland was worked extensively, as the three-field rotation was planted in the wooded steppe and the even more flexible *perelog* and *zalezh* system was evolved in the grassland. Until population pressure on the land became severe, there was little thought to or notion of conservation. When it became clear in the late 19th century, at least to scientists and government officials, that measures had to be taken to alter the use of the land, the bulk of the peasantry were trapped. Where holdings were small and highly fragmented, little improvement could be made. Nor was there any traditional wisdom that the peasants could fall back on. If possible, the peasantry had to survive, and from their lowly perspective that meant using the land as their fathers had done, and their fathers before them.

The clearing of the land in the forest belt had long before spelt the end of slash-and-burn cultivation. Although fields unsuited to farming had returned to forest and brush, the Swidden concept was impractical in a region dotted with villages and characterized by growing towns and city settlements. The only alternative was the development of animal husbandry and the improvement of the feed base. For the most part this was not possible for the bulk of the non-chernozem peasantry, though Baltic farmers made progress.

Geographically, the western provinces of Russia were the first to abandon the traditional and backward systems of farming. In western Europe when the three-field rotation declined, it was superseded generally by the adoption of *multiple cropping* (which in Great Britain was alled the "Norfolk system").[13] This revolution encouraged the raising of livestock. By putting half the land in grains rather than two-thirds, as was the rule under the three-field system *and* the rest in tubers, grasses, and other feed crops, *with little or no fallowing* (unnecessary in humid regions) it was possible to enhance the quality of livestock raising (Table 24). But, on peasant holdings (and even on small private farms) in Russia, the abandonment of three-field rotation did *not* result in a significant increase in animal fodder. Too much land continued to be left in fallow and livestock were turned loose on inferior pastures or onto fields after harvest.

"Good harvests are rare," one writer noted of northwestern Russia in 1875, "due to infertility or exhaustion of the soil; the fields are little manured because insufficient stock are kept; stock are few and weak due to the lack of fodder obtained from meadows and pasture, which far from satisfy all needs."[14]

Only in the Baltic area where the influence of West European farm practices was stronger, was there any improvement in livestock raising. Indeed, a healthy dairy economy formed the bases of Baltic agriculture in the two decades of independence between the world wars.

If peasant tradition tended to illuminate the backwardness of agricultural technique in rural Russia, commercial farming showed what could be achieved. Larger field size facilitated mechanization, more flexible cropping practices, the use of fertilizers, and the introduction of new strains of crops produced on tsarist experiment stations. During the period 1906-12, the value of agricultural equipment imported into Russia increased by more than three times, whereas imports of fertilizers (1900-12) rose from near 9,000 to more than 57,000 tons. In Russia the production of phosphates also improved.[15] Much of the new equipment and the fertilizers were destined for the commercial farms—the grain farms in southern Russia (and Siberia), the dairy farms in the Baltic region, and the expanding sugar beet farms in the central-western wooded steppe.

The principal media for the dissemination of information on farm management in tsarist Russia were the growing number of agricultural fairs and agricultural publications. Agricultural associations and societies were also formed. In addition to the social and political writers who expressed a deep concern for the plight of the peasantry, there were others—agronomists, geographers, soil scientists, and the like—who understood the nature of the rural problem and urged solutions. Specialists like P. A. Kostychev (1845-95),

A. A. Izmailsky (1851–1914), and V. V. Dokuchaev (1846–1903), among others, urged the regulation of small rivers to reduce flooding of farmland, the control of gulley erosion, the development of supplemental watering to improve dry pastures, and the use of artesian wells to combat drought. They also saw the value of and recommended the planting of trees to conserve soil moisture and to prevent steppe soil deflation. Such developments or recommendations had little meaning for the broad mass of the peasantry.

Effectiveness of Conservation Measures

Measures to combat drought had begun early in the 19th century, but such measures were largely confined to the estates of the gentry. Tree plantings or shelter belts were introduced in the Ukraine and, during the subsequent century, spread toward the droughty Volga basin. In 1898 a planimetric survey of sandy wastes was initiated by the government which undertook to plant grasses, especially along the lower Volga, to hold the sands. Mapping the extent of soil erosion began in 1900 when the first soils map of European Russia was published.[16] A soil conservation program was well established by 1913.[17]

In the forest belt where glaciation had left large tracts of poorly drained land, efforts were undertaken to make more profitable use of the agricultural potential. As early as 1874, work began on the drainage of the Pinsk marshes of Belorussia.[18] Additional reclamation, but on a smaller scale, occurred in the region northwest of Moscow.

EXISTING TRADITIONAL-RESOURCE USING SYSTEMS

The Emergence of a Scientific Concern

The emergence in Tsarist Russia of a scientific concern for resource utilization and management has persisted to the present. Perhaps no other government in modern times has instituted so much legislation relevant to resource use and the environment as has the Soviet. However, until the 1960s, much of the legislation—for a variety of reasons— was difficult to enforce. The regime, despite lip service to the principles of conservation was committed to a higher task, that of constructing a powerful industrial base. Moreover, since the Soviet Union encompasses about a sixth of the earth's surface, the notion of unlimited resources, a myth that understandably arose in decades past, survived the revolution to color much of official thinking.

In the realm of agriculture, the Soviet regime has, as far as can be determined, eliminated the patterns and systems of traditional farming in Russia. The seeds of that transformation lay in the revolution itself, although official pronouncements were never very clear as to what the future of Soviet agriculture was to be.

The initial step, upon seizure of power by the Bolsheviks in 1971, was the nationalization of all land and the abolition of private farming. The estates of the gentry and the large commercial farms were seized. Where they were not converted into state-directed or collective enterprises, they passed into the hands of the village.

The 1920s was a period of peasant farming—but there was a difference over preceding decades. The hugh majority of peasants farmed the land on a communal basis, and this, especially in the north-central agricultural regions of Russia, meant three-field rotation.[19] Even by 1927, at least 95% of the land in the Russian Republic was farmed under the communal system. Fully enclosed farms accounted for only a small fraction of the land, while socialist associations controlled even less. In any case, neither the socialist enterprises nor the enclosed farms represented much advance technically over the communal holdings of the village.

Newly established land codes in the early 1920s prohibited the purchase, sale, mortgage or inheritance of land. Some equalization of land among village communities occurred, while subdivision and fragmentation of holdings were restricted by law. On the other hand, the consolidation of holdings that began with the Stolypin reforms in 1906 did continue to a degree. The Soviet regime was opposed to the expansion of individualistic tendencies in farming, but there was ambivalence (Table 25). When general economic conditions worsened in the 1920s, the regime was inclined to favor agriculture and the peasantry. Instructions were issued to local authorities to the effect that peasants who possessed two horses should not be penalized (i.e., not treated as *kulaks* or capitalist farmers). The strategy seemed to be to support individual initiative among the class of middle peasants who were generally held, at least in the early 1920s, to be the foundation for a general reconstruction of farming and especially of animal husbandry. However, as soon as the economic situation improved, the main objective of Soviet agricultural policy was to fight "bourgeois" tendencies or *kulakism*. According to the saying: "The sheep's wool is growing once more, and the beast must be shorn."[20]

The revolution brought into existence socialist-type farming enterprises, but few

Table 25. Changing Size of Peasant Holdings, as Demonstrated in the Central Agricultural Region South of Moscow

Farms (dessiatines)[a]	Tula Goberniya (%)		The region as a whole (%)	
	1917	1919	1922	1926
Without crops	6.5	1.8	1.5	1.1
Up to 1.0	6.2	8.0	6.5	5.7
From 1.1–2.0	14.2	14.9	16.8	12.1
From 2.1–4.0	28.3	39.0	41.0	36.2
From 4.1–6.0	20.0	24.9	23.1	27.1
From 6.1–8.0	11.5	10.0	7.9	11.5
From 8.1–10.0	6.3	3.6	2.2	4.0
From 10.1–16.0	4.2	1.4	0.9	2.0
From 16.1	1.2	0.1	0.1	0.2

Note:
[a]1 dessiatine = 2.7 acres.
Sources: O zemle. Sbornik statey o proshlom i buduschem zemelnokhozyaystvennogo stroitelstva, Vol. 1 (Moscow, 1929), pp. 26–27; P. N. Sharova, *Kollektivizatsiya selskogo khozyaystva v tsentralno-chernozemnoy oblasti 1928-32 ff.* (Moscow, 1963), p. 51.

households opted to join. Except for the development of cooperative relationships among communities, the new socialist farms—*artels*, state farms, and communes—were in no position to make improvements on traditional practices. If anything, they may have been a step backwards. Such enterprises were often poorly equipped, had little financial support from the regime, and offered little return to the more self-reliant peasant.

The beginning of widespread collectivization of the village lands in 1928, however, began the process that was to transform the rural cultural landscape. All holdings were forcibly merged into large fields surrounding the villages. Peasants who resisted were sent into Siberian exile or executed. Collectivization succeeded, above all, in eliminating the better peasant cultivators from the agricultural scene. The poor, the less competent, the ideologues, inherited the land in the name of the people. Collectivization decreed that henceforth the market as a regulator in determining how the agricultural resource was to be used, was to be abolished. The state would determine what was to be produced and where it was to be produced. In place of the market mechanism, state planning through an intellectual device known as "regionalization" was advanced as the means whereby Russia's agriculture could be made and kept productive to satisfy the requirements of the state as a whole.

Laying the Foundation for Rationality

Collectivization revolutionized the Soviet countryside and by creating large collective (*artel*) and state farms, laid the foundations for universal mechanization and rationality, but the effects of the early years of the reorganization were nothing less than catastrophic. Planning and the application of scientific principles to farming could not proceed without substantial governmental investment. The latter was not forthcoming. Moreover, the regime had to deal with the question of a recalcitrant peasantry. There was no incentive to work on the farm.

The socialist form of farming had come into existence as early as 1918, but until 1928 such enterprises had never amounted to more than about one percent of the farm households of the Soviet Union. In 1929 the Communist Party under the firm grip of Joseph Stalin called for all-out collectivization of peasant holdings. Over the next year more than 10 million households were forced to give up their lands, livestock and equipment to the collectives. Resistance was met with Siberian exile or death. The *kulaks* or the more progressive peasantry were liquidated as a class—perhaps anyone who showed an unwillingness to cooperate. So disastrous were the immediate consequences that Stalin was forced to retreat. Stalin described the collectives as "voluntary associations" with the result that the peasants promptly abandoned them. However, those that withdrew got only a fraction of their former holdings back and none of their livestock; and tax burdens increased. Inability to survive outside the collective forced the recalcitrant peasants back in. By the mid-1930s there were nearly 86,000 collective farms in the USSR, containing nearly six million households, or 23.6% of all farm households. By 1937, more than 243,000 collective farms had replaced the holdings of 24 million peasant families.

The first state farms were set up in 1918 near Moscow on estates or portions of estates that escaped seizure by the peasants. By the end of 1921 there were over 4,000 such farms, the greatest concentration being around Moscow and in the grasslands. Average size was about 1,350 acres (500 hectares), although in the droughty Volga basin they reached 4,500 acres (1,400 hectares). By 1938 there were in all the USSR 3,961 state farms.

During the 1930s there was an attempt on the part of the regime to institute recommendations originating within the scientific community and compatible with party considerations. Among these was a program designed to promote, by regions, specialization in crop and livestock raising. After 1937, the regime shifted gears and the focus was directed towards regional self-sufficiency.[21]

The concern for regional specialization reflected the goal implicit in the shift from small-scale peasant cropping to large-scale mechanized farming.[22] Regions best suited for the production of specific crops were to be given over to that objective. However, the tempo with which the program was forced on the peasantry, already numbed by collectivization, intensified the agricultural problem. Not only were fertilizers unavailable but the necessary rotation systems had not been devised for the regions. The attempt to intensify led in some areas to almost total disaster. Lip service had been paid at official levels to the need for scientific farming, but the practice was an altogether different story.

The shortage of grain that materialized in the traditional breadbasket of southern Russia led Joseph Stalin to inaugurate a wheat program for the non-chernozem zone.[23] Under traditional three-field cultivation, winter rye had been the basic grain. Stalin sought now to expand the growing of wheat (mainly spring sown), not necessarily at the expense of rye, but through the plowing of little used and brush land. Wheat became, as a consequence, an important grain statistic by 1937, but contrary to the regime's expectations the increasing sowings came not so much through the use of waste land, but through the unfortunate plowing of pastures and meadow lands. The latter reduction worsened an already impoverished animal feed base. The area sown to rye and other crops also declined. On the other hand, wheat yields were low due to soil acidity; the quality of the grain was poor. Damp summers encouraged rust and Swedish fly infestations. The weakest component of the non-chernozem wheat program was that it failed to gain peasant interest or confidence. When in 1939 on the threshold of World War II, the regime gave the collective farms some choice as to the crops they might grow, they returned to those which they knew were adapted to non-chernozem soil and climatic conditions.

Improper land management had contributed to rural chaos. Specialization in crop and livestock production created special problems that could not have been resolved at the time without substantial investment in agriculture *and* transportation. At the same time the rapid pace of industrialization, together with a phenomenal rural-urban migration, had begun to alter the demand patterns for foodstuffs. Stalin had referred to this trend as early as 1934 in a speech to the 17th Party Congress:[24]

> We no longer have exclusively agrarian regions to supply grain, meat and vegetables to the industrial regions; nor have we exclusively industrial regions which can hope to obtain all the necessary produce from other regions...This means that the Ukraine, the North Caucasus, the Central Chernozem (Black Earth) Region, and other formerly agrarian districts can no longer supply the industrial centres with as much produce as they supplied in the past because now they have to feed their own towns and their own workers, whose number will be increasing. But from this it follows that every region will have to develop its own agricultural base, so as to have its own supply of vegetables, potatoes, butter and milk, and, to some extent, grain and meat if it does not want to get into difficulties.

What in effect this statement implied was that every major region of the Soviet Union, within some broad state guidelines, would have to take it upon itself to feed its own people. This theme was certainly a retreat from the more ambitious goal of regional specialization, announced in 1930.

Perhaps nowhere can this failure be better observed than in the operations of the farms in the districts near the major cities of European Russia. Commencing with the December Plenum of the Central Committee of the Party in 1929, the regime had persistently called for the establishment of suburban agricultural zones to provide the cities with fresh vegetables and potatoes. In 1931 a newly-organized State Fruit and Vegetable Trust outlined a number of measures that were to be undertaken to achieve the goal. In 1934 and again in 1939 resolutions called for the setting up of suburban agricultural bases. In the discussions pertaining to the Third Five-Year Plan (1938-42), it was noted that the major cities had to be fully assured vegetables, potatoes and, to a significant degree, meat and milk. The war followed.

After the war, the regime was nowhere nearer a solution than it had been before. Quotas were established in potatoes and vegetables and distributed among suburban collective farms, but allocations were such that each farm ended up with only small areas of each food item, precluding mechanization and proper crop rotations. Frequently, collective farms nearer the cities were granted smaller quotas than those at more distant locations, and frequently the quotas were set too low. Moreover, there was a good deal of cross-hauling of potatoes and vegetables between districts and thus between suburban areas. As late as 1955, a United Nations' publication noted that 70 to 80% of the fruit and vegetables, over 50% of the meat and 30% of the consumer purchases of dairy products (apart from the hotel and restaurant trade) were made in open or collective farm markets and supplied by the peasants from their private gardens and plots—outside the socialist sector![25]

In the years that followed, however, the regime made a firmer commitment. In 1956 the prices paid by the state to the farms for commodities were raised to stimulate production. Then, in 1958, there was a substantial shift of state farms in suburban districts entirely into vegetable and potato production. Subsequently, many collectives, having been merged and consolidated, were converted into state farms serving urban needs.

Soviet authors have complained about the "incorrect specialization on farms around cities;" but the development of suburban agriculture by decree saw a marked improvement only by the 1960s. Still the Soviet regime has not overcome the problem of seasonal production and winter shortages. Hot frames and hot houses, by lengthening the growing season, have done much to overcome the problem in the non-chernozem (Figure 35). The production of early vegetables and potatoes in southern steppe regions is handicapped by the sharp rise in summer air temperatures and the lack of adequate moisture, offset to some extent by the development of irrigation in the river valleys and especially in the North Caucasus.

In the 1930s, despite its support in theory of scientific farming, the regime embarked on programs that simply confused the peasantry, already reduced to apathy if not outright hostility, that set Soviet farming back decades. The expansion of the crop area from 1928 to 1937 through widespread plowing of little used or zalezh land, unimproved land, and pastures, which reduced livestock forage, necessitated—or so the party believed—the growing of grasses. What was intended here was the transfer of the production of hay

Fig. 35. Environmental modification in the forest zone. Since World War II, there has been a significant attempt to over-come the handicaps of a short growing season in the non-chernozem zone. In some regions hot frames have been constructed. Here near Vladimir, an industrial city northeast of Moscow, a large network of hot houses is visible from the highway.

from natural meadows and pastures to cultivated grasses, sown in rotation under a system known as *travopolye*.[26]

The *travopol* or grass-field system was advanced by the Soviet scientist, V. R. Williams, who claimed that the soil must first be improved structurally before it can be enriched chemically. He discouraged, therefore, the use of chemical fertilizers in favor of manure. Williams had undertaken his research in the wooded-steppe region south of Moscow. There the cultivation of grasses, including timothy and clover, was seen to be effective in enhancing soil fertility. The Soviet regime, however, undertook to apply the system indiscriminately to other regions of the country. In the acidic soils of the non-chernozem, the grass rotation failed. Clover, the most important element in the grass mixture, did not survive. The result was a mix of timothy and weeds; it neither provided adequate nourishment to livestock, nor did it do much for the soils.

In the grasslands of the Ukraine, the increase in grass rotation on collective farms led rather ill-advisedly to a reduction both of winter wheat and feed grain. The belief that spring grains should follow grasses in rotation resulted in some expansion of lower-yielding spring wheat at the expense of the winter variety. In an attempt to rectify the stiuation, more winter wheat was sown but at the expense of feed for cattle. Because there was a shortage of cattle feed, especially for the private herds of the farmers, the latter were forced to sell to the socialist sector. In any case, there was no substantial increase in the application of manure to fields.

The indiscriminate cultivation of grasses throughout the farm belt of European Russia finally came under attack in 1954.[27] By then, Khrushchev had found a new solution to the persistent feed problem and corn, by fiat, became "queen of the fields," especially in the Ukraine where the possibilities for grain production, because of warmth, were greater than elsewhere. Even so, grasses remained—perhaps in part through administrative or farm inertia—an important component in the rotation system. In 1962, however, grasses were downgraded as corn and pulses (and, for a short time, sugar beets) were heralded as the new and official basis of the Soviet livestock economy.

Farming by decree, especially with respect to the raising of socialist livestock (as distinct from the collective farmers' individual animals), failed to bring sustained improvement. The imbalance between the growth in the number of livestock and the country's ability to feed, was noted at the 19th party congress in 1952. To Nikita Khrushchev, corn seemed to provide an answer, and a corn program surfaced at about the same time the virgin and idle lands program got under way (1953-54). Corn was a new crop to most of Russia's farmers and in many districts, in the non-chernozem and the droughty steppe, a laughable exercise.

The virgin and idle lands program, which put millions more acres of existing *zalezh* and little used land into spring wheat, also had serious environmental consequences, even though the effort yielded more grain. The reduction of *zalezh* (principally in the steppe between the Volga basin and the Altay Mountains in Siberia) was *not* accompanied by an increase in short-term or summer fallowing. Indeed, under Khrushchev even the latter was reduced as state grain quotas required that more and more land be planted annually to wheat. Dust storms in the North Caucasus, the Volga basin, and east of the Urals, the loss of topsoil, and fluctuations in crop output, were frequent.

REGION IN TRANSITION

The overall stagnation that characterized Russian agriculture by the early 1960s contributed to the downfall of Khrushchev. Farming by central decree had led to the plowing of all readily available cropland, had failed to require the necessary preparatory work as scheme gave way to scheme, had led to further mismanagement of soils in droughtier parts of the steppe (due to overcropping), and had seemed incapable of any widespread qualitative improvement.

Yet, certain measures were taken to continue the battle against drought in the grasslands. One cannot be certain as to the degree of success achieved with the planting of shelter belts. Of the 7.4 million acres (3 million hectares) in such plantations up to 1956, only 2.5 million acres (one million hectares) survived (Figure 36). The usefulness of such belts depends on their height and depth, but where precipitation falls below 15 in. annually plantings fail to achieve desired size. The expanding irrigation network seems to have brought desired results. There had been little irrigation in steppe regions before 1928. By 1965, it is possible that some 3.7 million acres (1.5 million hectares) of cropland (notably grain) in southern European Russia were receiving supplemental supplies of water.

Gully erosion, despite efforts to hold the soil by tree or shrub plantings remained a problem. As Silvestrov observed in 1963: "Historically extensive erosion and deflation... reflected the faulty use of agricultural lands prior to the October Revolution, but such use has not been completely eliminated even today."[28] Part of the problem was due to the inadequate measures taken to combat gullying. In the non-chernozem, work

Fig. 36. Cattle grazing in harvested fields. In rural Russia, the raising of cattle has always been a difficult task. This is due in part to the climatic conditions; but in the non-chernozem zone pastures have been of low quality, whereas in the chernozem zone (shown here), pastures were plowed under for cropping. One practice has been to turn the cattle loose in the fields after harvest, with supplemental feeding of corn, other grains, and cultivated grasses. Note the shelter belt along the crest of the slope.

proceeded on the drainage of wet soils, but the use of such improved lands is impeded by their heaviness and the shortness of the growing season (Figure 37).

Before the revolution, the lands lying under and around the peasants' cottages were not subject to periodic redistribution as were the scattered holdings they obtained through the *obshchina*. These lands were worked as gardens by the peasants for their own table. During collectivization, the cottage gardens were not taken over by the collective but remained in the hands of the household.[29] In 1935 these small plots of land, to which every family was entitled, were officially described as separate from the collectivized land and confirmed in peasant usage. These "private plots" varied in size up to about an acre (2.471 hectares); in drier areas where cattle raising was more important they were often twice the size (Figure 38). The collective farmers were permitted to retain some livestock for their own use, usually a cow, a pig, a goat, chickens and geese. In the feeding of their animals, the collective farmers enjoyed *de facto* pasture rights to collective farm pastures.

Fig. 37. Vast stretches of the forest belt suffer from poor drainage. Here, northwest of Moscow, are fields through which drainage canals have been cut. Such drainage fields are often given over to livestock, since the soils remain too heavy for cropping.

Since the 1930s the private plots in the Soviet Union have amounted to between three and five percent of the total cropland of the country. Yet worked intensively, the plots have yielded nearly a third of the total agricultural product. By working his household plot with care, the farmer provides for his own family's needs and sells his surplus to the collective farm or to the populace in the neighboring town or city through the collective farm market. In terms of value, the bulk of the private sector's output consists of animal products, *but* for feed the farmer depends almost entirely on the socialist sector.[30] The Brezhnev regime has tended to favor the private sector in a way not countenanced by Khrushchev, but as the rural population declines the importance of the private plots will continue a decline already appparent in 1965. As the culture of the village changes, and the influence of the city grows it seems likely that farm households will increasingly abandon their dependence on the plot. The consolidation of collective farms, underway since 1950, together with the reconstruction of the rural village, will undoubtedly sweep away one of the last vestiges of traditional village life in Russia. Once achieved, the Soviet regime will have realized at last its goal of separating the workers on the land from the land itself.

On the whole the Brezhnev regime has fared better than its predecessor. A substantial increase in state investment since 1965 has brought about a generally higher level of farm performance. The era of physical expansion has ended, the adoption of improved systems

Fig. 38. Private plots or gardens in the village of Yasnaya Polyana, south of Tula. The soils are loamy and fertile, probably of a degraded chernozem type. The plots on the far side of the pond are suggestive of the widespread strip farming characteristic of this region before collectivization. The villagers were assured the use of these "back-yard" plots in the 1930s, but the rest of their holdings were consolidated into large fields.

of land management based on an understanding of regional natural conditions has been encouraged, and measures to combat drought in the steppe have been intensified while a new program to expand the production of green fodder in the non-chernozem zone has been adopted. Through more generous pricing policies, the regime has been able to stabilize farm income at higher levels, offering the farm population stronger incentives to work through guaranteed wage systems. Grain imports continue (averaging 19.7 million metric tons in 1972-73), but steps have been taken—the success of which it has been difficult to assess—to improve livestock feeding by creating interfarm production combines and feed lots.

CONCLUDING REGIONAL ASSESSMENT

The Bolshevik revolution put an end to the development of the private family farm and interrupted the advance toward modern land utilization practices on the larger market-oriented farms. Although there were variations in the pattern from region to region, the majority of Russia's peasants (up to 90% of the households) returned to or continued to participate in the village communal land-holding system. Holdings remained scattered in widely separated fields, with redistribution and some consolidation taking place.

During the 1920s the three-field system continued to be practiced throughout the central-northern regions of Russia, simply because innovation did not fit village tradition or arrangements. As late as 1928, some 5.5 million households, as Alec Nove, the British economist notes, still used the wooden plow (*sokha*), half the grain was reaped by sickle or scythe, and 40% was thrashed with flails.[31]

Between 1924 and 1928 the peasant enjoyed a degree of freedom of choice that encouraged him to consume more of his produce and market less. Their output, moreover, was paid for in fixed prices which became steadily smaller in relation to the prices the peasant had to pay for what he needed. These unfavorable terms of trade encouraged consumption which reduced marketings generally, but the better-off peasantry were in a position to use the situation to their advantage by striving for marketable surpluses. Even so, it would not be an exaggeration to say that Russian agricultural land use in the 1920s was decades behind that of western Europe.

Collectivization (with mechanization) was designed to pull from the earth the food-stuffs needed to feed the cities destined to emerge in the new industrial revolution. Certainly it transformed the face of the countryside. The better-off peasants, dubbed *kulaks*, were "liquidated," leaving Russia's new consolidated farm enterprises to be managed by the former farmhand. The Communist theoretician, Nikolai Bukharin, described the new rural land relationship as "military feudal exploitation of the peasantry."[32]

Collectivized farming never won the allegiance of the peasantry even though a half century has passed since it was widely instituted. This lack of confidence—indeed, outright hostility—was not simply peasant opposition to any attempted improvements in farm management. It was that the land was no longer theirs, nor did they have any voice as to how the land would be used. They worked by *diktat* and state decisions were arbitrary. They were aliens organized to work their historic holdings.

There is much of old Russian culture that has been lost by the revolutionary changes of the past 60 years. There is much that would have further enriched the lives of post-revolutionary generations had they been allowed to survive or tolerated. However, it is doubtful that there was anything in the use of Russia's resources—agricultural land or other—that merited preservation. The tender care that Russia's farm households have devoted to their intensively-worked backyard gardens suggests, nevertheless, that had Russian agriculture been permitted to evolve, land utilization would have righted itself (at least to a degree) in response to the growing urban market. Certainly, Soviet Russia might have been spared the many costly resource blunders perpetrated in the name of the people for the survival of the people from 1930 to about 1965. In any case the consequences of the attempt to sever traditional human relationships to the land may be a consideration that modern states will take to heart when they seek to promote goals that enslave an important segment of the population.

NOTES

[1] The question of agricultural resource management in pre-revolutionary Russia has never been fully explored. Some references to problems of conservation generally may be found in Philip R. Pryde,

Conservation in the Soviet Union (Cambridge: University Press, 1972). One of the first detailed Soviet studies of natural resources to appear is I. P. Gerasimov, D. L. Armand and K. M. Yefron, eds., *Natural Resources of the Soviet Union: Their Use and Renewal.* Translated from the Russian by Jacek I. Romanowski. English edition edited by W. A. Douglas Jackson (San Francisco: W. H. Freeman & Co., 1971).

[2]*Zasukhi v SSSR, ikh proizkhozhdeniye povtoriaemost i vlyaniye na urozhay* (Leningrad, 1958), pp. 10-70; V. V. Zvonkov, *Vodnaya i vetrovaya eroziya zemli* (Moscow, no date), p. 87 and map.

[3]There are several excellent accounts in English of the effect of emancipation on peasant cultivation. An understanding of the effect is difficult to grasp because the results varied significantly from province to province. See Geroid T. Robinson, *Rural Russia Under the Old Regime* (New York: Mac-Millan, 1961); A. Gerschenkron, "Agrarian Policies and Industrialization, Russia 1861-1917," in *The Cambridge Economic History of Europe*, Vol. VI, Part II (Cambridge: University Press, 1965), pp. 706-800; George Pavlovsky, *Agricultural Russia on the Eve of the Revolution* (London: George Routledge & Sons, Ltd., 1930); Peter I. Lyashchenko, *History of the National Economy of Russia to the 1917 Revolution* (N.Y.: MacMillan, 1949). See also Wayne S. Vucinich, ed., *The Peasant in Nineteenth Century Russia* (Stanford, Calif.: Stanford University Press, 1968). An excellent Soviet source is N. V. Bochkov et al., *Istoriya zemelnykh otnosheniy i zemleustroystva* (Moscow, 1956).

[4]N. I. Kozlov, *Zemleustroystvo (po zemelnomu kodeksu)* (Moscow-Petrograd, 1923), p. 7.

[5]M. Pershin, "Formy zemlepolzovaniya," in *O zemle. Sbornik statey o proshlom i budushchem zemel'no-khozyaystvennogo stroitelstva*, Vol. 1 (Moscow, 1921), p. 54.

[6]I. V. Chernyshev, *Agrarnyy vopros v Rossii (1861-1917)* (Kursk, 1927), pp. 22-23. Whereas in 1877 gentry estates embraced a total of 73.1 million dessiatines (197.4 million acres), by 1905 they had been reduced to 53.2 million dessiatines (143.6 million acres).

[7]Pershin, op. cit., note 5, pp. 69ff. According to informed opinion the minimum size required for a private consolidated farm in the wooded steppe and steppe regions was considerably above the actual average size. See Launcelot A. Owen, *The Russian Peasant Movement 1906-1917* (N.Y.: Russell & Russell, 1963), pp. 85-87.

Province	Requirement (acres)	Actual average (acres)
Wooded steppe		
Orel	40.5	19.0
Tula	40.5-135.0	17.0
Ryazan	27.0-135.0	18.0
Steppe		
Tambov	22.0-135.0	19.0
Voronezh	40.5-81.0	16.0
Samara	67.5-81.0	53.0
Yekaterinoslav	50.0	25.0
Chernigov	27.0-40.5	17.0
Non-chernozem		
Nizhegorod	35.0	20.0
Kazan	43.0-81.0	23.0

[8]V. E. Den, *Kurs ekonomicheskoy geografii*, 3rd ed. (Moscow-Leningrad, 1928), p. 123.

[9]The three-field system is believed to have spread into Russia through Lithuania. See R. A. French, "The Three-field System of Sixteenth-Century Lithuania," *Agricultural History Review*, Vol. 18, Part II (1970), pp. 106-128. An eye-witness account of the system in Russia in the late 19th century is afforded by Luigi Vellari, *Russia—Russia of Today* Vol. III (Boston and Tokyo: J. B. Millet Co., no date), p. 176: "The obsolete three-field system is still predominant throughout the greater part of agricultural Russia—winter wheat (or rye) is grown one year, other cereals in the second, and in the third the land lies fallow. In the steppes the land is cultivated for five years and left fallow for the next fifteen. In the northern forest region a tract is cleared of forest, cultivated for a few years, and then allowed to relapse into forest."

[10]Stephen P. Dunn and Ethel Dunn, *The Peasants of Central Russia* (N.Y.: Holt, Rinehart & Winston, 1967), afford some insight into the life of the Russian peasant from serf to collective worker.

[11] L. M. Saltsman and N. P. Makarov, eds., *Organizatsiya sotsialisticheskikh selsko-khozyaystvennykh predpriyatiy* (Moscow, 1963), p. 250.

[12] A. N. Chelintsev, *Russkoye sel'skoye khozyaystvo pered revolyutsiyey* (Moscow, 1928), p. 41.

[13] Folke Dovring, "The Transformation of European Agriculture," in *The Cambridge Economic History of Europe*, Vol. VI, Part II, pp. 636ff.

[14] Quoted in R. A. French, "The Reclamation of Swamp in Pre-revolutionary Russia," *Transactions and Papers*, The Institute of British Geographers, Publication No. 34, 1964, p. 176.

[15] P. I. Lyashchenko, *Istoriya narodnogo khozyaystva SSSR*, Vol. II (Moscow, 1952). pp. 91–92.

[16] A thoughtful study of soil erosion on the upland south of Moscow is found in Ihor Stebelsky, "Environmental Deterioration in the Central Russian Black Earth Region: The Case of Soil Erosion," *Canadian Geographer*, Vol. XVIII (1974), pp. 232–249. Soviet writers complain that between 1899 and 1917, attempts to control erosion affected only 26,900 acres (10,900 hectares), and work on flood control was in its infancy. See *Agrolesomelioratsiya* (Moscow, 1956), p. 7.

[17] Den, op. cit., note 8, pp. 81–84.

[18] French, op. cit., note 14, pp. 175–188.

[19] D. J. Male, *Russian Peasant Organization before Collectivization* (Cambridge: University Press, 1971).

[20] A. Yugoff, *Economic Trends in Soviet Russia* (London: George Allen & Unwin, Ltd., 1930), p. 137.

[21] W. A. Douglas Jackson, "The Problem of Soviet Agricultural Regionalization," *Slavic Review*, Vol. XX (1961), pp. 656–678. The Russian literature of the 1920s contains a number of references to agricultural regionalization and specialization. However, there seems to have been no attempt, at least before collectivization, to devise a comprehensive scheme of regions that might serve as anything other than an illustration of existing and pre-revolutionary patterns (based essentially on peasant farming). What most of the writers of the period realized, however, was that both the market and transportation were important in determining patterns of land use and ultimately land management. It is likely that the work of von Thunen had an influence on their thinking. See T. A. Studenskiy, *Problemy ekonomiki i geografii sel'skogo khozyaystva* (Moscow, 1927), pp. 16–19. Also B. Bruk, "O selskokhozyaystvennom rayone," *Vestnik sel'skogo khozyaystva*, Nos. 11–12 (1923), pp. 5–7. Additional reference may be found in Henri Chambre, *L'Amenagement du Territoire en U.R.S.S.* (Paris: Mouton & Co., 1959), p. 167.

[22] Ya. A. Yakovlev, *Kolkhoznoye dvizheniye i podem sel'skogo khozyaystva* (Moscow-Leningrad, 1930), pp. 33–34; P. Mesyatsev, "Sotsialisticheskaya rekonstruktsiya i razmeshcheniya selsko–khozyaystvennogo proizvodstva po vtoroy pyatiletke," *Planovoye khozyaystvo*, No. 1 (1932), pp. 102–103.

[23] W. A. Douglas Jackson, "The Russian Non-Chernozem Wheat Base," *Annals*, Association of American Geographers, Vol. 49 (1959), pp. 97–109.

[24] Jackson, "Soviet Agricultural Regionalization," note 21, p. 667.

[25] W. A. Douglas Jackson, "Comment," in Jerzy F. Karcz, ed., *Soviet and East European Agriculture* (Berkeley: University of California Press, 1967), pp. 100–102. A more recent study on this problem is Francis M. Leversedge and Robert C. Stuart, "Soviet Agricultural Restructure and Urban Markets," *Canadian Geographer*, Vol. XIX (1975), pp. 73–93.

[26] Ihor Stebelsky, "Soviet Agricultural Land Resource Management, Policies, and Future Food Supply," in W. A. Douglas Jackson, ed., *Soviet Resource Management and the Environment* (Columbus: American Association for the Advancement of Slavic Studies, 1978), p. 174. See also David Joravsky, "Ideology and Progress in Crop Rotation," in Karcz, op. cit., note 25, pp. 156–172.

[27] Naum Jasny, *Khrushchev's Crop Policy* (Glasgow: George Outram & Co., Ltd., 1963); Jeremy Anderson, "A Historical-Geographical Perspective on Khrushchev's Corn Program," in Karcz, op. cit., note 25, pp. 103–134.

[28] Stebelsky, op. cit., note 16, p. 243.

[29] Karl-Eugen Wadekin, *The Private Sector in Soviet Agriculture* (Berkeley: University of California Press, 1973).

[30] Keith Bush, *Soviet Agriculture: Ten Years Under New Management*, Radio Liberty Research Supplement, May 23, 1975, pp. 28–31.

[31] Alec Nove, "The Decision to Collectivize," unpublished manuscript, University of Glasgow, p. 2.

[32] William Henry Chamberlain, "The Ordeal of the Russian Peasantry," in Philip E. Mosely, ed., *The Soviet Union 1922-1962*. Published for the Council on Foreign Relations (New York-London: Frederick A. Praeger, 1963), pp. 124–125, 127.

Chapter 7

Europe

Warren A. Johnson

Traditional methods of resource management in Europe reached their most complete development in the Medieval Era which ended some 500 years ago. The Renaissance that followed marked the beginning of a long process of modernization that accelerated as the centuries passed, especially after the Industrial Revolution. Today, most traditional practices in Europe have been replaced by modern, energy-intensive techniques, although the European landscape still contains much to remind us of the traditional heritage. But because traditional practices have largely disappeared in Europe, this chapter has a somewhat different structure than the others in this book. The discussion of existing traditional resource using systems, which is to be found in the middle of other chapters, appears here as a part of the final section entitled Concluding Regional Assessment, that will also evaluate the possible usefulness of traditional methods if resource scarcities were to increase in the future.

THE RESOURCE BASE

Europe is well endowed with considerable natural and cultural diversities which constitute a great ecological advantage. Scandinavia in the North is much different from Spain and Italy on the Mediterranean. Moving from the East to West, the diversities become more apparent in examining the nature of Poland, Germany, France or England. Moreover, the European environment is remarkably favorable for human life. The European continent's endowment is well summarized by Shackleton in her regional geography text.[1]

[Europe] contains a greater proportion of land suited to agriculture than any other continent, and, unlike the others, had practically no desert. Its mineral wealth is considerable and varied, and is especially rich in coal and iron. Its mountain chains, though high, are not impassable barriers. Moreover, the continent is deeply penetrated by arms of the ocean such as the Baltic, Mediterranean, and Black Seas, so that in proportion to its area it has the longest sea-coast of any continent, and therefore the greatest opportunities for ocean transport, and most economical form of bulk conveyance. Although Europe on the north extends well within the Arctic Circle, the winters are remarkably warm for these high latitudes, especially in the northwest, so that settlement and cultivation have been carried nearer the Pole than anywhere else in the world. The great diversity of environment, especially west of the USSR, provided opportunities for the accumulation of different types of experience and for active exchange of goods and ideas.

The advantages of Europe's physical diversity cannot be over-emphasized. Perhaps the easiest way to illustrate this is to compare the biomes of Europe with areas of more extensive, single biomes, such as the Great Plains of North America, or the vast forests and steppes of Russia (Figure 39). When a single biome predominates, only a restricted range of resources and environmental opportunities exists for the people in the area. For example, the early settlers of the Great Plains had to cope with severe shortages of wood (for building, cooking and heating) and winter winds that swept across the wide open, lonely spaces. In contrast, let us consider the productive potential of a small, gentle valley of the kind commonly found in Europe. The river that flows through it can be used to power mills, to fish, or serve as an easy mode of transportation. Water meadows along its banks provide pasture for grazing animals while still offering resistance to erosion by flood. Farther from the water, the dryer bottom lands are usually well suited for the cultivation of grains. And as the land begins to rise toward the hillsides, there will be less danger from late spring frosts so that orchards and vineyards can be safely planted. The well-drained slopes are also likely sites for towns and villages, especially when there is a southern exposure to take full advantage of the low winter sun. Manure from the barns and waste from the houses goes onto the kitchen gardens that surround the village, and any nutrient laden run off drains toward the bottom lands. These areas are also suitable for roads and tracks since they remain usable even during the wettest seasons. Higher up the hillsides are woods for timber and firewood, and springs or small streams for gravity-fed water supplies. When patches of better soils are encountered on the hills, permanent pastures can be encouraged at the expense of woods to provide additional grazing for sheep and other animals. These diverse sources of sustenance were not available to the settler on the Great Plains or to the Russian peasant.

The ultimate in environmental diversity would be an island that rose gently from the sea to thousands of feet, providing every ecological niche, from tropical and maritime, through temperate, and on up to alpine with permanent snowfields to provide a steady source of water, so that every kind of food could be produced. This, of course, does not happen. But when we say that Europe benefited from its diversity, we suggest that in comparison with other areas, traditional societies in Europe were blessed with a relatively wide array of these ecological niches and thus able to provide themselves with much of the material basis necessary for a good life (without extensive transportation— always an expensive process in traditional societies). Part of the great attractiveness of today's Europe is due to the relative self-sufficiency of each region, and to the evolution of different styles of architecture, building materials, crops, foods, clothing styles, and crafts that this self-sufficiency encouraged.

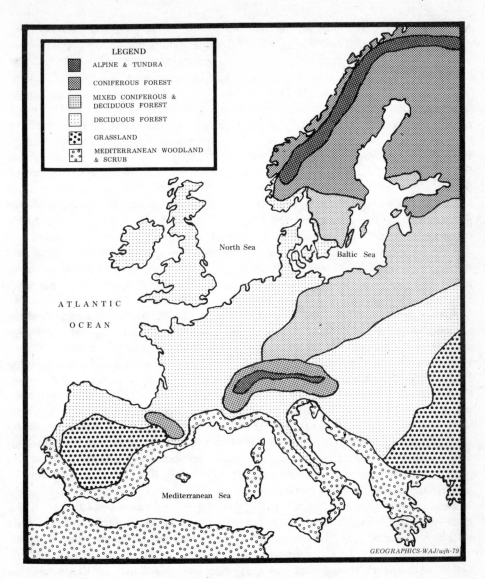

Fig. 39. The major biomes of Europe.

A diverse natural environment also provides many specialized ecological niches that can be used quite satisfactorily if trade is possible. The Swiss settled in the Alps, grazing their animals high on steep pastures in the summer and cutting and storing hay to turn into cheese and other products during the long winters (to be exchanged later for things they could not produce themselves); it was virtually the only way the high Alpine lands could be utilized. Fishing villages occupied protected harbors along rocky coasts, and seafood—usually salted—was carted to inland market places. Marshes were the source of reeds for thatched roofs and baskets, also used to raise geese and ducks, as well as for fishing. Ores were mined for the small amounts of metals used, stone was quarried, and clay roofing tiles were fired in kilns. In places where there was an overabundance of forests without soils suitable for farming or grazing, woodcutters turned wood into charcoal, to use in making iron or to transport to areas where wood was scarce.

But towards the periphery of Europe, conditions became more difficult and population densities were lower. A thin population on a landscape usually means that it was an unproductive area, poor and backward, compared to the heartland areas, the more hospitable ones that supported larger populations. Sweden provides a good example. Even today, the dominant impression received by the traveler to Sweden is one of vast forests, here and there broken by lakes and farmlands, but also broken in places by bare, glacial-smoothed rocks. The relatively recent departure of glaciers left the soils immature, often poorly drained, and less fertile than farther south. The northern latitude meant a short growing season. And while today the timber and iron ore are valuable exports, this trade was not possible in the past when transportation was limited and demand for industrial goods was modest. Considering how modern and advanced Sweden is today, it is surprising how relatively primitive and backward Sweden was in the rather recent past. Its main export, along with the rest of Scandinavia, were fierce barbarian invaders, the feared Norsemen that raided Europe and Russia.

East of the favored heartland of Western Europe, the winters become colder and the summers hotter as the maritime climate changes into the continental. In Poland, the large areas of lowland forest start to appear, becoming so intimidating farther east in Russia. Eastern Europe also suffered from being in the path of invasion into Europe from the east, and then later in the shatter belt between western and eastern parts of the continent. Farther toward the south and east are the Balkan countries, which are often mountainous, with hot summer winds, moderate rainfall, and frequent droughts.

Since the focus of this chapter will be on Europe north of the Mediterranean, where there is adequate rainfall during the summer growing season, more will be said in this section about the Mediterranean area. The unique and rather severe problems this region provided to the traditional resource manager led to a significantly different pattern of resource use than in the lands to the north.

Mediterranean Europe advanced earlier than the rest of Europe, not because it was more amenable to human habitation but because it was on the main transportation route by which civilization reached Europe, from the east by way of the Mediterranean Sea. The difficulties in southern Europe were not limited to the dry summers of the Mediterranean climate, even though that was a major problem. Mediterranean Europe also has a higher proportion of hilly and mountainous land, and a greater variability in rainfall; torrential rainfall is as apt to cause soil erosion as inadequate rainfall is to wither crops. The hills were usable mainly by nomadic herders, and the tendency was toward overgrazing, the damaging of the vegetative cover, and often irreversible environmental degradation. The few level coastal areas were frequently poorly drained, and in the warm southern latitudes, this meant that they were malarial and therefore virtually uninhabitable if not drained. At times this was accomplished and the coastal areas were made safe. But the drainage systems required constant maintenance, a task that became difficult and ultimately impossible when flood waters from the overgrazed mountains caused the drainage systems to fill with sediment or when civil authority broke down and maintenance stopped. It was not until modern times, when powerful machinery became available, that the coastal lowlands could be permanently reclaimed and turned into safe, productive areas for human settlements.

With the coastal lowlands malarial and the mountains suitable only for grazing, the intermediate hilly areas offered the main areas for permanent human habitation. Water resources were of critical importance, and intensive agriculture developed in the few areas where perennial springs were available (such as in the Po Valley below the Alps in Italy). But the large dams and canal systems that exist today were not possible.

In fact, the main form of water management was not irrigation works but terracing. A terrace should actually be understood as a dam designed to collect water and silt during the winter and spring rains, except that water is stored in the soils behind the terrace rather than in a reservoir behind a dam. Equally important, terraces served to increase soil depth on the hillsides, concentrating the soil behind the terraces. A crop of winter wheat or barley could be raised, and with better soils fruits and vegetables could be grown as well, often intercropped with grains. Crops such as olives, figs, and grapes that could withstand summer droughts were particularly favored.

Terraces not only required a great deal of work to build—much rock and dirt had to be handled to create an acre of usable land—but also were difficult to cultivate with draft animals. They were vulnerable to heavy rainfall, and had to have some type of protective device to let surplus water escape without their destruction (a "spillway" to follow the analogy with a dam). Continuous maintenance was essential. With limited land to produce fodder for animals, it is not surprising that the Mediterranean diet contained less meat and dairy products than in other parts of Europe, and that most animal protein came from sheep and goats that could graze on the rocky hills and mountains. Even the Mediterranean Sea itself was sparing in its offerings; the mountains plunge down into the water, leaving little continental shelf with which to support a rich sea life and almost no currents to bring nutrients towards the surface to support plant growth and thus fish life. The Roman Empire quickly came to provide its food needs by importing grains from North Africa rather than trying to produce them in Italy.

Yet with all the labor required to wrest a living from the Mediterranean environment, the long years of occupance has led to many sustainable and productive land-use methods. Moreover, Mediterranean countries are attractive to the eye as well, made more so by the bright summer weather that makes agriculture difficult. This is the measure of cultural evolution, that it can produce such satisfactory solutions to such difficult environmental challenges.

EVOLUTION OF A TRADITION

With such cultural and environmental diversity, it is rather impossible to speak of a single tradition in Europe. But while there are many different traditions, a common pattern is discernible in Western Europe north of the Mediterranean.

Historical Roots of the Tradition

The story begins with tribes of hunters and gatherers who, based on archeological evidence, had adopted elements of shifting agriculture by 6000 B.C. With polished stone tools they began making clearings in the vast primeval forests of northern Europe. Always, their life was closely associated with animals and hunting, and archeological remains also seem to mediate an attraction to violence and warfare unusual among primitive peoples.

Civilization (an urban-based society) came to Europe slowly and erratically from the east. The pace quickened with the expansion of Roman authority, which was backed up with disciplined and well-armed legions. The security of the Roman Empire north of the Alps, however, was no easy matter. When Rome weakened and collapsed centuries later, the barbarians (non-Romans) still retained their primitive vitality, reinforced by continued invasions of new peoples from the east. The veneer of civilization had not gone very deep in northern Europe; without the Roman authority, order broke down into the Dark Ages.

In the words of Kenneth Clark, European civilization was saved by "the skin of its teeth."[2] It fell to the church to preserve the saving remnants. During the Dark Ages that followed the fall of Rome, monks from the periphery of Europe, primarily Ireland, gradually worked their civilizing ways across Europe, converting the barbarians to Christianity. The Franks, Goths, Saxons, Angles, and Scandinavians were all turned into good Europeans, but it was a long, slow and often difficult task. To maintain Christian standards of conduct among proud, warlike people still emerging from primitive ways was no easy task. But slowly, the battle was won and a new order was achieved in the period known as the Medieval Era. This era opens around 700 A.D., but the process of change was not completed for several centuries, especially on the periphery of Europe. The Medieval Era reached its fullest development in the 12th and 13th centuries; it was the time when traditional methods of resource management in Europe had their fullest expression.

Traditional Resource Management in England

England is a convenient country to use as an example of a process that went on all over Europe, not only because it contains many of the elements found throughout northern Europe, but also due to the fact that Anglo-Saxon elements in our own heritage make it somewhat easier to understand; English terms such as "acre," "furlong," "landlord," "parish," or "enclosure," help us visualize these distant times.

The Stone Age farmers of Europe occupied lands that were easiest to till. In England these were the open limestone hills in the south known as downs. The more fertile lowland areas of England were avoided not only because of the tangled forests, but also because of heavy clay soils and frequent marshy areas. The earliest settlers seem to have been seafaring peoples who came from the direction of Spain. As time passed, other peoples came across the English Channel from northern Europe. The tin discovered in England, one of the components of bronze which was traded widely, seems to have been an early attraction. The Celtic people arrived sometime between 1000 and 500 B.C., but by this time the great stone circle at Stonehenge had already been built.

Julius Caesar made a foray into Britain in 55 B.C. The land, however, was not occupied by Roman legions until 43 A.D., after which Romans stayed for three and one half centuries. Even though this was a relatively long time, Roman influences in England actually constituted a relatively thin cultural overlay. After the legions were called back to defend Rome, the cities, the fine straight roads, and the administrative structure built by the Romans were largely abandoned. The Romano-British culture that was left behind after the legions departed was no match for the barbarian invaders from northern Germany. The Angles, Saxons, Jutes, and later the Danes, took over the land and pushed the Celtic peoples to the marginal lands on the west coast, to places with greater share of mountains, moors and heavy rains, such as Wales and Cornwall that even today remain Celtic. The Anglo-Saxon invaders shunned the cities whose refinements they despised as effete.

The bias of many historians in favor of Roman civilization has tended to mask the extraordinary achievement of barbarian groups in Europe. These people came as settlers rather than as colonialists (as the Romans) bent on exploiting the land. Anglo-Saxons came to England in communal groups, and one of their first tasks was to systematically lay out a pattern of settlements that was used extensively throughout northern Europe—still a model of planning and foresight. It survives today as the age old *parishes* that continue to be the basic political units of England (in German, the analogous unit is called the *mark*). Each unit was defined so as to provide a communal group of settlers with everything they needed: water, land suitable for cultivation, and "waste," or what is more correctly described as rough woodland. That this was an orderly process in England is demonstrated by the shape of the parishes. Some are roughly square while others are long and thin, all clearly laid out to provide the basic necessities of settlers. Size varies according to the productivity of the land; with good land, four square miles was common but in poorer areas, such as at higher elevations, the size became larger.[3]

The moldboard plow. Of great importance in utilizing the most fertile heavy clay soils of northern Europe, was a piece of new technology that slowly spread throughout Europe during the Dark Ages. It was the moldboard plow. This plow had a knife-like cutter (called a coulter), which was followed by the moldboard which turned over the soil cut loose by the coulter. The plow was able to work the heavy clay soils that the light Roman plow (also called the scratch plow because it merely scratched the surface) could not. The Roman plow was logical in the Mediterranean where the hot, dry summers caused minerals to be concentrated at the surface of soil by evaporation. But in northern Europe and England, rainfall carried the nutrients deeper into the soil, and the moldboard plow was necessary to bring them back toward the surface, as well as to aerate the soil.[4] White argues that the moldboard plow must have been developed by the Slavic people of Eastern Europe prior to the 6th century, since 26 of the technical terms that describe the plow are Slavic in origin.[5]

To pull the moldboard plow through heavy soils required a number of oxen, usually eight. While no single farmer could provide such a team, the Anglo-Saxon settlers with their communal organization were able to put a plow and team together. Each individual contributed at least one ox or the plow, and used the team in proportion to this contribution. A plowman who contributed an ox or the plow could plow with it for a day, and then turn it over to the next individual, until it reverted back to him by rotation.

If it were necessary to select one reason why the United States is described as an Anglo-Saxon country (rather than Romano-British) it could well be the moldboard plow (as well as the social organization of Anglo-Saxons that permitted them to use it effectively). Without this plow, it would not have been possible to utilize the best English soils, and England would have remained a marginally productive and marginally populated country. It would also have remained highly vulnerable to the inroads or more powerful groups from the Continent. Instead, England evolved into a strong country, with its "fields full of folk" as described in *Piers Plowman*, the great Anglo-Saxon epic. The tangled forests were slowly removed, and the country began to appear more the way we think of it today.

It is difficult to resist the temptation to ascribe more importance to the moldboard plow than it deserves. Still, the plow is capable of providing a thread that ties a number of elements together in the Medieval experience. If for no other reason than to encourage an understanding of evolution of a tradition, it is useful to follow this thread along.

The open field system of agriculture. A plow pulled by eight oxen is an awkward operation, especially slow in turning it around. The plowman must leave the plow, go to the front oxen and lead it around (or have a helper do it). This takes time and requires much space at the end of the field. Thus, fields were laid out in substantial lengths to reduce the necessary turning. What we now call an *acre* is a measure of land that could be plowed during the course of an average day. Its oddly defined shape—660 by 66 feet— reflects these long fields; 660 feet is a furlong, a "furrow long," or one eighth of one mile.

Excess rainfall, rather than drought, is England's major water problem, especially affecting the clay soils that drain so slowly. The Anglo-Saxon method of plowing led, perhaps inadvertently, to a drainage system that was of great help in draining wet soils. Comprising one of several critical advantages of this method of agriculture, the drainage system is quite interesting.

It is not possible for a farmer who uses a moldboard plow to plow in one direction, turn around, and plow back adjacent to the previous pass because the furrows would be turned in different directions. Each pass of the plow had to be in the same direction, so that the plowed furrow would be turned into the space made available by the previous pass. In order to do this is was necessary to make two initial cuts (Fig. 40A) and then throw each subsequent cut toward the initial ones from both sides (Fig. 40B). After a number of passes, a small ridge was left in the middle and two unfilled furrows on the sides. As this was repeated over the years, the advantageous ridge and furrow pattern was slowly formed (Fig. 40C). Thus, low places acted as drainage for the fields, and crops could be planted on the ridges without fear of being drowned by particularly heavy or continuous rainfall. The ridges and furrows tended to vary in width depending on the amount of clay in the soil (in poorly drained soils with high clay content, the furrows were closer together than on well drained lands). They also served to distinguish between the strips of land in common fields farmed by different individuals, and reduced the need for fencing. The large unfenced fields characterized the entire farming method which became known as the *open field system*. Today, the ridges and furrows can be clearly identified in many parts of England where grass replaced farming after the traditional system went out of use (modern plowing eliminates ridges and furrows). They are amazingly even and graceful, attesting to the skill of the Medieval plowman.

Strips worked by one farmer were scattered throughout the open fields as the ox team and plow were alternated between the contributing farmers. At one time, it was assumed that the reason for this was to facilitate each farmer's equal access to all lands in a field—to those with good soil and to those with the bad. This was interpreted as a reflection of the egalitarian nature of Anglo-Saxon society. However, recent scholarly work which disputes this contention,[6] emphasizes the more practical advantages of the open field system. By present standards, the system was not highly productive. It should be understood as a form of agriculture that is somewhere between slash and burn

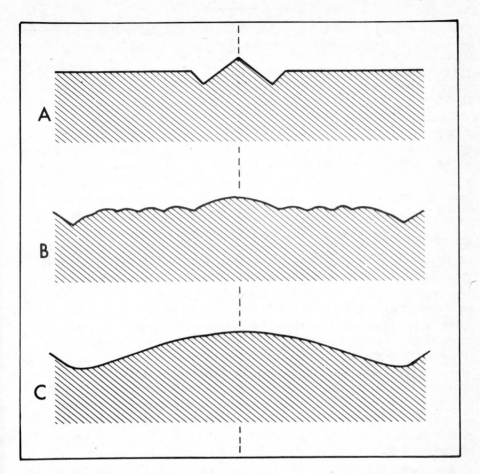

Fig. 40. Formation of the ridge and furrow pattern in Medieval fields. A. Initial passes of the plow leave the soil laid together in the middle of the plow strip. B. Subsequent passes of the plow continue to move the soil toward the middle of the strip, filling furrows left by previous passes, and leaving the last furrow unfilled on the sides of the plow strip. C. Pattern formed by continuous repetition of plowing in this manner.

and the highly intensive methods farmed for longer periods of time to support higher population densities. In the open field system, half of the fields were initially left fallow (unused) each year to let their fertility recover (the two-field system). Later on, as population increased, only one field in three was left fallow each year (the three-field system).

The role of fallowing, or leaving fields unused, in improving soil fertility merits considerable consideration. Since all manure was in any event normally put back on the fields, fallowing would have had no effect on this main form of fertilization. And while leaving land fallow would mean that no soil nutrients would be taken off with crops, there would still be no nutrients put back into the soil by the mere absence of cropping.

The modest benefits of fallowing suggest why agricultural productivity was low. It contributed to soil fertility in two principal ways:

(1) It replenished nitrogen through nitrogen fixing bacteria in the soil. Of the three essential plant nutrients—nitrogen, phospherous, and potassium—nitrogen is the most elusive. It can be leached away by water as well as lost to the atmosphere in the form of a gas. The only source of nitrogen to replace the loss is in the air, but it can only be fixed by bacterial action (or through application of energy with modern industrial technology). The most important nitrogen fixing bacteria are found on the roots of legumes, and peas and beans were grown very early in Europe.[7] But grains were the basic source of food—bread was indeed the staff of life—and grains do not fix nitrogen. Therefore, fallowing allowed time for the other nitrogen fixing bacteria that live in the soil to do their task, and to provide a modest amount of nitrogen for the subsequent year's crop.

(2) Weathering of parent material provided other nutrients. Although this is a slow process, the nutrients released in this manner—phospherous, potassium, and trace elements—are not so likely to be lost as easily as nitrogen. Although weathering is a continuous process, it did not produce enough nutrients to support annual cropping, even when supplemented by manuring. To say it differently, with land relatively abundant (clearing such land was the major cost item) it was easier to fallow it to provide the necessary nutrients than to perform the laborious process used in heavily populated countries such as China to maintain soil fertility under continuous cropping.

Compared to the large amount of nutrients added to soil through chemical fertilization in modern agriculture, the nutrients available in traditional European agriculture were very modest. We can now make organic gardening productive in our backyards only because we have huge surpluses of useable organic waste. Such was never the case in traditional societies as organic materials was very scarce and usually hoarded. Since most nutrients are in organic materials rather than free in the soil, an important function of domestic animals was to eat plant wastes and process nutrients from an organic into a mineral form which plants could utilize for their growth. This manuring function of animals has traditionally been highly valued, because it served to reduce the amount of nutrients tied up in vegetable matter and yield a form that plants could use. Animals would graze down the stubble left after harvesting; they were often "folded" or penned up at night so that manure could be collected and used where it was most needed.

The low agricultural yields notwithstanding, one fourth of the crop had to be reserved for next year's seed, because much of it tended to be lost to birds, insects, and animals; the seed drill, developed much later, placed it below the surface of the soil, thus greatly reducing such loss.

The grain crop was a matter of survival to the community. If one single food staple is to be relied upon for survival, grains which are known to provide a better balance of energy and nutrients than other foods are undoubtedly the best choice.[8] This is due to the fact that grain is the seed of a new plant. The embryo (germ) must be supplied with all nutrients that the young plant needs until it can get its leaves up into the sun and its roots down into the soil where it can find nutrients and thus provide for itself. The young plant's sustenance is also that of human beings. In addition to bread, the Europeans also used grains for beer. The harvest festival was a time of true thanksgiving if the crop was adequate for the year, whereas an insufficient crop produced a deep foreboding of the oncoming winter. Vegetables and fruits were consumed in much smaller amounts than today, and only during the time of the year when they ripened because preserving them was rarely possible. Nor was meat especially important, except in the fall when animals which could not be fed during the winter were slaughtered. Whatever feed was available had to be first reserved for the oxen, and only the balance of available hay and pasture could be used for other animals. Half-wild pigs that rooted in the forest provided most of the available meat. Pork could be preserved by salting and smoking, while the northerly climate reduced disease hazards which, in warmer climates, were responsible for the notion that pigs were unclean. Oxen were selected primarily for their value as draft animals, rather than as a source of beef or dairy products.

Medieval agriculture did not provide a high material standard of living, but it was a critical pioneering accomplishment. Thick woods had been penetrated, the heavy wet soils drained and put to use and in a manner that preserved the land's productivity. Through man's activities, in fact, the soil had been improved, primarily due to provision of drainage. Trade was minimal, and each village was largely self-sufficient. Conversion to Christianity smoothed many of the rough edges of a proud and sometimes violent people. The moot courts held in each village and attended by all villagers determined how the communal fields were to be operated. They levied fines on those who used the land improperly or did not adequately control their animals, and enforced the laws that evolved out of custom and usage. Out of this system of common laws evolved the English legal system—and thus our own.[9]

Feudalism is basicaly a military concept, and it came in various ways to different regions in Europe. Generally, it was a product of the Dark Ages, when people willingly put themselves under the control of a powerful military figure, giving up their freedom for safety from maurading bands. The Anglo-Saxons, protected by the English Channel, avoided this for a long time, only to be conquered by the Normans in 1066, and placed under their rigid feudal yoke.

William the Conqueror claimed all of England as a result of his victory over the English. He allotted large areas of it to his barons in return for their services in conquering it initially and defending it thereafter. The noblemen then granted each parish to a knight or a soldier who became the *lord* of the parish. The Anglo-Saxons who were forced into serfdom, were given the right to work the land in return for rendering services to the lord. At this level, such services were not military but economic. The serfs were to work the lord's land, called the *demesne* (pronounced similar to "domain"), and to provide other services. At the village level, feudalism is more correctly termed manorialism, since it is an economic concept more than a military one.

In order to control England effectively, the Normans were forced to incorporate many Anglo-Saxons institutions into their system, which to a degree softened the otherwise heavy impact of the Norman Conquest on the country. They brought much with them from the Continent in the form of new building techniques, new crops, as well as expanded communications with the rest of Europe. And while the serfs had obligations to the lord, the lord had obligations to his serfs as well, primarily to provide a stone-built church in the Norman style, a priest, and a mill to grind grain. Village courts (henceforth called manor courts) were continued and held in the great hall of the lord's house. After the rights of the lord were incorporated into the common law, he too, just as any commoner, was subject to the power of the manor court. Even the King, while considered to be under no man, was still under the law, as finally established by the Magna Carta in 1215. The traditional system of resource management continued to evolve, and the villages began to look more and more like they do today. With transportation still very limited, the village remained the center of the resource management system.

Medieval Village as an Effective Resource Management System

The houses of the medieval village were clustered together around the church, the market place, or some open gathering place where goods were exchanged. Somewhat away from the village was the manor house, substantially more impressive than the cottages in the village and surrounded by the lord's demesne. Around the village were the open fields, with their ridges and furrows marking off the various strips of land that were tilled by different farmers. Beyond the open fields was the waste, the rough woodlands. Crude tracks led away from the village in several directions, to adjacent villages, to market towns where craftsmen produced goods that the village could not, to the seat of the county government, or to holy places to visit on pilgrimage. Each element in the system played its essential role. But in addition to the agricultural, there were also several other elements of the resource management system.

The waste had several important functions. It was a source of wood for fuel and building materials, of rough grazing, and a reserve out of which additional fields could be cleared as population expanded.

Woods for timber production were managed quite differently than those for fuel. For building timbers, it was desirable to have large trees with straight trunks and limbs suitable for conversion into frames for a house (the familiar half timbered house in which a frame was filled in with other materials). Coppicing was generally used for fuel; deciduous trees were periodically cut back at the ground, and their stumps then allowed to sprout in many places. Sprouts grown into branches several inches in diameter could be easily cut into firewood. Cutting was easy because it was done right on the ground level, and sawing and splitting of larger members was not needed. With coppicing, wood could be harvested frequently, and regrowth was rapid because the roots were left in place and all growth could go into regeneration of branches. A similar technique was used along roads and tracks, except that firewood was harvested at a higher level, some 8 feet up, in order not to obstruct passage along the road. Called pollarding, it left attractive rows of trees along roads with large knots out of which the sprouts grew and developed.

In a carefully managed wood, both objectives of timber and firewood production could be combined in a system called coppice and standard. The large trees for timber production were allowed to grow straight up and lower branched removed in order to leave space for coppiced trees on the ground. This system reached its maximum development in the 16th and 17th centuries when the growing demand for timber for England's navy and also for charcoal to produce iron placed a heavy strain on the country's woodlands. But even earlier this system was advantageous because, in addition to making woodlands highly productive, it reduced the need for transportation to supply the wood to the village.

Pigs played an important role in the clearing of woods for new fields. They fed on acorns and beech mast, the seeds that otherwise would have led to new trees. And if young trees did appear, the pigs would eat them too, or trample them. When allowed to graze freely in the waste, they effectively eliminated the young trees. Thus, if mature trees were cut down and the stumps burned, the land would be virtually cleared. In early medieval times, there was generally a surplus of waste and pigs played an important role in clearing the land as well as providing the main source of meat.

When villages grew too large, it was common to establish so called "daughter villages" in the waste which were new villages started with assistance of the parent village. Areas with infertile soils were the last to be cleared and settled, and there were a number of areas with sandy soils that were considered impossibly "hungry" because rainfall rapidly leached out the nutrients. Similarly, areas of higher elevation and high rainfall were likely to be unused. In England, the Norman kings forbade settlement in a number of these areas, and established royal "forests" to preserve their favorite sport of hunting. In many cases they were not forests at all, but open moorlands. The word "forest" originally meant a hunting area, and not necessarily a place with trees.

Unlike the attitudes toward wilderness today, forests were considered dangerous, often valueless places. They were frequently the refuge of bandits, "witches" and others who had been ostracized, or cast outside the protection of the common law, i.e., outlaws. The legend of Robin Hood of Sherwood Forest probably has some source of reality, as a group of outlaws who resisted despotic Norman authority, aided the commoners and found refuge in the forests of Nottinghamshire.

Grazing. The available evidence suggests that winter forage was an important limiting factor in medieval times.[10] Young animals were usually slaughtered in the fall in order to leave the available forage to feed the oxen, which were so important to the agricultural system. Water meadows, or wet areas that produced a rich stand of grass, were considered very valuable because the grass could be cut and dried for winter hay to feed animals. Beyond that, the only feed was the stubble left after the fields were harvested, the volunteer on the fallow fields, the rough grazing in the waste, and whatever other common grazing land was available. The fields to be planted in the spring were plowed in the fall, to let winter frosts pulverize the lumps of clay to provide a better seed bed. It was not until the agricultural advances of the 18th century that supplies of winter feed, primarily root crops, became widely available. Until then oxen were bred to pull plows rather than for meat or milk production.[11] As recently as 1840, some farmers in England deemed oxen superior to horses as draft animals.

Sheep grew increasingly important in Medieval England because wool was one of the few commodities valuable enough per unit of weight to be exported. English wool was known to be the best in Europe, largely because the Atlantic Ocean moderated temperatures so that grass stayed green all year long, and sheep could survive without shelter. With income from the sale of wool, a farmer could purchase goods that could not be produced in the village, as well as the imported products that slowly began to appear in England during medieval times. Although trade generally remained quite modest, the profits generated from wool led to efforts to fit sheep into the grazing system wherever possible. Later on, this became a major source of conflict in England, but while the manor court remained effective, wool production was not allowed to interfere with the welfare of the village.

One of the major tasks of the manor court was to regulate all grazing on common lands. Various duties were assigned each year to enforce rules established by the manor court—the hayward to look after fences, the woodward to look after the use of the woods, and the shepherd, cowherd, and swineherd to enforce the limits of the number of animals each commoner was allowed to graze on the commons. Common laws, based on the precedents from the past, ruled here as they ruled so much of medieval life. The controls on the use of the commons are generally considered to have worked well at this time, and it was later, when the manorial system lost its effectiveness, that the controls broke down, and the "tragedy of the commons" occurred.[12]

Because of wool's trade value, most garments were not made of wool. Leather was widely used, and each village garden contained a section of flax, with its lovely blue flowers, to be converted into linen.

Building. The Medieval Era is frequently characterized as a time of relative stability when compared to other periods of Western civilization. The permanence of its buildings fully reflects this characterization. Europe's towns and villages are today still the sites of many houses, hundreds of years old, often with structures built of wood. Since the medieval way of life seemed unchangeable, houses were built to give service to many generations. In contrast to present times, when a house a few generations old begins to deteriorate, the achievements of traditional builders seem quite impressive.

Stone, used whenever available within reasonable distance, was the preferred building material because of its permanence. Bricks were fired, but it was not until after the Medieval Era that firing temperatures were high enough to produce brick that could stand by itself (during medieval times brick structures were supported by timber framing). Slate and tile were preferred for roofing; thatch and shingles would have to be replaced many times on a house that lasted several centuries. Defense works and bridges were rebuilt in stone to replace wood as soon as possible, and building in stone developed to a very high degree, an art that reached its zenith in the structure of medieval cathedrals.

Because of limited transportation and the weight of stone, it was only used for building if it could be quarried nearby. Most cottages were built with the half-timbered method. Oak, which was the preferred building wood for half-timbered houses, was generally allowed to cure for 30 years before use. It was found that if it were incorporated into a building sooner, it would not adequately resist rot (small timbers could, of course, be cured more rapidly). It mattered little if the timber cured into irregular shape; solidly mortised and pegged together, the timber structure was solid even if crooked. The frame was then filled with various materials, the most common being wattle and daub, or woven sticks and twigs plastered with mud and finished with a limestone wash. The poorest houses skipped the timber framing altogether, and these are the ones of which no trace can be found today.

Glass was rare and expensive until the 18th century. As a result, windows were small and covered with shutters which could be opened or closed, or with animal membranes which let in some light but not the view. Roofs were commonly of thatch, which had to be replaced every 10 to 20 years, depending on the type of thatch used. It did provide better insulation than slate, which compensated to a degree for its impermanence. Today's architects describe it as the perfect roof, covering the house like a warm blanket, which is probably why some retirees in the English countryside take off slate roofs and replace them with thatch; the poor man's roofing of the past is now a status symbol.

Waste generation and disposal. One advantage of a very modest material standard of living is that the amount of waste generated is very modest, and virtually all of it is useable in some way or another. The amount of nonbiodegradable materials to dispose of was almost infinitesimal. Iron was expensive enough to be salvaged for innumerable uses even after it was worn out in its original purpose. Glass was rare and costly, as was brass, virtually the only metal in use besides iron. Wood waste could be burned, and the ash went into the soil. Any stone waste was useful on the roads and tracks to help cope with the everpresent mud of rainy periods.

With organic waste, the first response was to feed it to animals, not only to reduce it to a form where the nutrients were more available for plant growth as manure, but also to get some benefit in terms of animal growth or work. That which could not be fed to animals was returned to the soil in one way or another, usually as mulch or compost. In fact, in the village world it was virtually impossible to do anything else with the waste; the land was where even indiscriminate disposal took place. But the nutrients tied up in organic waste were valuable, and in the absence of vast supplies of nutrients in chemical fertilizers, wastes were hoarded. In some countries even today the size of a farmer's manure pile is considered to be a measure of his wealth.[13] In towns and cities, waste disposal was more of a problem, and it was here that the custom of men walking on the street-side of women developed, in order to protect women from the slop that might be thrown out of upper story windows.

Many medieval villages in Europe had a fishpond situated on the low side of the village, the area toward which run-off from the village would flow. Since it was inevitable that some nutrients would escape collection, the fishponds were designed to catch and fix them in aquatic plants in the pond, which would then be eaten by fish, ducks or geese. The effect of the fishpond was to turn what would have been water pollution into high protein foods.

The completeness of the utilization of a slaughtered animal provides another illustration of why waste disposal was not a problem. Again, there was virtually no waste and almost everything was used. In addition to the familiar uses of meat, hide, and organs, there were many more. Headcheese was made by cooking the contents of the animal's head; blood sausage was made from its blood; the stomach was cooked as tripe, and smaller intestines were used as sausage skins; oxtails were used for soup; tallow (the hard fat), was used for candles, soap, cooking, and as a lubricant. Even the bones, the sinews, and the offal—the contents of the intestines and other wastes—were utilized in the soil for the nutrients.

When we speak of the "spaceship earth" concept, it is meant to suggest the total reutilization of everything we carry with us on this planet. The term suggests a highly sophisticated process, as a real spaceship would have to be to achieve this goal. However, the medieval village approached the same goal using a very different approach. Whether the spaceship ideal can be achieved with sophisticated technology remains to be seen, but at least we have the self-sufficient village to use as a model if the sophisticated model does not work out.

Effectiveness of Traditional Conservation Measures in Europe

In modern times stability is often considered to be a negative quality, as synonomous with stagnation, the absence of progress, and lack of opportunity. However, as we become more and more concerned with the consequences of uncontrolled growth and change, stability is gaining as a positive quality; no longer is change considered to be synonomous with progress. Even though freedom and opportunity are clearly desirable, they create problems as well: With resource management, the key would seem to find some way to control the excesses in our use of resources and the environment without moving toward excesses in government to control resource use.

Medieval Europe, in many respects, achieved this objective. Certainly the evidence remaining today from Europe's past suggests that a stable balance was created with the environment. Tourists still admire the attractive countryside, the villages, the market towns, and the soaring architecture of the cathedral cities. Any culture that is able to create such a satisfying cultural landscape, as well as one in which human activity was largely in ecological balance with the environment, must have something to say to us. When combined with the written documents of the era (such as Chaucer's *Canterbury Tales*) with its earthy, bawdy flavor but suffused with deep religious beliefs, one gets a different impression of the Medieval Era than many history books tend to give.

Conservation as a reflection of its cultural milieu. The Medieval Era has been described as an interruption in the characteristic qualities of Western civilization, of creativity on the one hand, and a tendency toward violence on the other. This volatile quality of Western civilization was interrupted by the disintegration of the Dark Ages, which gave the church an opportunity to become a strong institutional force, strong enough to restrain the equally strong appetites of Europeans, at least until broken by the Renaissance. The church had a key role in the stability of the Medieval Era, a role that included the use of resources.

Medieval society was static for the most part; people were born to a station in which they were expected to stay. The church reinforced this static quality. The powerful had obligations to the common people, while the poor were expected to accept their place in the scheme of things. With opportunities for advancement so limited, the pressure to strive and achieve was also limited. The values honored in a static society are those that support traditional obligations and accept the inherited rights of others.

In the towns there was a greater degree of freedom than in the countryside, but even in the towns restraints were everywhere. Craft guilds existed to make sure that all craftsmen used proper workmanship and materials, to control prices, and to restrict entry of new craftsmen into the trade. The church required that a "just price" be established for all goods, a price that provided a fair income to the craftsman but no unearned, or speculative, profit. Traders and merchants were always regarded with a great deal of suspicion; they were allowed to receive a fair compensation for the work they did, such as transporting goods from one place to another, but no more. Since this was difficult to enforce, the church reinforced it through religious sanctions, by emphasizing the Biblical prohibition against wealth for selfish purposes. Wealth was acceptable if it was used for the benefit of others, but hell was the reward for greed and avarice, and it was necessary to picture it very graphically in order to encourage acceptable behavior. Usury, the loaning of money at interest, was forbidden to Christians since it produced income for the lender without his doing any productive work for it. This at least left an economic niche open for the Jews, but one that earned them enmity.

The ideals established by medieval Christianity were designed to turn people's thoughts from material goods to spiritual matters. To exploit the environment, as well as other people, was discouraged and wealth was to be used for the glory of God. Money and lands were given to establish monasteries, to build cathederals or village churches, and to outfit them with silver and gold vessels for the sacrament, stained-glassed windows from France, and fine vestments. With its resources, the church also provided what we would call today the welfare functions, of caring for the needy, the sick, the orphaned, and the dying. The hierarchy of values is perhaps best expressed in the cultural landscape by the soaring churches of the time, dwarfing the modest shops and houses that clustered around them.

There were coercive elements in medieval Catholicism, of course, but the positive elements were the ones that held society together, the ones that invested the lives of simple, unlettered people with beauty and significance. The great festivals marked the passage of the year: Christmas on the darkest day of the year; Easter at spring, the time of rebirth; at Rogantide when the fields were blessed by the priest; and at Lammas, when the first loaf of the harvest was placed on the altar. There were some 30 to 40 holy days (holidays) per year which were occasions for feasts or fasts.[14] Meaning and individual satisfaction came from other things rather than high levels of material consumption.

A static society was easier to sustain at a time when trade was so limited. Without crushed rock or asphalt to surface roads, ruts were cut into the dirt, especially when the roads were wet, and hardened into bone-rattling bumps when dry. Goods were carried on carts pulled by oxen, and money was regularly debased by kings reducing its gold or silver content to make it go farther. All of this was a major factor in discouraging resource exploitation since it was not possible to move bulky goods such as timber or grains to distant markets and still make a profit. The manor lord, while he could accumulate grains and other goods that could be produced in the parish, found it difficult to exchange them for the expensive goods that were beginning to reach Europe from the Orient. With trade so limited, there was less incentive for the greedy exploitation of resources since it was difficult to benefit from it. One of the reasons why there was so many festivals and feast days during this time was that it was often the only way that surplus grains held by the manor lord or the church could be disposed of.

In such a stable situation, risks were minimized to the individuals involved. Traditional ways of using land and resources had stood the test of time and were fixed in common law. To stay with them meant that people could at the least be assured of survival, even if it was at a modest level. There was little danger that some new, untried activity would undermine the communities sustenance and interfere with known and familiar ways of life.

But as time passed, this became less and less of an advantage. By the 14th century pressures were beginning to emerge that would, over a long period of time, lead to the passage of the medieval village economy.

MEDIEVAL EUROPE IN TRANSITION

For a system as firmly established as that of medieval Europe, change is very difficult. The forces of change must exert a strong, growing pressure. In Europe, it came from a gradual change in the underlying relationship between man and the land. Some came from population growth, some from technological advance and some from explorations to the ends of the earth, but all fundamentally affected the nature of European society.

By today's standards, European population was low in the 14th century. Four million people lived in England and Wales, and even though this was only 8 percent of the present population, it could still be considered close to being overpopulated given the simple technology in use at the time.[15] It has been suggested that the Black Death, in which the population of Europe was reduced by one third, was an ecological adjustment to over-population in the 14th century.

Whether true or not, the Black Death weakened the manorial system. Labor became scarce, and lords relaxed their requirements in order to attract labor. Many villagers left their manors to take advantage of more attractive opportunities elsewhere. Since the plague had hit the towns and cities the hardest, many urban opportunities had been opened up. The rental of land for cash appeared as an alternative to the provision of services to the lord. In effect, the plague loosened the ties that held the feudal system together.

But the economic alternatives were still small as long as trade was so limited. The main factor that changed this way of life was the Age of Discovery.

Initially, it was the more advanced Mediterranean countries, especially those that were also well situated on the Atlantic (Spain and Portugal) that capitalized on their location and made major discoveries and conquests. But, during Elizabethan times in the 16th century, England also began to take advantage of its location on the Atlantic, initially to prey on gold-laden Spanish galleons coming from the New World, and then, using the profits of this piracy, to build a powerful maritime fleet.

The British Empire was born with the defeat of the Spanish Armada in 1588. Rather suddenly, there were many economic opportunities for Englishmen, as seamen, soldiers, traders, and suppliers of the foreign operations. Demand for shipbuilders and ironworkers expanded, skills that would later be used for the Industrial Revolution. With the Age of Discovery, the center of activity in England began to shift from agriculture to maritime and commercial activities. Great wealth was created, and the new rich quickly emulated the old rich (the landed aristocracy) by acquiring land in the country and building lavish estates. In many cases, the Crown awarded large estates to individuals as a reward for services in establishing the British Empire, following the precedent established by William the Conqueror five hundred years before.

Since Anglo-Saxon times England has always employed the tradition of primogeniture, the passing of land to the eldest son. This discouraged the fragmentation of land into small holdings that occurred elsewhere in Europe, while at the same time encouraging younger sons to clear more land or start new daughter villages in their forest. In Eliza-bethen times, primogeniture had the very useful function of providing manpower for England's worldwide adventures. As so many tales began, a younger son would "set out to make his fortune," and if their families were wealthy enough to outfit them with a ship to get started as a privateer, it indeed could lead to fame and wealth.

The landed class was, to a degree, bypassed by many of these commercial opportuni-ties. The landed artistocracy looked down on commercial ventures and the commercial classes; no matter how wealthy this new class became, they could never become "gentle-men" or "ladies." But with all the fine things that were reaching Europe—the silks, spices, wines, tobacco, sugar, cotton—the landed classes began to look around for ways to make more income off their lands. Wool was the logical choice, but everywhere the landlords looked, they ran into commoners with their rights to the land; the villagers were only interested in continuing a way of life, and they were suspicious of the lord's motives, correctly so, as it turned out.

The enclosure of the common lands into private property was the step that marked the transition from the feudal to the modern, from a contract economy based on inherited rights, obligations, and common law to a market economy based on private land, wages, and free trade. Through enclosure the common lands were divided into separate parcels of private land and distributed to those who had rights to use it. It is generally considered to have been a necessary step to increase agricultural productivity, since under the communal open field system of agriculture the conservative commoners, fearful of losing their rights, had prevented the adoption of new techniques, new crops, and the improved breeding of animals. But the process of change itself caused tremendous suffering among those without rights to land, and civil war threatened, off and on, especially during the French Revolution.

In England, the King and Parliament controlled the enclosure process, but the lords generally had a great advantage. A commoner seeking to obtain his small piece of land, had to pay his share of the costs of enclosure, which included legal fees plus the cost of dividing the land, building walls or hedges, and sometimes constructing drainage works. Without the necessary capital, many were forced to sell to the lord. Those without common rights received nothing and were turned away from the only places most of them had ever known. Whole villages were razed to the ground. Hundreds of lost villages have been identified by aerial photography.[16]

Thus began the pauperism, the begging, and the stealing by the landless who could not find laboring jobs. It was said that the land was raising sheep instead of men. The majority of enclosures were between 1760 and 1820, but the process began much earlier and continued sporadically for centuries, fluctuating with Parliamentary favor and the price of wool. The people who were turned off the land between 1760 and 1820 provided a ready source of labor for the nascent industrial revolution, which transformed England from a rural country into an industrial nation (a process vividly described by Karl Polanyi in *The Great Transformation*). But this transformation was not completed without a great deal of unrest and peasant revolt, including that of the Levellers, who cut down the hedges and filled the ditches which marked the boundaries of the new fields, and the Diggers who invaded enclosed land and planted vegetables.

The small fields that travellers see today in the English countryside are largely the product of the enclosure movement. Bounded by hedges and with frequent hedgerow trees and wildflowers, these attractive sites provide good habitat for wildlife. Today, only four percent of the land is subject to common rights, and much of it has management problems due to lack of control. Recreation, rather than agriculture, is the major use of the remaining common lands.

With the enclosure movement, England experienced the Agricultural Revolution that had begun on the Continent, especially in the Netherlands, and which was based on the same scientific and technological advances as the Industrial Revolution. Both revolutions led to tremendous changes in man-land relationships, not only milltowns, mines, and railroads, but to the depopulation of the countryside as well.

A number of changes increased agricultural productivity significantly, particularly in animal husbandry. Clovers were introduced which fixed nitrogen and made fallowing unnecessary. Root crops, such as turnips and rutabaga, produced animal fodder that could be stored through the winter, making the traditional fall slaughter of so many animals unnecessary. Enclosure permitted controlled breeding of animals, improving immensely the quality of sheep, cattle, hogs, and horses. Improved grasses for permanent pasture could support good numbers of grazing animals all year long. But most importantly, after the Industrial Revolution was underway, it became possible to import cheap grains from North America.

All these activities meant that fewer farm workers were needed compared to earlier times, and wages dropped. And another root crop—the potato—introduced from the New World, was found to be capable of keeping agricultural labor alive with less land. The rural poverty of the time led to greater and greater dependence on potatoes. In Ireland, a failure of the potatoe crop in the 1840s reduced Ireland's population by one half, partly through starvation and partly through emigration. Bread, the traditional staff of life, was less available to the growing class of rural poor as more land was given over to sheep and other cash crops.

For a while, the rural economy received some support from the landed aristocracy who until 1870 effectively held political power in England. The aristocracy used some labor in their stately homes and stables as well as in their fields. For the most part, the aristocrats were vigorous and well educated people who did not disdain public service like the French aristocracy. The naturalistic gardens built in England after 1720 are greatly admired as artistic creations, but it is difficult to go as far as Ian McHarg does, in *Design with Nature*, in ascribing great ecological merit to them, given the large number of dispossessed agricultural laborers on which they were based. And the incomes of the landed aristocracy were also based on agriculture, which made them vulnerable to falling agricultural prices.

As the Industrial Revolution expanded, power slowly but surely gravitated toward the urban commercial classes. "Free trade" was the cry of the capitalists against the privileges of the aristocracy, and the key battle was over the Corn Laws that restricted the importation of inexpensive grains from America and elsewhere. Finally in 1846, the Corn Laws were repealed, throwing rural England into a depression that would last until World War II. The economic base of the small farmer as well as of the landed aristocrat was destroyed by the imports of cheap grains. Many farms were abandoned, and much of the remaining arable land was turned to grass. Farm buildings and improvements deteriorated, and stately homes were turned into schools, hospitals, or retirement homes, while many were abandoned and are today in ruins. Industry became more profitable than agriculture. Britain fell from a position of being roughly self-sufficient in food production in 1860 to the point in the 1930s when only 35% of its food was produced at home, a situation that produced great hardships during World War II.

This transition from the traditional to the modern had taken centuries to develop. As with any change of such magnitude, it was a painful process, as villagers were first impoverished and finally left with few alternatives to turn to other than long hours in the factories of industrial cities. In a sense, the United States was fortunate in that it was not necessary here to break down an age-old traditional system in order to develop as we have. Without such obstacles, the U.S. came to be the clearest reflection of the modern era. Yet at the same time we do not have (while Europe does) the benefit of a long heritage of traditional methods of resource management to help us today. A number of these, as we shall see, are quite valuable.

CONCLUDING REGIONAL ASSESSMENT

Lapsed Attitudes and Practices that Could be Revived

It is unlikely that, under current economic circumstances, traditional resources management practices will be revived in Europe. Today's world is radically different from the Medieval world. In one case it was suggested that a form of opera field agriculture be reestablished in order to let small farmers share in the use of expensive large equipment which they could not afford individually, removing fences and hedgerows to let the larger equipment operate efficiently. But complex agricultural equipment is not like a plow and ox-team. It is vulnerable to mechanical problems, especially with several operators, and this otherwise logical suggestion has not been adopted.

But our world is changing, particularly the availability of energy at low costs. Energy is what permitted the full development of modern ways, and severe energy scarcity (to the degree it becomes a reality) will surely force radical changes in modern practices.

As the cost of energy increases and other resource shortages appear, certain responses can be expected. They are: (1) more labor intensive practices and less use of energy; (2) less transportation, leading to population decentralization, smaller scale economic enterprise, and less international trade; (3) lower incomes, less waste, and more reuse, and (4) reduced personal mobility leading to more responsibility to one's environment.[17] These are all qualities of traditional European society and even though the future will be different from the past the realities of environmental contraints may be similar to those of the past. It will be interesting to see what form the cultural response takes. Given the tendency to revert to familiar way from a culture's own past rather than adopting untried ways, it may be that traditional ways will reappear.

Current Practices and Attitudes

Town and country planning in England. The English have never felt especially comfortable in cities, owing primarily to the unpleasant industrial environments that for many was the first urban experience. They prefer to think of themselves as villagers, and have gone to great lengths to preserve the rural scene that is the context for this self-image. And because England has made such a great effort to reduce dependency of imported food since World War II, agricultural production has been encouraged, and the countryside is once again well tended, after years of neglect.

This attractiveness of the English countryside—indeed of all of Europe—is especially impressive when population densities are considered. England and Wales together with a population of 47 million, are roughly the same size as Illinois or one third the size of California. In the U.S. only New Jersey has a higher population density, but England has still been able to preserve the attractive quality of its rural areas. The English countryside remains a major tourist attraction. How were they able to do this?

One legacy of the feudal era is the acceptance of the idea that the community has the primary role in land use decisions; it is not just a matter for the landowner. Remember that private ownership of land, as we know it today, is a relatively recent phenomenon in England, dating from the enclosure movement. Since 1947, England has had a strong Town and Country Planning Act, which gives the government the power to restrict the use of land far more extensively than would ever be allowed in the U.S. For instance, residential developments can be prohibited around cities to form greenbelts without compensating the landowners involved. And when residential developments are permitted, the land owner must pay a tax of one half of the increased value of the land for residential purposes compared to agricultural. If England's countryside appears very attractive to the visitor today, it is largely because of its effective preservation under the Town and Country Planning Act and the feudal precedent for its land use controls.

The English national park is simply an area that is especially attractive and in which the planning legislation is strictly enforced to preserve it that way.[18] No land is purchased, as is the case in the U.S., and the government saves the huge sums of money now necessary to acquire land for a national park here.

We in the United States have always felt blessed to have an abundance of land, but that is by no means an unmixed blessing. England demonstrates some of the advantages of a shortage of land. With land scarce and populations high, England has had to initiate strict conservation practices and to make the most of the land it possessed. In contrast, in this country it has always been hard to justify conservation measures because there was always more land elsewhere, and people could argue that laws to control resource use were not necessary. If we had problems, there was always more land farther west, farther away from deteriorating cities, or farther away from the devastated forest or the eroded farm land. As a result, even though we started with a magnificent, fertile landscape, we have in all too many places treated it poorly. In most cases, this did not happen in Europe with its very high population densities.

Public right-of-ways. From Anglo-Saxon times, systems of public right-of-ways have developed across the English countryside in response to local needs. A few were planned, but most evolved as simple routes to accommodate movements from farm or cottage to village, church, or mill. Later, as the fields were enclosed, right-of-ways were provided for farmers whose fields were away from existing roads or paths to gain access to their fields by certain specified routes. Some right-of-ways have grown in use until they are now roads, while many remain as footpaths, and some have ceased to be used altogether.

The public is allowed to use these right-of-ways today, and they are a priceless recreational asset. It is possible to walk virtually anywhere in the countryside because of these right-of-ways, although a map is often necessary since many are not actually marked out on the ground. But because of the system of right-of-ways, walking in the countryside is a major form of recreation, far more common than in the U.S. where private property is a major barrier to walking.

The royal forests. The Normans, with their great interest in hunting, established royal preserves over a large area of England, up to one third of all the land according to some estimates.[19] In general, the forests were areas of poor land which were not intensively used before the Norman Conquest. These wooded, scrubby wastes and moorlands were, however, the best remaining wildlife habits. The rights of the few farmers who lived in the forests were maintained, but they were subjected to harsh forest laws which forced them to protect the king's wildlife. Many woodlands and natural areas were preserved until today because of the forest laws. A number form the heart of the national parks, places such as Dartmoor, the Peak District, and the Lake District. Only one is still functioning as a royal forest, the New Forest near Southampton on the south coast, which was established in 1079 and still covers 145 square miles. The Crown has long since changed its activities from hunting to forestry, but it permits extensive recreational activities in the forests, which contain much open hearthland and sandy areas.

The great estates. While many stately homes have deteriorated, been torn down, or gone into institutional uses, the finest ones have been preserved. More often than not, they are open to the public, as their owners struggle to raise revenues to maintain these elaborate structures. Many are associated with great names of English history, whose ancestors often still own them. Virtually all are set in fine parks that admirably serve the public. In some cases, even when the great house is gone or in ruins, the park around it remains to serve a public function as it served its private function in the past. When an owner can no longer maintain an estate, it is not uncommon for the family to donate it to the public as a park, receiving in return substantiated tax advantages.

Traditional Ways and the Modern Resource Manager

The history and environment of Europe combine to make it a unique illustration of a region with a very different environmental experience, one with a strong traditional heritage that, although largely overwhelmed by modernization, still influences the way the environment is perceived and used. Moreover, the quality of medieval attitudes and institutions still holds an attraction, particularly for those disillusioned with modern life.[20] The impact of Europe's traditional ways may be felt increasingly in the future if resource scarcity slowly erodes the vitality of the modern industrial economy. If this happens, the role of resource managers will also change. They will be less the specialist representing a distant government, and more a member of a smaller community, intimately aware of its resources, and concerned largely with the ongoing productivity of the environment on which they and their descendents depend.

NOTES

[1] Margaret Reid Shackleton, *Europe: A Regional Geography* (London: Longmans, 7th ed., 1964), p. 1.

[2] Kenneth Clark, *Civilization* (New York: Harper & Row, 1969), pp. 1–17.

[3] L. Dudley Stamp, *Man and the Land* (London: Collins, 1964), pp. 40–41, 60–61; C.S and C. S. Orwin, *The Open Fields* (Oxford: Clarenden Press, 1967), pp. 24–27.

[4] E. Estyn Evans, "The Ecology of Peasant Life in Western Europe," in *Man's Role in Changing the Face of the Earth*, William L. Thomas, ed. (Chicago: University of Chicago Press, 1956), p. 228.

[5] Lynn White, Jr., *Medieval Technology and Social Change* (Oxford: Oxford University Press, 1962), p. 49.

[6] Orwin, op. cit., note 3, pp. 6–10.

[7] Stamp, op. cit., note 3, pp. 107–108.

[8] Paul Mangelsdorf, "Wheat," *Scientific American*, July 1953, p. 50.

[9] Arthur Bryant, *The Medieval Foundation of England* (New York: Doubleday, 1967), pp. 42, 164–165.

[10] Stamp, op. cit., note 3, p. 40; Orwin, op. cit., note 3, pp. 56–59.

[11] Stamp, op. cit., note 3, p. 124.

[12] Garrett Hardin, "The Tragedy of the Commons," *Science*, Dec. 1965, Vol. 162, pp. 1243–1248.

[13] John Frazer Hart, "The Geography of Manure," in *Land Economics*, Vol. 32 (1956), pp. 25–38.

[14] Bryant, op. cit., note 9, p. 175.

[15] Stamp, op. cit., note 3, p. 90.

[16]W. E. Tate, *The English Village Community and the Enclosure Movement* (London: Victor Gollancz, 1967).

[17]See Warren A. Johnson, *Muddling Toward Frugality* (San Francisco: Sierra Club Press, 1978) for an explanation of why the trends listed can be expected.

[18]Warren A. Johnson, *Public Parks on Private Land in England and Wales* (Baltimore: Johns Hopkins Press, 1971).

[19]A. G. Tansley, *Britain's Green Mantle* (London: George Allen & Unwin, 1965), p. 34.

[20]Michael W. Foley, "Who Cut Down the Sacred Tree?", *Co-Evolution Quarterly*, Fall 1977, pp. 60–67.

Chapter 8

North America

Ned H. Greenwood

Traditional agricultural resource management in North America prior to the European settlement was surprisingly uniform compared to the number of existant linguistic and cultural patterns. In nearly all environmental regions with temperature conditions suitable for the cultivation of domestic plants, the Indians practiced a horticulture based upon maize (*Zea mays*), beans (*Phaseolus vulgaris*), and squash (*Cucurbita* species). Each of these crops had originated south of the North American cultural region (the United States and Canada), but adapted well to conditions here.

The management of these crop resources was deliberate and usually well planned. But because it was executed with a digging stick and stone tools we tend to consider it primitive. The carry over of the Indian techniques into subsistence agriculture where European settlers used a plow pulled by draft animals rather than a digging stick is considered an advancement. The progress, however, is confined to shifting part of the human labor to another form of energy conversion and does not necessarily include a greater energy efficiency based upon calorie output per calorie input.

Farmers would later substitute fossil-fuel powered tractors for fodder-powered oxen, again shifting the composition of energy conversion. A system makes the transition from "traditional" (palaeotechnic) to "modern" (neotechnic) when the majority of the energy input is brought from outside the system in the form of fossil fuels. There is a tendency to equate traditional agriculture with subsistence or self-sufficiency. The degree of self-sufficiency is usually high in traditional agriculture. "Traditional," however, refers to the nature of the energy inputs used by the system and "subsistence" is related to how much of the farmers consumption is obtained from within the system (Figure 41). The economic importance of the kitchen garden is usually a valid indicator of traditional energy application. The kitchen garden is almost always found in traditional systems from subsistence to the economic level where commercial (cash) agriculture takes over.[1]

Fig. 41. "Traditional" agricultural management refers to the nature of energy inputs. Human labor contributes a large part of the energy conversion of such a system. This 19th century photo shows wheat being cut with scythe and cradle (*Source*: U.S. Department of Agriculture).

Subsistence is usually the most primitive, economic form of traditional agriculture. A subsistence farmer, when given the opportunity, will generally produce a cash crop to provide greater access to modern economic amenities. From there the logical sequence is specialization and full commercial agriculture.

By nature traditional agricultural resource management requires a great deal of human and animal labor input, and excludes the use of fossil fuels, synthetic fertilizers, sophisticated pesticides, and hybrid seed stocks. Based upon these exclusions, North American agriculture could be considered predominantely traditional until after 1920. Most farmers were still largely self-sufficient in the means of production as well as consumption. Horses and mules were the dominant source of power except for threshing which was done with the aid of steam engines. Soil fertility was supplied through the application of animal manures, green manures, and rotating row crops with close-grown crops of grasses and legumes. Crop yields had scarcely changed in a century. A typical acre in 1920 produced only 26 bushels of corn, 14 of wheat, or 170 pounds of cotton, comparable to the yields of the early 19th century.[2]

Between 1920 and 1950, North America made the transition from a predominantely traditional pattern of agriculture to one that was modern. This left only two valid remnants of traditional agricultural resource management—the village horticulture of some Southwest Indian groups and the subsistence farming of Canada's Atlantic Provinces (Figure 42).

In barely three decades North America had become a continent of urbanites, scarcely aware of the meaning of "self-sufficiency" and confident that their highly educated

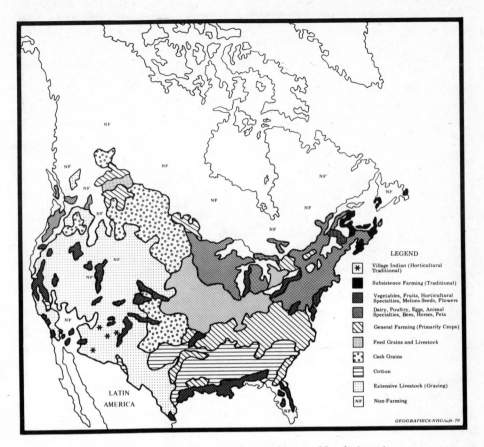

Fig. 42. Generalized types of agriculture in North America.

farmers and advanced energy technologies could feed not only this continent but much of the world besides. Fossil fuels were cheap, abundant, and the basis for the "industrial" food system that had been pioneered here. Never had the ordinary man been able to eat so well so cheaply. Much of the abundance is attributable to technology, but it should not be overlooked that North America is highly favored with fertile soils, moderate climates, and a relatively plentiful crop land.

THE RESOURCE BASE

At least 8 major biomes are recognized in North America (Figure 43). These biomes represent associations of ecosystems in which the role of climate and vegetation largely determine the fertility of the soil and the potential for agriculture.

The deciduous forest biome was originally a complex of broadleaf forest ecosystems extending from Tennessee to Ontario. In the north it is dominated by a humid continental climate with cold winters, warm summers and adequate precipitation through

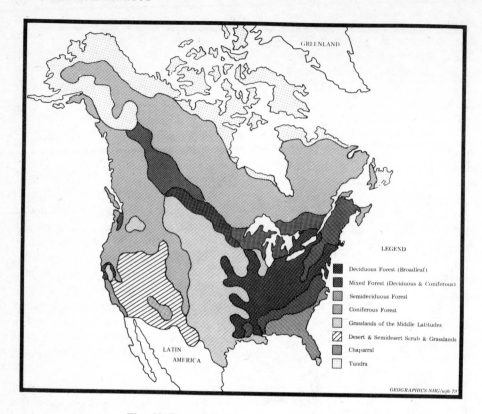

Fig. 43. Principal biomes of North America.

the year. The dominant soils are gray-brown forest soils (Alifisols) which are widely noted for their "staying" power.[3] They are mildly acidic and not as rich in nutrient elements as the soils of dryer areas, but they have good structure and tilth, and are able to withstand much of the compaction caused by tillage. This was the best part of the aboriginal cultural region of the Northeastern Woodland Indians. Further east and north this cultural region was dominated by mixed and coniferous forests with less fertile and more acidic Boreal forest soils (Spodosols).

The southern part of the deciduous forest biome extends into the former cultural region of the Southeastern Woodland Indians. Here the lands are influenced by a humid subtropical climate. The soils are less fertile, red-yellow forest soils (Ultisols). These soils have relative good structure, but require more ammendments than the gray-brown forest soils. Winter erosion of agricultural fields tends to be a problem because they lack constant snow cover and frequently have no winter cover crop. Further south and east this biome gives way to a mixed forest, and a semideciduous forest biome in the coastal plain. Unfortunately the same infertile soils and erosion potential exist throughout.

The grassland biome, in its tall-grass prairie ecosystem, contains the richest agricultural potential on earth. Most of this potential was effectively locked away from Indian horticulture as well as from the first European farmers. The continuous sward and deep interlocking roots of the bluestem prairies blocked early attempts to turn the virgin sod. These prairies were a biological enigma, existing in the same humid continental climate with as much precipitation as produced forests in adjacent areas. When the agricultural potential of the prairie soils (Mollisols) were finally unlocked, with the aid of a steel plow in the decade after 1837, it produced some of the best crop yield in agricultural history.

The prairie Mollisols were nature's masterpiece of fertility, containing a bounty of nutrients and an abundance of humus and secondary clays (montmorillonite) in which to store them. The grasslands had been the realm of the Plains Indians who tapped their riches with the aid of the buffalo (*Bison bison*) because their cultural repertoire like that of early European farmers was not adequate to deal first hand with the sod.

The short-grass ecosystems were not so productive as the prairies. Nutrient elements were abundant and the physical structure of the soils were good, but the high variability of precipitation reduced the reliability of agriculture. In wet years crops were abundant. In dry years farmers often lost their entire crop. The high plains lost thousands of cattle in the blizzards of the 1890s and suffered severe wind erosion, as the "Dust Bowl," in the 1930s. Even now falling ground-water tables threaten the grain sorgham agriculture which had replaced wheat as the dominant crop.

Further west the desert and chaparral biomes precluded most agriculture except where water could be found for irrigation. Desert soils (Aridisols) are adequate for agriculture, though they tend to accumulate salt due to poor irrigation practices and inadequate drainage. Aridisols require intensive management and heavy capital inputs in order to remain productive.

Most of the coniferous forest biome is unsuitable for farming because of short growing seasons and acid soils (Spodosols). Neither Indian nor modern agricultural techniques have been able to overcome nature's resistences in these areas. Later on it will be seen that the Indians who did not practice horticulture were largely found in the coniferous forest zones. The major exceptions were the Indians of the Great Basin and the California Pacific Drainage. The latter area now contains some of the world's most productive agriculture. The tundra biome like most of the coniferous forest creates an absolute barrier to agriculture because the growing season is too short and the soils too acidic and waterlogged.

In summary, the North American resource base contains some of the best potential for traditional agriculture on earth. Many environmental regions were only marginally utilized by the Indians. Low population density was the major reason for this favorable man-land relationship. The causes of low density are not completely understood, however, it does not appear to be related to the horticultural system which many tribes employed. In fact, the horticulture was well adapted to the environments in which it was practiced. Likewise traditional agriculture is still plausible in most biomes from an environment basis. It is the economic influence of our high consumption society that now excludes it from North America except for a few remnants.

EVOLUTION OF TRADITIONAL RESOURCE MANAGEMENT

Traditional resource management systems in North America today are only remnants of their past importance, yet it is still possible to find complete systems of the Indian's

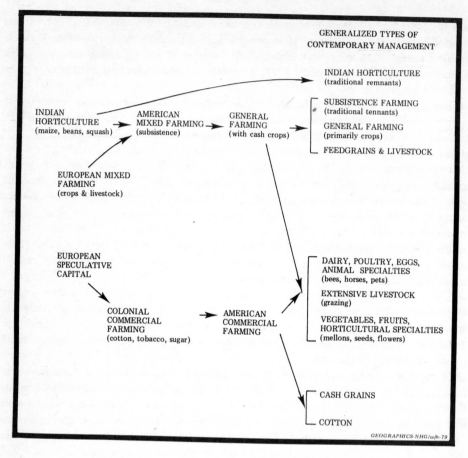

Fig. 44. The evolution of farming in North America.

maize, bean, squash horticulture in the Southwest and subsistence (mixed) farming in the Atlantic Provinces of Canada. The reasons for both remnants are largely environmental, which will be discussed later.

Modern agricultural management systems owe much to their traditional roots. One contemporary system is derived directly from its horticultural past and seven agricultural systems have at least part of their roots in American mixed-farming (Figure 44). American mixed farming evolved as a combination of Indian horticulture and European mixed farming which was introduced piecemeal between A.D. 1600 and 1800.

Indian Horticulture

As mentioned initially Indian horticulture in North America was almost exclusively maize, beans, and squash. The diversity of cultigens in pre-Columbian North America was far less than that found in Latin America. In fact at least 4 important crop groups and numerous lesser cultigens originating in the Americas had either failed to spread north of Mexico or had not been widely accepted by American cultures. The missing crop groups included: potatoes (*Solanum tuberosum*), tomatoes (*Lycopersicon esculentum*), peppers (*Capsicum frutescens*), and sweet potatoes (*Ipomoea batatas*). Since Columbus all of these groups have become major commercial crops in North America.

Domestic food animals were limited to dogs (*Canis familiaris*) and turkeys (*Meleagris gallopavo*), neither of which constituted a major food supply. Animal protein was mostly obtained through hunting and fishing. Gathering of wild plants was also universal, especially for condiments and to supplement poor harvests. Plant cultivation was the primary cultural tool, with stalking and gathering used for augmentation.

In the Arctic, sub-Arctic and Boreal forest, where inadequate frost-free periods precluded horticulture, the Indians and Eskimos were forced to rely upon hunting and fishing. Stalking and trapping became the dominant cultural tools. Even plant gathering was limited to a few favorable locations along the southern edges of these harsh environments.

The other environmental extreme, lack of moisture, did not preclude horticulture as the dominant resource pattern. The practice of irrigation and moisture conservency supported the same pattern of maize, beans, and squash.

Raiding as a cultural force existed throughout North America, but it seemed to have been most highly developed in areas of greatest environmental stress. In the far north it was common practice for one group to raid the traps of others. In the Plains the stealing of another tribe's horses brought great honor. But in the Southwest raiding developed into a delicate symbiotic relationship as the Athapascan-speaking Apaches and Navajos obtained much of their livelihood by raiding the agricultural stores of the Pueblo cultures.

Northeastern Woodland Indians. The area which extends from what is now Virginia northward into Quebec and Labrador and westward into Iowa, Minnesota, and Manitoba was at the time of European Colonization the domaine of horticultural Woodland Indians (Figure 45). The development of horticulture appears to have occurred sometime after 400 B.C. with the gradual introduction of maize growing as a supplement to hunting and gathering by the Adena and Hopewell cultures. These cultures reached their peak in the Ohio and Mississippi Valleys between 200 B.C. and A.D. 200. Horticulture in this area began and continued as "rainfall cultivation" practiced for the most part on valley bottom soils. These soils were usually soft, sandy and gently sloping. Digging sticks and stone implements did an adequate job of tillage. Apparently population densities were low enough that slope terracing and similar practices used to increase arable land were not necessary.

The addition of beans and squash to the maize culture probably occurred before A.D. 600 as the Mound Builders were superceding the older Hopewell. This was a period when cultural concepts from Mexico were readily received. Sometime between A.D. 500 and 1300 the Mound Builders reached their zenith, following the period in which horticulture became the dominant source of sustenance.

By 1600, the Northeastern Woodland Indians comprised 2 linguistic stocks and nearly 25 cultural entities. The Algonquian linguistic group was the larger with more than 16 tribes occupying southern Canada from the Atlantic to Lake Winnipeg with extensions northward to Hudson Bay and down the Atlantic seaboard to Cape Hatteras. There was little political unity among the Algonquian tribes, but they shared common resource practices which were based on maize, bean, squash horticulture. On either side of the

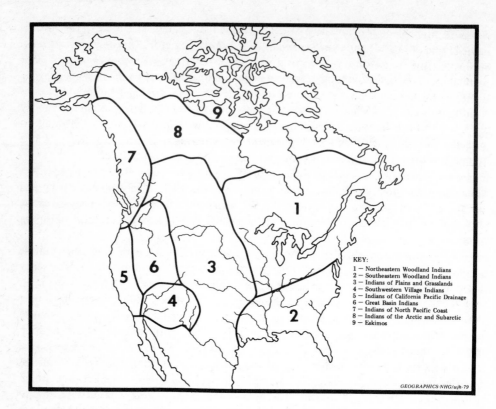

KEY:
1 — Northeastern Woodland Indians
2 — Southeastern Woodland Indians
3 — Indians of Plains and Grasslands
4 — Southwestern Village Indians
5 — Indians of California Pacific Drainage
6 — Great Basin Indians
7 — Indians of North Pacific Coast
8 — Indians of the Arctic and Subarctic
9 — Eskimos

GEOGRAPHICS-NHG/wjh-79

Fig. 45. Aboriginal cultural regions of North America, A.D. 1600-1700.

St. Lawrence River maple syrup and sugar had become an important adjunct to horticulture. The Algonquian-speaking Menominee had pioneered this development which later spread to the Iroquoian tribes as well. Along the St. Lawrence River and westward into Minnesota the Algonquians, especially the Chippewa, continued to supplement horticulture by gathering wild rice (*Zizania aquatica*).

Intermixed with the Algonquians were the Iroquoian speakers. This group called "The Longhouse" by the French were heriditary enemies of the Algonquians, yet their horticultural practices were basically identical. At least 6 tribes of Iroquoians were scattered in this broad region with more important concentrations located in the valleys of the St. Lawrence and Susquehanna, with outliers in the Appalachian highlands and the tidewater areas of New York and New England.

The Iroquois were perhaps better horticulturalists than the Algonquians. They lived in palisaded villages with adjacent agricultural plots. Their system consisted of planting 3 or 4 kernels of corn and a few beans in a hill separated from other hills by a minimum of 3 feet in all directions. As the corn grew its stocks served as support for the bean vines. At the margin of each plot, squash and pumpkins were planted in hills separated by more than 4 feet in all directions.

Fertility was ammended by the application of ashes, organic wastes and fish. Even so shifting cultivation was necessary to accommodate the rapid depletion of fertility in the lighter (sandy) soils which were preferred because of easier tillage. Domestic crops were augmented by hunting, fishing, and the gathering of wild plant materials. Berries were particularly important, so the patches were frequently burned to improve the stand and reduce competing plants.

In most years horticulture supplied over 75% of the food consumed.[4] Because maize was so important to this system its Iroquoian name was "our life."[5] A typical family required 3 to 6 acres of tilled land besides its hunting grounds in order to sustain itself.[6] Today few among the Northeastern tribes practice agriculture. Many work in modern industry—most noted are the Mohawks in steel construction. The closest thing to traditional resource management would be scattered areas of poor quality, part-time agriculture.

Indians of the southeastern forests. In the area from what is now Louisiana and Arkansas eastward through the Carolinas, Georgia, and Florida the Mississippi culture complex had evolved largely from the old Hopewell culture. The most notable advances in horticulture occurred between A.D. 700 and 1200. By the time of European contact the Muskhogean linguistic stock, with at least 6 cultural divisions, dominated the area. Most of the tribes later associated with the Creek Confederation.

In late pre-Columbian times their horticulture was basically the same as that practiced by the Northeast Woodland Indians. To the maize, beans, and squash, however, they added sunflowers, tobacco, and gourds. At least 4 varieties of maize were commonly planted. Hunting and fishing supplemented the protein intake. Root garthering and tree products including plums, persimmons, chestnuts and hickory nuts were common fare.[7] "Black drink" a tea made from the shrub *Ilex Cassine* may have been the most widely used plant product.[8]

Horticultural plots, typically quarter acre in size, were hacked and burned out of the forests. A family would use several of these. A shifting sequence of field-use was practiced when ammendments and fallowing no longer maintained enough fertility to make continuous tillage worthwhile. There is little in the historical record as to the amount of land required by a family or individual, but it was likely less than in the northeast (3 to 6 acres per family) due to less severe winters and longer growing seasons.

The Creek peoples readily adopted European management techniques including slave holding, cotton farming, and loom weaving. Most were later displaced westward into "Indian Territory," but the remnants left behind in the Carolinas and Georgia now include many successful farmers growing fieldcrops on a commercial basis.

Plains Indians. Traditional resource systems in North America's great grassland biome were enigmatic. Vast biological potentials were locked in the soil by a nearly inpenetrable sod. The introduction of the horse, sometime between A.D. 1540 and 1700, and the rapid cultural impaction caused by tribes bring displaced Westward as European settlers claimed the wooded portions of eastern North America had turned the grasslands into a vast shatterbelt of cultural interactions.[9] These grasslands extended from northern Alberta, Saskatchewan, and Manitoba all the way to southern Texas. In the 18th and 19th centuries, cultural conflict was most acute in the lands adjacent to the Missouri River and its tributaries.

The pressures of white men, for example, on the Algonquian-speaking Chippewa had started a ripple of displacement from the Ohio River to the Rocky Mountains.

Siouan-speaking peoples especially the horticultural Dakota and Hidatsa were forced into what is now Minnesota where they displaced Algonquian speaking Cheyenne and Arapohoe. These western Algonquians, who had progressed from hunting and gathering wild rice to horticulture and permanent villages, were then forced onto the plains migrating all the way to the edge of the mountains sometime before A.D. 1700.

There, contact with the Comanchee (Uto-Aztecan Stock) introduced them to the horse, tepee, and nomadic hunting of the buffalo. The Hidatsa and Mandan became the earliest earth-lodge, horticultural people on the upper Missouri.[10] So it went, the Kansas, Missouri, Iowa, Osage, and Quapan tribes of Siouan stock, the Pawnee of Caddoan stock, the Kiowa of Tanoan stock and the Blackfoot of Algonquian stock all gave up settled villages and horticulture to become nomadic hunters using horses to hunt the buffalo.

So ingrained had hunting become that attempts to reintroduce farming after the near extinction of the buffalo, could not prevent death by starvation of nearly a quarter of the Piegan tribe of the Blackfoot. Since then, the Blackfoot like most other Plains Indians, have accepted the white man's agriculture and stock raising. Many became successful farmers, but cattle raising was the more appealing, probably because of greater ties to the old nomadic livelihood.

Southwestern Villiage Indians. The earliest horticulturalists in North America lived in the desert and plateau areas of the Southwest (Figure 45). Maize which originated in Mexico was known in this area prior to 2000 B.C. as evidenced in Bat Cave in western New Mexico. Squash was represented in Bat Cave by 2000 B.C. Beans had probably dispersed into the area by 1000 B.C.[11] Horticultural dominance was, however, slow to spread.

Hunting and gathering desert cultures eventually gave rise to the horticultural Mogollon and Hohokam peoples (Uto-Aztecan linguistic stock) sometime around A.D. 200. The Mogollon culture utilized rainfall and floodwater diversion to grow their crops. The Hohokam practiced irrigation.

The Hohokam built extensive canal and diversion systems bringing water from permanent streams to supply their irrigated horticulture. Maize, beans, squash, and cotton were introduced in order. Tansy mustard, little barley grass, horse parslane, amaranths (pigweed), and chenopods (spinach-like plants), while not cultivated directly were allowed to grow in Hohokam fields and were undoubtedly used for food.[12]

At the peak of development the Hohokam had constructed over 200 miles (320 kilometers) of main canals which averaged 7 feet (2.25 meters) in depth and 30 feet (9.23 meters) in width, and watered over 200,000 acres (81,000 hectares). It is estimated that 13 acres (5.25 hectares) per person of irrigable land may have been available, though it is doubtful that so much land was actually cropped at any one time. The productive capability of the Hohokam peaked sometime in the 13th century, declining rapidly thereafter as the canals silted in and the social structure fell apart. Today many among the Hohokam remnants, the Pima and Papago, practice floodwater farming to produce corn, beans, squash, cotton, wheat and vegetables. For the others, the use of modern irrigation using electrically-pumped water, fossil-fuel mechanization, and heavy synthetic fertilization have placed them in the mainstream of commercial agriculture.

Sometime before A.D. 800 another horticultural group called "Basket Makers" was developing in southeastern Utah. They spread eastward and southward into present day

Colorado, Arizona, and New Mexico developing the culture we now called Anasazi. Meanwhile the Mogollon culture was moving northward. The two cultures interacted across the broad mountainous area of east central Arizona and west central New Mexico. By A.D. 1000 the Mogollon was in the final stages of decline, its remnants being absorbed into the flourishing Anasazi or Puebloan culture which gave root to the present Hopi, Zuni and Rio Grande puebloes, some of which will be discussed later in their modern context.

Non-horticultural groups. In the area of California coastal drainages, Hokan–Coahuiltecan-speaking tribes practiced gathering, fishing and hunting. The acorn was the primary staple. In the Great Basin areas of California, Nevada, Utah, Idaho, and Oregon, Shoshonispeaking peoples eked out a bare existence gathering pinon nuts, mesquite beans, agava and anything else they could pick or catch.

From the coastal reaches of the Columbia River northward to Alaska dwelt the richest fishing, hunting and gathering peoples of pre-Columbian North America. Wild food was so abundant that there was never much stimulus for these peoples to tie themselves down with horticulture. Here the Salishan linguistic stock with at least 8 cultural units, and the Athapaskan-speaking Haida, Tlingit and other closely related tribes fished, hunted and gathered plant foods. Foods included sprouts, roots, and bulbs of at least a dozen species and fruits and berries from over 20 species. Ten different mollusks and 20 species of fish including Pacific salmon, steelhead trout, sturgeon and halibut were used. Sea mammals, deer, elk, bear and water fowl rounded out their abundant larder.[13] Food in such abundance gave rise to a vastly different attitude toward resources. Important leaders tried to elaborate their prestige by giving away or destroying resources in one of the strangest adjuncts to traditional resource management ever devised—the potlatch. Today most of these Indians work at fishing, and lumbering. Very little agriculture is practiced.

In the Boreal forest zone stretching from the Klondike past Great Slave and Yellowknife lakes to the western shores of Hudson Bay live hunting and trapping peoples of two linguistic groups. In the western parts, Athapascan linguistic tribes such as the Kutchin, Nahani and Yellowknife still hunt a variety of animals, but depend most heavily upon the caribou. Further east the Algonquian-speaking Cree also hunt the caribou, but moose, deer, rabbits, and ptarmigan are important. Today trapping for fur is the dominant economic activity of these sub-Arctic tribes.

The Arctic proper serves as home to the Eskimos who continue to live by hunting (mostly sea animals) and fishing. Their traditional resource management practices remain little changed. The impact upon the resource base has, however, greatly increased with the availability of high powered rifles and motor launches.

Indian Impact

Taken as a whole, pre-Columbian North America suffered little pressure of population against the land resource base. To be sure, certain resources were occasionally over utilized. Hunting by early man probably caused or contributed to the extinction of certain large mammals such as the *Bison antiquus, Mastodon Americanus*, and *Camelops*. But this occurred long before maize, bean, and squash horticulture became established. Once horticulture began it was sometimes necessary to move plots as soil depletion and erosion took a limited toll. It was probably the rigors of hunting, warfare and disease rather than limited land resources which restrained life expectancy and held human production in check.

It is estimated that at the time of European discovery only about 1 million people inhabited 4.8 billion acres (7.5 million square miles or 2.9 billion hectares). Of this total nearly 1 billion acres (405 million hectares) were potentially arable—1000 tillable acres per inhabitant. In fact very little damage could have occurred because of such a thin population load. Today this same land area supports some 250 million individuals who cultivate between 500 and 550 million acres (200-220 million hectares) each year.

American Mixed Farming

The maize, bean, squash resource system which had served the Indian well, became the transitional mainstay to which the first European settlers gradually added a system of mixed farming with livestock and old world cultigens. Subsistence was the initial thrust of this mixed or general farming pattern from Maryland to New Foundland. In the Southern colonies commercial agriculture, made possible by heavy capital investment from England and based upon commercial staples like tobacco, cotton, sugar and indigo was more important than subsistence almost from the beginning. This did not preclude subsistence, it simply made it less appealing initially. The pioneering of the southern Appalachians was dominated by subsistence economic patterns.

As European settlers gained dominance the Indians were dessimated, their cultures torn apart, and the forced impact of one tribe upon another's land eventually destroyed the old reliable maize, bean, squash horticulture. Its remnants, however, continued in the frontier of a new America. Here three agricultural frontiers came to be recognized: (1) the Atlantic coastal plain—A.D. 1600-1800, (2) the trans-Alleghenies (Heart of the Continent) frontier—A.D. 1800-1840, and (3) the trans-Mississippi frontier—A.D. 1840-1890. In the first two, a subsistence, mixed farming dominated other resource systems. The latter was forged in a mold of capital intensity. It was a frontier of fur trapping, mining and finally wide open ranges where only those without capital backing would rely upon subsistence agriculture. Yet ironically it was the traditional farmer who ultimately made the west stable economically and politically.

Atlantic Seaboard agriculture. The degree to which British agricultural systems dominated the Atlantic Seaboard was greatly affected by a poor land base. The deep glacial advances of the Quartenary period left thin stoney soils which have become acidic and leached under an abundant rainfall, cold winters and coniferous forest cover. The rocky hills were never able to sustain the prosperity typical of England or even the colonies further to the south.

This area suffered badly from what Aubrey Land termed a "sea change."[14] The agricultural traditions of England were never wholly tenable in this more rigorous environment. In spite of Puritan traditions and the help afforded by Indian horticulture, Yankees and Down Easterners found their economic reprieve not in agriculture but in fishing, shipping, and timber extraction. Agriculture was from the first a second sister forced to wait for westward migration before blossoming into fulfillment and vigor.

A combination of heavy yielding Indian corn (maize) and fish fertilizer sustained the northeastern colonies while they were developing a new tradition. The Iroquois also taught them the practice of field rotation and the application of dung as well as muck and ashes to sweeten and restore fertility to the soil—all of this before Jethro Tull and Turnip Townshend (discussed later). Indian horticulture plus the practice of curing salt hay for livestock fodder were the changes that "Americanized" colonial agriculture.

Pennsylvania agriculture. Even though the coastal plain from Long Island to the Chesapeake Bay was being converted to Commercial agriculture during the last quarter of the 17th century, a resolute strain of land-hungry peasants, mostly of German origin, were gravitating into southeastern Pennsylvania and northern Maryland. There they practiced a largely self-sufficient type of mixed farming.

Capital formation came easier here than in New England, attested by sturdy stone barns and well-made fences. Kitchen gardens, orchards, flowers and herbs flourished with grain and livestock in a fusion of heritages. Germans, Dutch, Swedes, Scots and others lent their cultural inputs to the system. But it was the spirit and temperament of the stolid German peasants that dominated the fusion, and influenced future developments of general farming in North America. Frugality and industry were its guidelines which were carried into and across the mountains. It was in the valleys of the Ohio drainage that the Pennsylvania and New England roots of mixed farming blended and eventually became a modern feed grain and livestock agriculture (Figure 42).

In the South and eventually the West traditional agricultural resource management followed the general patterns dictated by subsistence. The types of modern agriculture that developed from these patterns were molded by the physical environment, locational factors and economics.

Subsistence. The American system of self-sufficiency had numerous weaknesses, but it related fairly well to the variety of physical environments in which it was practiced. Equally important was its fundamental practice of returning nutrients and organic matter to the soil which created a potential steady-state ecosystem.

Self-sufficiency was the key. Each farm family produced their own supplies of food, clothing, shelter, house furnishings, and farm implements, returning all by-products to the land from which they came. Little was sold from the farm so there was little loss of nutrient elements and organic matter as long as erosion was controlled.

Traditional American agriculture borrowed much from the Iroquois and other Indian tribes, but it owed a debt to the 18th century work of Englishmen like Jethro Tull and Turnip (Charles) Townshend who developed the technologies we now call the Norfolk Revolution.[15] The introduction of turnips and alfalfa or clover into English field agriculture was a major advance from the medieval fallow system. The Norfolk System included a four-part rotation of crops on a given field which usually included turnips, barley, clover, rye grass, and wheat. This practice restored fertility to the soil so that wheat yields on badly jaded fields were increased by 3 or 4 times.

Crop rotation was slow to be accepted in North America, but when it was, the early patterns usually went: wheat, potatoes, wheat, barley, and peas and clover. By 1840 farmers were becoming conscious of the need to improve management techniques. Capital investment in barns, houses, and roads made it advisable to stay with the "old" land. The observation that it was cheaper to buy a new acre than manure an old one no longer held. The Norfolk Revolution was, by default, incorporated into traditional American agriculture. Grasses, turnips, buckwheat, and clover were increasingly mixed with maize, wheat, and cash crops.

Fertilizers were frequently neglected, but better farmers applied manure when it was available and improvised when it was not. The rule of thumb for manure application was 4 tons per acre every other year. In coastal areas "rockweed" was gathered after high storms or pulled from the rocks and plowed into the fields usually in April. Whitefish were seined and applied to the soil.[16] Limestone, marl and gypsum were commonly used. The rule for liming was to apply half as much lime as manure (2 tons per acre) every fourth year. Traditional agriculture utilized a variety of soil ammendments, but animal manures were the main source of organic matter and nutrient elements. Crop rotation and green manures rounded out the system of fertility management.[17]

Subsistence had gradually given way to less penurious forms of traditional agriculture, especially between 1840 and the end of the century. Much of the food, feed and fuel needed by the family were still produced on the farm, but a cash crop brought in more consumer goods. The lure of monetary returns continued to chip away at all forms of traditional agriculture. Sometime between 1920 and the end of World War II traditional agriculture almost disappeared from North America.

The Impact of American Traditional Farming

Land abandonment following the advance of America's agriculture frontier is one of the ugliest spots in our heritage of traditional resource management. The process started with Colonial farmers who left their wornout and eroded fields to occupy virgin soils further west.[18] Exploitation and abandonment as a facet of traditional agriculture seems to have lasted as long as the tradition itself, apparently culminating in the Dust Bowl migrations of the 1930s.

By 1939 an estimated 450-500 million acres (180-200 million hectares) of North American cropland had been affected by some degree of erosion.[19] Charles Kellogg felt that 75 million acres (28 million hectares) of this were too worn out to return a living wage under any system of farm practices.[20] There were ugly faces of traditional resource management history, but they helped to stimulate a greater environmental consciousness, and a technical application of soil erosion control which has largely carried over into modern agricultural practices.[21]

PRESENT DAY TRADITIONAL RESOURCE MANAGEMENT

Traditional agricultural resource management techniques have largely disappeared from North America except for two quite dissimilar systems—Southwestern Indian horticulture in Arizona and New Mexico and a subsistence agriculture of mixed farming and kitchen gardens found in Canada's Atlantic Provinces of New Foundland, New Brunswick, Prince Edward Island and Nova Scotia. Southwest villagers now number about 40,000 people and utilize over 100,000 acres (40,000 hectares). Atlantic subsistence in 1966 numbered about 80,000 individuals on 17,000 farms utilizing 2.3 million acres (930,000 hectares) or 49.4% of all farm land in those provinces.[22] Farmers in other regions probably utilize scattered elements of traditional management, but for the most part commercial agriculture prevails.

Commercial farmers have become so specialized that they make little attempt to integrate traditional practices even to the extent of keeping a kitchen garden. A dairy farmer in Ontario, a wheat farmer in Kansas, and an urbanite in San Francisco are all apt to buy their groceries in the same type of supermarket. Convenience is the dictator. Cash flow in traditional systems is too limited to permit the buying of groceries on a regular basis. Ready access to garden vegetables and fruits smooths the rough spots of the economic cycle and provides the base from which other management practices stem.

Slope management. Slope management was apparently not practiced nor needed to any significant extent by pre-Columbian horticulturalists in the humid parts of North America. The Indians did not trigger accelerated erosion in their cultivation, simply because the size of their fields and the agglomerate demand was not of sufficient extent to create a problem.[23] The exploitation of agricultural resources by white settlers is another matter. The first white settlers in North America arrived in Virginia in 1607 and by 1685 there was a serious increase in flooding caused by forest clearance.

With the rapid depletion of soil fertility in Tidewater land many settlers moved on to the Piedmont where they mostly repeated their exploitive errors. However, a few Piedmont farmers plowed on the contour and built terraces to control runoff. These practices seem to have been borrowed from Scotland.[24] This may have been the starting point for extensive contouring accomplished throughout North America during the disasterous droughts and blows of the 1930s.

In the arid Southwest, terracing was practiced from pre-Columbian times through the present, primarily as a technique of water management. Additional advantages of erosion control were mostly incidental. The Hopi and other village horticulturalists still practice terracing. The increase of livestock grazing by Indians, Mexicans, and whites between 1870 and 1935 caused a rapid denudation of arid and semiarid grasslands followed by accelerated sheet and gully erosion. Check dam construction and terracing of adjacent slopes was fostered by soil conservation organizations to help rangeland in the way that contour plowing was conserving tilled lands. These "depression" programs were traditional in that they were accomplished with draft animals and much human labor (Figure 46). Slope management practices have carried over into modern agriculture, modified primarily by nothing more than the application of mechanized equipment.

Water management. Irrigated horticulture in pre-Columbian North America was practiced only by the village agriculturalists of the Southwest. It survives today with the Hopi, Zuni, Pagago, Pima, and Rio Grande villages. The Hopi have maintained the greatest elaboration of the basic concept.[25] Their field systems integrate soil characteristics, slope and water sources with water conservancy. Four patterns are recognized:[26] (1) floodwater cultivation, (2) rainfall culture in dune fields, (3) utilization of subsurface seepage, and (4) irrigation from springs.

Floodwater farming, using surface runoff, is usually practiced on alluvial fans, at the mouths of tributary arroyos, or in the valleys of the main arroyos. Crops are planted in low-lying terraces which are watered when thunder storms cause the fan or arroyo to flood. Small dams are frequently placed in the watercourse to increase the amount of moisture diverted.

Rainfall culture is used on fields too high to receive floodwaters. Fields for this practice are selected on the basis of a silty-clay horizon overlain by a layer of 4 to 6 inches of coarse, wind-blown sand. Sand mulching is the practice of planting below this thick layer of sand to conserve moisture (Figure 47). Fields using subsurface seepage are located near the mesa edge. They tend to be small and quite steep. Surface irrigation from springs

Fig. 46. Traditional slope management practices utilizing hand labor are still widely used (*Source:* U.S. Department of Agriculture).

is conventional, similar to irrigation practiced anywhere in the arid zone. Sand mulching may be used in all Hopi field systems (Figure 48). Three main field types are recognized:[27] (1) *peesa pasa* (dune fields, largely watered by rainfall and flood water), (2) *ak-chin* ("at the arroyo mouth"), and (3) *naya pasa* ("good fields" found in the level areas of the main valleys).

Traditional planting methods and seed stocks acquired through the centuries are geared to sand mulching. Weeds are first removed from the fields. A shallow layer of loose soil is pushed aside with the foot to create a small depression. The planter drops to a knee and digs a smaller hole to a depth of 10 or more inches so that the seed will be within the layer of moist soil. The moist soil is loosened with a rotary motion of the digging stick.[28] A handful of seed, 8 to 20, are placed in the hole. Moist soil is replaced first then the remaining hole is loosely filled. This loose sand becomes part of

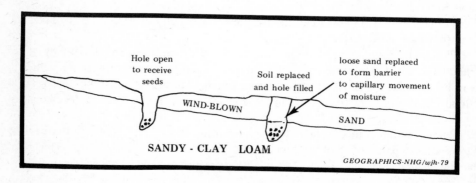

Fig. 47. Sand mulching as practiced by Hopi farmers.

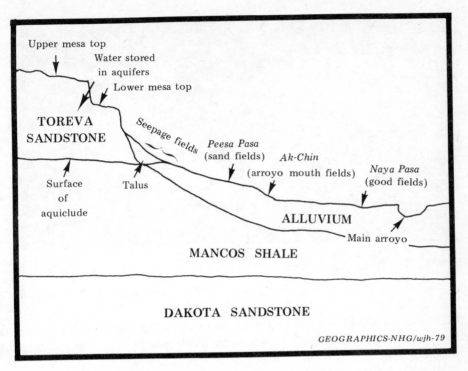

Fig. 48. Hopi agricultural field placement.

the mulch layer. Deep seeding and–sandy surface layers optimize water availability.

The utilization of subsurface seepage by the Hopi is made possible by rather specific natural conditions. In this broad area of the Colorado Plateau thick beds of Mesa Verde (Toreva) sandstone dip gently from north to south. This sandstone forms a vast reservoir which slowly feeds the springs and seeps along the southern edge of the mesas (Figure 48). Droughts may last for months at a time, yet the flow continues because of the great capacity of the sandstone.

Moisture control by other Southwest Indians is not so elaborate as that of the Hopi. Floodwater farming is the principle management technique. Alluvial fans and aprons of the Sonoran Desert make ideal places to trap runoff from spring freshets or summer thunder showers. Floodwater diversion has been the mainstay of desert Indians since the canals of the Hohokam were silted-in during the 14th century.

Water management for Atlantic subsistence farmers is a problem of keeping fields dry enough to plant, produce, and harvest. Three land types are recognized: uplands, dyked lands and intervales.[29] Uplands need little water management. Dyked lands require complete control. These were formerly intertidal marshes located in the esturaries of the coastal plains. Dyking begins by driving logs (piles) into the ground where the tide enters the marsh. Sluiceways through the dyke are fitted with clapper valves to allow the flow of fresh water seaward, but prevent saltwater from reentering the low ground.[30] Around these piles, earthworks are built to insure the integrity of the reclaimed land

Fig. 49. Dyked agricultural lands in Nova Scotia (*Source:* Nova Scotia Communications and Information Centre).

(Figure 49). Most of these dykes were built before 1930 with communal labor which is reflected in present ownership. Maintenance is controlled by user organizations, but cropping is on an individual basis.

The intervales are found along rivers and between the marshes and uplands. These areas require ditching (open drain collectors) to alleviate water-logging. Plow patterns used in Great Britain and eastern North America take care of excess surface water (Figure 50). Soils in the intervales and marshes are heavier (more clay) than the uplands so they require fewer amendments.

Cropping patterns reflect the nature of the soils in the various drained areas. The better uplands, with rich alluvial loam, are used for hay, cereals, and vegetables. Lighter (sandy) soils are pastured by sheep. The intervales are frequently used for apples and

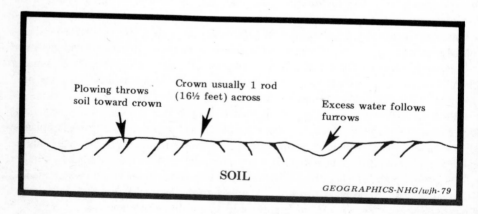

Fig. 50. Plow patterns used to increase surface drainage for hay and meadow.

small fruits. Dyked lands are cropped for grains, peas, and vegetables. An interesting and early practice of sowing wheat and peas together is still occasionally used.

Good farming soils are limited to river valleys and small sections of the coastal plains. Rocky ridges, barren uplands and porous soils separate these bits of low-lying arable land. Water management is essential to the continuance of agriculture in the Atlantic Provinces.

Soil fertility management. The use of fertilizers in the Southwest have always been minimal. Some native farmers use kitchen refuse and crop wastes to replace organic matter and nutrients. No doubt human wastes are occasionally used, although there does not seem to be a consistent practice as such. In some Hopi villages the privies are built over the edge of a cliff so that urine and fecal matter drop onto the slope below. Some nutrient elements and organic matter may find their way to low lying fields, but there seems to be little direct utilization.

The only consistent replacement of nitrogen, potassium, and other elements results from the annual deposition of silts and clays carried by floodwaters from higher lands. *Ak-chin* and *naya pasa* fields benefit from this. *Peesa pasa* fields are not reached by annual floods, so shifting cultivation is used on these (Figure 48). Fortunately leaching losses are minimal in this semiarid climate. Synthetic fertilizers are not used in any significant quantities by Southwest traditional horticulture.

Atlantic subsistence by contrast has a severe leaching problem. Liming of acidic soils is a common practice. Manures are used to maintain organic matter and nutrients. Other natural fertilizers include mussel mud, seaweed (rockweed), peat, marsh mud and fish offal.[31] Synthetic fertilizers are used on commercial farms, but seldom on subsistence units because of cost. Crop rotation is practiced, particularly between root and forage crops. Atlantic subsistence farmers have adequate knowledge of fertilizers and soil amendments, but calcium and potassium deficiencies continue to plague them.

Microclimate management. Microclimate modification is inter-related with numerous other practices. When the Hopi builds a windbreak or terraces a slope there is an automatic modification of the microclimatic environment. Windbreaks change evapotranspiration rates. Terraces alter slope aspects, hence solar receipt and warming. No management practice operates in isolation and traditional farmers have learned to optimize moisture and warmth for the benefit of their crops.

Atlantic subsistence farmers improve soil temperatures by drainage. This is especially important in the spring when drier soils warm up more quickly than water-logged areas. Winter cover crops and mulches are used to reduce erosion, but provide additional benefits by keeping the soil warmer. Coldrames and hotbeds are used to give seed germination and seedlings a head start for the short growing season, but they also counteract the injuries of windy springs. Microclimate management has been and continues to be a traditional way to ameliorate the extremes of macroclimates.

Kitchen gardens. The term "garden" in most of North America is synomous with "kitchen" or "vegetable garden." It is essentially a small plot, generally less than ½ acre in extent, in which a wide variety of vegetables are grown, primarily for household use (Figure 51). The sale of produce is not excluded, but it is definitely of secondary importance. Among the Southwest Indian farmers there may not appear to be a clear distinction between gardens and field agriculture. Fields range in size from ¼ to 10 acres. But a careful check of who tends the patch reveals that women care for small

Fig. 51. Kitchen gardens are a microcosm of traditional agriculture. Here Zuni horticulturalists prepare the seed beds for their famous "waffle" gardens (*Source:* Heye Foundation, 1920).

plots close to the village which produce a greater variety of products. Kitchen gardens are apt to contain chili, onions, cabbages, watermellons, safflower, coxcomb (for food dyes), and occasionally tomatoes in addition to small amounts of maize, beans and squash.[32] These plots supply the day to day needs of the household during the growing season. Surplus is frequently traded fresh or placed with the harvest from the main fields for winter storage.

The Atlantic subsistence farm has a definitive kitchen garden in which carrots, parsnips, beets, turnips and cabbage are the basic vegetables. If potatoes and rutabagas are not produced as field crops then they are apt to be included in the garden.

Kitchen gardens remain the heart of traditional resource management in North America. They are ecologically stable with a great deal of nutrient recycling as food wastes, vegetable choppings and ashes are worked back into the soil. Animal manures, when available, are tilled into the garden plot on a rotating basis. Crop diversity and the practice of shifting the plot from year to year especially in conjunction with the application of animal manures combine to maintain high fertility. The common practice of manuring is to apply the manure in the fall or winter. A field crop such as oats is grown during the first and sometimes the second year following application. The long residual of nutrients in the manure and a slow transition to humus optimizes conditions in the third or fourth year.

Kitchen gardens are a microcosm of traditional agriculture. They are frequently used as the heart of a nearly self-sustaining economic unit or as a supplement to part-time employment elsewhere. In any case the garden allows a maximization of human labor input and the minimization of external application of capital and energy. It also optimizes economic and ecological security in small scale agriculture. The kitchen or household garden, for these reasons, will continue as the heart of low-energy, traditional agriculture as it is found in North America.

Fruit gardens. Fruit gardens, though not as essential to traditional agriculture as vegetable gardens, are used where possible. Hopi and Zuni plantings which always include peaches, introduced by the Spanish in the 16th century, now have a sprinkling of apricots, apples, cherries, and grapes. Fruit trees belong to individual women and like vegetable gardens are cultivated by women. Management of perennial trees is primarily wind control through shelter belts, rock walls and selection of sheltered sites. Young fruit stocks are hand watered until deep roots become established in the moist seepage areas. Extremely high summer temperatures prevent the Pima and Papago from growing fruit with traditional methods.

Fruit culture in Atlantic subsistence is controlled by length of the growing season. In Newfoundland blueberries and strawberries are the most dependable. Further south, especially in Nova Scotia, diversity is greater with apples, small fruits such as cherries and plums, and a wide range of berries including gooseberries and currants. Management practices include planting on slopes to insure air drainage for frost protection. East slopes are considered best because they also give shelter from prevailing winds and optimize spring warmth. Well drained soils enhance earlier warmth in the spring.

Livestock. Livestock in pre-Columbian North America was limited to domestic turkeys and dogs. The Spanich introduced sheep, goats, burros, and horses to the Southwest during the 16th century. All are integrated into traditional Indian systems at present. Burros and horses are used to haul firewood and crops, but little used in field preparations. Sheep caused a more direct change in crop practices in that cotton cultivation in the Pueblo areas ceased after wool became readily available. Domestic animals rely primarily on forage, even so there must be some storage of corn fodder and even wild-grass hay for winter sustenance.

Animal husbandry in the Atlantic tradition is second only to the garden as an economic stabilizer. Dairy cattle, sheep, chickens, hogs, and horses are found on nearly all farms. Most animal products except for some milk is consumed on the farm as there is little local or national market. The Canadian government has tried to stimulate the commercial production of beef in this area, but with little success because of market isolation and unfavorable climates.

Seed selection. The purchase of commercially-grown seeds can be a burden for a farm with minimal cash flow. This problem is compounded by the predominance of hybrid seeds having a usefulness of a single year. So most traditional farmers save their own seeds.

Hopi seed saving is typical. Maize, as the main crop, receives most attention. As late as 1937 the Hopi lacked a specific knowledge of cross pollination, yet intuitively they avoided planting seeds from ears thought to be mixed varieties.[33] So careful was selection that 97 varieties were recognized. Two very beneficial characteristics have resulted from this selective breeding: (1) the mesocotyl in Hopi corn averages 11 inches in length compared with 5 inches in most maize, this allows the plant to live with the deep sand mulch, and (2) a deep thrusting radicle has replaced the numerous and shallow seminal roots allowing access to deeper soil moisture.[34] The ownership of seed varieties, the right to grow that variety, is vested in the women who are also responsible for seed selection. Thus maize varieties have become virtually hereditary by household.

Atlantic subsistence farmers are not as definitive in seed selection, but most have a knowledge of germination testing and seed selection. The best ears and heads of corn and wheat are saved. With maize it is further refined, saving only the uniform kernels from the center of the ear. Likewise seed potatoes are selected on the basis of size, uniformity, and the quality of the eye (sprout bud).[35]

Seed selection may seem a minor technology among the diversity of practices used in traditional agriculture, but the tendencies of genetic drift can devastate productivity and disease resistence in a few generations if a farmer is not careful to maintain a good gene pool.[36] The medieval English practice of exchanging seeds with farmers in another parish at Michaelmass each year helped to maintain a varied breeding pool. Present traditional systems are more apt to maintain variation by commercial supplements. Among the Hopi 16% of their total seed supplies were purchased from commercial sources. Specific varieties ranged from 70% for mellons to none for blue corn and white corn. Blue corn seed came mostly from the woman's clan (66%), 22% from the man's clan, and 8% by exchange.[37] Through careful selection of seeds from various scources the traditional farmer is able to maintain both type integrity and an adequate gene pool.

Size of operation. Two acres of maize and ½ acre of vegetables and fruits are required to support the average Hopi villager.[38] Requirements have changed little over the centuries except to accommodate the introduction of peaches and domestic animals in the 16th century.

The typical Atlantic subsistence farm in 1931 consisted of some 125 acres (50 hectares) of which 28 acres (4 hectares) were cultivated—hay 17.4, oats 6.4, potatoes 1.8, buckwheat 1.2, and vegetables and fruits 1.2 acres. The typical livestock complement included 6 cows, 4 sheep, 2 horses, 3 hogs and 44 chickens.[39] Average farm size in 1966 had only increased to 135 acres (54 hectares) of which 37% was improved.[40] Hay still occupies over half of the improved land. Livestock categories have changed little, neither has their management. Atlantic subsistence farmers have long been accused of "small patch plots and small patch mentality."[41]

Summing up traditional farming. In spite of certain obvious advantages such an energy efficiency and ecological stability, traditional farming in North America could not survive as a widespread resource system. The pressures of economic growth, the easy availability of fossil fuels, good transportation networks and the desire for higher consumption standards have always worked against traditional farming especially in its most self-sufficient forms.

Subsistence is dependent upon farmers producing crops for their own food supply. It does not preclude the marketing of surplus. On the other hand it optimizes survival through diversification of crops and animals, crop rotation, recycling of plant nutrients and organic matter, and the ability to integrate human ecosystems with natural systems. Balance is more important than profit. This, however, creates a problem in money supply. Traditional farmers cannot depend on commercial banks to carry their debts because profits are low and most dare not risk their real capital of land and buildings to secure loans. Thus they are forced to remain at more or less the same level of productivity.

In order for traditional agriculture to maintain itself land must be cheap, taxes low, additives inexpensive or free except for labor and the competing job market must be adequate. All of these conditions fall upon the Hopi and other Indian villagers who elect to remain at home. They must accept an extremely limited job market. Their land is cheap because they live on the reservation, with no taxes. Use rights are essentially inherited. Few if any additives are purchased. Most soil fertility replacement comes from annual flooding. Economically the villagers remain somewhat isolated, thus forced to near subsistence. Many opt to leave for the advantages of Phoenix or Los Angeles, but those who remain behind have little choice but to conform to traditional methods and social stringencies of an extremely old and conservative culture.

In the Atlantic Provinces economic forces of isolation are also at work. The area has long been outside the mainstream of Canadian or New England economic life. Land is cheap because of chronic depression. Governments dare not raise taxes since it would only force people to abandon their lands. Some additives are cheap but not well utilized. Heavy labor input in the application of animal manures slows their application even though monetary costs are low. Soils are widely deficient in calcium and potash. The system is far from a steady state, but it still retains a basic economic security for those involved. Most heads of families must work part-time away from the farm in timber or fishing industries. But wages are low and seasonal so they dare not give up the security of their land.

Traditional farmers try to balance their risks, hedging their bets that if one crop does not yield a good return another will. They use a variety of soils and microclimates to enhance the possibility of at least a partial harvest. Productivity per man hour remains very low, but the opportunity to utilize the labor supply is constant. Stability then depends upon an ability to optimize the factors most readily available—cheap labor and great diversity.

REGIONAL ASSESSMENT

The transition from traditional to modern agricultural resource management is more nearly complete in North America than in any other world region except northwest Europe. Farm population in the United States in 1978 was at a low of 7.8 million, just 3.6% of the population. This is indicative of high productivity and adequate distribution systems. Modern farming is still hard work, but food production per man hour is high because management is able to focus a wide range of energy and capitalization techniques upon the basic land resource. Recent and rapid increases in energy costs will cause this to change. Energy costs have not yet been reconciled in current management practices, but a greater conservation of fossil fuels must develop.

The restoration of selected traditional technologies is one way to reduce fuel demands. The restitution of crop rotation, a full utilization of farm manures, and a greater input of hand labor are obvious first steps.[42] Unfortunately such measures will increase the costs of food, but so will the continued high dependency upon fossil fuels. Given a choice of where to accommodate the increased food costs, it is better to make adjustments by withdrawing carefully and steadily from high fossil-fuel dependency.[43]

Draft animals could conceivably return to American agriculture, but the advantage they offer is couched in a dilemma. Some of the land now in food production would be required for feed production. The use of tractors in North America has released 70 to 80 million acres of cropland which would otherwise be used to feed horses and mules. Less crop land equals less profit. Horses are slower and less powerful than tractors. More

Fig. 52. Labor-intensive agriculture based on traditional management practices may become very important to future food production in North America (*Source:* U.S. Department of Agriculture).

work by horses means more human time devoted to tillage. Labor costs would go up. Draft animals should be the last resort in conserving fossil fuels.

Land costs, however, have become the ultimate factor that precludes traditional agriculture in most areas of North America. A farmer who pays high land costs is forced to use the most profitable measures available no matter how wasteful of energy or other resources. Traditional farmers, forced off their lands in great numbers during the 1930s, stayed to work in the cities during World War II and never returned to the land.

Some veterans returning from the same war went into small scale agriculture.[44] Inspite of favorable loans and hard work they were forced either to give up agriculture or move into increasingly intensive methods to keep up with the growing tide of consumerism. This meant more land at higher costs, more equipment, more fertilizers, and spray chemicals.

Farmers have been on an economic treadmill ever since. The average size farm in the United States in 1974 and 534 acres (214 hectares) up from 138 acres (55 hectares) in 1910. Capitalization costs also keep rising, forcing profit conscious farmers into larger operations. By 1976 a farm in Yolo County, California would have to have been at least 2,600 acres (1,050 hectares) to maximize the economics of scale gained from capital inputs of machinery, fertilizer and spray chemicals.

Obviously this pattern of high capitalization and heavy energy inputs cannot continue. At some point agriculture must revert to greater human input which means selectively adopting many traditional practices. Hopefully this does not mean a reversion to complete subsistence, but an integration of the best from traditional with the best of modern agriculture.

The economics of the late 1970s are a long way from those that influenced traditional resource systems in the 1920s and even further from the subsistence of the American Frontier. As mentioned earlier, the cost of land is perhaps the most crucial factor. Costs, as related to productivity have become extremely distorted. The old rule of thumb, used in land economics, was "that the cost of land should be no more than 10 times its annual return." It is now impossible to buy agricultural land under such favorable conditions, therefore many are looking to smaller holdings where labor-intensive techniques may be used to counter high capitalization costs and compensate for this distortion.

A new strata of farming is developing. At the micro-agricultural level many manage a minimum acreage while working part-time at other jobs. In 1970, 63% of farm residents supported themselves from farming only. By 1978 the figure was less then 54%. Nearly one half of American farmers had to work part-time away from the farm in order to live. This trend may be more beneficial than economists would like us to believe. There is a measure of security found in part-time agriculture not found in many occupations, including full-time agriculture. More important to the economy as a whole is the potential for saving fossil fuels. Indeed the future of food production in North America may well hinge upon our ability to integrate small, labor-intensive, traditional units within the mainstream of commercial agriculture (Figure 52).

The mark of a good resource system, though often forgotten, is its ability to sustain and renew itself indefinitely. Small and part-time, traditional farmers are more likely to work within the steady-state capabilities of their land use. It is easier for them to maintain a balance between plant and animal husbandry, to use manures to ammend the soils, to rotate crops and resist the urge to mine soils for short term gain.

Traditional farming as a resource system in North America most certainly reached a low point in the mid-decades of the 20th century. The tradition is still alive and with some modifications it may well re-emerge with more vigor than it has shown in more than 50 years. The appeal and value of small scale and part-time traditional agriculture cannot be denied, so it should be incumbent upon society and government to stimulate its development.

NOTES

[1] The importance of the kitchen garden in American resource tradition was recognized in early agricultural literature, e.g., Thomas Bridgeman, *The Kitchen Gardener's Instructor* (New York: C. M. Saxton & Co., Agricultural Book Publishers, 1857).

[2] Donald D. Durost and Warren R. Bailey, "What's Happened to Farming," *Contours of Change*, Yearbook of Agriculture 1970 (Washington, D.C.: Government Printing Office, 1970), pp. 2–9.

[3] At the Rothamsted Agricultural Experiment Station in England these types of soils have been planted to wheat for over 100 consecutive years without fertilization and still produce 10 bushels per acre.

[4] Conrad E. Heidenreich, "The Indian Occupance of Huronia, 1600–1650," in R. Louis Gentilcore (ed.), *Canada's Changing Geography* (Scarborough, Ontario: Prentice-Hall of Canada, 1967), p. 25.

[5] Matthew W. Sterling, *Indians of the Americas* (Washington, D.C.: National Geographic Society, 1955), p. 46.

[6]William Nelson Fenton, "Iroquois," *Encyclopaedia Britannica*, 1966, Vol. 12, p. 638.

[7]John R. Swanton, *The Indians of Southeastern United States*, Bulletin 137 (Washington, D.C.: Bureau of American Ethnology, 1946), p. 265.

[8]Sterling, op. cit., note 5, p. 63.

[9]John C. Ewers, *The Horse in Blackfoot Indian Culture*, Smithsonian Institution, Bureau of American Ethnology, Bulletin 159 (Washington, D.C.: Government Printing Office, 1955), pp. 332–36.

[10]David I. Bushnell, Jr., *Villages of the Algonquian, Siouan, and Caddoan Tribes West of the Mississippi*, Smithsonian Institution, Bureau of American Ethnology, Bulletin 77 (Washington, D.C.: Government Printing Office, 1922), p. 125.

[11]Herbert W. Dick, *Bat Cave*, Monograph No. 27 (Santa Fe: School of American Research), pp. 95–99.

[12]Paul S. Martin and Fred Plog, *The Archaeology of Arizona* (New York: Doubleday/Natural History Press, 1973), p. 168.

[13]Wayne Suttles, "Variation in Habitat and Culture on the Northwest Coast," in Yehudi A. Cohen (ed.), *Man In Adaptation: The Cultural Present* (Chicago: Aldine, 1968), pp. 91–112, reprinted with permission from *Proceedings of the 34th International Congress of Americanists* (1960).

[14]Aubrey C. Land, "A Modified Heritage: The Colonial Economy and Social Order as Seen in the Literary and Non-literary Sources," in Alan Fusonie and Leila Moran (eds.), *Agricultural Literature: Proud Heritage–Future Promise*, A Bicentennial Symposium, September 24–26, 1975 (Washington, D.C.: Associates of the National Agricultural Library, Inc. and the Graduate School Press, U.S. Department of Agriculture, 1977), p. 13.

[15]Jethro Tull, *Horse-hoeing Husbandry: Or, an Essay on the Principles of Vegetation and Tillage. Designed to Introduce a New Method of Culture; Whereby the Produce of Land Will Be Increased, and the Usual Expense Lessened. Together with Accurate Descriptions and Cuts of the Instruments Employed in it.*, 3rd. ed. (London: A. Millar, 1751).

[16]Percy Wells Bidwell and John I. Falconer, *History of Agriculture in the Northern United States, 1620–1860* (New York: Peter Smith, reprinted with the Permission of the Carnegie Institution of Washington, 1941), pp. 87–89.

[17]Green manuring is the practice of planting a cover crop, preferably legumes such as sweet clover, then plowing it into the soil while the plants are still tender and rich in nitrates.

[18]Isaiah Bowman, *The Pioneer Fringe*, Special Publication No. 13 (New York: American Geographical Society, 1931), p. 29, and Herman R. Friis, *A Series of Population Maps of the Colonies and the United States, 1965–1790*, Mimeographes Publication No. 3 (New York: American Geographical Society, 1940), pp. 12–13.

[19]Hugh Hammond Bennett, *Soil Conservation* (New York: McGraw-Hill, 1939) p. 73.

[20]Charles E. Kellogg, *The Soils that Support Us* (New York: Macmillan, 1941), p. 58.

[21]The rise of environmental consciousness is seen in two landmark works separated by nearly a century of time, George Perkins Marsh, *The Earth as Modified by Human Action* (New York: Scribner's, 1882) and Aldo Leopold, *A Sand County Almanac*, enlarged ed. (New York: Sierra Club and Ballantine, 1970).

[22]Alan Macpherson, ed., *The Atlantic Provinces*, for the 22nd International Geographical Congress, Montreal 1972 (Toronto: University of Toronto Press, 1972), p. 108.

[23]A. F. Gustafson, *Conservation of the Soil* (New York: McGraw-Hill, 1937), p. 6.

[24]A. R. Hall, *Early Erosion Control Practices in Virginia*, Miscellaneous Publications No. 252 (Washington, D.C.: U.S. Department of Agriculture, 1938), pp. 4–7.

[25]Hopi field and planting techniques are well illustrated in Jerry Jacka, "The Miracle of Hopi Corn," *Arizona Highways*, Jan. 1978, pp. 3–15.

[26]John T. Hack, "The Changing Physical Environment of the Hopi Indians of Arizona," papers of the Peabody Museum, Harvard University (Cambridge: Harvard University Press, 1942), Vol. 35, No. 1, p. 26.

[27]Maitland Bradfield, *The Changing Pattern of Hopi Agriculture*, Occasional Paper No. 30 (London: Royal Anthropological Institute, 1971), pp. 17–18.

[28]Bradfield, op. cit., note 27, p. 5.

[29]National Development Bureau, Department of the Interior, *The Maritime Provinces of Canada*

(Ottawa: F. A. Acland, Printer to the King's Most Excellent Majesty, 1930), pp. 21–25.

[30] Andrew Hill Clark, *Acadia: The Geography of Early Nova Scotia to 1760* (Madison: University of Wisconsin Press, 1968), pp. 238–42.

[31] National Development Bureau, op. cit., note 29, pp. 26–36.

[32] Alfred F. Whiting, "Hopi Indian Agriculture: I, Background," *Museum Notes* (Flagstaff: Museum of Northern Arizona), Vol. 8 (1937), No. 10, p. 53.

[33] Alfred F. Whiting, "Hopi Indian Agriculture: II, Seed Source and Distribution," *Museum Notes* (Flagstaff: Museum of Northern Arizona), Vol. 10 (1937), No. 5, p. 13.

[34] Bradfield, op. cit., note 27, p. 5.

[35] Traditional seed saving techniques are elaborated in M. G. Kains, *Five Acres and Independence*, revised and enlarged ed. (New York: Dover Publications, 1973), pp. 243–52.

[36] The danger of loosing standard seed stocks and increasing genetic variation are discussed by Wilson Clark, "U.S. Agriculture Is Growing Trouble as well as Crops," *Smithsonian*, Vol. 5 (1975), No. 10, pp. 59–65.

[37] Whiting, op. cit., note 33, p. 14.

[38] Bradfield, op. cit., note 27, p. 21.

[39] Thomas Griffith Taylor, *Canada: A Study of Cool Continental Environments and Their Effect on British and French Settlement*, 2nd. ed. (London: Dutton, 1950), p. 388.

[40] Macpherson, op. cit., note 22, p. 105.

[41] R. Louis Gentilcore, "Agriculture in Eastern Nova Scotia," *Annals*, Association of American Geographers, Vol. 46 (1956), p. 402.

[42] Details of potential energy savings are contained in an excellent article, David Pimental, et al., "Food Production and the Energy Crisis," *Science*, Vol. 182 (1973), pp. 443–49.

[43] Howard T. Odum foresees a time when urbanites will commute to the countryside to work on farms and the economic system will be based upon labor intensive, land intensive agriculture. See "Odums Law," *Newsweek*, Jan. 13, 1975, p. 54.

[44] Ed and Carolyn Robinson, *The "Have-More" Plan for a Little Land—a Lot of Living* (New York: Macmillan, 1947).

Chapter 9

Latin America

William M. Denevan

Latin America is characterized by extreme environmental variability as well as by great cultural diversity, time depth, and persistence. Consequently, as might be expected, there exists a wide range of traditional (palaeotecnic) methods of resource management. These are methods which make little or no use of machinery, fossil fuels, and chemicals, but which are not necessarily simple, extensive, or unchanging. Most have an origin in the colonial and aboriginal past. They have survived because they are viable adaptations by people to specific environmental, demographic, and economic conditions. They may not be as efficient and as productive as modern (neotecnic) agricultural systems, but they do minimize subsistence risk and they are relatively stable ecologically. These methods are summarized in Tables 26-30 below. The emphasis here is on management of the major agricultural natural resources: water, soil, and climate, and also slope.[1]

Latin America is considered to consist of those nations of the Western Hemisphere south of the United States. Historically, the southwestern United States is part of Latin America but will not be included here. Latin America can be subdivided into South America (south of Panama) and Middle America consisting of Mexico, Central America, and the Caribbean Islands. Because of space limitations, less attention will be given to the islands.

Culturally and racially, the over 350 million population of today consists of roughly 7% Indian, 45% mestizo and mulatto, 33% white, and 15% black. The European influences are predominantely Spanish and Portuguese and are strongest in southern South America. English, French, and Dutch elements exist in the Caribbean and fringing mainland. The largest Indian survivals are in the Andes and in Mexico-Guatemala. Blacks dominate the Caribbean and the east coast of South America. Traditional resource management techniques are most prevalent in the Indian and mestizo culture areas.

An indication of the continuing importance of traditional agriculture in Latin America, despite considerable efforts towards modernization, is provided by the following data for Mexico. Of all farm units, 40.5% are traditional semi-commercial, and 52.4% are traditional subsistence. The two categories take up 80% of the total crop land.[2]

THE RESOURCE BASE

The principal biomes (large ecosystems) of Latin America are shown on Figure 53. The physical aspects of natural vegetation are the basic criteria of differentiation since they largely reflect conditions of rainfall, temperature, drainage, soil, and elevation.

The tropical forest (rainforest and semi-deciduous or seasonal forest) of Amazonia and the tropical coasts of Latin America have no period of frost and have moderate to heavy rainfall; the soil is mostly poor, leached of soluble minerals, with limited areas of superior alluvial, volcanic, and other young soils. The tropical rainforest has little or no dry season, while the tropical seasonal forest has several dry months of little or no rainfall. Land use in both is dominated by shifting cultivation. The tropical and mid-latitude scrub forests vary from a low, closed scrub forest to more open scrub savanna with grass between the low trees and thorn bush; rainfall is low, and soils are variable. Most of this biome is only used for extensive livestock grazing, but there is some agriculture where soils are good and seasonal rainfall is adequate or irrigation possible. The tropical savannas are grasslands with or without scattered trees. They occur in Amazonia, northern Columbia, the Orinoco region, the Guiana Highlands, and in patches in Cuba and on the east and west coasts of Central America. Most have a long dry season, with soils characterized by severe leaching or by hard pans and poor drainage. Large portions have been converted from forest by human action, while others seem natural as a result of seasonal flooding or particular soil conditions. Most are used for livestock and agriculture is rare, although there is evidence for considerable pre-Columbian cultivation.

The deserts, obviously, are characterized by little or no rainfall and little or no vegetation; there are both modern and traditional forms of irrigation agriculture as well as no use at all. The middle-latitude grasslands, Mediterranean type scrub forest of central Chile, and middle-latitude deciduous and coniferous forests of southern South America are mostly used for modern agriculture and pasture, but there is still considerable traditional agriculture in the middle-latitude forests and grasslands of Mexico. The coniferous forests of southern Chile and Mexico-Central America are used mostly for wood products, with some traditional agriculture and grazing. The Andean highlands contain varied and highly mixed biomes, ranging from montane tropical forest to temperate basins to desert and tundra. Traditional agriculture survives here in some of its most interesting forms, along with livestock raising and with modern agriculture in the more favored basins.

Thus, it is in the tropical lowlands and the mountains where traditional agriculture has most frequently survived, in part because of greater isolation and in part because these areas are less attractive to commercial, modernized agriculture because of isolation and unfavorable soils and climate. The mountain lands often have steep slopes, progressively colder temperatures, thin soils, and rainfall extremes from arid to very wet, while the tropical lowlands have heavy rain, high temperatures, infertile soils, and poor drainage. The people who live in these biomes must utilize ecologically sound resource management

Fig. 53. Principal biomes of Latin America.

techniques which can reclaim what is mostly difficult land for agriculture and which can maintain or improve soil fertility. It must be kept in mind that "marginal" lands are not marginal for all agricultural systems, only for certain technologies and economic forms.

EVOLUTION OF TRADITIONAL RESOURCE MANAGEMENT

The traditional resource management techniques found in Latin America today were mostly developed in pre-Columbian times by the native peoples of the hemisphere.

Changes subsequent to the arrival of the Europeans were primarily in crops and tools, rather than cultivation techniques.

The most fundamental of all agricultural resources were the wild plant species which evolved under man's guidance into cultivated plants, a process taking thousands of years. The first clearly identifiable domesticated seed plants appeared by 5000 B.C. in central Mexico (maize, gourd, squash), with many others appearing between 3400 and 5000 B.C. (beans, cotton, chili pepper, amaranth). In coastal and highland Peru the oldest known crops date to 3000 to 5600 B.C. (gourds, squash, beans, cotton, potato), with others appearing between 3000 and 5000 B.C. (maize, peanuts, achira, chili pepper, sweet potatoes). In the humid tropical lowlands, domesticates may be even older than in Mexico and Peru, but because of poor preservation the evidence is poor. Manioc, the major staple of Amazonia, was probably a well developed crop by 3000 B.C.[3]

The initiation of plant domestication and cultivation, however, did not result in an agricultural revolution. Rather, for several thousand more years, hunting, gathering, and fishing continued to be more important for food than was agriculture. In the dry Tehuacán Valley in central Mexico, for which we have a detailed archaeological sequence for subsistence, settlement, and demography, the first domesticated crops date to about 7000 B.C., but sedentary populations making major use of crops are not present until 1500 B.C., and agriculture doesn't provide 50% or more of the diet until 850 B.C.[4] The change from hunting and gathering to substantial agriculture probably can be attributed in part to increasing population densities, as can the development of new and more intensive agricultural resource management techniques.[5] By the time states and cities appear, two major crop complexes are present: a seed crop tradition (maize, beans, squash) in Mesoamerica and the north and west coasts of South America, and a root crop tradition (dominated by manioc in the lowlands and the potato in the highlands) in the Caribbean, eastern Central America, tropical South America, and the Andes. For each complex, a wide variety of both extensive and intensive cultivation methods were practiced.

The earliest forms of agriculture are unknown but probably consisted of rainfall cultivation, house gardens, floodwater farming, and shifting cultivation, with little or no soil or water management. Riverine sites would have been preferred because of aquatic resources and water for household needs. Soils were utilized that were reasonably fertile and easily planted. As population pressures increased, an increasingly wider variety of ecological niches were used for farming. Techniques were developed to increase (a) the quantity of land used by reclaiming marginal land (steep, dry, wet, low fertility), and (b) the quantity of production and the frequency of cultivation by improving or maintaining soil fertility. The native farmers discovered by the Europeans were as sophisticated in terms of complex techniques and ecological understanding as any in the world.

The agricultural technologies of pre-Columbian Latin America can be described with some reliability because of the accounts left by the early Europeans, archaeological evidence, and especially because of the survival of remains of millions of once cultivated fields which were characterized by major landscape engineering. The more numerous and spectacular forms of ancient agriculture are associated with the great states of central Mexico, Yucatan, and the Andes, where populations were the densest. However, the tropical lowlands, deserts, and highlands elsewhere also had localized intensive farming systems.

Fig. 54. Vertical aerial photograph (scale c. 1:20,000) of hilly landscape covered by sloping-field agricultural terraces near Lake Titicaca and the city of Puno in highland Peru. Most of the terraces are of pre-Columbian origin, but are still maintained and cultivated in maize and wheat. Along the streams a few non-terraced, flood plain fields can be seen (*Source*: Instituto Geografico Militar, Peru, 1955).

Terracing. The most intensive and still visible pre-Columbian agricultural resource management techniques were terracing of slope land, irrigation of dry lands, and drainage of wet lands with raised fields and ditches. Terracing involves the construction of stone walls or ridges on slopes and functions to provide more level surfaces, to reduce erosion, to control water, and to accumulate soil (Figure 54). Ancient terracing was widespread throughout the uplands of northern and central Mexico and extended into the Mayan regions of Chiapas, Yucatan, Belize, and Guatemala. The largest and most elaborate terraces in the New World are the Inca staircase, cut-stone wall *andenes* of central Peru, whose floors measure up to 5 meters or more in width, with back walls up to about 4 meters high. The Mayan terraces in Yucatan, although found over an area of 10,000 square kilometers, were only recently discovered and described. There is clear evidence that the Maya civilization was sustained by sophisticated, permanent agriculture rather than by shifting cultivation.[6]

Terraces are difficult to date, but suggested antiquity includes 200–300 B.C. in the Teotihuacán Valley of Mexico, 300 B.C.–100 A.D. for Oaxaca and Chiapas in Mexico, 500–600 A.D. for Yucatan, and by 200 B.C. in the central Andes.[7]

Terraces are classified in Table 26. It should be emphasized here that (1) while terrace agriculture is still common in Latin America, it mainly involves the maintenance of ancient terraces rather than the construction of new ones, and (2) that many terraces have been abandoned completely, especially on higher and more inaccessible slopes. Terrace agriculture is virtually unknown today in Chiapas, Yucatan, and Belize, and in the central Andes I would estimate that over 50% of the terraces are no longer farmed. Most are abandoned in northern Chile and Argentina. Also the check-dam terraces in northern Mexico are seldom maintained or built, and many of the semi-terraces of central Mexico have been abandoned. Much of the excessive hillside erosion in these areas can be attributed to the collapse of terrace and check-dam systems.[8]

Irrigation. The development of the high cultures of central Mexico and the central Andes was closely associated with the development of complex irrigation systems.[9] Canal irrigation in Mexico dates between 850 B.C. and 150 B.C. at Tehuacán, to before 200 B.C. in Puebla, and probably to 1500 B.C. in the Moche Valley of coastal Peru.[10] Non-canal forms of irrigation such as floodwater farming and manual irrigation were undoubtedly substantially earlier. Watertable farming in coastal Peru has been dated to about 100 B.C. in the Viru Valley.[11]

Irrigation was carried out in pre-Columbian times in coastal Peru, the central Andes, central and northern Mexico, and highland Guatemala. In the tropical lowland regions with long dry seasons, irrigation was practiced in a few areas such as northern Honduras, northern Yucatan, lowland Venezuela, and Hispaniola. Raised fields in the tropical lowlands may have served the combined functions of drainage and irrigation. Most canal irrigation systems in the Andes and Mexico were simple diversion operations managed on the local level, and most have continued in use to the present (Table 27). However, in coastal Peru in particular, local systems gradually expanded into valley-wide systems and then megasystems linking two or more river valleys and moving huge amounts of water long distances through large canals. The Moche Valley received water from the Rio Chicama via the La Cumbre canal (now abandoned) which was 80 kilometers long. Further north, the Lambayeque complex irrigated 100 kilometers of the coastal plain by an interconnected canal system utilizing five different drainage basins. This

Table 26. Slope Management: Terracing

Form[a]	Examples	Form[a]	Examples[b]
Check-dam terraces[b]	North Mexico Yucatan, Mexico Oaxaca, Mexico Andes	*Sloping-field terraces*	Highland Guatemala Colombian Andes Southern Andes Coastal Peru

Semi-terraces
   Maguey hedges[c]
	Central Mexico	*Bench terraces*[e]
		   Stone wall
			Central Mexico
			Southern Andes

Sloping-field terraces[d]	Central Mexico Chiapas, Mexico Yucatan	*Andenes*[f] *Valley floor terraces*[g] Coco terraces	East Andes, Peru Central Andes Central Andes Bolivian yungas

Notes:

[a]Most types of terraces may be dry field (rain watered). Check-dam terraces are irrigated by floodwater. Sloping field and especially bench terraces are often irrigated from canal systems. Construction materials may consist of earth, piled stone, stone slabs, or cut stone. Most types are ancient as well as present day. For a detailed classification of terraces, see J. E. Spencer and G. A. Hale, "The Origin, Nature, and Distribution of Agricultural Terracing," *Pacific Viewpoint*, Vol. 2, No. 1 (1961), pp. 1–40.

[b]Small stone walls built across ravines to trap silt, settle water, or spread water. Also known as weirs, cross-channel terraces, channel-bottom terraces, *trincheras, muros,* and *presas.*

[c]*Bancales* or *metepantli.*

[d]Cropping surfaces are less steep than the natural slope but are not flat.

[e]Flat floored with vertical back walls; linear, contour, irrigable terraces.

[f]Large staircase or tier terraces.

[g]Valley floor terraces have very broad planting surfaces and serve to facilitate canal irrigation by water drawn off at a higher location.

Coco terraces (*gradas*) are stone or earth ridges backed by a trench in which rain water is trapped and where the coco seedlings are planted.

Sources: Broadbent, "Agricultural Terraces in Chibcha Territory, Columbia," *American Antiquity*, Vol. 29 (1964), pp. 501–504; Cook, "Staircase Farms of the Ancients," *National Geographic Magazine*, Vol. 24 (1916), pp. 474–534; Donkin (*note* 7); Engel, "New Facts About Pre-Columbian Life in the Andean Lomas," *Current Anthropology*, Vol. 14 (1973), pp. 271–280 (ref. on pp. 275–278); Field, "A Reconnaissance of Southern Andean Terracing," unpublished Ph.D. dissertation (University of California, Los Angeles, 1966); Guzmán, "Las terrazas de los antiguos Mayas montañeses, Chiapas, México," *Revista Interamericana de Ciencias Sociales*, Vol. 1 (1962), pp. 398–406; Hopkins (*note* 7); Howard and Griffiths, *Trinchera Distribution in the Sierra Madre Occidental, Mexico*, Technical Paper No. 66-1 (Denver: Department of Geography, University of Denver, 1966); Isbell, "New Discoveries in the Montaña, Southeastern Peru," *Archaeology*, Vol. 21 (1968), pp. 108–114; Kirkby, *The Use of Land and Water Resources in the Past and Present Valley of Oaxaca, Mexico*, Memoirs of the Museum of Anthropology, No. 5 (Ann Arbor: University of Michigan, 1973), pp. 36–38; Patrick, "A Cultural Geography of the Use of Seasonally Dry, Sloping Terrain: The Metepantli Crop Terraces of Central Mexico," unpublished Ph.D. dissertation (University of Pittsburgh, 1977); Turner, "Prehispanic Terracing in the Central Maya Lowlands: Problems of Agricultural Intensification," in Normand Hammond and Gordon R. Willey, eds., *Maya Archaeology and Ethnohistory* (Austin: University of Texas Press, 1979), pp. 103–115. West, "Population Densities and Agricultural Practices in Pre-Columbian Mexico, with Emphasis on Semi-terracing," in *Verhandlungen des XXXVIII Internationalen Amerikanistenkongresses* (Müchen, 1970), Vol. 2, pp. 361–369; Wilken (*note* 8); Wilken, "Food-Producing Systems Available to the Ancient Maya," *American Antiquity*, Vol. 36 (1971), pp. 432–448. **For additional details pertaining to sources, see** *note 49.*

Table 27. Water Management: Irrigation

Form	Examples	Form	Examples
Floodwater: uncontrolled	Viru Valley, Peru[a]	*Canal irrigation*	
	Northwest Mexico[a]	River fed: flatlands	Coastal Peru[a]
Floodwater: controlled			Central Mexico[a]
Partitioned fields	Viru Valley[a]		*See* Table 26
With canals	Oaxaca, Mexico	River fed: terraced	Viru and Moche, Peru[a]
Check dams	*See* Table 26	Fed from ponded groundwater	Michoacán, Mex.
Groundwater		Fed from lakes	Tehuacán, Mex.
Sunken fields[b]	Coastal Peru[a]	Fed from springs	Central Mexico
High water table	Coastal Peru[a]	Fed from reservoirs	Oaxaca
	Oaxaca	Fed from wells	Teotihuacán[a]
	Teotihuacán, Mex.[a]	Fed from check dams[c]	Northern Chile
		Underground canals	Southern Peru[a]
Manual irrigation			Tehuacán[a]
Container (pot, bucket)	Oaxaca		Puebla-Tlaxcala, Mex.[a]
	Tlaxcala, Mexico	*Tablones*[d]	Highland Guatemala
	Highland Guatemala	Drained fields[e]	*See* Table 28
	El Salvador		
	Viru Valley		
Splash irrigation	Highland Guatemala		
	Central Mexico		

Notes:

ªPre-Columbian, but often still current.

ᵇSunken fields are depressions dug down to ground water level. In Peru they are called *pukios, mahamaes, hoyas,* or *canchones.*

ᶜQanats.

ᵈTablones are splash-irrigated platform terraces. On flat, poorly drained ground they also serve for drainage.

ᵉDrained fields often serve both for irrigation and for drainage.

Sources: Armillas, "Land-Use in Pre-Columbian America," *Arid Zone Research, Vol. 17: A History of Land Use in Arid Regions* (Paris: UNESCO, 1961), pp. 255–276; Kirkby (*see Sources, Table 26*); Knapp, "The Sunken Fields of Chilca," unpublished Master's thesis (University of Wisconsin, Madison, 1979); Kosok, *Life, Land and Water in Ancient Peru* (N.Y.: Long Island University Press, 1965); Kus, "Selected Aspects of Irrigated Agriculture in the Chimú Heartland, Peru," unpublished Ph.D. dissertation (University of California, Los Angeles, 1972); Mathewson, "Specialized Horticulture in the Guatemalan Highlands: The Tablón System of Panajachel," unpublished Master's thesis (University of Wisconsin, Madison, 1976); Moseley (*note 10*); Parsons and Psuty, "Sunken Fields and Prehispanic Subsistence on the Peruvian Coast," *American Antiquity,* Vol. 40 (1975), pp. 259–282; Price (*note 9*); Sanders (*note 7*); Sanders, *The Cultural Ecology of the Teotihuacán Valley* (University Park: Department of Sociology and Anthropology, Pennsylvania State University, 1965), pp. 33–35; Sanders, "Hydraulic Agriculture, Economic Symbiosis and the Evolution of States in Central Mexico," *Anthropological Archeology in the Americas* (Washington, D.C.: Anthropological Society of Washington, 1968), pp. 88–107; Seele, "Galerías filtrantes en el área de Acotzingo-Tepeaca: Estado de Puebla," *Boletín del Instituto Nacional de Antropología y Historia,* Vol. 35 (1969), pp. 3–8; Smith, "Agriculture, Tehuacán Valley," *Fieldiana: Botany,* Vol. 31 (1965), pp. 49–100; Troll, "Qanat-Bewässerung in der Alten und Neuen Welt," *Mitteilungen der Österreichischen Geographischen Gesellschaft,* Vol. 105 (1963), pp. 313–330; West (*note 11*); West, "The Use of Agricultural Resources in an Andean Coastal Ecosystem," *Human Ecology* (in press); West (*note 47*); West and Augelli, *Middle America: Its Land and Peoples* (Englewood Cliffs: Prentice-Hall, 1976), p. 271; Wilken (*see Sources, Table 26*); Wilken, "Manual Irrigation in Middle America," *Agricultural Water Management,* Vol. 1 (1977), pp. 155–165; Wolf and Palerm, "Irrigation in the Old Acolhua Domain, Mexico," *Southwestern Journal of Anthropology,* Vol. 11 (1955), pp. 265–281. For additional details pertaining to sources, see *note 49.*

system has long been out of use, but recently a major desert reclamation scheme, the Tinajones-Taymi Project, has been attempting to reactivate one of the major inter-valley canals using modern engineering methods.

In coastal Peru, most of the ancient irrigation systems have been abandoned or are only partly operational. Many have been replaced by modern irrigation works associated with commercial agriculture. Nevertheless, the amount of land irrigated, especially on the northern coast, is generally less than was irrigated in pre-Columbian times. The difference is 40% less for both the Viru Valley and the Moche Valley.[12] The difference partly reflects higher water demands by the different crops grown now (especially sugar cane). Also, land was abandoned due to natural factors (dune encroachment, flooding, tectonic uplift), management factors (salinization, siltation), and to conquest and de-population. However, the difference may also reflect a lower efficiency of modern water management technology.

Raised fields. The third major form of ancient agricultural landscape engineering is the raised field (Table 28). Raised fields include any prepared land involving the transfer and elevation of soil above the natural surface of the earth in order to improve cultivating conditions. In Latin America they functioned primarily to improve drainage of seasonally flooded tropical savannas and highland basins, waterlogged soils, and as garden islands in shallow lakes. Other functions include soil aeration, concentration of organic matter and top soil, temperature modification, erosion control, and moisture retention or irrigation. Although widespread, these fields have only recently received attention, partly because they are not readily noticeable except from airplanes and on air photos. In fact, most of these fields were not discovered until after 1960.

Raised fields take many forms, including ridges, platforms, and mounds; they form a variety of distinctive patterns on the landscape; and they range in size from very small up to about 20 meters in width, 1000 meters in length, and one meter in height.[13] In contrast to terraces and irrigation works, which remain part of traditional agriculture, the larger raised fields are known mainly as relics from pre-Columbian times. Surviving examples still cultivated, of limited extent, are the *chinampas* in the lakes around Mexico City, the drained fields of Tlaxcala, Mexico, and the *tablones* of highland Guatemala.

Relic agricultural ridges and platforms have been found in the seasonally inundated savannas of Mojos in northern Bolivia, the Guayas Basin of Ecuador, the San Jorge region of northern Colombia, the coast of Surinam, the Orinoco Llanos of Venezuela, in Belize, and in Vera Cruz, Campeche, and Quintana Roo in Mexico (Figure 55). In Andean basins they occur on the Lake Titicaca plain of Peru and Bolivia, in Ecuador, and in the Sabana de Bogotá of Colombia. They number in the millions. They cover 200,000 acres of land around Lake Titicaca, 240,000 acres in northern Colombia, and over 50,000 acres in northern Bolivia. Many more are buried by alluvium, or are covered by forest.

The remains of large, raised fields are indicative of a form of agriculture that supported substantially larger populations than at present. They date back to at least 1000 A.D., and the chinampas of Mexico may have originated as early as 1300–800 B.C.[14] Most were probably abandoned with the massive Indian depopulation that came with European conquest. Some may have been abandoned earlier due to changing levels of flooding or for other reasons. Harrison suggests that the raised fields in the *bajos* of Yucatan filled with sediment from erosion on surrounding slopes and were abandoned as a result, contributing to the collapse of Classic Maya civilization.[15]

Table 28. Water Management: Drainage

Form	Examples	Form	Examples
Raised fields		Ditched fields	Sabana de Bogotá
Ridged fields	South America[a]		Venezuelan Llanos
	Campeche, Mex.[a]		Viru Valley, Peru
	Belize[a]		Highland Peru
Chinampas[b]	Basin of Mexico[a]	*Diking*	Lake Titicaca, Peru[a]
	Tlaxcala, Mex.		Aztec Mexico[a]
	Antigua,	*Natural drainage*	
	Guatemala	Playas	Amazonia
Tablones	*See* Table 27		Orinoco
		Lagoons	Orinoco Llanos[a]

Notes:

[a]Pre-Columbian, but often still current.

[b]*Chinampas* are platform fields, usually in shallow lakes or on lake shores.

Sources: Armillas, "Gardens on Swamps," *Science*, Vol. 174 (1971), pp. 653–661; Denevan, William M., personal observations; Denevan (*note 13*); Denevan and Bergman, "Karinya Indian Swamp Cultivation in the Venezuelan Llanos," *Yearbook of the Association of Pacific Coast Geographers*, Vol. 37 (1975), pp. 23–37. Denevan and Schwerin (*note 48*); Higbee, "The River Is the Plow," *Scientific Monthly*, Vol. 60 (1945), pp. 405–416; Parsons and Denevan, "Pre-Columbian Ridged Fields," *Scientific American*, Vol. 217, No. 1 (1967), pp. 92–100; Price (*note 9*); Siemens and Puleston, "Ridged Fields and Associated Features in Southern Campeche: New Perspectives on the Lowland Maya," *American Antiquity*, Vol. 37 (1972), pp. 228–239; Siemens, "Some Patterns Seen from the Air," *Journal of Belizean Affairs*, No. 5 (1977), pp. 5–21; Smith, Denevan, and Hamilton, "Ancient Ridged Fields in the Region of Lake Titicaca," *The Geographical Journal*, Vol. 134 (1968), pp. 353–367; West (*see Sources, Table 27*); Wilken, "Drained-Field Agriculture: An Intensive Farming System in Tlaxcala, Mexico," *Geographical Review*, Vol. 59 (1969), pp. 215–241; Wilken (*see Sources, Table 26*); Zucchi and Denevan, Campos elevados e historia cultural prehispánica en los llanos occidentales de Venezuela, (Caracas: Universidad Católica, in press). **For additional details pertaining to sources, see** *note 49.*

Most of these areas are not cultivated today. The lowland savannas are empty or sparsely populated, although livestock grazing is common. Soils and drainage are considered too poor for farming. In the highland basins, populations are dense but cultivation is mainly on the better lands. At Lake Titicaca the old fields are in pasture, and at Bogota they have been destroyed by modern drainage works and plowing.

Other forms of agriculture. Because they left visible remains, we know more about terraces, irrigation, and raised fields than other forms of pre-Columbian land use. We do have some information on the latter from early European accounts, and inferences can be made from the practices of surviving Indians. Certainly shifting cultivation was a common means of cultivation in the tropical forests as well as in many other forested areas. The playas or sandy shores and islands of rivers were cultivated annually when water levels dropped. Rain farming was practiced in the grasslands of the Mexican highlands and parts of the Andes, with or without fallowing depending on soil conditions and pest and weed problems.

Soil fertility. The complex agricultural engineering techniques described for pre-Columbian America were highly labor intensive. High labor inputs were required to

Fig. 55. Pre-Columbian raised fields (ridges and mounds) in the seasonally flooded Llanos de Mojos in northeastern Bolivia. The ridges are about 20 feet wide (Photograph by Tony English, July 1961).

establish terraces, canals, and raised fields, and considerable additional effort was required to maintain them. It is very unlikely that these fields would have been utilized under long-fallow rotation systems, although brief fallowing may have occurred after long periods of cropping. To make possible what was permanent or near permanent cultivation, often on soil that was of poor fertility or of shallow depth, soil improvement techniques were applied.

Little is known about these techniques, but they probably included most of the methods of present day traditional farmers, including the use of ash, house refuse, faunal remains and manure, green manure, mulches, compost, and the incoporation into the soil of weeds, grasses, and leaves (Table 29). The Peruvian Indians used fish heads as fertilizers in sunken fields. Chinampas and other raised fields were fertilized with aquatic vegetation and muck from the canals between fields. In Peru bird guano from the coastal islands was used for fertilizer, and the birds were protected to assure a continuing supply. The Aztecs rotated house sites over their fields to obtain the fertilizing effect of house and human refuse. One form of fertilizer used in pre-Columbian times, rarely used today, was human manure. It was reported in the Valley of Mexico by the early Spaniards, and it was used on maize fields in the Andes after drying and pulverization. By use of such natural fertilizers, continuous moderate levels of productivity were possible in areas of dense populations.

The European impact. The pre-Columbian agricultural resource management techniques were intentional adaptations to specific environmental conditions, developed over centuries of trial and error under increasing demographic pressures and the need to exploit new habitats. They reflect a successful "folk" knowledge of ecological processes, variation, and possibilities for food production.

This is not to say that there were no ecological disasters resulting from maladaptation or mismanagement of resources. For example, it has been argued that population pressures in central Mexico had already resulted in massive erosion and land failure by the time the Spaniards arrived.[16] Nevertheless, pre-Columbian systems of resource management were for the most part successful. They supported populations with local densities in the hundreds per square kilometer, with numbers in some areas far exceeding those of the present. The total Indian population of Latin America in 1492 probably reached at least 50 million and possibly 100 million.[17]

The arrival of Europeans brought significant overall changes. First of all, there was a massive depopulation of the Indians, mainly from the introduction of epidemic European diseases, to less than 5 million by the year 1600. With depopulation, much of the intensive, high-labor indigeneous agriculture was abandoned, and simpler less labor demanding agriculture was relied on. Depopulated, abandoned farm lands were reoccupied to a large extent by European livestock (cattle, sheep, goats, horses).[18] Overgrazing contributed to severe erosion on previously well managed terrain. Where human populations were re-established by the 20th century, it might be expected that former farm land would be returned to cultivation, but often this has not been the case due to land holding interests which favored continuation of livestock raising.

European, Asian, and African crops were introduced, the most important being wheat, barley, rice, citrus, coffee, sugar cane, and bananas. While new crops have entered the diets of traditional farmers, they have tended to be more important in commercial agriculture and of secondary importance in subsistence (with the major exceptions of the banana and rice which are staple foods in some areas).

European tools were introduced starting in the 16th century. Most important for the traditional farmer was the ox-pulled Spanish plow (the ard or scratch plow), which often replaced the native foot plow (Andean *chaquitaclla*), digging stick, mattock, and spade (*coa*), especially in the bottom lands and on gentler slopes.[19] The use of the plow has contributed substantially to the greater rate of post-Columbian erosion, in contrast to the native hand tools which tend to manipulate individual plants rather than the entire soil surface. In many areas, however, the native tools or European metal hand tools such as the hoe, machete, and ax have continued in use to the present. Water lifts were introduced for irrigation, but they remained rare, although today many peasant irrigation

Table 29. Soil Fertility Management

Form	Examples	Form	Examples
Organic Fertilizers		Compost	Aztec Mexico[b,e]
Animal manure and urine[a]	Highland Guatemala	Grass, weeds, leaves, straw, crop residues[l]	Widespread
	Andes	*Other methods*	
	Mexico (widespread)	Leguminous trees	Highland Guatemala
Bird guano	Peru[b]	Accelerated fallowing	Highland Guatemala
Human manure[c]	Aztec Mexico[b]	Multiple cropping[m]	Widespread
	Inca Peru[b]	Liming	Northeast Brazil
	Highland Guatemala	Sodium nitrate	Northern Chile
Animal remains		Texture improvement	
Fish heads	Inca Peru[b]	Sand or clay addition	Tlaxcala
Bones and shells	Widespread	Rock sifting	Highland Guatemala[n]
Ash and charcoal[d]	Widespread	Rock removal	Northwest Argentina
Household refuse	Aztec Mexico[b,e]	Soil transfer	
	Amazonia	From valleys	Centr. Andean terraces[a]
	Widespread	From woodlands or relatives' fields	Centr. Mexican semi-terraces
Rotation of house plots within fields	Highland Guatemala	By truck or burro	Central Mexico
Use of former village sites for fields[f]	Basin of Mexico[b,j]	Soil theft	Tlaxcala
Mixed garbage/manure[g]	Raised fields[b,k]	Organic swamp sediment	Widespread
Forest litter[h]	Tlaxcala, Mex.	Top soil concentration	Belize[a,o]
Aquatic vegetation and muck[i]			Anc. raised fields (probable)

Notes:

[a] Manure and urine of cattle, sheep, goat, llama, horse, pig, chicken, Guinea pig. Sheep and cattle dung may be carried to the fields from stables, corrals, or pens, or temporary small pens may be rotated over the fields (folding). Dung is often mixed with stable debris, leaf litter, or other organic materials. Sheep and

other urine are often considered to be beneficial (especially when mixed with other organic materials), tending to offset field losses of nitrogen caused by bacterial action in the decomposing litter.

[b] Pre-Columbian, but often still current.

[c] Outhouse rotation in gardens as well as rotation of defecation areas within fields is widespread.

[d] From swidden fires, kitchen fires, and burnt crop residues.

[e] Widespread today.

[f] This is the *terra preta* or black earth of former Indian village sites along the lower Amazon River.

[g] Refuse is collected in piles around houses, pens, and stables and transferred as piles or broadcast onto fields. Contents include kitchen garbage, floor sweepings, ash, animal manure and urine, stable cleanings (straw and droppings), poultry feathers, and garden weeds, as well as non-organic refuse such as tin cans, broken ceramics, plastic, and glass.

[h] Forest litter, called *broza* in Guatemala, consists mainly of leaves which are carried from forests to vegetable plots to improve fertility, tilth, and moisture retention.

[i] Includes water hyacinth, water cress, tule, algae, sediment, fish and animal feces and remains, and water-bourne nutrients.

[j] *Chinampas.*

[k] See Table 28.

[l] Cut vegetation material may be composted, placed on the field surface as a mulch, mixed into the soil, or buried as a layer within the soil.

[m] Also crop rotation, intercropping, planting of leguminous crops.

[n] *Tablones.*

[o] Ancient terraces.

Sources: Armillas (*see Sources, Table 28*; Cook (*see Sources, Table 26*); Denevan, William M., personal observations; Field (*see Sources, Table 26*); Harvey, "Public Health in Aztec Society," *Actes du XLIIe Congrès International des Américanistes* (in press); Hopkins (*note 7*); Kelly, "Land-Use Regions in the Central and Northern Portions of the Inca Empire," *Annals of the Association of American Geographers*, Vol. 55 (1965), pp. 327–338; Mathewson (*see Sources, Table 27*); McBryde, *Cultural and Historical Geography of Southwest Guatemala*, Institute of Social Anthropology, Publication No. 4 (Washington, D.C.: Smithsonian Institution, 1947), p. 20; Sternberg, *The Amazon River of Brazil*, Geographische Zeitschrift, Beihefte, No. 40 (1975), pp. 32–33; West (*see Sources, Table 26*); Wilken (*note 22*); Wilken (*see Sources, Table 28*); Wilken, "Integrating Forest and Small-Scale Farm Systems in Middle America," *Agro-Ecosystems*, Vol. 3 (1977), pp. 291–302; Williams, "Aztec Soil Science," *Boletín, Instituto de Geografía*, Vol. 6 (1976), pp. 115–120; Williams, "Tepetate in the Valley of Mexico," *Annals of the Association of American Geographers*, Vol. 62 (1972), pp. 618–626; Winterhalter et al., "Dung as an Essential Resource in a Highland Peruvian Community," *Human Ecology*, Vol. 2 (1974), pp. 89–104. **For additional details pertaining to sources, see note 49.**

Table 30. Other Agricultural Resource Management Techniques

Form	Examples	Form	Examples
Shifting cultivation	Widespread	Multiple cropping/intercropping[f]	Widespread
Ox-drawn plowing	Widespread in uplands	Multi-layering of crops[g]	Widespread
House gardens	West Indies	Altitudinal crop zonation	Highland Peru
	Darién, Panama	Weeding	Widespread
Microclimate management[a]	Widespread	Pest control	
Vegetation rows[b]		Birds	Widespread
Living fences	Sonora, Mexico	Human theft	Highland Peru
	Mexico, Guatemala	Minor agricultural landforms	
Tree rows, wind breaks	See Table 26	Lazy beds[h]	Highland Colombia
Maguey terraces	Widespread		Peru
Hedges	Middle America		Hispaniola[j]
Mulching[c]	Highland Peru	Montones[i]	Mojos, Bolivia[j]
Crop rotation	Widespread		Northern Brazil
Space management[d]	Widespread		Middle America
Crop scheduling[e]		Maize mounds[k]	Highland Guatemala
Seed beds	Chinampas, Mexico		Coastal Peru
	Tablones, Guatemala	Pits for individual plants[l]	Central Mexico

Notes:

[a]Microclimate functions include temperature control, dew inducement, shading, windbreaking, reduction of evapotranspiration, reduction of rain impact, and infiltration control, as well as the major means of water control listed in Tables 27 and 28.

[b]Vegetation row functions besides windbreaking and living fences, include erosion control, reduction of evaporation, shading, source of mulch and vegetative fertilizer, stabilization of raised fields, fuel, and habitat for wildlife which can help minimize crop losses from pests.

[c]Mulching with grass, straw, weeds, crop residue, leaves, and even rocks serves to moderate temperature extremes, reduce moisture loss from soil, absorb the energy of rain and hail, and provides an organic fertilizer.

d Space, both horizontal and vertical, is an agricultural resource, little studied, which can be managed for maximum utilization.

e Crop scheduling refers to management of the time of the year and the length of time a crop is in the field.

f Multiple-cropping functions include pest and disease control, optimum use of space, and optimum use and cycling of soil nutrients. Intercropping refers to systematic alternating of two or more crops.

g Multi-layering functions include temperature control, wind protection, soil protection, shading, weed reduction, reduction of evapotranspiration, optimum use of surface and subsurface space.

h Lazy beds (eras, huachos) are narrow ridges (ca. 1 meter wide), mainly used for potatoes, both on slopes and on flats, whose major functions are breaking up grassland soil, aeration, destruction of grasses, drainage of waterlogged soil, green manuring of buried grass, and raising temperatures.

i Montones are large manioc mounds which have functions similar to those of other raised fields, but montones may occur in well-drained areas where there is no drainage problem.

j Pre-Columbian, but often still current.

k Maize mounds seem to serve for protection against windthrow, for tillering, improved soil drainage and aeration, decreased evaporation, and weed control.

l Round or square depressions dug to irrigate individual trees or other crops. Called pit terraces (when on slopes) or cepas in Mexico. Also found in coastal Peru and highland Guatemala.

Sources: Armillas (see Sources, Table 28); Andrews, "Ridged Fields in the Andes of Peru," El Dorado, Vol. 1, No. 1 (1973), pp. 50–56; Blank, "Macusi Indian Subsistence, Northern Amazonia," unpublished Master's thesis (University of Wisconsin, Madison, 1976), pp. 95–96; Brierley, "Kitchen Gardens in the West Indies, with a Contemporary Study from Grenada," Journal of Tropical Geography, Vol. 43 (1976), pp. 30–40; Brush (note 28); Covich and Nickerson, "Studies of Cultivated Plants in Choco Dwelling Clearings, Darién, Panama," Economic Botany, Vol. 20 (1966), pp. 285–301; Denevan, The Aboriginal Cultural Geography of the Llanos de Mojos of Bolivia, Ibero-Americana, No. 48 (Berkeley: University of California Press, 1966), p. 89; Dickinson (note 42); Gade, "Ecología de robo agrícola en las tierras altas de los Andes centrales," América Indígena, Vol. 30 (1970), pp. 3–14; Gade, Plants, Man and the Land in the Vilcanota Valley of Peru, Biogeographica, Vol. 6 (The Hague: W. Junk, 1975), pp. 43–44; Hatch (note 31); Innis, "The Efficiency of Jamaican Peasant Land Use," Canadian Geographer, Vol. 5, No. 2 (1961), pp. 19–23; Kimber, "Dooryard Gardens of Martinique," Yearbook of the Association of Pacific Coast Geographers, Vol. 28 (1966), pp. 97–118; McBryde (see Sources, Table 29); Mathewson (see Sources, Table 27); Nabhan and Sheridan, "Living Fence Rows of the Río San Miguel, Sonora, Mexico: Traditional Technology for Floodplain Management," Human Ecology, Vol. 5 (1977), pp. 97–111; Sturtevant, "Taino Agriculture," in Johannes Wilbert, ed., The Evolution of Horticultural Systems in Native South America, Causes and Consequences: A Symposium (Caracas: Sociedad de Ciencias Naturales La Salle, 1961), pp. 69–82; Watters (note 24); West, "Ridge or 'Era' Agriculture in the Colombian Andes," Actas del XXXIII Congreso Internacional de Americanistas (San José, 1959), Vol. 1, pp. 279–282; Wilken (note 8); Wilken (note 21); Wilken (note 23); Wilken (see Sources, Table 29); Wilken, "Management of Productive Space in Traditional Farming," Actes du XLIIe Congrès International des Américanistes, Vol. 2 (Paris, 1978), pp. 409–419. For additional details pertaining to sources, see note 49.

farmers have small gasoline pumps. Reservoir irrigation, which was rare in pre-Columbian times, was introduced by the Spaniards to central Mexico.

In summary, pre-Columbian resouce management techniques were effective, relatively stable ecologically, moderately productive, and often supported large populations. The basic Indian techniques have almost all survived to the present, but are used on a much smaller proportion of the land. Some ancient farm lands have never been reoccupied; others are now in pasture, have been destroyed by erosion, or are in commercial or subsistence crop production utilizing modern rather than traditional management techniques.

PRESENT DAY TRADITIONAL RESOURCE MANAGEMENT

Traditional resource management techniques are today dominated by elements which are either pre-Columbian or were introduced from the Old World during the colonial period. Now, most traditional farmers also include some elements of modern farming within their traditional practices—use of machinery, pesticides, chemical fertilizers, hybrid seeds, well water for irrigation. Actually, in distinguishing between traditional and modern, it is best to speak in terms of individual techniques rather than farmers who are "traditional" or who are "modern." In fact, much of what is considered modern commercial agriculture in Latin America retains elements of traditional land mangement.

Given the great diversity of traditional techniques in Latin America, they will only be briefly discussed here. Tables 26 to 30 list the major techniques and indicate some of the areas where each occurs.

Slope management.[20] The farmer working on a slope is faced with problems of excessive erosion, water control, and shallow soil depth. The common means of coping with slope in the uplands of Latin America is the terrace, as discussed earlier (Table 26). There are other, minor slope control landforms such as the lazy bed, which is widespread throughout the Andes, usually involving potato cultivation. These are narrow ridges commonly made with the Andean foot-plow. Lazy beds usually occur on steeper slopes where oxen or machine plows are not feasible.[21] Contour plowing with oxen occurs in many regions of Latin America but is not as universal as might be expected. On many cultivated slopes there is no erosion control method today, in some cases because soils are not susceptible to erosion, in other cases with disastrous erosion occurring.

Water management. Irrigation agriculture is widespread throughout the arid and semi-arid lands of Latin America (Table 28). However, while indigeneous forms of irrigation have survived, most irrigation has been modernized and commercialized and involves the use of pumping, lined canals, reservoirs, and mechanized cropping. Traditional, small scale irrigation has survived mainly along the rugged slopes of the Andes, where commercial agriculture is impractical, and as splash and container irrigation in the upland basins of Mexico and Guatemala (Figure 56). Drained-field cultivation, in contrast, has rarely been modernized nor has it survived in traditional form; rather it has been abandoned in both the tropical lowlands and in the uplands (Table 27). There are a few instances of modern drainage using canals, dikes, tiles, and pumping, such as in the Sabana de Bogotá in Columbia, in the Orinoco Delta, and in the coastal polders of the Guianas.

Soil management. The great diversity of organic fertilizers used in Latin America is indicated in Table 29. Composting with manure, garbage, and plant material is widespread.

Fig. 56. Splash irrigation (using gourds) of a garlic crop on tablones at Aguacatán in highland Guatemala. The tablones are raised planting beds separated by ditches which serve both drainage and irrigation. Note the pile of crop residue in the foreground, which will be used for fertilizer (Photograph by Kent Mathewson, 1974).

Particularly important is livestock manure. The integration of livestock and crops is much more common in Latin America than realized, although the two activities may take place separately. Traditional farmers are very knowledgeable about soil characteristics and potentials in relation to agriculture, and they know how to manipulate soils by using the varied organic and inorganic materials from their immediate environment.[22]

Microclimate management. We readily envision traditional farmers attempting to control climate through prayer, rain dances, and offerings to the gods. However, all farmers modify local climate by technological means which are both intentional and unintentional. Irrigation and drainage are obvious means of controlling moisture, but actually most farming methods have an effect on microclimates. Shade is managed; radiation and moisture penetration and retention are increased or decreased by given plant or soil surfaces and by surface geometry; wind is modified by rows of trees or by planting pits; temperatures are raised by mounding; tillage and mulching affect temperature and moisture; dew formation can be increased, local evapotranspiration is influenced, etc. Traditional farmers are by no means helplessly at the mercy of climate, but their varied means for achieving a degree of control have been little studied.[23]

Shifting cultivation. The most widespread system of traditional agricultural resource management in Latin America is shifting cultivation which probably supports at least 50 million people.[24] It is still found throughout the forested tropics as well as in the montane and mid-latitude forests. It survives, despite low productivity, since most land is in fallow, because labor requirements are low, and because it is effective on marginal soils. On the other hand, shifting cultivation can be destructive of forest, soil, and water resources and is a leading cause of the rapid disappearance of the Amazon rainforest. Under sparse populations abandoned fields regrow in forest and soil fertility is renewed, but this seldom happens today as worn out or weedy fields are usually converted to pasture.

Shifting cultivation involves clearing forest, allowing the debris to dry out and then burning it, cropping for a few years, and then abandonment to forest, scrub, or grass (Figure 57). Traditional farmers, especially Indians or those with an Indian heritage who have adapted to local conditions over time, usually carry out intercropping, crop diversification, and layering of crops, with adequate fallowing ("stable shifting cultivation").[25] The soil is minimally disturbed, and recovery is rapid. Nevertheless, colonists, who dominate much of tropical forest farming, more so in Latin American than in Asia and Africa, and who are traditional farmers only in a superficial way, tend to practice monoculture; they crop too long and either fallow too short or follow crops with pasture, with permanent land deterioration resulting ("unstable shifting cultivation"). Mechanized land clearing can lead to severe erosion, whereas erosion is minimal, on steep slopes under traditional management.[26] Thus the dilemma of shifting cultivation: it can be either resource conservative under traditional management and sparse populations, or it can be very destructive.

House gardens. Although somewhat taken for granted and little studied, house gardens, or dooryard gardens, are found throughout Latin America. Associated with rural areas, small farmers, and with workers on commercial farms, they are also common in towns and even cities, especially with poor people who lack steady employment. They serve for supplementary food as well as for basic food when field crops fail or wage employment is lacking. Such gardens are also sources of fuel, fertilizer, ornamental plants, and other products.

Fig. 57. Shifting cultivation by Campa Indians in the Gran Pajonal region of eastern Peru. A patch of montane tropical forest has been cleared and the debris dried out and partly burned (Photograph by William M. Denevan, 1966).

House gardens range from a few fruit trees up to large plots with over 50 different useful plants in them and sufficient productivity to provide for most of a family's food needs. Some of the best developed gardens are in the densely populated islands of the Caribbean, such as Hispaniola, Jamaica, and Martinique. They occur on a wide variety of soils, including what were originally very impoverished ones. Regardless, they are as permanent as the house sites which they surround. Some are hundreds of years old. Well-established house gardens are ecologically stable and very productive. Soil structure and fertility are maintained by nutrient recycling from house and garden (cut weeds, garbage, kitchen fire ash, manure from dooryard animals, and human manure), crop diversity, intercropping, and layering of crops. Erosion is minimized and soil moisture is sustained. Optimum use is made of space, and different crops are efficiently scheduled, so that there is a plant cover over the soil for most or all of the year. The varied crops have different requirements for nutrients, shade, and moisture. Pests are minimal so that there is greater production than from a single crop. Trees help bring up nutrients from considerable depth. Labor inputs are high, but considerable time is saved because travel is nil.

General characteristics of traditional farming. Traditional methods of cultivation usually promote ecological stability (equilibrium of production), with minimal external inputs, through diversification of crops and crop varieties, intercropping, layering of crops, recycling of nutrients from organic materials in the local environment, and by hand methods that minimally disturb the soil. Soil quality is thus maintained or improved. Pests (weeds, insects, diseases, rodents, birds) are minimized by diversity, rather than by chemicals. Ecological stability does not necessarily mean that the natural environment is not disturbed, but rather that the created agroecosystem is relatively stable. Most forms of agriculture completely remake the habitat, replacing wild plants with cultivated crops and creating new soils and microclimates. Also, traditional agriculture is energy efficient because human and animal energy is relied on rather than fossil fuels for fertilizers, pesticides, machinery, and irrigation. For example, for the village of Nuñoa in the Peruvian altiplano, the cultivation system produces 11.5 times as many kilocalories of energy as the energy expended in the agricultural work.[27] Shifting cultivation is even more efficient, with an output to input ratio of 15–20:1. Food production in the United States, in contrast, is very inefficient due to heavy dependence on fossil fuels, with a negative output to input ratio of 1:5 or less.

The traditional farmer is usually a subsistence farmer (though he markets his surplus), who by definition is dependent on his own crop production for his food. He, therefore, must minimize risk ("subsistence risk") in order to survive, and this is his first priority rather than a high quantity of production for marketing purposes. He minimizes risk by diversifying his crops and by planting several fields where soils and microclimates are different. In the Andes, for example, a farmer may plant in different altitudinal zones.[28] Thus, if one crop or one farm has a bad year, success elsewhere can assure adequate food. The fully commercial farmer, in contrast, is more concerned with total production, which usually means monocropping with chemical additives to control resulting pests. He can count on economic institutions (loans, savings, insurance) to carry him through bad years.

The traditional farmer has little or no capital investment in his farming, since he makes little or no use of chemicals and machinery. This means that he is not dependent on the uncertainties of credit and prices. The small farmer who is dependent on credit stands a good chance of losing his real capital, his land, when he cannot repay loans. Millions of such farmers in Latin America have been forced off their lands to the cities where few employment opportunities are available. Highly capitalized modern farming may result in higher productivity, but it also means the destruction of the small farmer, whether in Wisconsin or Peru. In Wisconsin there are industrial jobs available for the former farmer but seldom so in Peru.

The advantages of traditional farming, of course, have to be weighed against the major disadvantage of lower production levels under mixed cropping without the use of chemical fertilizers and pesticides. This can be partly offset by expanding the area under cultivation, by more frequent cropping, by minimizing unused space within a farm by greater use of local organic and inorganic additives, and by intercropping. For example, intercropping two or more crops may produce higher total yields without reducing the size of the major crop, because of more efficient use of solar radiation and available soil nutrients, and lower losses to pests.[29] Labor inputs are also much higher under traditional cultivation in contrast to mechanized agriculture. Productivity per man hour is low under hand methods, and income is thereby limited. On the other hand, mechanization eliminates farm labor and leads to rural depopulation.

LATIN AMERICA IN TRANSITION

As elsewhere in the world, traditional agriculture is giving way to modernized methods of resource management, or as previously indicated, elements of both are being combined. Thus a farmer may pump water from a well to his field, paying a fee to do so, because that is his only access to water or because he can thereby greatly increase production, while at the same time he still uses oxen for plowing.

The motivations behind change are several. First, agricultural change is an ongoing process within all agricultural systems. A wide range of technical knowledge is available to most farmers. A farming strategy is selected from this knowledge which will minimize risk and which will be efficient in terms of energy expended and other costs. Why build terraces on mountain sides or drain swamps, at the expense of great effort and time, if there is plenty of well-drained flat land available? However, as population pressure increases on limited land, it becomes necessary to crop more frequently (or to reclaim marginal land). A continuum of increasing agricultural intensity thus can be postulated, from long fallow to permanent cropping with several crops a year, with increasingly greater labor inputs along the continuum.[30] As population or other production pressures increase or decrease in an area, cultivation methods can change drastically to accommodate changing needs and still maximize efficiency.

Second, agricultural methods may change to meet commercial opportunities, which require higher output, certain crops, certain qualities of crops, or certain conditions for effective management and harvesting.

Third, traditional agricultural methods may be abandoned because of social and institutional pressure. Farmers are told by development agencies (FAO, AID, agricultural extension) that their methods are backward and low yielding, whereas modern methods are progressive and high yielding. It is difficult for an impoverished farmer to resist the "brain washing" involved when he is taken to an experimental farm where he sees corn growing over his head and producing 10 or 20 times the yields on his own farm. He is told that he too can join the Green Revolution if he will buy hybrid seeds, chemical fertilizer and pesticide, and irrigation water, and that he will be given loans to buy these things if he is a "good" farmer. He is not told about the problems and risks involved, that some farmers will become prosperous but that most will fail.[31]

Finally, traditional practices may decline because the costs of hand labor become too high (e.g., because of deteriorating soils and increasing weeding), or because modernizing inputs become affordable. "In other words, traditional practices fail not necessarily because they lose their relative effectiveness, but because traditional farmers become less traditional."[32]

As the costs of energy rapidly increase, thereby raising the costs of chemical, mechanized agriculture, it is the traditional and intermediate technologies that are going to have to produce most of the staple food in Latin America, as they already do.[33] It is essential, then, that traditional methods be preserved, encouraged, and improved rather than being discouraged and abandoned. This must begin in the agricultural schools of the developed countries where agricultural technicians and administrators responsible for promoting agricultural change in Latin America are trained. Seldom is any attention or respect given in these schools to traditional agriculture which is viewed as something that must be replaced. Not surprisingly, such attitudes carry over and dominate development thinking in Latin America (as well as in Africa and Asia). Cultural geographers, anthropologists, and ecologists are the scientists most knowledgeable about traditional agriculture. On the other hand, agronomists, agricultural economists, and rural sociologists, who dominate development planning, are not. Thus, part of the problem lies in the organization, control, and distribution of knowledge, attitudes about people and customs, and communication between disciplines.

If food production is to increase, with energy availability decreasing and unemployment increasing, then compromises must be sought. The answer would seem to lie in working for changes that: (1) minimize machinery and use hand labor, thereby maintaining employment,[34] (2) seek to increase productivity by using local fertilizers, maximizing space and time efficiency, and (3) develop systematic methods of intercropping to keep pest levels relatively low and production reasonably high. Above all, change should work within the existing traditional systems, rather than completely replace such systems. It is also essential that traditional farmers themselves participate in decisions involving change.

REGIONAL ASSESSMENT

Traditional methods of managing agricultural resources in Latin America have deep roots in the aboriginal and colonial past. Most can still be found, at least locally, but they have been abandoned over large areas. In particular, the once common raised-field system is virtually a lost technique in Latin America, although it is still widespread in the Old World tropics.[35] Clearly it could be revived to reclaim uncultivated wetlands, and experimental efforts are being made to accomplish this objective in Belize and in Tabasco, Mexico.[36] Terracing is another ancient technique of soil and water management that has been abandoned in many areas where it could be profitably reestablished. Abandoned farm lands occur mainly in areas that are remote and sparsely populated, and which have poor soils, too little or too much water, or steep slopes. Given no local pressure for increasing food production through land reclamation, with the costs of such reclamation being too high to justify commercial production which can be undertaken more cheaply elsewhere, it is not surprising that land resources remain unused today (in contrast to the past).

There are many specific traditional practices still current which should be preserved in the face of pressures for modernization, in order to reduce subsistence risk, avoid dependence on fossil fuels and chemicals, for soil and water conservation, and to minimize losses to diseases and pests. Possibly the most important is diversification of crop species, crop varieties, and growth form, since such diversity protects both crops and their habitat and maximizes production.[37] In tropical Latin America it is biological competition that is usually the major limiting factor in agriculture, even more so than soil. For a monoculture this competition is intense, and the costs of controlling it are so great that usually only high value export crops (such as bananas, sugar, and coffee) are economically feasible.

For the production of food crops multiple cropping systems growing more than one crop on a field in the same year, seem to be the best procedure, even though mechanization is difficult.[38] We need to develop and promote agroecosystems that extend the advantages of the house garden to larger fields, an integration of food staples (such as maize and manioc) into a single, ecologically stable, sustained-yield system that includes vegetables, legumes, root crops, dooryard animals, livestock, and useful non-food plants. The house garden itself, in a highly productive form, needs to be greatly encouraged (e.g., through inexpensive, simple-to-read and well-illustrated manuals designed for environments, crops, and cultures of Latin America; a good model which has had a useful impact is *The Samaka Guide to Homesite Farming* in the Philippines).[39]

When compared to unstable shifting cultivation, stable shifting cultivation with its ecological advantages needs to be encouraged and improved in order to reduce the length of fallowing. Shifting cultivation is probably the most widespread form of traditional agriculture, and it is steadily increasing rather than decreasing. It can be made more stable and productive by zero tillage; by use of mixed crops of high yielding varieties resistant to pests; by use of organic fertilizers and compost from kitchen and stable; by cropping legumes (cowpea, lima bean, winged bean, peanuts) which fix nitrogen in the soil; by control of acidity through careful use of ash or lime if available; and by planting deep-rooted fallow trees which can bring nutrients from depth to the surface. Mulches of plant residues need to be used to suppress weeds, reduce erosion, lower soil temperatures, and add nutrients. The mulch can be enriched by bringing in organic debris from nearby forests.[40]

Another variation would be the development of agro-silvicultural systems that emphasize production of mixed trees which are environmentally protective, provide a sustained yield, and are locally useful and/or commercially profitable. Such trees are found throughout the tropics and might be brought together in viable, highly productive combinations. These anthropogenic or artificial rainforests may once have existed with the Maya in Yucatan and along the Pacific coast of Central America, containing productive food trees such as the ramón or bread nut, chicle, papaya, cacao, the pejibaye palm, and many others.[41] The ramón may have been a major food staple for the Maya. Why food producing trees, in contrast to the industrial and luxury product trees dominating plantation agriculture, are not more important is a historical mystery (the banana is a major exception). Certainly the possibilities can be seen in house gardens that invariably include fruit and nut trees.

While such systems, on a systematic basis, have been attempted experimentally, and their ecological values pointed out, they still are not a significant component of agricultural development research, planning, and implementation.[42] Nevertheless, this is the direction in which development must move if it is agreed that a large number of people are going to have to be fed by small farmers producing from their own immediate ecosystems rather than drawing upon the resources of the entire earth as does modern, neotecnic agriculture.[43] Agricultural science need not be neglected in this scenario, but it should be directed toward making viable traditional farming systems more productive and not towards the establishment of variations on midlatitude, industrialized monoculture.

Ultimately, the question of modern versus traditional methods of agricultural resource management must be viewed in terms of permanence.[44] Most traditional systems and techniques have survived for hundreds if not thousands of years because they are relatively stable, minimally polluting, and not dependent on external subsidies. As such, they can be projected far into the future. Modern systems in contrast exhibit highly tenuous existences. A reversion to the traditional world is not the answer to today's food and environmental problems, as that world has its own problems of health, well being, and opportunity. Nevertheless, we must seek out the "essence of palaeotechnic permanence" and apply it to our use of the earth's resources if we want to avoid the collapse of society as we know it.[45] The necessary changes for an economics of permanence will require, in the words of Schumacher: "a profound reorientation of science and technology, which have to open their doors to wisdom...," as well as a very different way of thinking by western man about environment, food production, and the quality and quantity of levels of living.[46]

NOTES

[1]For a brief, general survey, see Gene C. Wilken, "Some Aspects of Resource Management by Traditional Farmers," in Huntley H. Biggs and Ronald L. Tinnermeier, eds., *Small Farm Agricultural Development Problems* (Fort Collins: Colorado State University, 1974), pp. 47–59.

[2]Edwin J. Wellhausen, "The Agriculture of Mexico," *Scientific American*, Vol. 235, No. 3 (1976), pp. 128–150.

[3]Barbara Pickersgill and Charles B. Heiser, Jr., "Origins and Distribution of Plants Domesticated in the New World Tropics," in Charles A. Reed, ed., *Origins of Agriculture* (The Hague: Mouton, 1977), pp. 803–835.

[4]Richard S. MacNeish, "Speculation About How and Why Food Production and Village Life Developed in the Tehuacán Valley, Mexico," *Archaeology*, Vol. 24 (1971), pp. 307–315.

[5]Mark N. Cohen, *The Food Crisis in Prehistory* (New Haven: Yale University Press, 1977), pp. 279–286.

[6]B. L. Turner, II, "Prehistoric Intensive Agriculture in the Mayan Lowlands," *Science*, Vol. 185 (1974), pp. 118–24. Also see P. D. Harrison and B. L. Turner, II, eds., *Pre-Hispanic Maya Agriculture* (Albuquerque: University of New Mexico Press, 1978).

[7]William T. Sanders, "The Agricultural History of the Basin of Mexico," in Eric R. Wolf, ed., *The Valley of Mexico: Studies in Pre-Hispanic Ecology and Society* (Albuquerque: University of New Mexico Press, 1976), pp. 101–59 (reference on p. 130); Joseph W. Hopkins, III, "Prehispanic Agricultural Terraces in Mexico," unpublished Master's thesis (University of Chicago, 1968), p. 43; Turner, op. cit., note 6, p. 121; Gordon R. Willey, *An Introduction to American Archaeology, Vol. 2, South America* (Englewood Cliffs: Prentice-Hall, 1971), p. 131. Less certain dates as early as 800 B.C. have been suggested for both central Mexico and the central Andes: R. A. Donkin, *Agricultural Terracing in the Aboriginal New World*, Viking Fund Publications in Anthropology, No. 56 (Tucson: University of Arizona Press, 1979), p. 18.

[8]Gene C. Wilken, "Traditional Slope Management: An Analytical Approach," *Hill Lands: Proceedings of an International Symposium* (Morgantown: West Viriginia University Books, 1979), pp. 416–422.

[9]Barbara J. Price, "Prehispanic Irrigation Agriculture in Nuclear America," *Latin American Research Review*, Vol. 6, No. 3 (1971), pp. 3–60.

[10]MacNeish, op. cit., note 4; Melvin L. Fowler, "A Preclassic Water Distribution System in Amalucan, Mexico," *Archaeology*, Vol. 22 (1969), pp. 208–215 (reference on p. 215); Michael E. Moseley, "An Empirical Approach to Prehistoric Agrarian Collapse: The Case of the Moche Valley, Peru," in Nancie L. Gonzales, ed., *Social and Technological Management in Dry Lands* (Boulder: Westview Press, 1978), pp. 9–43 (reference on p. 20).

[11]Michael West, "Early Watertable Farming on the North Coast of Peru," *American Antiquity*, Vol. 44 (1979), pp. 138–144.

[12]Gordon R. Willey, *Prehistoric Settlement Patterns in the Viru Valley, Peru*, Bureau of American Ethnology, Bulletin 155 (Washington, D.C.: Smithsonian Institution, 1953), p. 394; Moseley, op. cit., note 10, p. 24.

[13]William M. Denevan, "Aboriginal Drained-Field Cultivation in the Americas," *Science*, Vol. 169 (1970), pp. 647–654.

[14]Sanders, op. cit., note 7, p. 136.

[15]Peter D. Harrison, "The Rise of the Bajos and the Fall of the Maya," in Norman Hammond, ed., *Social Process in Maya History* (London: Academic Press, 1977), pp. 469–508.

[16]Sherburne F. Cook, *Soil Erosion and Population in Central Mexico*, Ibero-Americana, No. 34 (Berkeley: University of California Press, 1949), p. 86.

[17]William M. Denevan, ed., *The Native Population of the Americas in 1492* (Madison: University of Wisconsin Press, 1976), pp. 2–4, 290–291.

[18]Lesley B. Simpson, *Exploitation of Land in Central Mexico in the Sixteenth Century*, Ibero-Americana, No. 36 (Berkeley: University of California Press, 1952).

[19]For discussions of Indian agricultural tools, see Robin A. Donkin, "Pre-Columbian Field Implements and Their Distribution in the Highlands of Middle and South America," *Anthropos*, Vol. 65 (1970), pp. 505–529; and Daniel W. Gade and Roberto Rios, "Chaquitaclla: The Native Footplough and Its Persistence in Central Andean Agriculture," *Tools and Tillage*, Vol. 2 (1972), pp. 3–15.

[20]See, in particular, Wilken, op. cit., note 8; and Donkin, op. cit., note 7.

[21]For other agricultural land forms to control slopes, see Gene C. Wilken, "Minor Agricultural Landforms in Middle America," unpublished paper, Annual Meeting of the Association of American Geographers, Salt Lake City, 1977.

[22]The only comparative study of traditional soil management in Latin America is that by Gene C. Wilken, "Studies of Resource Management in Traditional Middle American Farming Systems, No. 7, Soil Management: Part 1, Organic Amendments; Part 2, Inorganic Amendments," unpublished report to the National Science Foundation, 1977.

[23]Gene C. Wilken, "Microclimate Management by Traditional Farmers," *Geographical Review*, Vol. 62 (1972), pp. 544–560.

[24]The most comprehensive survey of shifting cultivation in Latin America, focusing on Mexico, Venezuela, and Peru, is by R. F. Watters, *Shifting Cultivation in Latin America*, FAO Forestry Development Paper No. 17 (Rome: UNESCO, 1971).

[25]Detailed studies of Indian systems of shifting cultivation include William E. Carter, *New Lands and Old Traditions: Kekchi Cultivators in the Guatemalan Lowlands* (Gainesville: University of Florida Press, 1969); William M. Denevan, "Campa Subsistence in the Gran Pajonal, Eastern Peru," *Geographical Review*, Vol. 61 (1971), pp. 496–518; Kenneth Ruddle, *The Yukpa Cultivation System: A Study of Shifting Cultivation in Colombia and Venezuela*, Ibero-Americana, No. 52 (Berkeley: University of California Press, 1974); William J. Smole, *The Yanoama Indians: A Cultural Geography* (Austin: University of Texas Press, 1976).

[26]Pedro A. Sanchez, *Properties and Mangement of Soils in the Tropics* (New York: John Wiley & Sons, 1976), p. 363.

[27]Michael A. Little and George E. B. Morren, Jr., *Ecology, Energetics, and Human Variability* (Dubuque: W. C. Brown, 1976), pp. 66–67.

[28]Stephen B. Brush, *Mountain, Field, and Family: The Economy and Human Ecology of an Andean Valley* (Philadelphia: University of Pennsylvania Press, 1977), pp. 1–16.

[29]Sanchez, op. cit., note 26, p. 511. In Jamaica, a potato field which commonly produced 800 lbs. of potatoes per acre could also produce 300 lbs. of yams, 2 bushels of beans, and some taro without decreasing the amount of the potato crop: Donald Q. Innis, "Traditional Versus Modern Methods of Increasing Tropical Food Production (in India and Jamaica)," *Proceedings of the 23rd International Geographical Union*, Vol. 6 (Moscow, 1978), pp. 203–208.

[30]Ester Boserup, *The Conditions of Agricultural Growth* (Chicago: Aldine, 1965).

[31]For an excellent case study of the problems faced by traditional farmers attempting to modernize, see John K. Hatch, *The Corn Farmers of Motupe: A Study of Traditional Farming Practices in Northern Coastal Peru*, Land Tenure Center Monographs, No. 1 (Madison: University of Wisconsin, 1976).

[32]Wilken, op. cit., note 22.

[33]By "intermediate technologies," we mean methods which make some, but limited, simple, and inexpensive, use of machinery and chemicals.

[34]William C. Thiesenhusen, "Latin America's Employment Problem," *Science*, Vol. 171 (1971), pp. 868-874.

[35]William M. Denevan and B. L. Turner, II, "Forms, Functions and Associations of Raised Fields in the Old World Tropics," *Journal of Tropical Geography*, Vol. 39 (1974), pp. 24-33.

[36]Dennis E. Puleston, "Experiments in Prehistoric Raised Field Agriculture: Learning from the Past," *Journal of Belizean Affairs*, Vol. 5 (1977), pp. 36-43; Arturo Gómez-Pompa and Raúl Venegas, "La chinampa tropical," *Informa, Instituto de Investigaciones Sobre Recursos Bióticos* (Mexico), No. 5 (1976), 4 pp.

[37]In addition, the preservation of crop varieties is essential to maintain the gene pool that modern agricultural genetic research is based on. Green revolution agriculture that stresses high yielding, single variety hybrids is destroying the great diversity within maize, potato, and other crops that exists in traditional agriculture in Latin America.

[38]For a classification of multiple cropping systems, see Sanchez, op. cit., note 26, p. 481.

[39]Colin M. Hoskins, *The Samaka Guide to Homesite Farming* (Manila: Samaka Service Center, 1954).

[40]D. J. Greenland, "Bringing the Green Revolution to the Shifting Cultivator," *Science*, Vol. 190 (1975), pp. 841-844.

[41]B. Leroy Gordon, *Anthropogeography and Rainforest Ecology in Bocas del Toro Province, Panama* (Berkeley: Department of Geography, University of California, 1969), pp. 69-81; Frederick M. Wiseman, "Agriculture and Historical Ecology of the Maya Lowlands," in P. D. Harrison and B. L. Turner, II, eds., *Pre-Hispanic Maya Agriculture* (Albuquerque: University of New Mexico Press, 1978, pp. 61-115, reference on pp. 85-89).

[42]L. R. Holdridge, "Ecological Indications of the Need for a New Approach to Tropical Land Use," *Economic Botany*, Vol. 13 (1959), pp. 271-80; Joshua C. Dickinson, III, "Alternatives to Monoculture in the Humid Tropics of Latin America," *Professional Geographer*, Vol. 24 (1972), pp. 217-22; David H. Janzen, "Tropical Agroecosystems," *Science*, Vol. 182 (1973), pp. 1212-19; Sanchez, op. cit., note 26, pp. 478-532; Martin Kellman, "Some Implications of Biotic Interactions for Sustained Tropical Agriculture," *Proceedings of the Association of American Geographers*, Vol. 6 (1974), pp. 142-145.

[43]In Colombia and Central America 70% of the food consumed is produced on small farms (less than 5 hectares): Sanchez, op. cit., note 26, p. 480. In Mexico 55% of the total agricultural production is on traditional farms: Wellhausen, op. cit., note 2, p. 139.

[44]William C. Clarke, "The Structure of Permanence: The Relevance of Self-subsistence Communities for World Ecosystem Management," in Timothy P. Bayliss-Smith, ed., *Subsistence and Survival* (London: Academic Press, 1977), pp. 363-384. For a good review of the problems of modern agricultural technology, see Edward Groth, III, "Increasing the Harvests," *Environment*, Vol. 17 (1975), pp. 28-39.

[45]Clarke, op. cit., note 44, p. 377.

[46]E. F. Schumacher, *Small is Beautiful: Economics as if People Mattered* (New York: Harper & Row, 1975), p. 31. In recent years there have been numerous indications of a change in thinking in this direction by development planners; e.g., World Bank advisor Charles Weiss, Jr., "Mobilizing Technology for Developing Countries," *Science*, Vol. 203 (1979), pp. 1883-1889.

[47]Robert West, *Cultural Geography of the Modern Tarascan Area*, Institute of Social Anthropology, Publication No. 7 (Washington, D.C.: Smithsonian Institution, 1948), p. 47.

[48]William M. Denevan and Karl H. Schwerin, "Adaptive Strategies in Karinya Subsistence, Venezuelan Llanos," *Antropologica* (in press).

[49]In the manuscript, each specific form of resource management and each example thereof was correlated with a detailed bibliographic entry. In order to conform with the presentation of similar tables in other chapters of this book, all sources pertaining to Tables 26, 27, 28, 29, and 30 were set in type in an abbreviated form. Researchers interested in any complete bibliographic reference pertaining to any specific form of management and example thereof can obtain it by writing to Prof. William M. Denevan, Department of Geography, University of Wisconsin, Madison, WI 53706.

Chapter 10

Oceania

Gary A. Klee

Many South Pacific islanders possessed and continue to possess a wealth of environmental knowledge, including traditional systems of resource management. Taboos, bans, seasons, wildlife preserves, marine preserves, land and lagoon tenure systems, systems of time reckoning, social stratification, religion, and population control (overseas voyaging, suicidal voyages, celibacy, prevention of conception, abortion, and infanticide) undoubtedly function in conserving island resources. Several of these inadvertent or recognized conservation practices were distinctly effective in terms of conserving resources, and, if those appropriate were supported or adapted to modern conditions, they could continue to be so. Yet, little time remains to identify, record, and possibly preserve some of these traditional systems of conservation management.

THE RESOURCE BASE

The Pacific Ocean contains about 25,000 islands, more than in all the rest of the world's oceans combined. The ocean itself is the dominant influence in the area, thus accounting for its regional title of "Oceania." The sea acts as a barrier (preventing the spread of most terrestrial life), link (connecting land masses that are thousands of miles apart), source of food (providing a habitat for food resources), and communication media (providing an avenue for trade, colonization, and exploitation). Only the interior of the large land masses of Australia, New Guinea, and New Zealand escape the influence of the sea.

Despite its pervasive influence, it is not the ocean itself that warrants most of our attention, but rather the land masses of Australia, New Zealand, Micronesia, Melanesia, and Polynesia, for the land is man's main source of livelihood (Figure 58). The largest

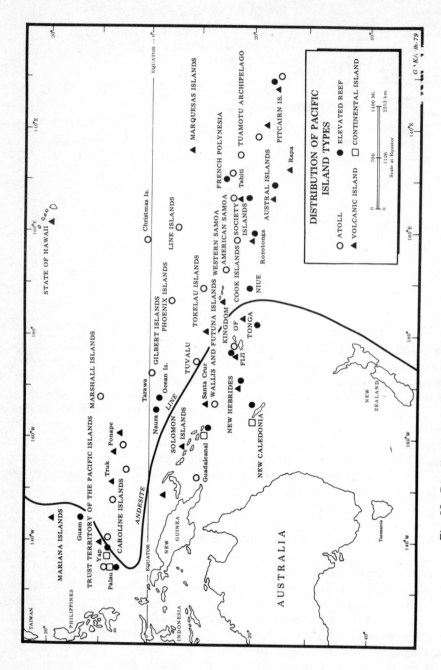

Fig. 58. Distribution of Pacific island types (based on Dahl, *see* note 106).

land mass of the Pacific area is the continent of Australia, approximately of the same size as the 48 contiguous U.S. states. Situated 1,400 miles southeast of Australia are the large island groups of New Zealand, the southernmost nation in the Eastern Hemisphere.

Almost all small islands of the Pacific lie between latitudes 30°N and 30°S, extending longitudinally from southeast Asia to Easter Island. Beyond this, the rest of the Pacific Basin is practically empty. The great triangle of Polynesia, with its corners at Hawaii, Easter Island, and New Zealand, encompasses the island arcs and clusters of the Ellice, Samoan, Tongan, Cook, Society, Tuamotu, Tokelau, and Marquesas islands. "French Polynesia" refers to the French settlements and related influences in the Society, Tuamotu, and Marquesas island groups. Situated north of the Equator and west of the International Date Line are the numerous small islands of Micronesia. The principal island groups in Micronesia include the Marianas, the Carolines, the Marshalls, and the Gilberts. In the southwestern corner of the Pacific lie the islands of Melanesia. New Guinea, the second largest island in the world, dominates the region. The other important island groups of Melanesia include the Solomon, New Hebrides, Fiji, New Caledonia, and the Bismarck Archipelago (New Britain, New Ireland, and the Admiralty Islands).

Within the warm tropical belt lie the romaticized calcareous reefs built by coral polyps and calcareous algae which require warm (64.7° to 75°F), relatively shallow (90 to 150 feet), and clear 80% saline water. Thus, coral reefs are absent near river mouths where the sea is diluted by fresh water.

The major coral reef-building organism is the coral polyp. Coral reefs are massive calcareous structures built by large numbers of coral polyps that secrete lime from sea water in order to build a protective outer skeleton. Some such skeletons (reefs) are razor sharp posing a serious hazard to swimming and diving, local fishermen, and ship navigation.

The coral polyps that create reefs occur in uncountable billions in the tropical waters of the Pacific, but they must attach themselves to something solid before building their compound skeletal structures. Volcanoes often provide the necessary base for coral polyps to gain a foothold. Their upward growth on a subsiding platform is referred to as "Darwin's Subsidence Theory," which is still the most accepted explanation of the different reefs and associated island types. Fluctuating sea levels resulting from glacial melt have also had an effect on coral reef build-up.

Coral reefs, which comprise the "low islands" of the Pacific, have been morphologically classified into eight types according to their stage of development: apron reef, fringing reef, almost barrier reef, barrier reef, almost atoll, atoll, almost table reef, and table reef. Besides these "low islands" of carbonate rock, there are three other major island types within the Pacific Basin: (1) "Continental Islands," all outside the andesite line, such as New Guinea and the two main islands of New Zealand; (2) "High Islands," of volcanic origin, such as Moorea in French Polynesia, and the Big Island of Hawaii; and (3) "Uplifted Coral Platforms," which are usually only slightly larger than coral islands. Examples include Ocean Island, Nauru (West-central Pacific), and Makatea (in the Tuamotus).

As a habitat for humans, the Pacific Ocean and its islands (Table 31) provide a resource base that is extremely diverse (Figures 59 and 60). "Continental Islands" have the greatest variety of natural resources and land-use potential. The other three island types make up for their occasional resource deficiencies by the glowing personality and "tourist attracting" character of their physical landscapes: brillant beaches, towering

Table 31. Biotic Provinces and Island Types of the Pacific

Biotic province		Island type			
		Continental	Volcanic	Elevated	Low
I	New Guinea	*	*	*	*
II	Bismark Archipelago		*		*
III	Solomon Islands		*	*	
IV	New Caledonia-Loyalty	*	*	*	*
V	New Hebrides-Santa Cruz		*	*	*
VI	Norfolk-Lord Howe-Kermadec				
VII	Fiji		*	*	*
VIII	Tonga-Niue		*	*	
IX	Samoa-Wallis		*		*
X	Tuvalu-Takelau				*
XI	Gilbert-Nauru			*	*
XII	Mariana Islands		*	*	
XIII	Caroline Islands	*	*	*	*
XIV	Marshall Islands				*
XV	Phoenix-Line-Northern Cook				*
XVI	Cook-Austral		*	*	*
XVII	Society Islands		*	*	*
XVIII	Tuamotu			*	*
XIX	Marquesas		*		
XX	Pitcairn-Gambier-Rapa		*	*	*

palms, warm tropical waters, multi-colored coral reefs, peaceful lagoons, elegant shore birds, varied marine creatures, torrential rainstorms, giant rainbows, and exquisite sunsets.

EVOLUTION OF A TRADITION

Approximately 25,000 years ago, the ancestors of today's Pacific Islanders migrated out of Southeast Asia in search of less crowded land. The division of the Pacific Islands into Melanesia (islands of dark-skinned people), Polynesia (many islands), and Micronesia (small islands) correspond with the exploration and settlement of this region and roughly equate with major cultural groupings.

Although the earliest known ancestors of the Pacific People were hunters and gatherers who walked, waded, or floated on crude rafts across to Australia and New Guinea during the last glacial period when sea levels were much lower, most Pacific migrations must be associated with seafaring voyages. Micronesia received voyagers from the Philippines, Indonesia and islands north of New Guinea between 3000 and 2000 B.C., whereas Polynesia received its first known settlements in Tonga and Samoa about 1000 B.C. In all voyages, these Pacific ancestors brought with them their domesticated plants and animals as well as traditional slash and burn and sedentary systems of agriculture. The most important plants introduced were taro (*Colocasia*), breadfruit (*Artocarpus altilis*), yam (*Dioscorea*), coconuts (*Coco nucifera*) and several varieties of bananas (*Musa*). Dogs, chickens, and pigs were the three most important domesticated animals introduced.

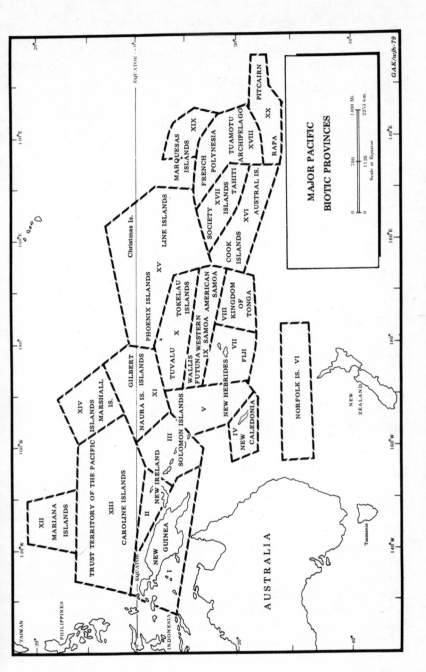

Fig. 59. Major Pacific biotic provinces (based on Dahl, *see* note 106).

Biome / Biotic province	New Guinea	Bismarck Archipelago	Solomon Islands	New Caledonia-Loyalty	New Hebrides-Santa Cruz	Norfolk-Lord Howe-Kermadec	Fiji	Tonga-Niue	Samoa-Wallis	Tuvalu-Takelau	Gilbert-Nauru	Mariana Islands	Caroline Islands	Marshall Islands	Phoenix-Line-Northern Cook	Cook-Austral	Society Islands	Tuamotu	Marquesas	Pitcairn-Gambier-Rapa
Lowland rain forest	*	*	*	*	*		*	*	*				*	*		*	*	*	*	*
Montane rain forest	*	*	*	*	*		*	*	*				*	*		*	*	*	*	*
Bamboo forest	*	o	*	*	*		*						*	*		*	*		*	o
Cloud forest	*	o	*	*	*		*		*				*	*			*			
Riverine forest	*	*	*	*	*		*		*				*	*			*		*	*
Swamp forest	*	*	*	*	*		*		*					*						
Seasonal forest	*								*					*		o				
Semi-deciduous forest																				
Subtropical rain forest						*									o					
Mangrove forest	*	*	*	*	*		*	*	*	*	*	*	*	*		*			*	
Atoll/beach forest	*	*	*	*	*		*	*	*	*	*	*	*	*	*	*	*	*	*	*
Woodlands	*	*	*		o		*	*					*	*		*	*			
Scrub	*		*	*	*	o	*	*					*	*	*	*	*	*	*	*
Serpentine vegetation				*																
Dwarf-shrub heath	*			*									*	*					*	
Bog				*			*							*						
Woodland savanna	*			*					*				*	*						
Tree savanna	*						*	*					*	*						o
Shrub savanna		*		*			*	*					*	*						
Grassland	*	*	*	*	*	*	*	*					*	*		*	*	*	*	*
Flood savanna	*											o	*	*						
Fresh water marsh	*	*	*	*	*		*	*	*			o	*	*		*	*	*	*	
Tidal salt marsh	*				*		*	*					*	*		*				
Non-tidal salt marsh	*				*		*	*						*	*					
Rock desert		*			*		*	*					*	*	*				*	*
Sand desert					*								*	*	*					
Floating meadows	*						*							*						
Reed swamp	*							*						*						
Submerged aquatics	*						*							*						
Floating aquatics	*												*	*						
Permanent lake	*	*	*	*			*	*				*	*	*		*	*			
Intermittent lake													*							
Brackish lake			*										*							
Mountain stream	*	*	*	*	*	*	*		*				*	*			*		*	*
Lowland river	*	*	*	*	*		*		*				*	*			*		*	*
Seabird rookeries	*	*	*	*	*	*	*	*	*	*			*	*	*	*	*	*	*	*
Sea turtle nesting areas	*	*	*	*	*		*	*	*	*	*	*	*	*		*	o	*	*	*
Cave	*	*	*	*	*		*	*	*	*	*	*	*	*	*	*	*	*		
Algal bed	*	*	*	*	*		*	*	*	*	*	*	*	*		*	*	*	*	*
Sea grass bed	*	*	*	*	*		*	*	*	*	*	*	*	*	*	*	*	*	o	*
Animals in sediments	*	*	*	*	*		*	*	*	*	*	*	*	*		*	*	*	o	*
Algal reef	*	*	*	*	*		*	*	*	*	*	*	*	*		*	*	*	*	*
Coral reef	*	*	*	*	*		*	*	*	*	*	*	*	*	*	*	*	*	*	*
Windward atoll reef	*			*			*	*	*	*	*	*	*	*		*	*	*		*
Leeward atoll reef	*			*			*	*	*	*	*	*	*	*		*	*	*		*
Barrier reef	*	*	*	*	*		*	*				*	*	*		*	*			*
Fringing reef	*	*	*	*	*	*	*	*	*			*	*	*		*	*	*	*	*
Lagoon reef	*	*	*	*	*		*	*		*	*	*	*	*		*	*	*		*
Dead reef	*											o								
Drowned reef				*				o	*	*		o					*			
Rocky coast	*	*	*	*	*	*	*	*	o		*	*	*			*	*		*	*
Beach	*	*	*	*	*	*	*	*	*			*	*	*		*	*		*	*
Saline lagoon																				
Open lagoon	*	*	*	*	*		*	*		*	*	*	*	*		*	*		*	*
Closed lagoon							*			*	*	*	*	*		*	*		*	*
Dilute lagoon			*				*			*	*	*	*	*		*	*			
Brackish lagoon							*													
Fresh water lagoon																*				
Estuary	*	*	*				*	*												
Marine lake							*	*					*	*				*		
Marine cave					*		*	*					*	*						
Offshore terrace							*							*						
Offshore slope	*	*	*		*		*	*				*	*	*		*	*		*	*
Continental shelf	*	*			*		*													
Submarine canyon	*																			
Continental slope	*				*		*													
Abyssal plain	*	*	*		*	*	*	*	*		*	*	*		*	*	*		*	*
Submarine trench				*		*	*						*	*						
Submarine ridge						*							*	*						
Seamount	*	*	*		*	*	*	*	*	*		*	*	*		*	*		*	*
Inshore circulation cell															*					
Larger circulation cell																				
Upwelling system																				

Fig. 60. Matrix of biome occurence, by biotic region (based on Dahl, *see* note 106).

Key: * present, o probable.

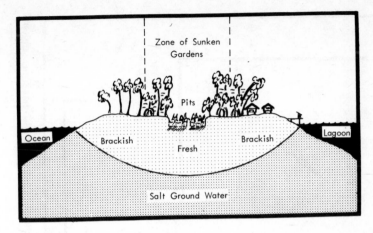

Fig. 61. Cross-section of a typical atoll islet with sunken gardens.

Perhaps the most significant traditional system of agriculture that evolved in the Pacific is the "Sunken Garden," or water-table excavation.[1] Since atolls lack lakes and freshwater streams that could be diverted to irrigate crops, tapping underground water supplies was a major cultural innovation that allowed atolls to be successfully inhabited. The method consists of excavating a pit down to the water table and planting crops (usually *Cyrotosperma chamissonis*—a form of taro) at the bottom of the pit. Since atolls contain ground water that is almost entirely brackish except for a fresh water lens near the center of the islets, pits are always centrally located (Figure 61). An aerial view of an inhabited islet dramatically illustrates the close association between ground water salinity and plant zonation (Figure 62).

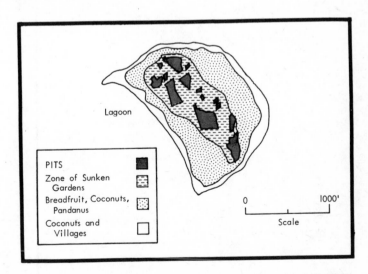

Fig. 62. Aerial view of typical atoll islet showing vegetation belts and proximity of sunken gardens within center of islet.

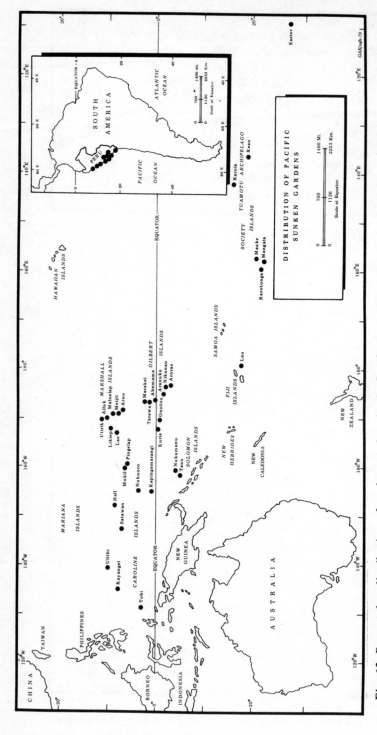

Fig. 63. Present-day distribution of sunken gardens in the Pacific Basin. Note that Peru in South America also has some sunken gardens.

252

Water-table excavation is a traditional agricultural technique that is still practiced widely in Oceania (Figure 63). Associated with its efficient use of water resources, there is also a soil conserving technique worth noting. For example, in the Gilbert Islands, the farmer places each individual plant in a bottomless basket woven from twigs. The "basketed" plants are then placed in the mud at the bottom of the pit and are filled with miscellaneous organic material which acts as natural fertilizers and soil conditioners. These floating baskets, for all practical purposes, duplicate the swampy lowland environment from which the plant originated.

The sunken garden is merely one traditional system of resource management that played an important role in the migration and settlement of the Pacific Islands. What follows is a closer look at those types of past and present traditional resource-using systems that are associated with Oceania.

PAST AND PRESENT TRADITIONAL RESOURCE-USING SYSTEMS

Types of Traditional Conservation Practices

Environmental awareness was central to most forms of traditional conservation practices in Oceania. The native islanders by necessity lived close to nature and had the ability to read the diurnal, monthly, and seasonal cycles of their environment. To the Polynesia, Micronesian, and Melanesian the heavens and the phases of nature served as a clock and calendar to be read and sometimes acted upon.[2] The position of the sun, the rising and setting of stars, the moon, the ebb and flow of tides, changing wind directions, the height of the breakers on the reef, the natural smells within the village, the seasonal variances of terrestrial flora and fauna, and the aquatic cycles all served as a system of time-reckoning, consequently, playing a major role in the understanding of life histories, mating seasons, habitat requirements, and other basic knowledge of plants and animals within their environment. With this high degree of environmental awareness, many island cultures were able to regulate their harvest and use of wild plants and animals on a sustained yield basis. Hence, daily activities were geared to the cycles of nature.

Marine resources. The types and importance of marine conservation in Oceania dwarf all other forms of traditional conservation practices—as one might expect of peoples who live along the margins of the sea. In most areas of the Pacific, fishing, the gathering of shellfish, the hunting of different kinds of sea mammals, and the capture of turtles provided an important source of protein which supplement a diet of terrestrial plants and animals. These aquatic resources were safeguarded by skilled conservation officers and master fishermen, a complex system of marine tenure, food preservation methods, magico-religious taboos, and strict fines and punishment (Table 32).

Since fishing was the most cyclical of human activities, it was carried out according to the reading of the heavens as well as the phases of nature. The moon, tides, stars, and fish migrations had a direct bearing on the movement and activities of island fishermen. Since the reef, lagoon, and sea were primarily the domain and habitat of men, it was natural that men led a life that was closest to the cycles of nature. Although women would occasionally comb the tidal flats for shellfish, sea urchins, sea cucumbers, and some varieties of small fish, their activities were primarily concentrated on the land in the cultivation of taro, an activity that varies little with the seasons.

Table 32. Traditional Marine Resource Management

Examples (left panel):

Form	Ancient	Present
Traditional fisheries ecologists[a]	Samoa Lau (Fiji) Lamotrek Society	Palau Gilberts
Marine tenure systems Fishing rights to specific areas[b]	Marshalls Papeete Society	Pukapuka Hawaii
Specific species regulation[a]	Guam Hawaii Mangareva	Yap
Optimum fishing seasons according to traditional time reckoning[a]	Society Mangareva Tokelau Niue Kapingamarangi Fiji Trobriand Palau	Palau
Closed seasons[a]	New Zealand Hawaii Society Mangareva Pukapuka	Yap

Examples (right panel):

Form	Ancient	Present
Food avoidances[c]	Society Hawaii Pacific	Yap
Conservation of sea food[a] Traps and ponds	Pukapuka Mangareva	
Preservation	Pukapuka Tokelaus Hawaii	Palau
Magico-religious taboos[a]	Samoa New Zealand Society Tokelau Hawaii Marquesas Mangareva Pukapuka Truk Ponape Palau Marshalls Hawaii	Woleai
Fines and punishment[a]	Mangareva Pukapuka	

Notes:

[a] Recognized conservation practice.

[b] Recognized conservation practice in some cultural groups and inadvertent in other.

[c] Inadvertent conservation practice.

Sources: Alkire (*note 3*); Allen (*note 3*); Barrau (*note 35*); Beaglehole (*note 20*); Buck (*note 10*); Catala (*note 33*); Cumberland and Whitelaw (*note 8*); Elliott (*note 61*); Emory (*note 2*); Falanruw (*note 2*); Fischer (*note 13*); Handy (*note 18*); Johannes (*note 5*); Klee (*note 2*); Klee, personal observation in 1972; Loeb (*note 61*); Lundsgaarde (*note 7*); Macgregor (*note 7*); Mead (*note 19*); Melinowski (*note 2*); Meller and Horwitz (*note 2*); Owen (*note 7*); Reinman (*note 28*); Sauder (*note 6*); Titcomb (*note 8*); Tobin (*note 6*); Williamson (*note 9*). For correlation of sources with form and examples, see note 120.

Master fishermen that acted as fisheries' ecologists and conservation officers were predominant in Polynesia, Micronesia, and Melanesia.[3] In the Lau Islands, for example, Allen records the following interesting data:[4]

> Each of the Lau Islands also enjoyed the services of a *ndau ni nggoli*, a master fisherman and authority on the island's fish lore and fishing techniques. The master fisherman's job was to act as a fisheries' ecologist, studying the habits of all the edible marine species, the state of the fishing grounds, the incidence of toxic plants that might render fish poisonous, and all other matters affecting fisheries. No large, organized fishing parties were formed without his permission, and he led all communal turtle hunts. The master fisherman thus protected the island's marine resources from over-exploitation, and, by taking advantage of his knowledge of the optimum conditions for fishing, ensured an optimum take.

Remnants of the position of "master fisheries ecologist" can still be found in the Pacific. In my own field studies in the Palau Islands, it was quite easy to identify the master fisherman (Figure 64). Whereas most men fished at one time or the other for their families, only a handful were considered regular fishermen. The other male members of the community were involved in such enterprises as administering the village's local government, running the village sawmill, or cooking noon meals for the school children. Other male members of the community were ministers, teachers, or farmers. Of those classified as regular fishermen, only one was so thoroughly versed in reading the heavens and the phases of nature that he could name and determine the feeding habits, movements and times and places of spawning of over 300 species of finfishes.[5] Although other factors (such as population size and lack of trading contacts) may be equally important in limiting demands on the resource base, the importance of the Master Fisherman must not be overlooked.

Fig. 64. In 1972, Malsol (Ngiraklang) was one of two or three remaining Master Fishermen in Palau, Micronesia.

Marine tenure systems that placed restrictions on geographic area, season, specific species, and food type also helped regulate the harvesting of aquatic resources.

Fishing rights to specific areas (marine reserves) surrounding an island were often controlled by local chiefs or simply claimed as their own personal property.[6] In the former case, islanders would have to ask permission of the chief to fish in the lagoon, on the reef, and out at sea. In the latter, villagers were completely restricted from the chief's choice fishing spots. In both cases, some form of regulation was involved. Such traditional marine reserves are still maintained by the islanders of Pukapuka and Woleai.[7]

The opening and closing of fishing season was also a tool in managing marine exploitation. Sometimes the restriction was for economic reasons to allow a depleted supply to recover or to conserve the supply for some festival in the near future.[8] At other times, it was applied as a mark of respect in the death of the ruler or some other ethical or religious purpose.[9] Closed seasons were also applied to reserve particular aquatic life for the ruler or high chiefs.[10]

Specific species regulation also was incorporated into traditional tenure schemes of marine management. During their spawning season, specific fish such as albacore, bonito, and rock cod were protected in the Society Islands.[11] Buck records the regulation of more exotic aquatic life, such as the octopus, in the Mangareva Islands.[12] In order to keep this "royal fish" in abundant supply, the Mangareva islanders would erect a tree branch as a sign to warn others that a particular islet on the outer reef was restricted territory for octopus fishing. After a closed period of time, a master fisherman would then gather some octopuses and present them to the king. The restriction was then withdrawn.

In Yap, Falanruw has recently observed the opening and closing of fishing seasons, specific species regulation, and elements of social stratification that continue to conserve marine resources.[13]

> One such example is the "bungud of the lupuu" as is done on Yap. When fish become scarce and small, a sign is put up in the lagoon prohibiting certain kinds of fishing, or all fishing there. When fish have regained their former size and abundance, this ban is removed ... Social stratification also results in a diversified use of the island resources. If some items, such as turtles, are available only to the high classes while other foods such as eels are eaten only by low classes (as is the case in Yap), then both turtles and eels are protected from exploitation by all inhabitants of the island. This would tend to insure their continued productivity.

Food avoidances also played a role in maintaining aquatic resources. Some species could only be eaten by chiefs, or chiefs and priests.[14] In other cases, certain animals were restricted to members of particular tribes, each tribe having a few such restricted species.[15] Food avoidances according to one's sex or class were also prevalent in the Pacific. In the Marquesas Islands, for example, yam, coconut, breadfruit, and most kinds of fish were free to everyone; but bananas, pigs, and such marine life as turtle, cuttle-fish, bonito and albacore were prohibited to women and lower class men.[16]

Most marine tenure systems were integrally dependent upon the political authority of village elders and were buttressed by a set of ethical rules proclaimed by the religious leaders within the community. Areal, seasonal, specific species, and food restrictions placed on aquatic resources were reinforced by a complex set of magico-religious taboos.

Taboos could be issued in the form of chieftain decrees, clan taboos, or private ownership taboos.[17] In the latter case, those villagers who owned sections of a reef would periodically institute taboos on fishing to allow the fish to multiply.[18] Master fishermen could also put a taboo on fishing at certain times; these traditional fisheries ecologists had power beyond that of mere advising.[19]

In addition to those mentioned above, taboos were also placed on the reef, lagoon, or sea for a variety of other reasons. They were decreed to regulate the numbers of fishermen on the reef at any particular time. For example, the fishermen of Ngake Village in Pukapuka would announce that they might fish in the lagoon for one night. For that period the lagoon was taboo (off limits) to all other villages except Ngake; other villages got their turn to harvest the reef on subsequent nights.[20] Taboos were issued placing regulations on the first fishing expeditions of the season.[21] On the death of a king or clan member, the sea was declared taboo and fishing was prohibited.[22] Taboos even existed that barred women from participating in particular types of fishing.[23]

To illustrate the close relationship between tenure system (in this example, reef rights in the Marshall Islands) and the workings of magico-religious belief systems, the following passages are selected from Tobin's field work in Micronesia:[24]

> Throughout the Marshalls the reefs were claimed by the *iroij* (king or paramount chief) as *emo* (forbidden, taboo) or personal property if the fishing was good around them . . . After this tabu was instituted, no one else was permitted to fish that particular reef . . . Other people were afraid to disobey the tabu until it was lifted by government edict . . . Small islands were also occasionally tabooed, e.g., Kaben, a small island with a few trees on it on Wotto Atoll, was taken by the *iroij* for his personal use because of the abundance of coconut crabs on it. *Emo* (forbidden) fishing sites were in existence on every atoll.

These magico-religious taboos that governed Pacific island tenure systems were enforced by strict fines and punishment. Offenders could sometimes expect severe if not fatal punishment for what seems a trifling matter. In Pukapuka, Beaglehole recorded that trespassers in a fishing reserve that belonged to another village might be punished by fines in nuts levied by the guards of the village whose reef was violated.[25] But, if one trespassed on tabooed fishing reserves in the Marshall Islands, one could expect the penalty of death or expulsion from the island.[26] Severe punishments for taboo violations were recorded in Hawaii and Mangareva, as well as many other islands throughout the Pacific region.[27] These penalities for breaking taboos held the people in strict obedience.

The conservation of sea foods was the final major means by which Pacific islanders conserved their aquatic resources. Traps and fish ponds were used to capture, raise, and maintain fish or turtles until needed or until they reached the desired size. Taro fields were also used to provide a flooded area in which shrimp and small fish were maintained.[28]

Food preservation methods were widespread and helped stretch the available supply of aquatic resources. Basically, the following methods were used: sun drying, smoking, salting or combinations of salting, soaking in brine, and sun drying.[29]

Soil and water resources. Traditional resource-using systems such as taro production in the Cook Islands, yam-raising in the Ponape Islands, and "pot cultivation" in the Gilbert Islands have been reported by Barrau to have excellent soil/water conservation techniques that need further documentation.[30] In his study of the Tsembaga, Rappaport recorded the various conservation aspects of swidden agriculture as practiced by these New Guinea tribesmen.[31] In a recent study by Randolph Thaman, the conservation features of Pacific "Urban Agriculture" were highlighted.[32]

In today's Pacific, a variety of specific traditional soil and water conservation techniques are practiced (Table 33). As previously mentioned, planting in pits or sunken gardens to efficiently tap ground water resources is predominant in the Gilbert, Ellice, Marshall, Phoenix, and Line Islands as well as French Polynesia.[33] Mounding is of particular importance in New Guinea.[34] Terracing is well represented in New Caledonia, New Guinea, and the New Hebrides.[35] Mulching has been reported in New Guinea and the Eastern Caroline Islands.[36] The practices of preserving certain stretches of natural vegetation (e.g., beach-scrub vegetation) to intercept salt spray and prevent beach erosion has been recorded on Kapingamarangi Atoll.[37]

Leaving tree and shrub stumps within the garden after initial clearing is still practiced in New Guinea.[38] Some New Guinea tribes even plant trees within the garden site for soil erosion control, nitrogen enrichment of the soil, as well as providing additional timber.[39] Certain tribes in New Guinea also have the technique of arranging felled trees or rubbish in transverse rows on hillsides.[40] In the New Hebrides, and elsewhere, felled trees are used to outline the garden site, thus helping to keep out wild animals.[41] Using pigs for rooting and soil fertilization is still practiced in New Guinea.[42] In New Guinea, Clarke also recorded the use of bodily wastes to enrich the fields.[43] In the Gilbert and Caroline Islands various types of leaves and shrubs are cut and mixed together to make a fertilizer to enrich the soil (Figure 65).[44]

Rotating fields to leave certain lands fallow for periods at a time is a practice that continues in Yap, Guam, Samoa, as well as New Guinea.[45] Burning fields to release

Fig. 65. In Palau, Micronesia, women still gather various types of leaves to fertilize their agricultural fields.

Table 33. Traditional Soil and Water Resource Management

Form	Examples of recognized conservation practice		Form	Examples of recognized conservation practice	
	Ancient	Present		Ancient	Present
Terracing	Fiji	New Hebrides, New Guinea, New Caledonia	Arranging felled trees or rubbish in transverse rows on hillside	Pacific	New Guinea
Mulching	Pacific	New Guinea, East Caroline Isl.	Restricting extensive digging of large plots to lowlands	Pacific	
Leaving tree seedlings and shrub stumps after initial clearing	Pacific	New Guinea	Field rotation	Samoa, New Zealand	Yap, Guam, New Guinea
Planting trees within gardens		New Guinea	Fertilizer uses	Polynesia, Micronesia	Gilbert Isl., East Carolines
Planting in individual isolated holes, pits, or mounds	Pacific	Pacific, Gilbert, Ellice, Caroline, Marshalls, French Oceania, Fanning, Garden, Hull, Washington, New Guinea	Using pigs for rooting and fertilization	New Zealand	New Guinea
			Burning to release nutrients into soil		New Guinea
			Using bodily wastes to enrich fields	New Zealand	New Guinea
			Alteration of soil to improve texture	Rapa	
			Using silt to change soil texture	Hawaii	
			Shelterbelts	New Zealand	
			Different crop intercultivation[a]		New Guinea
			Knowledge of soil types	New Zealand	New Guinea
			Restrictive taboos[b]	New Zealand	New Guinea

Notes:

[a]Practice of intercultivating different crops with different maturation periods for erosion control and nutrients.

[b]Inadvertent conservation practice in some cultural groups.

Sources: Barrau (*note 30*); Barrau (*note 35*); Catala (*note 33*); Clarke (*note 39*); Crocombe and Hide (*note 36*); Cumberland and Whitelaw (*note 8*); Dagodag and Klee (*note 1*); Falanruw (*note 13*); Fischer (*note 18*); Fosberg (*note 69*); Lundsgaarde (*note 7*); Mead (*note 19*); Olliver, Drover and Godelier (*note 50*); Rappaport (*note 31*); Siwatibau (*note 53*); Spoehr (*note 45*); Waddell (*note 34*). **For correlation of sources with form and examples, see** *note 120.*

nutrients into the soil is practiced in New Guinea as well as many other areas.[46] In New Guinea and the Loyalty Islands, shelterbelts are created to cut down wind erosion.[47] To conserve soil moisture, the careful construction of ditches and drains is well represented in New Caledonia and New Guinea.[48] To further erosion control, some New Guinea tribes inter-cultivate different crops with different maturation periods.[49] As is the case of New Guinea, all of these techniques and more are probably founded on a traditional soil knowledge that stresses types and proper use.[50] Magico-religious taboos coupled with fines and punishment for offenders enforced the proper management of soil and water resources.

Forest and garden crop resources. Traditional means to protect forest and garden crop resources existed and continue to exist in the Pacific (Table 34). A number of Pacific Island cultures had "forestry ecologists" that acted as conservation officers; they watched over trees, garden crops, and made ecological decisions. Allen cites an interesting example from Melanesia:[51]

> In the Lau Islands of Fiji, the *Vaka Vanua* was custodian of forest produce and of crops. His duties were to watch his island's food supply, and as each major food crop (whether wild or cultivated) matured, to place a *tapu* on it. When the crop custodian judged the crop to be ready for harvest, he lifted the *taboo*. He saw that the initial harvest was distributed correctly, with portions going to the chief and, in equal shares, to each of the clans. If the harvest was a good one, some of this initial take was set aside to be fermented and stored against time of scarcity. Once the initial distribution had been made, the people harvested the rest of the crop, as they required it, from their own lands.

With the use of taboos and degrees of punishment for offenders, these traditional forestry ecologists could control the cutting of particular trees or entire stands, the harvesting of fruits, leaves, bark, or any other product of the tree, and the planting of trees as crops.[52] In the following passage, Siwatibau discusses the planting of tree crops as a traditional resource-conserving system in itself.[53]

> Tree crops, except for coconuts, were generally never planted in large single stands, but in mixed stands, often interspersed with native tree species. Tree cropping involved little initial clearing and even less consequent clearing. It is fair to assume that most of the inhabited islands originally supported forests. Tree cropping therefore simply emulated the structure of natural vegetation and as a consequence the physical environment was not as extensively altered as would otherwise be the case. A sufficient diversity of species of plant forms remained to continue to provide a diversity of habitats for associated fauna and flora. This ensured a store of predators for any introduced agricultural pests.

Trees, forests, and garden crops continue to be protected by a variety of traditional restrictions. In Kapingamarangi, Emory has noted that present day islanders continue to respect coconut leaf signs that restrict use of particular trees.[54] On the same atoll, Niering noticed that the inhabitants had come to terms with their severely limited resources, and, consequently, developed functional conservation practices: "This is evidenced by their selective management policies and further emphasized by their reluctance to sell canoes to outsiders since it would mean the loss of another large productive breadfruit tree."[55] Mangrove trees are still appreciated as "fasteners-of-the-shore" in Truk and Ponape, and, consequently, are traditionally protected.[56] In the New Hebrides, if

Table 34. Traditional Forest and Garden Crop Resource Management

Form	Examples of recognized conservation practice[a]	Form	Examples of recognized conservation practice[a]
Forestry ecologists	Fiji	Sacred groves[d]	Kwajalein
Tree reserves	Pukapuka		New Guinea[b]
Planting tree crops	Pacific	Storage reserves for garden crops	Fiji
	New Guinea[b]		Samoa
Protecting tree seedlings within swidden gardens	Samoa	Magico-religious taboos	Pukapuka
Closed seasons for harvesting fruits or other tree portions	Pukapuka[c]		Fiji
Single species protection		Fines and punishment	Tokelau
			Samoa

Notes:

[a] Ancient unless otherwise indicated.

[b] Present-day.

[c] Examples of present-day practice include Kapingamaringi, Eastern Carolines and Palmerston.

[d] Inadvertent conservation practice in some cultural groups.

Sources: Allen (*note 3*); Beaglehole and Beaglehole (*note 20*); Clarke (*note 39*); Elliott (*note 61*); Emory (*note 2*); Fischer (*note 18*); Lundsgaarde (*note 7*); Macgregor (*note 52*); Niering (*note 37*); Rappaport (*note 31*); Siwatibau (*note 53*); Williamson (*note 9*). **For correlation of sources with form and examples, see note 120.**

someone with strong rights and claims to a tree desires to prevent trespassing, he can still place a tabu on it—thus restricting its exploitation until he lifts the tabu.[57] Clarke has observed that the Maring clans of New Guinea have what they call *Komung*: spirited-inhabited sacred groves that are restricted.[58] Rappaport found that the Tsembaga farmers of New Guinea are well aware of the importance of regenerating trees, and, consequently, practice the sparing of tree seedlings and small tree trunks when clearing a garden to ensure a more rapid redevelopment of the forest canopy.[59] He also found that the maturing tree seedlings and small tree trunks act as a clock and calendar to warn the tribesmen when to abandon their gardens, so that the soil would not be depleted:[60]

> Above the ground the developing leaves and branches not only provide additional protection for the thin forest soil against tropical downpours but also immobilize nutrients recovered from the soil for release to future gardens. However, they also make it increasingly difficult for gardeners to harvest and weed. As a result the people are induced to abandon their gardens before they have seriously exhausted the soil, even before the crops are completely harvested. The developing trees, whose growth they themselves have encouraged, make harvesting more laborious at the same time that it is becoming less rewarding . . . It is clear that the Tsembaga support not only the garden species that provide them with food but also the species on which they ultimately depend—those of the forest, which sustain their gardens.

Wildlife resources. Traditional Pacific Island cultures also had a variety of methods that undoubtedly had an affect on restoring, maintaining, and increasing game populations (Table 35). Habitat maintenance, game reserves, game laws (such as hunting seasons and bag limits), and prohibitions against certain sacred plants and animals all played a role in conserving wildlife resources.[61] With the effects of the U.S. pet store trade on wildlife extinction coming more into the news, it is interesting to note that some island cultures even specifically forbid the keeping of animals as pets.[62]

As with marine, soil/water, and forest/garden crop resources, traditional island cultures enforced the above restrictions on wildlife exploitation by a series of magico-religious taboos and penalities.[63] A few select passages from Tobin's field study in the Marshall Islands illustrate the interrelatedness of game reserves, religious ritual, and avifauna and marine resources:[64]

> The Northern Radak atolls at Bikar, Bokak (Taongi), Toke, the island of Jemo, and the islands of Erik and Luij in Erikub atoll have been used from time immemorial as game reserves. These areas are the habitat of myriads of sea and nesting fowl. Periodically, turtles, turtle eggs, birds and their eggs were taken . . . Jemo is the home of myriads of turtles and birds whose flesh and eggs have been a valuable source of protein for the neighboring atolls . . . Before the party commenced their search for eggs, etc., divine sanction was requested. Everyone assembled on the beach before proceeding inland and cut a leaf of coconut frond. With the *iroij* (high chief) leading the way they walked toward Lawi Jemo (the Kanal tree) in single file, each individual carefully stepping in the footprints of the person in front of him so that only one set of footprints would appear as if only one person had been there.

Traditional means of managing wildlife resources still exist in the Pacific. For example, Allen has observed that the Council of Elders still regulates bird collection in the Tokelau Islands, and that traditional game reserves are kept in the Pukapukas.[65]

Table 36. Traditional Wildlife Resource Management

Form	Examples of recognized conservation practice[a]	Form	Examples of recognized conservation practice[a]
Habitat maintenance Game reserves	Australia Pukapuka[b] Marshalls New Guinea[c]	Prohibition of sacred plants[d] Regulations pertaining to pets[d]	Niue Marshalls Pukapuka

Game laws
  Hunting seasons
  Bag limits
	Tokelau[c]
	Pacific
	Micronesia
		Magico-religious taboos	Australia
			Pukapuka
			Tonga
			Niue
			Micronesia
			Tokelau

Prohibition of sacred animals[d]	Tonga Samoa Society Hawaii Niue	Fines and punishment	Niue Marshalls

Notes:
[a] Ancient unless otherwise indicated.
[b] Also present-day practice.
[c] Present-day.
[d] Inadvertent conservation practice.
Sources: Allen (*note 3*); Beaglehole and Beaglehole (*note 20*); Clarke (*note 39*); Elliott (*note 61*); Gifford (*note 63*); Handy (*note 14*); Loeb (*note 61*); Owen (*note 17*); Powell (*note 61*); Tobin (*note 6*). **Also see** *note 120* **for correlation of sources with forms and examples.**

Clarke observed that the *komung* (sacred groves) of the Maring serve not only as a source for seed for the recolonization of rainforest trees, but also as hunting preserves:[66]

> Because the *komung* are remnants of a habitat something like the primary rain forest, they also serve as places where rain forest birds and animals can be hunted close at hand. In the basin this function is expanded by the presence of a "false komung," which is a plot of rain forest not charged with spiritual danger but left uncut as a kind of private hunting preserve for its claimant.

Population control. Various natural and cultural controls have traditionally kept Pacific Island cultures in relative equilibrium with their restricted land base. Natural calamities such as typhoons, tidal waves, droughts and consequent famine have played an important part in controlling island populations in the past—particularly on low lying atolls.[67] Researchers have also found that venereal and other diseases have played an important role in preventing large population increase in the past.[68]

In addition to natural catastrophes and diseases, a variety of cultural practices influenced population control (Table 36). An entire range of fertility control mechanisms was practiced by Pacific Island cultures. In prevention of conception, moral restraints (often connected with taboos) and to a lesser degree withdrawal (coitus interruptus) appear to have been the most predominant.[69] Frequent periods of ritual celibacy also occured.[70]

Table 36. Traditional Population and Food Resource Management

Form	Examples of recognized conservation practice[a]	Form	Examples of recognized conservation practice[a]
Fertility control[b]		*Socio-political control*	
Moral restraints[c]	Pacific Society	Adoption[c]	Micronesia Australia
	Micronesia	Importing/exporting people	
	Kapingamarangi	In case of natural calamity	Pacific[e]
	Marshalls		East Carolines
Coitus interruptus	Micronesia	In case of critical sex ratio	Pacific
Ritual celibacy[d]	Pacific	imbalance[c]	
	Micronesia	Regulating presence of	Ulithi[f]
	Tikopia	outsiders	
Abortion[d]	Pacific	Planting nonsubsistence	Pacific
	Pukapuka	crops[d]	
	Yap	Food preferences[d]	Pacific
	Truk	Overseas voyages	Pacific
	Kapingamarangi		Tikopia
	Australia	Warfare[d]	Pacific
Infanticide[c]	Pacific		Pukapuka
	Australia		New Guinea[e]
		Human sacrifice[d]	Mangareva

Notes:
[a]Ancient unless otherwise indicated.
[b]Prevention of conception.
[c]Recognized practice in some cultural groups and inadvertent in others.
[d]Inadvertent conservation practice.
[e]Also present-day practice.
[f]Present-day practice.

Sources: Beaglehole and Beaglehole (*note 20*); Bodley (*note 69*); Buck (*note 10*); Buck (*note 78*); Crocombe and Hide (*note 36*); Emory (*note 2*); Falanruw (*note 13*); Firth (*note 87*); Fischer (*note 18*); Fosberg (*note 69*); Gladwin (*note 71*); Knudson (*note 74*); Lessa (*note 79*); Rappaport (*note 80*); Schneider (*note 68*); Tobin (*note 6*); Williamson (*note 9*); Yen (*note 110*). **Also see** *note 120* **for correlation of sources with forms and examples.**

If conception did occur, abortion was the cultural control mechanism most often practiced in Melanesia, Polynesia, and aboriginal Australia.[71] During 1947–48, a team of anthropologists studied the problem of depopulation on Yap Island.[72] They found that self-induced abortion was a factor in keeping down the fertility rate and in prolonging the underpopulated state of the island. Yapese women under thirty who became pregnant induced abortion by one of three major techniques: (1) magical manipulations, (2) drinking boiled sea water, and (3) the plug-and-injury method. Since the latter technique was believed to be the most effective, it was most frequently used. It consisted of placing a thick rolled plug of hibiscus leaves (which expand when moist) into the mouth of the cervix. Injury was then managed by scratching with a stick, stone, fingernail or other sharp object until blood was drawn. The massage method, a technique common in Melanesia and Polynesia, was apparently unknown on Yap. A number of Pacific cultures also practiced infanticide.[73]

Social and political mechanisms also existed that allowed for the redistribution of people on the land. Local pressure was sometime relieved through the practice of adoption or the importing or exporting of groups or individuals in case of typhoon destruction or critical imbalance in a community's sex ratio.[74]

Food preferences and the planting of nonsubsistence crops were also cultural controls that helped maintain population well below any theoretical maximum carrying capacity based on the ultimate limits of food production. According to Bodley, the critical population ceiling in the Polynesian outlying atolls seems to have been set by the environmental limits to taro production.[75]

> Taro was a daily element in the diet and a prime measure of the overall adequacy of the food supply. If cultural preferences were not a factor, then presumably these cultures might have simply switched to crops which provided more calories per acre or per unit of labor such as coconuts, and supported even denser populations. However, it appears that the ideal was for taro to supply approximately 50% of the calorie intake, and it was culturally intolerable for it to drop below 25%.

The planting of nonsubsistence crops (such as ritually important tumeric) displaced food crops and, consequently acted as a possible further cultural control of carrying capacity.

If the above mentioned natural calamities and cultural controls failed to keep the people and land in balance, other cultural mechanisms went into effect. Overseas voyages were also relied upon when inner-island redistribution measures failed to relieve population pressure.[76] If such voyages failed to fine new lands, they often became unintentional "suicidal voyages." If population pressure continued, warfare often erupted over violations of taboos on food reserves, bickering over divisions of the reserves, or quarrels over food divisions.[77] Warfare, obviously, resulted in a certain amount of reduction in population though the number of deaths was usually small. Human sacrifice for religious purposes also slightly reduced the number of individuals in a community.[78]

Population and food resources continue to be traditionally regulated on a number of Pacific Islands. Ulithians still have *etap* (taboos or prohibitions) that protect the food supply and regulate the presence of outsiders arriving from other islands. Despite some loosening of the traditional restrictions since World War II, Lessa has observed that most *etap* continue in force today.[79] In highland New Guinea, ceremonial cycles help maintain a balance between human population, pig herds, and the natural environment.[80] The critical growth of the pig herd, the connected ritual warfare and eventual pig slaughter have been all reduced to a computer simulation model and analyzed by various specialists.[81]

The northern Cook Islands provide one of the finest examples of traditional population/food resource regulation under modern conditions. In his analysis of the area, Allen observed that the traditional communal control of reserve lands in Pukapuka is far superior to the land tenure system found in the southern Cook Islands:[82]

> The Pukapukans regard bird nesting and resting areas, the barrier reef and all fishing grounds on the reef, continuous areas of sea, the lagoon, coconut groves, and taro and *Cyrtosperma* beds as reserve lands. Reserve lands are controlled by three "companies," which in effect are Pukapuka's three villages. The *ariki* (village leaders) are the executives of the companies, and they decree when reserves shall be opened and how much of the reserves' resources—coconuts, taro, crabs, sea birds or fish—shall be taken. All adults receive equal shares (and children equal part-shares), except for the *ariki* who are given an extra supply of coconuts in recognition

of their position. To ensure that the constraints imposed by the *ariki* are not abused, the companies operate a system of guards, in which adult members of each village take turns at guard duty. The guards patrol the reserves throughout the day to keep away thieves, to protect the nuts, pandanus trees and other reserve flora, and to keep wandering pigs and chickens from damaging the taro and *Cyrtosperma* beds. This control system has proved capable of expansion as in the case of the island of Nassau, purchases by the Pukapukans to increase their resources, and now treated as a reserve. More significantly, perhaps, the system has proved adaptable to the exploitation of resources sold for cash, in particular copra. When a boat is expected, the *ariki* open the reserves for harvest, having inspected them to determine how much the harvest should be. An equal number of nuts is assigned to each villager for preparation, who received an equal share of the profits.

Inadvertent vs. Recognized Conservation Practices

Many of the aforementioned techniques were employed consciously and explicity for conservation purposes.[83] However, a number of practices were frequently bound up in religious and social rituals and customs, and, consequently, were not actually recognized for their conserving qualitities. Other practices were only occasionally carried out for their conserving qualities.

Marine resources were mostly consciously conserved by the methods noted in Table 32. Clearly inadvertent practices that conserved aquatic resources comprised the restricting of certain foods to selected social classes, sexes, or clans and prohibiting fishing on the death of an important individual. Certain practices such as allocating fishing rights to specific areas and opening and closing of fishing seasons were sometimes but not always initiated for the purpose of conserving resources. In the first case, fishing rights to specific areas were often claimed by local chiefs for strictly selfish reasons. On the other hand, master fishermen occasionally controlled fishing rights to an area for the express purpose of regulating the exploitation of aquatic resources. In the second case, the opened and closed fishing seasons were for the express purpose of allowing a depleted supply to recover; this measure was at times merely instituted as a sign of respect for a dead ruler.

Soil and water resources were conserved primarily by recognized practices, such as those noted in Table 33. Although inadvertant practices might have existed, none were identified by this author.

Forest and garden crop resources were also conserved primarily by recognized practices (Table 34). The keeping of "sacred groves" was the only practice not always done for its conserving benefits; whereas some island cultures consciously tried to conserve particular groves of trees, other cultures were merely restricting access to religiously sacred or tabooed tree species.

Wildlife resources were conserved by recognized as well as inadvertent practices (Table 35). Such conservation practices as prohibiting the capture of certain sacred animals, prohibiting the picking or harvesting of certain sacred plants, and forbiding the keeping of animals as pets were more inadvertant than recognized.

Population control, both recognized and inadvertent had an effect on reducing the demand on all resources (Table 36). Clearly inadvertant population practices were ritual celibacy, prefering to eat only certain foods, and lessening population pressure through warfare.

Such practices as restraint due to morals, adopting children, and importing or exporting people due to a critical imbalance in a community's sex ratio were at times initiated for conservation purposes as well as at times for other reasons. For example, moral principles that regulate the spacing of children were recognized cultural controls of population growth; other kinds of community morals were not related to conservation, and, consequently were not recognized as such. In some cultures, child adoption was for the purpose of equally distributing the people on the land; in other cultures, adoption was for the sake of adding wealth or prestige to a marriage that lacked children. Migration to regulate an imbalance in a community's sex ratio was for the purpose of creating an equal distribution of people to resources. In certain cultures, however, it was merely practiced to provide a male in one group with a female partner from another.

Degree of Effectiveness

Examination of past forms of traditional resource management in Oceana would seem to indicate that most of the region's people were effective conservationists. Several authors have specifically cited the effectiveness of traditional marine conservation techniques.[84] Johannes, a marine biologist, states the problem most clearly.[85]

> Certainly not all practices worked, any more than all western conservation measures work. But I am confident that some *did* work. The inhabitants of Oceania have had centuries to test these measures by trial and error. Even in Hawaii, where the fishermen, by virtue of their more intense contact with the West, have probably lost more of their traditional marine lore than elsewhere in Oceania, their knowledge of marine ecology clearly surpasses that of the marine biologists in some ways. I went as a consultant to a fisherman's meeting in Hawaii a few months ago and came away having learned more from them than they learned from me.

The effectiveness of traditional forest/garden crop and wildlife conservation techniques has also been cited in the literature.[86] Several authors have also referred to the effectiveness of traditional forms of population control in Oceania.[87] Emory's note of child spacing in Kapingamarangi was most interesting. Traditional Kapingamarangi peoples believed that the mother of a baby should not become pregnant for at least a year after its birth, or the baby would somehow suffer. The husband was considered "weak" if he had intercourse with his wife during this period. Emory's census figures of typical families on Kapingamarangi bear out the fact that in most families the children were spaced two or three years apart.[88]

This is not to say, however, that traditional Pacific Island cultures always did what was best in terms of conservation management. Nor should one infer that the mere citing of a few authors brings hard evidence to bear supporting the effectiveness of traditional systems of resource management. Two contrasting evaluations of the Maori in New Zealand should make this point clear: Cumberland writes, "he hunted, gathered and fished but always within the limits composed by the *taboo* and an inherent reverence for nature. His keen sense of conservation meant that he made little long-term impression on the land's surface."[89] Yet, another New Zealand specialist has this to say about the Maori as a conservationist:[90]

I am a little skeptical of some studies of traditional conservation practices as they have not always distinguished between the traditional idea and the reality of what happened. For example, the New Zealand Maori has been acclaimed as a great conservationist and in theory this may be true but in fact they succeeded in de-foresting a large part of the country with fire, often wontonly lit, while according to tradition showing great reverence for the forest.

Although one could possibly argue the fact that burning improves hunting conditions in many cases, thus improving wildlife resources, the significance of Ward's comment remains valid.

In sum, Pacific Island cultures had a variety of conservation techniques that were, in many cases, effective. As Ward has so perceptively stated, the problem of future researchers dealing with past forms of traditional conservation management will be one of trying to "distinguish between the traditional idea and the reality of what happened." This will be no easy task, but one certainly worthy of pursuit.

REGION IN TRANSITION

Traditional Pacific islanders generally lived in relative equilibrium with their environment. Geographic isolation due to the insular character of island environments, consequent slow rate of culture change, and limited demands on resources were factors in providing a comparatively stable socio-economic system. Subsistence agriculture with hunting and fishing sufficed. Their high degree of environmental awareness provided much knowledge of the conservation requirements of plants, animals, and man.

A "father-to-son" system of education passed this environmental knowledge down to subsequent generations. It was an education system that not only ensured an awareness of the environment, but also the survival tactics necessary to maintain and conserve that society in that environment for perpetuity. Furthermore, this environmental knowledge was ingrained in a magico-religious conservation ethic that was administered and often ruthlessly enforced. An efficient administration and enforcement system used a complex variety of taboos (conditions, rules, regulations) and penalities for offenders to maintain controls on population growth and ward off the over-exploitation of resources.

The factors that held traditional island cultures in relative equilibrium (a comparatively stable socio-economic system, a high degree of environmental awareness, an efficient educational system, and an efficient administrative and enforcement system), suddenly began to break down.

Factors that Break Down Traditional Conservation Techniques

There are several elements of cultural change that have a profound effect on breaking down the traditional time-honored ways of conservation management in Oceania. The following is a closer look at each of the major factors.

Increased cultural contact. Increased contact with outsider cultures had a tremendous impact on traditional conservation ethics and practices. "With the coming of European man all this disappeared. A culture based on accumulation of wealth, equality of opportunity, complete individualism and greed was unsuited to a conservation ethic."[91] Ship captains spread goats and other hoofed animals to almost every island in the Pacific, resulting in animal population explosions that degraded forests, eliminated wildlife habitats, brought on serious soil erosion problems, and generally disrupted ecosystems that had evolved in the absence of such animals.

In addition to the environmental havoc brought on by the introduction of exotic plants and animals, the ships brought hundreds of missionaries that substituted a religion that had neither a conservation ethic nor any tolerance for traditional customs or practices that regulated and protected marine preserves, soil and water resources, forest and garden crops, wildlife sanctuaries, and human population/land ratios. Tobin's field study in the Marshall Islands provides an excellent illustration of missionaries at work:[92]

> The early missionaries successfully used their prestige and persuasive powers to discourage the worship of Lawi Jemo and the other *ekjab*. This kabun (ritual) was last performed at Jemo during German times, according to a reliable informant, shortly after which the tree, Lawi Jemo, was cut down for boat timber. Today people gather turtle eggs and birds' eggs, etc., at any time of year and walk wherever they wish on Jemo. None of the tabus are observed as far as may be determined. This is true for the other bird islands as well.

Similar cases have been recorded in Melanesia, Polynesia, as well as other parts of Micronesia.

During World War II, military activity swept through the Pacific region bringing drastic degradation to island ecosystems. Not only did the war bring devastating damage to a great many islands (naval bombardment sometimes left scarcely a tree remaining on some atolls), but it also increased the pace and degree of contact with alien cultures. Once the war was over, many Pacific island territories came under the influence and "protection" of foreign cultures, which had a further deteriorating effect on traditional values and attitudes.

Military interests remained in the Pacific during the post World War II period. The use of atolls as sites for the testing of atomic weapons caused almost total destruction to certain islets, reefs, and lagoons, and also required the separation and relocation of some Pacific communities from one island to another. Relocation had a shattering effect on such communities. In 1968, nine Bikinians were taken to inspect their atoll. They were there three days looking at the remnants from the United States' presence: rusted equipment, buildings, and concrete bunkers. The Bikinians searched in vain for something that would indicate to them that this area was their home; the only sign of the pre-bombing era was the native graveyard. The thatched-roofed huts were gone, along with the church and meeting house. Also gone were the rows of coconut palms that had lined the shores and the pandanus and breadfruit trees that were once abundant. In their place grew thick vegetation composed of shrubs and vines. All this prompted the leader of the Bikinians, Alab Lore, to stop and say, "Everything has changed; everything has gone."[93]

There were other drastic changes on Bikini: sunken U.S. Navy ships were on the lagoon floor; low islets on the southern rim were now connected to form an airstrip; four islets on the northern rim were made into one large island in order to provide for a series of test facilities; one entire island, and parts of two others, had disappeared in the explosions. Bikini was an entirely different atoll than that which existed before the bombings began in 1946. For a culture that once read and geared its activities to the cycles of nature (e.g., the blossoming of flowers, trees, and shrubs; the migration and spawning cycles of fish within the lagoon), all these indicators were either drastically disrupted or totally eliminated. Traditional ways of doing things obviously had to be modified.[94]

The search for natural resources was a further impetus for foreign interest and exploitation in Oceania, and consequent destruction of traditional cultures. Bodley clearly stated and documented this fact: "Overconsumption by the industrial nations not only destroys the physical environment, but it has also been the primary cause of the almost total destruction of primitive cultures over the past 150 years."[95]

Most recently, tourism and volunteer groups such as the American Peace Corps have had an effect on increasing island contact with outside cultures. Hundreds of jumbo jets descend on the major urban centers of the Pacific, unloading thousands of Asian, European, and American tourists. Although the average tourist does not usually stray too far from the central cities, numerous American Peace Corps volunteers (the author a case in point) penetrate the outer most sections of islands where tourists rarely tread. The impact of tourism and overseas volunteer agencies on traditional island cultures is only now beginning to be assessed.

With increased contact with outside cultures comes the aspiration to imitate the higher standard of living of the observed culture. This, in turn, often leads to greater demands on local resources as a result of the collapse of basic traditional systems.[96]

Increased population. Increased rates of population growth in Oceania have also had their effect on breaking down traditional conservation practices. Island populations were usually drastically reduced due to foreign contact and the ensuing changes in diet, succumbing to new diseases, acquisition of firearms, and breakdown of cultural systems.[97] Only a few places, such as the Gilbert Islands, Mokil, Pingelap, and Fiji have had population problems in the early stages of colonization.[98]

The demographic picture drastically changed once state intervention took hold.[99] Traditional population control mechanisms were eliminated. Missionaries halted abortion and infanticide practices and the new government curbed intertribal warfare. The entire system of taboos that so carefully regulated resource exploitation was considered "pagan," and gradually eliminated over time. The state also provided medical and health services and even incentives for population growth. By encouraging a labor-intensive agricultural system for cash crops, a large family became more advantageous for a traditional farmer than a small one. With elimination of traditional cultural controls on population growth, the introduction of western medicine, and creation of new incentives to increase the size of families, rapid population growth was the inevitable consequence.

Increased population pressure further modified any remaining traditional conservation practices. For example, swidden agriculture which so nicely fit into the ecological scheme of things for centuries, became practiced in a new way with harmful consequences.

Failing education, administrative and enforcement systems. New education systems in the Pacific failed to teach traditional environmental knowledge, thus further stimulating the breakdown of traditional cultural controls over resource management.[100] Only a few remaining village elders still read and use the cycles of nature; in the young, traditional attitudes towards resources and their utilization are lacking.

The failure of new administrative systems in the Pacific to incorporate aspects of traditional resource management and enforcement also led to further deterioration of traditional cultural controls over resources.[101] Few, if any, observers have stated this more precisely than Allen:[102]

Unfortunately, the British did not understand this remarkable institution, and so did not incorporate it into the new administrative structure they created when they established indirect rule. As a result, the office of *vaka vanua* (forest and garden crop ecologist) lost most its authority and prestige, the number of forest and garden crops placed under *tapu* declined, parts of the crops were eaten before they were ready for harvest, and thus their nutritional contribution was reduced ... Each of the Lau Islands also enjoyed the services of a *ndau ni nggoli*, a master fisherman and authority on the island's fish lore and fishing techniques ... Again, unfortunately, the British did not understand this institution, and the *ndau ni nggoli* has lost status.

Elements of Cultural Change that Might be Supportive of Traditional Systems

Several social indicators support the possibility of at least partial retention of some remnants of traditional systems of resource management in Oceania: the presence of traditional social structures and resource controls under modern conditions; the increased recognition of the value of traditional forms of resource management; the rebirth of conservation mindedness and resurgence of ethnic pride in the Pacific; and the "fallowing" of rural resource areas.

Presence of traditional conservation techniques. Isolated cases of the successful retention of traditional social structures and resource controls under modern conditions have been recorded. Force observed that "features of language, culinary practices, religious beliefs, and kinship usages are areas of traditional culture which often survive and bulwark the individual faced with the uncertainties and unfamiliar aspects of a new and complicated social milieu."[103] In another work, his findings counteract much of the pessimism regarding the retention of traditional island social structures:[104]

> Because urban life is in many ways different from traditional village life, we tend to emphasize the islanders' sociocultural change, or their adjustment to new forms or new ways. Preoccupied with the impressive overt evidence of change, there is a tendency to overlook the need to assess the extent to which Oceanians have changed because of their residence in urban centers. The suspicion grows stronger with mounting evidence that, despite adaptive change, there is a significant retention of older values and behaviors in a new environment with new trappings.

Allen has observed that although modern leaders or councils lack the sanction of religion that once supported their system of taboos, this is not likely to be a problem:[105]

> The principal constraints on their effectiveness on Raroia, Tokelau and other islands where controls have broken down, appear to be (a) the general collapse of traditional attitudes to resources; (b) the absence of any specific allocation of responsibility for controls over natural resource consumption to the leader or council; and (c) the fact that ownership of nesting and resting areas is not specifically vested in the whole community ... This is born out by two examples of the successful retention of traditional controls, even under modern conditions. In the case of Tokelau, bird collection from *communal* property, such as of frigates from Palea islet on Fakaofo atoll, is still regulated by the Council of Elders. However, the most impressive example comes from Pukapuka in the northern Cooks, where traditional controls in only slightly modified form have continued to be effective even when applied to a cash crop such as copra.

Even more interesting is the retention of specific conservation techniques in modern times.[106] Tables 31-36 include a variety of resource conserving methods still present in Oceania.

Increased recognition of traditional systems. Local, regional, and international organizations are now recognizing the need to identify, evaluate, and possibly preserve various traditional systems of resource management in Oceania. A relatively recent symposium on conservation in South Pacific issued a strong recommendation.[107] which recognized "that South Pacific islanders possess a rich store of knowledge of their environment; and that the traditional conservation practices of many South Pacific cultures were once highly effective and, if supported or adapted to modern conditions, could continue to be so." It expressed concern "that, in some parts of the region, traditional knowledge is being lost and traditional conservation practices displaced." The symposium meeting addressed itself to governments and international organizations, urging that:

> ... traditional knowledge of the environment be collected immediately, making use in particular of those individuals who are or have been the traditional custodians of this knowledge ... that any additional measures that may be necessary to support effective traditional conservation practices be taken as a matter of urgency; and that traditional environmental knowledge, and information on traditional conservation practices, be disseminated widely—especially at the village level—through appropriate education and public awareness programmes.

Considering that such symposia meetings have numerous indigenous representatives and participants in addition to outside scientists, it can be assumed that the value of traditional conservation techniques is now being recognized by both parties.

Re-birth of conservation mindedness and resurgence of ethnic pride. Many parts of the Pacific are experiencing a re-birth of conservation mindedness. In Micronesia, for example, "more and more Palauans are becoming active conservationists—in their yards and neighborhoods and in support of communities, villages, and also with efforts to make man's environment more attractive and pleasing."[108]

The Palau superport controversy is a contemporary case in point.[109] Japanese, Iranian, and American interests were negotiating with the native Palauans over the possibility of establishing a supertanker port on Kossol Reef, which is located north of Babelthaup Island in Palau, Micronesia. The controversy is over the unknown effect of such a facility on the ecological and cultural systems of the Palau Islands.

The proposal generated much concern and debate in Palau. In this case, the desired Palau resource is not the oil, but rather the island's strategic location. The Palauan culture represents a mere 14,000 people, and its traditional leaders are fighting the proposal. The facility, they claim, would deal a crushing blow to a way of life much cherished by the people and adapted to its physical setting. Regardless of the outcome of this important issue, island cultures such as Palau are now beginning to show a renewed interest in the preservation of their cultures and island environments.

Another social indicator supporting the possibility of preserving traditional systems of resource management in the area is the sweeping resurgence of ethnic pride in the Pacific. Many school systems are now encouraging the teaching of traditional values, attitudes, and skills.[110]

The "fallowing" of rural resource areas. This "fallowing" process constitutes one positive effect of the current migration of Pacific peoples to the city. Although the depopulation of outer-island areas may bring on a number of negative trends (like abandonment of traditional techniques of agriculture), the opportunity to conserve valuable natural resources is at hand. Douglas Yen, an ethnobotanist, clearly illustrated this point:[111]

> There has been a tendency to deplore, without qualification, the depopulation of rural and outer island areas in Oceania, with its accompanying effects. However, the aspect of "fallowing" may be one of the positive values of this trend, allowing a conservation of the natural terrestrial (and, perhaps, marine) resources. For such areas are "banks," whose topographies and soils best fit them for the readaptation of traditional crops and forms of agriculture under a new economic and political order emanating from the towns. Ideally, the adoption of new crops and a new technology would include an over-all consciousness of conservation.

CONCLUDING REGIONAL ASSESSMENT

Lapsed or Recessive Attitudes and Practices that Might be Revived and/or Reinforced

A few comments are called for before proceeding. First, some pre-European island cultures had numerous destructive as well as constructive and conserving practices; every traditional island culture did *not* live in blissful harmony with its environment. Cumberland's study of destructive practices of the Maohunter of New Zealand is a case in point.[112] What needs to be done is to identify and focus on the positive elements of these traditional cultures to see if there are conservation elements worthy of reviving and reinforcing.

Secondly, the modern-day resource manager is faced with a paradox. Westerners attempting to evaluate and possibly preserve traditional systems of resource management must move with extreme caution, for it is their ancestors (the European and North American) that were initially instrumental in breaking down these ecologically sound traditions.

Thirdly, in many cases it is most impractical to suggest that native islanders can revert to former ways of doing things. Pacific cultures are no longer isolated as they once were, as stated by Force, "Its people are *not* museum populations, nor do they wish to be."[113] Furthermore, a return to precontact tenure systems or subsistence agricultural systems, for example, is simply not plausible nor desirable in certain cultures, particularly those that have entered a cash economy.[114]

However, many aspects of these traditional methods of natural resource management remain appropriate to some cultures and might possibly be advantageous if adopted elsewhere. Allen illustrates this point in his discussion of ways in which to intensify cultivation by adopting a variation from some other culture:[115]

> There are so many different systems of cultivation practiced in the Pacific islands that there are no shortage of models for intensification of food production. Cultivation ranges from the semi-gathering of atoll cultures through extensive systems of slash-and-burn of shifting agriculture to intensive systems, often using irrigation, such as the linear contour, irrigable terraces of New Caledonia and the wet field terraces of Futuna. Population increase will necessitate change in agriculture, and probably the most practical strategy would be to intensify cultivation by adopting a variant of one of the more intensive techniques practiced elsewhere in the region. Indeed, it is possible that such techniques have already been practiced. For example, in the New Hebrides, archaeological research has identified terracing

systems in areas where shifting agriculture now predominates. Archaeologists concluded that populations were once much greater than they are today, and that despite considerable increases in numbers in recent decades, they are still significantly lower than they were before being decimated by contact with Europeans. There are numerous signs of pressure on natural resources throughout the Pacific. This pressure ultimately will only be relieved by stabilizing populations. However, there is room for relieving this pressure by retaining or reviving traditional practices.

It is possible to hypothesize about the lapsed or dying-out attitudes and practices that might be revived, reinforced, and/or modified (Table 37); it should be noted that the tabulation is not a complete list of traditional forms of resource management in Oceania.

Such marine conservation practices as fishing seasons, specific species regulation, traps and fish ponds, and methods of food preservation could probably be revived or reinforced within an area without too much difficulty or modification. Re-establishing the degree of environmental awareness, the concept of "master fisherman," fishing rights to specific geographic areas, magico-religious taboos, and related fines and punishment would often require a high degree of modification. For example, the "conservation ethic" behind an indigenous religion might be revived and reinforced without doing the same for the magical aspects (i.e., many Christians support the Ten Commandments without actually believing and supporting the origin of those ideas). The severity of fines and punishment might also be modified a bit to meet universal accepted humanitarian standards. Food avoidance based on class or sexual differences probably could not (and should not) be revived or reinforced as the notion of equality, as well as ethnic pride, is sweeping throughout the islands. However, if food avoidances according to class or sex lines remain to some degree in a particular culture, the practice should not be discouraged for it does play a role in conserving resources.

Almost all traditional soil and water conservation techniques that have been identified (e.g., terracing, mulching, rotating fields, and so on) could be likely revived without much difficulty. The practice of using fertilizers to enrich the soil might be revived as well as modified slightly to make it more productive. For instance, after an analysis of the ingredients of a particular fertilizer, modern soil scientists along with tropical botanists might be able to improve on the original mixture by only slightly modifying its contents with other existing local vegetation. The whole idea would be to take an existing culturally acceptable practice and modify it only slightly to make it more productive or efficient, thus hopefully avoiding any disruptive side effects.

Traditional wildlife resource practices such as habitat maintenance, game reserves, hunting seasons, bag limits, and regulations regarding the keeping of pets might be revived without too much difficulty. Traditional restrictions on sacred plants and animals might be slightly modified to include "endangered" plants and animals. Again, the conservation value of the indigenous religion must be identified and reinforced, though fines and punishment considered cruel and inhumane hopefully will be modified.

Controls over population and food supply ratios, such as coitus interruptus, adoption, and importing or exporting of groups of individuals for disaster relief, and food preferences might be revived with limited problems. Re-establishing moral constraints and abortion would require a major change, and, consequently be quite difficult. The revival of ritual celibacy, infanticide, importing or exporting of individuals or groups to alter

Table 37. Lapsed or Drying-out Attitudes and Practices that Might be Revived, reinforced, or modified

Attitudes and practice	Revived and/or reinforced	Modified	Not revived, not reinforced, nor discouraged
Marine resources			
Environmental awareness	*	*	
Master fishermen	*	*	
Marine tenure systems			
Fishing rights to specific areas	*	*	
Fishing seasons	*		
Specific species regulation	*		
Food avoidances			*
Traps and fish ponds	*		
Methods of food preservation	*		
Magico-religious taboos	*	*	
Fines and punishment	*	*	
Soil and water resources			
Terracing	*		
Mulching	*		
Leaving tree and shrub stubs after initial clearing	*		
Arranging felled trees or rubbish in transverse rows on hillsides	*		
Restricting extensive digging of large plots to low lands	*	*	
Capturing and using river silt for agricultural purposes	*		
Using fertilizers to enrich soil	*	*	
Rotating fields	*		
Burning fields to release nutrients	*		
Using shelterbelts to reduce wind erosion	*		
Alterating and improving soil structure	*		
Forest and garden crop resources			
Forestry ecologists	*	*	
Magico-religious taboos	*	*	
Fines and punishment	*	*	
Wildlife resources			
Habitat maintenance	*		
Game reserves	*		
Games laws			
Hunting seasons	*		
Bag limits	*		
Prohibition of sacred animals	*	*	
Prohibition of sacred plants	*	*	
Regulations regarding pets	*		
Magico-religious taboos	*	*	
Fines and punishment	*	*	
Population and food resources			
Fertility control			
Moral restraints	*	*	
Coitus interruptus	*		
Titual celibacy			*
Abortion	*	*	
Infanticide			*
Socio-political control			
Adoption	*		
Importing/exporting people			
In case of natural calamity	*		
In case of critical imbalance in sex ratios			*
Food preferences and planting of nonsubsistence crops	*		
Overseas voyages			*
Warfare			*
Human sacrifice			*

critical imbalances in sex ratios, overseas/suicidal voyages, warfare, and human sacrifice would be contrary to humanitarian standards and basic precepts of modern civilization.

Methods of Retaining Desirable Traditional Techniques

There are a number of measures that the field researcher can take to support effective traditional conservation practices. Once the data has been collected, analyzed, and written-up, the first order of business would be its dissemination within the region to appropriate administrative authorities.

With the research findings in hand, Oceanians could undertake a number of possible measures. Using Palau as an example, Trust Territory Government information manuals that effectively combine traditional and western conservation techniques could be produced and dispersed to District conservation officers, requesting that certain practices be revived and/or encouraged. These western-trained conservation officers, in turn, could work closely with the traditionally-trained "master fishermen," "forest ecologists," and other overseers of an area's resources—ideally, both learning from each other. Classroom materials could be reproduced and distributed to every elementary, secondary, and vocational school within the Palau District; environmental awareness and traditional conservation practices could then become a permanent part of a unit on the history and geography of the Palau Islands—a subject already taught to some degree in the District. Appropriate education and public awareness programs (radio broadcasts or portable video-tape units) could reach even the most remote village "to reinforce pride in traditional lifestyles and add ecological and other scientific reasons for supporting traditional practices that until the impact of Europe and North America had no need of objective validation."[116]

Any "retention" measures must involve public consultation in the planning process as well as careful monitoring of their effects. As with any new program, there is always the possibility of negative repercussions.

Lessons for the Western Resource Manager

First and foremost, the modern-day resource manager can heighten his own awareness of the local environment by mentally combining two culturally different temporal frameworks.[117] By combining his own system of time-reckoning (the Swiss watch and Gregorian calendar) with that of the indigenous culture's system (the movement of the sun, moon, stars, or tides), the modern-day resource manager should see the heavens and the phases of nature in new perspective.

To be more specific, the western marine biologist can gain a great deal of information: the lunar periodicity of the spawning of reef fish; the location and traditional regulation of marine preserves; the fishing grounds used by a particular village; the affect of rainfall, winds, currents, and temperatures on fishing conditions and the habits of certain fish; the times, places, and seasons of optimum fishing; the peculiarities of different islands and different parts of the coasts of larger islands on fish habits and migration; the incidence of toxic plants that might render fish poisonous; the traditional fishing rights, closed seasons, specific species regulation, and food avoidances; the optimum days for particular fishing techniques; the construction and proper use of traps and ponds for fish conservation; and the various methods of preserving fish. According to Handy and others, "the experienced native fisherman is possessed of a store of precise knowledge that may be truly characterized as natural science.[118]

The western soil conservationist and hydrologist could benefit from such information as: the names, types, locations, and uses of different soils; the materials used for mulching and fertilizing; the methods of improving existing soil structure; techniques of terracing, irrigation, use of windbreaks; and traditional conservation ethics and restrictions.

The western forest ecologist and agricultural specialist might increase his knowledge about the types, location, and seasonality of local indigenous and introduced flora; the optimum seasons for planting, harvesting, and crop rotation; methods of food preparation and storage; the planting of tree crops according to sound ecological principles; the proper harvesting of fruits, bark, and other tree products. As perceptively stated by Gourou, "The disasters brought on by agricultural methods which have taken no account of the treasures of wisdom and experience accumulated in the old tropical system are a sufficient proof of the latter's value."[119]

The modern-day wildlife biologist might benefit from such information as the life histories, feeding habits, mating seasons, habitat requirements and other basic knowledge of various forms of local wildlife; the types and migration cycles of avifauna; the breeding requirements and location of various insectum; the location and traditional regulation of wildlife reserves; and traditional hunting rights and practices, closed seasons, specific species regulation.

Some insight into traditional conservation ethics, restrictions, and related fines and punishment could be of benefit to all of the aforementioned western specialists.

The western demographer might further his understanding of island carrying capacity by studying traditional cultural controls over population growth. Future population control programs might benefit from such information as an area's attitudes towards birth control; practices and acceptability of abortion as a fertility control mechanism; concepts of density; past, present, and possible future systems of adoption; and requirements for inter-island relocation.

Many western conservation officers in Oceania are fully aware of the value of traditional conservation practices. Unfortunately, they just lack the time to go out and record this information, much less integrate it into a comprehensive management program. Field researchers can be of help by starting with the scattered bits of information already known to the western conservation manager. Then, under such a manager's guidance, the researcher can add additional indepth information, and ultimately arrive at some conclusions.

With the final report in hand, the local resource manager would be less likely to create regulations or make other decisions in conflict with traditional conservation practices. He would be in a position to prescribe regulations that have already stood the test of time, and finally might just learn some new ecologically sound principles in the process.

NOTES

[1]T. Dagodag and G. A. Klee, "A Review of Some Analogies in Sunken Garden Agriculture," *Anthropological Journal of Canada*, Vol. 11, No. 4 (1973), pp. 10–15.

[2]K. P. Emory, *Kapingamarangi: Social and Religious Life of a Polynesian Atoll* (Honolulu: B. P. Bishop Museum Press, 1965), p. 345; G. A. Klee, "Traditional Time Reckoning and Resource Utilization," *Micronesica*, Vol. 12 (1976), pp. 211-246; and B. Malinowski, *Soil-Tilling and Agricultural Rites in the Trobriand Islands* (Bloomington: Indiana University Press, 1965), p. 51.

[3]E. S. C. Handy, *Houses, Boats, and Fishing in the Society Islands* (Honolulu: B. P. Bishop Museum Press, 1932), p. 74; W. H. Alkire, "Lamotrek Atoll and Inter-Island Socioeconomic Ties," in *Illinois Studies in Anthropology* (Urbana: University of Illinois Press, 1965), p. 69; and R. Allen, "Ecodevelopment and Traditional Natural Resource Management in the South Pacific," paper presented at the Second Regional Symposium of Conservation of Nature, Apia, Western Samoa, June 14-17, 1976, p. 10. (mimeo.).

[4]Allen, op. cit., note 3.

[5]R. E. Johannes, "What the Tropical Marine Fisherman Can Teach the Fisheries Biologist," *Abstracts of Papers*, Thirteenth Pacific Science Congress, Record on Proceedings Vol. 1 (Vancouver: Pacific Science Association, 1975), p. 128; and G. A. Klee, "The Cyclic Realities of Man and Nature in a Palauan Village," unpublished doctoral dissertation, University of Oregon, 1972, p. 109-177.

[6]P. B. Sauder, "Guam: Land Tenure in a Fortress," in *Land Tenure in the Pacific*, Ron Crocombe, ed. (Melbourne: Oxford University Press, 1971), p. 192; and J. E. Tobin, "Land Tenure in the Marshall Islands," *Atoll Research Bulletin* (Washington, D.C.: Smithsonian Press, 1952), p. 11.

[7]Allen, op. cit., note 3, pp. 8-9; N. Meller and H. Horwitz, "Hawaii: Themes in Land Monopoly," in *Land Tenure in the Pacific*, Ron Crocombe, ed. (Melbourne: Oxford University Press, 1971), p. 26; H. P. Lundsgaärde, ed., *Land Tenure in Oceania* (Honolulu: University of Hawaii Press, 1974), p. 50.

[8]K. B. Cumberland and J. S. Whitelaw, *New Zealand* (Chicago: Aldine, 1970), p. 22; Meller and Horwitz, op. cit., note 7, p. 27; and M. Titcomb, *Native Use of Fish in Hawaii* (Honolulu: University of Hawaii Press, 1972), p. 13.

[9]R. W. Williamson, *The Social and Political Systems of Central Polynesia* (Cambridge: University Press, 1924), p. 250.

[10]P. H. Buck, *Ethnology of Mangareva* (Honolulu: B. P. Bishop Museum Press, 1938), p. 161.

[11]Handy, op. cit., note 3.

[12]Buck, op. cit., note 10, p. 302.

[13]M. V. C. Falanruw, "Conservation in Micronesia," *Atoll Research Bulletin* (Washington, D.C.: Smithsonian Press, 1971), p. 19.

[14]Meller and Horwitz, op. cit., note 7, p. 27; Williamson, op. cit., note 9, p. 146; and E. S. C. Handy, *Polynesian Religion* (Honolulu: B. P. Bishop Museum Press, 1927), p. 129.

[15]Handy, op. cit., note 3, p. 129.

[16]Williamson, op. cit., note 9, p. 147; and Titcomb, op. cit., note 8, p. 11.

[17]Alkire, op. cit., note 3; Handy, op. cit., note 3; and R. P. Owen, "The Status of Conservation in the Trust Territory of the Pacific Islands," *Micronesica*, Vol. 5 (1969), p. 303.

[18]J. L. Fischer, *The Eastern Carolines* (Connecticut: Pacific Science Board in Association with the Human Relations Area Files, 1957), p. 139.

[19]M. Mead, "The Samoans," in *Cooperation and Competition Among Primitive Peoples*, M. Mead, ed. (Boston: Beacon Press, 1961), p. 291.

[20]E. Beaglehole and P. Beaglehole, *Ethnology of Pukapuka* (Honolulu: B. P. Bishop Museum Press, 1938), p. 32.

[21]Williamson, op. cit., note 9.

[22]Buck, op. cit., note 10, p. 494; and Alkire, op. cit., note 3.

[23]Williamson, op. cit., note 9, p. 295.

[24]Tobin, op. cit., note 6.

[25]Beaglehole and Beaglehole, op. cit., note 20, p. 33.

[26]Tobin, op. cit., note 6.

[27]Titcomb, op. cit., note 8, p. 13; and Buck, op. cit., note 10, p. 494.

[28]F. M. Reinman, "Fishing: An Aspect of Oceanic Economy," *Fieldiana: Anthropology*, Vol. 56 (1967), p. 192.

[29]Ibid., pp. 192-193.

[30]J. Barrau, "Subsistence Agriculture in Polynesia and Micronesia," (Honolulu: B. P. Bishop Museum Press, 1961), p. 72.

[31] R. Rappaport, "The Flow of Energy in an Agricultural Society," *Scientific American*, Vol. 224 (1971), pp. 117–132.

[32] Personal communication with Randolph R. Thaman, Assistant Professor of Geography, University of the South Pacific, April 5, 1977.

[33] Dagodag and Klee, op. cit., note 1, pp. 11, 13–14; and R. L. A. Catala, "Report on the Gilbert Islands: Some Aspects of Human Ecology," *Atoll Research Bulletin* (Washington, D.C.: Smithsonian Press, 1957), pp. 67–75.

[34] E. Waddell, *The Mound Builders: Agricultural Practices, Environment, and Society in the Central Highlands of New Guinea* (Seattle: University of Washington Press, 1972).

[35] J. Barrau, "Subsistence Agriculture in Melanesia," (Honolulu: B. P. Bishop Museum Press, 1958), pp. 21–22, 41.

[36] R. Crocombe and R. Hide, "New Guinea: Unity in Diversity," in *Land Tenure in the Pacific* (Melbourne: Oxford University Press, 1971), p. 294; Waddell, op. cit., note 34, p. 135; and Fischer, op. cit., note 18, p. 90.

[37] Niering, N. A., "Terrestrial Ecology of Kapingamarangi Atoll," *Ecological Monograph*, Vol. 33 (1963), p. 144.

[38] Rappaport, op. cit., note 31, pp. 122–123.

[39] Lundsgaarde, op. cit., note 7, p. 29; Waddell, op. cit., note 34, p. 143; and W. C. Clarke, *Place and People* (Berkeley: University of California Press, 1971), p. 72.

[40] Crocombe and Hide, op. cit., note 36, p. 294; Lundsgaarde, op. cit., note 7, p. 23; Rappaport, op. cit., note 31, p. 127.

[41] Barrau, op. cit., note 35, pp. 41–42.

[42] Crocombe and Hide, op. cit., note 36, p. 294; Rappaport, op. cit., note 31, p. 128; and Waddell, op. cit., note 34, p. 135.

[43] Clarke, op. cit., note 39.

[44] Catala, op. cit., note 33, pp. 69, 70–71; and Fischer, op. cit., note 18, p. 90.

[45] Falanruw, op. cit., note 13, p. 19; A. Spoehr, "The Ethnology of War-Devasted Islands: Saipan," *Fieldiana: Anthropology*, Vol. 41 (1954), p. 155; and L. Holmes, "Samoa: Custom versus Productivity," in *Land Tenure in the Pacific*, Ron Crocombe, ed. (Melbourne: Oxford University Press, 1971), p. 95.

[46] Crocombe and Hide, op. cit., note 36, p. 294; Rappaport, op. cit., note 31, p. 120.

[47] Crocombe and Hide, ibid.; and Barrau, op. cit., note 35, p. 12.

[48] Crocombe and Hide, ibid.; Barrau, ibid., p. 22.

[49] Waddell, op. cit., note 34, p. 144.

[50] C. D. Olliver, D. P. Drover and M. Godelier, "Soil Knowledge Amongst the Baruya of Wonenara, New Guinea," *Oceania*, Vol. 62 (1971), pp. 33–41.

[51] Allen, op. cit., note 3, p. 9.

[52] Allen, ibid.; Williamson, op. cit., note 9, pp. 134–135, 137; and G. Macgregor, *Ethnology of Tokelau Island* (Honolulu: B. P. Bishop Museum, 1937), p. 61.

[53] S. Siwatibau, "Traditional Conservation Practices for Modern Pacific Societies," paper presented at the Second Regional Symposium on Conservation of Nature, Apia, Western Samoa, June 14–17, 1976, pp. 3–4. (mimeo.).

[54] Emory, op. cit., note 2, p. 128.

[55] Niering, op. cit., note 37, p. 145.

[56] Fischer, op. cit., note 18, p. 73.

[57] R. Lane, "New Hebrides: Land Tenure Without Land Policy," in *Land Tenure in the Pacific*, Ron Crocombe, ed. (Melbourne: Oxford University Press, 1971), p. 252.

[58] Clarke, op. cit., note 39, p. 66.

[59] Rappaport, op. cit., note 31, pp. 122–123.

[60] Ibid.

[61] H. F. I. Elliott, "Past, Present and Future Conservation Status of Pacific Islands," in *Nature Conservation in the Pacific*, A. B. Coston and R. H. Groves, eds. (Canberra: Australia National University Press, 1973), p. 217; E. H. Loeb, *History and Traditions of Niue* (Honolulu: B. P. Bishop Museum Press, 1926), p. 171; and J. M. Powell, "Conservation and Resourse Management in Australia 1788–1860," in *Australian Space/Australian Time*, J. M. Powell and M. Williams, eds. (Melbourne: Oxford University Press, 1975), p. 18.

[62] Beaglehole and Beaglehole, op. cit., note 20, p. 73.

[63] Owen, op. cit., note 17; Beaglehole and Beaglehole, ibid.; and E. W. Gifford, *Tongan Society* (Honolulu: B. P. Bishop Museum Press, 1929), p. 325.

[64] Tobin, op. cit., note 6, pp. 12–24.

[65] Allen, op. cit., note 3, pp. 8–9.

[66] Clarke, op. cit., note 39, pp. 66–67.

[67] Fischer, op. cit., note 18, pp. 81–82; and Falanruw, op. cit., note 13, p. 19.

[68] Tobin, op. cit., note 6, p. 32; and D. Schneider, "Abortion and Depopulation on a Pacific Island: Yap," in *Health, Culture, and Community*, D. B. Paul, ed. (New York: Russell Sage Foundation, 1955), pp. 211, 215.

[69] Emory, op. cit., note 2, p. 155; J. H. Bodley, *Anthropology and Contemporary Human Problems* (Menlo Park: Cummings Publishing Co., 1976), p. 162; and F. R. Fosberg, "Part, Present and Future Conservation Problems of Oceanic Islands," in *Nature Conservation in the Pacific*, A. B. Costin and R. H. Groves, eds. (Canberra: Australian National University Press, 1973), p. 211.

[70] Bodley, op. cit., note 69; and Falanruw, op. cit., note 13.

[71] B. Blackwood, *Both Sides of Buka Pasage: An Ethnographic Study of Social, Sexual, and Economic Questions in the Northwest Solomon Islands* (Oxford: Claredon Press, 1935), p. 117; T. Gladwin and S. B. Sarasan, *Truk: Man in Paradise* (N.Y.: Viking Fund Publications in Anthropology, 1953), p. 133; and Beaglehole and Beaglehole, op. cit., note 20, p. 267.

[72] Schneider, op. cit., note 68, pp. 211–235.

[73] Bodley, op. cit., note 69, p. 150; and Falanruw, op. cit., note 13, p. 19.

[74] Bodley, ibid., 143, 150, 152, 162; and K. E. Knudson, "Resource Fluctuation, Productivity, and Social Organization on Micronesian Coral Islands," unpublished doctoral dissertation, University of Oregon, 1970.

[75] Bodley, op. cit., note 69, p. 161.

[76] Falanruw, op. cit., note 13, p. 19; Fosberg, op. cit., note 69, p. 211; and Bodley, op. cit., note 69, p. 144.

[77] Beaglehole and Beaglehole, op. cit., note 20, p. 373; Bodley, op. cit., note 69, pp. 143, 150; and Crocombe and Hide, op. cit., note 36, p. 296.

[78] Buck, op. cit., note 10, p. 458; and P. H. Buck, *Mangaian Society* (Honolulu: B. P. Bishop Museum Press, 1934), p. 179.

[79] W. A. Lessa, "The Social Effects of Typhoon Ophelia (1960) on Ulithi," in *Peoples and Cultures of the Pacific*, Andrew P. Vayda, ed. (Garden City: The Natural History Press, 1968), p. 371.

[80] R. Rappaport, *Pigs for the Ancestors: Ritual in the Ecology of a New Guinea People* (New Haven: Yale University Press, 1968), Chapter 6.

[81] Bodley, op. cit., note 69, pp. 156–159; and S. B. Shantzis and W. Behrens, "Population Control Mechanisms in a Primitive Agricultural Society," in *Toward Global Equilibrium*, D. H. Meadows and D. L. Meadows, eds. (Cambridge: Wright-Allen Press, 1973), pp. 257–288.

[82] Allen, op. cit., note 3, pp. 8–9.

[83] Titcomb, op. cit., note 8, p. 12; Tobin, op. cit., note 6, p. 27; and Reinman, op. cit., note 28, p. 192.

[84] Allen, op. cit., note 3; Reinman, op. cit., note 28, pp. 192–193; and Owen, op. cit., note 17.

[85] R. E. Johannes, "Exploitation and Degradation of Shallow Marine Food Resources in Oceania," in *The Impact of Urban Centers in the Pacific*, R. W. Force and Brenda Bishop. eds. (Honolulu: Pacific Science Association, 1975), p. 60.

[86] Allen, op. cit., note 3, p. 9; Elliott, op. cit., note 61, p. 217; and Tobin, op. cit., note 6, p. 27.

[87] Beaglehole and Beaglehole, op. cit., note 20, p. 373; Crocombe and Hide, op. cit., note 36, p. 296; and R. Firth, *We the Tikopia* (N.Y.: Barnes & Noble, 1957), p. 414.

[88] Emory, op. cit., note 2, pp. 155–156.

[89] Cumberland and Whitelaw, op. cit., note 8, p. 3.

[90] Personal communication with R. Gerald Ward, Professor of Human Geography, Australian National University, September 27, 1976.

[91] Fosberg, op. cit., note 69, p. 212.

[92] Tobin, op. cit., note 6, p. 27.

[93] C. Mydans, "Return to Bikini," *Life*, October 1968, p. 32.

[94]L. Mason, "The Bikinians: A Transplanted Population," *Human Organization*, Vol. 9 (1950), pp. 5-55.

[95]Bodley, op. cit., note 69, p. 79; and J. H. Bodley, *Victims of Progress* (Menlo Park: Cummings Publishing Co., 1975).

[96]Barrau, op. cit., note 35, p. 9; and H. Wiens, "Some Effects of Geographic Location Upon Land Utilization in the Coral Atolls of Micronesia," *Proceedings of the Ninth Pacific Science Congress of the Pacific Science Association, Hulalongkorn University, Bangkok, Thailand, November 18 to December 9, 1957* (Bangkok: Secretariat, Ninth Pacific Science Congress, 1963), p. 157.

[97]Bodley, op. cit., note 69, p. 164; Cumberland and Whitelaw, op. cit., note 8, p. 31; and Schneider, op. cit., note 68.

[98]Fosberg, op. cit., note 69, p. 212.

[99]Bodley, op. cit., note 69, p. 164; and Fischer, op. cit., note 18, p. 82.

[100]Allen, op. cit., note 3, p. 8; Buck, op. cit., note 10, p. 405; and Klee, op. cit., note 2, pp. 245-256.

[101]Falanruw, op. cit., note 13, p. 20; Meller and Horwitz, op. cit., note 7, p. 40; and Tobin, op. cit., note 6, p. 12.

[102]Allen, op. cit., note 3.

[103]R. W. Force, "Pacific Urban Centers in Perspective," in *The Impact of Urban Centers in the Pacific*, Roland W. Force and Brenda Bishop, eds. (Honolulu: Pacific Science Association, 1975), p. 355.

[104]R. W. Force and M. Force, "Kith, Kin, and Fellow Urbanites," in *The Impact of Urban Centers in the Pacific*, Roland W. Force and Brenda Bishop, eds. (Honolulu: Pacific Science Association, 1975), p. 196.

[105]Allen, op. cit., note 3, p. 8.

[106]Ibid., pp. 9-10; Titcomb, op. cit., note 8, p. 17; and A. L. Dahl, "Regional Ecosystems Survey of the South Pacific Area," paper presented at the Second Regional Symposium on Conservation of Nature, Apia, Western Samoa, June 14-17, 1976. (mimeo.).

[107]"Recommendation No. 4: Traditional Environmental Knowledge and Conservation Practices; Second Regional Symposium on Conservation of Nature in the South Pacific, Apia, Western Samoa, June 14-17, 1976," *International Union for the Conservation of Nature and Natural Resources Bulletin*, August 1976, p. 2.

[108]J. S. Kochi, "Objectives and Importance of Conservation," *Atoll Research Bulletin* (Washington, D.C.: Smithsonian Press, 1971), p. 22.

[109]W. H. Moore, "Port Pacific: A Superport for Palau," *Sierra Club Bulletin*, June 1976, pp. 52-54.

[110]For example, this author's doctoral dissertation, concerned with the traditional system of time-reckoning that is dying out in Palau, was procurred by the Koror School District which is using copies as required reading in high school.

[111]D. Yen, "Effects of Urbanization on Village Agriculture in Oceania," in *The Impact of Urban Centers in the Pacific*, Roland W. Force and Brenda Bishop, eds. (Honolulu: Pacific Science Association, 1975), p. 178.

[112]K. B. Cumberland, "Moas and Men: New Zealand about A.D. 1250," *The Geographical Review*, Vol. 52 (1962), pp. 151-173.

[113]Force, op. cit., note 103, p. 351.

[114]Crocombe and Hide, op. cit., note 36, p. 375; and Barrau, op. cit., note 30, pp. 33-34.

[115]Allen, op. cit., note 3, p. 7.

[116]Ibid., p. 11.

[117]Klee, op. cit., note 5, p. 143.

[118]Handy, op. cit., note 3, p. 76.

[119]P. Gourou, *The Tropical World* (London: Longmans, Green & Co., Ltd., 1953), p. 32.

[120]Researchers interested in detailed references that correlate each particular *form* of traditional resource management with *examples* thereof, as given in Tables 32, 33, 34, 35, and 36, can obtain an expanded bibliographic listing by requesting it from Dr. Gary A. Klee, Department of Environmental Studies, School of Social Sciences, San Jose State University, San Jose, CA 95192.

Chapter 11

Traditional Wisdom and the Modern Resource Manager

Gary A. Klee

Many traditional cultures have disappeared under the onrush of change, but a good many are resilient and surviving and several of their ways of life have assets which seem especially valuable to modern-day ecological concerns. First of all, these cultures are well adapted to their environment. Their survival over thousands of years is proof enough that they were good conservationists. Secondly, they are generally small in scale and decentralized, thus allowing for a closer intimacy with their local surroundings. And thirdly, they rely upon local "income" or renewable resources, not upon "capital" or non-renewable resources as do most industrial societies. As the world moves into an age of resource scarcity, the wise dependence on renewable resources becomes all too apparent.

A few world-watchers now see the "paraprimitive solution" as perhaps the only viable answer to the problems now facing mankind. Whether an anthropologist calls it "paraprimitive," a biologist "de-development," a chemist "earthmanship economics," an economist "appropriate technology," or a geographer refers to it as "frugality," the concept remains essentially the same: an attempt to combine the best elements of industrial civilization with the obviously superior components of primitive cultures in order to establish a stable, more ideal society.[1] An example of a paraprimitive solution to our current agricultural problems would be farm decentralization, self-sufficiency, the use of organic fertilizers, and the practice of biological control for insect pests, as opposed to our existing heavy reliance upon the large centralized corporate enterprise that practices monoculture farming with its dependence on fossil-fuel based chemical fertilizers, herbicides, and pesticides.

Although not designed with this purpose in mind, it is interesting to see how closely the findings of our own research team fit and support one of the latest scenarios of the future. In *Muddling Toward Frugality*, Professor Warren Johnson maintains that industrialized countries *will* be able to transcend the approaching problems of resource

283

depletion.[2] However, he also states that these same countries will "muddle" (unplanned adaptation or social change) toward "frugality" (useful or fruitful utilization of resources), i.e., the paraprimitive solution. Johnson maintains that economics and ecology are inseparable, that affluence cannot increase indefinitely, that technology cannot answer all resource shortages, that cultural evolution may be marching in the wrong direction, that economic collapse is no more likely than reaching utopia, that society needs the restraint provided by resource limitations, and that high speed ground transportation, rapid transit, urban renewal, insecticides, and antibiotics are examples of failing or failed technologies.

The 21st century, as Johnson foresees it, will be a world where production is small-scale and labor intensive; mobility is reduced; small communities are revived; winning technologies based on renewable resources (sun, wind, water, land) overrun existing failing technologies based on non-renewable resources; repair businesses flourish; small neighborhood groceries return to residential areas; small-scale agricultural farms become economical; agricultural fields are hand sprayed; woodcutters return; pollution of all types decline as the consumption of resources in our economy declines; building styles reflect building materials available nearby; and regional styles of clothing, music, and dance reemerge with reduced mobility. In other words, we will have less income, less consumption, and less mobility in the 21st century. On the positive side, however, we will also have less mass production, less standardization, less centralization, and less pollution. The bottom line is that our lives will be richer, simpler, and more human in scale, thus more enjoyable. The age of scarcity, according to Johnson, has enormous benefits and should not be feared. If this cultural geographer/natural resource specialist is at all correct in his vision of the future, the importance of preserving traditional values, attitudes, and overall resource-using systems should be obvious.

However, little time remains to identify, record, and possibly preserve some of these traditional systems of resource management. The key village elders (the true custodians of information relating to past and present forms of traditional conservation practices) must be filmed, taped, and interviewed immediately, before this information passes with their deaths. Specific geographic locations and the conservation methods employed must be recorded for each cultural area. Much of what would be documented would come from the studies of ethnohistory, fossilized remains, and oral traditions. Knowledge of the workings of traditional land economies such as soil conservation techniques, techniques for storing and conserving water, forest reserves and conservation practices would need to be put in print. This information could then be disseminated widely through appropriate education and public awareness programs, in order that it be preserved within the local cultural area. To put it simply, traditional methods of managing resources should not be allowed to die.

Furthermore, entire cultures, not just their particular elements that seem desirable for our own immediate needs, should be nourished and protected, not disrupted or permanently changed. Our planet has millions of different plants and animals, yet there are only a few thousand human cultures. For the former, public awareness of environmental problems has been heightened by the Endangered Species List, which is a protection device under the Endangered Species Act. What we need is a kind of "Endangered Cultures List" that identifies specific cultures that are at the point of being the next victim of careless industrialization. The 14,000 people of Palau, Micronesia are a case in point. As mentioned in Chapter 10, American, Japanese, and Iranian interest have proposed a superport oil tanker facility for northern Palau. The social, economic, political, and ecological ramifications of such a facility raise the question of Palau's ability to survive as a unique cultural type.

Cultural ecologists and resource managers can play a major role in keeping tabs on possible endangered cultures. The final product might be a dynamic world map with orange dots for those cultures that are "threatened" (cultures likely to become endangered in the foreseeable future) and red dots for those cultures that are "endangered" (cultures facing a critical decision regarding their survival as a distinctive cultural type). Palau, for example, is now in the red dot stage. Current information on threatened and endangered cultures could be fed on a regular basis to world organizations that are involved in the protection of different places and people.

Modern-day resource managers have much to learn from the traditional systems of using the land, and it would behoove all researchers of the problem to *spend more time on recording and preserving traditional systems or resource management than devoting ones time to learning how to remove traditional obstacles to modernization.*

As if the above goals were not worthwhile enough, there is a final reason to record traditional systems of resource management throughout the world. In addition to providing valuable information to the modern-day resource manager, statistical compilation (population statistics, religious denomination types and rates of resource exploitation) along with cartographic compilation might just lead to some interesting correlations and relationships as well as unifying theories and/or prediction.

But before any serious cross-cultural analysis and theory building can be pursued, the core questions presented in this book must be asked on a culture by culture basis in the field. To date, the available information on traditional conservation practices is meager and anecdotal; past researchers, in most cases, have neglected to focus their studies on these essential questions. Further studies of world systems of traditional resource management are needed for they can be an important tool for the modern-day resource manager.

NOTES

[1] John H. Bodley, *Anthropology and Contemporary Human Problems* (Menlo Park: Cummings Publishing Co., 1976); Paul R. Ehrlich, *The End of Affluence* (New York: Ballantine Books, 1974); G. Tyler Miller, Jr., *Living in the Environment: Concepts, Problems, and Alternatives*, (Belmont: Wadsworth Publishing Co., 1975); E. F. Schumacher, *Small is Beautiful* (N.Y.: Harper & Row, 1973); and Warren Johnson, *Muddling Toward Frugality* (San Francisco: Sierra Club Books, 1978).

[2] Johnson, op. cit., note 1.

Index